international
review of
social history

Special Issue 25

Brazilian Labour History: New Perspectives in Global Context

Edited by Paulo Fontes, Alexandre Fortes, and David Mayer

Published by the Press Syndicate of the University of Cambridge
The Pitt Building, Trumpington Street, Cambridge, CB2 1RP
1 Liberty Plaza, Floor 20, New York, NY 10006, USA
10 Stamford Road, Oakleigh, Melbourne 3166, Australia

*A catalogue record for this book is available
from the British Library*

Library of Congress Cataloguing-in-Publication Data applied for

ISBN 9781108450898 (paperback)

Printed in the UK by Bell & Bain Ltd, Glasgow, UK.

CONTENTS

Brazilian Labour History: New Perspectives in Global Context

Edited by
Paulo Fontes, Alexandre Fortes, and David Mayer

IRSH 62 (2017), Special Issue, pp. 1–22 doi:10.1017/S0020859017000645
© 2018 Internationaal Instituut voor Sociale Geschiedenis

Brazilian Labour History in Global Context: Some Introductory Notes

PAULO FONTES

School of Social Sciences of the Fundação Getulio Vargas (CPDOC/
FGV), Praia de Botafogo, 190 – sala 1422, 14° Andar, Botafogo,
Rio de Janeiro, RJ, 22250-900, Brazil

E-mail: paulo.fontes@fgv.br

ALEXANDRE FORTES

Universidade Federal Rural do Rio de Janeiro, Department of
History, Av Governador Roberto da Silveira S/N, Nova Iguaçu,
RJ, Brazil

E-mail: fortes.ufrrj@gmail.com

DAVID MAYER

International Institute of Social History, Cruquiusweg 31, 1019 AT
Amsterdam, The Netherlands

E-mail: david.mayer@iisg.nl

ABSTRACT: This article introduces the main topics and intellectual concerns behind this Special Issue about Brazilian labour history in global context. Over the last two decades, Brazilian labour history has become an important reference point for the international debate about a renewed labour and working-class history. It has greatly broadened its conceptual scope by integrating issues of gender, race, and ethnicity and has moved towards studying the whole gamut of labour relations in Brazil's history. Furthermore it has taken new perspectives on the history of movements. As background to this Special Issue, this introduction embeds current Brazilian labour historiography in its development as a field and in the country's broader political and social history. Presenting the contributions, we highlight their connections with current debates in Global Labour History.

"The winds from the North don't move windmills", so states a verse from *Sangue Latino* (Latin Blood), an early 1970s Brazilian popular song that celebrates a continentalist vision of Latin America.[1] Many advocates of Global Labour History tend to believe that, currently, the "the winds from the Global South move windmills" in our field of studies. Moreover, the winds that blow from Brazil seem to be strong. Indeed, over the last two decades, Brazilian labour history has become an important reference point for the international debate about a renewed labour and working-class history. It has been cited as a "best practice" case (often alongside Indian and South African Labour historiographies) and an important instigator of the field of Global Labour History.[2] Labour historians from Brazil (but also international scholars working on Brazil) have succeeded in greatly broadening their conceptual scope by integrating issues of gender, race, and ethnicity and have moved towards studying the whole gamut of labour relations in Brazil's history – with a special emphasis on the manifold interconnections between free and unfree as well as formal and informal labour. This expanding scholarship has also shed new light on "classic" topics, such as strikes, unionism, or the role of labour policies in redefining workers strategies. Scholars have also expanded the geographical scope of their studies, which were originally con-fined to the main industrial areas (particularly, São Paulo and Rio de Janeiro), thus offering a much more complex picture of Brazil's regional diversity.

Brazilian labour history, at the same time, forms part of a continental, Latin American research community that, during the last two decades, has set out to revive and redefine the study of labour relations, workers, as well as labour and social movements. A recent congress celebrated in La Paz (Bolivia) has aimed to bring this continental community together.[3] The topics of the papers presented there have made clear that, apart from the two major continental centres of labour history – Argentina and Brazil – there is an increasing academic interest in a methodologically and conceptually renewed historical study of labour in a series of other Latin American countries. The conference included themes such as "representations and interpretations of work", "conflicts about work, uprisings, and revolts in pre-industrial periods", "struggles of workers and unions", or "free and unfree labour, slaveries, and their multiple transitions". This short list alone illustrates the degree to which labour history in Brazil can boast having anticipated and greatly contributed to this renewal – particularly in relation to a nuanced analysis of the whole gamut of historical labour relations going

---

1. "Sangue Latino", composed by João Ricardo and Paulo Mendonça, was a hit by the band Secos e Molhados in 1973.
2. Marcel van der Linden, *Workers of the World: Essays toward a Global Labor History* (Leiden [etc.], 2008), p. 3.
3. Congreso Latinoamericano y del Caribe de Trabajo y Trabajadores, 2–8 May 2017, La Paz, http://ctt2017.cis.gob.bo/inicio; last accessed 7 November 2017.

beyond the traditional focus on "double-free" wage labourers.[4] This list also makes clear that Latin American labour history has its own emphases and is not fully equivalent with the research focuses of labour historians in the Global North or in South Asia. For instance – and the contributions to this Special Issue provide several examples – topics of labour movement history are still (or again) running strong, often realized with new questions and approaches. Another difference is the (sometimes acute) "topicality" of the research done in Latin America: the political relevance of issues such as the co-existence of different labour relations or the trajectory of historical movements seems obvious both to scholars and their audiences.

A BRIEF SKETCH OF LABOUR HISTORIOGRAPHY IN BRAZIL

As in other countries, the development of labour history in Brazil has been closely interconnected with major political conjunctures, economic transformations, changes in the composition of the working class and the collective presence of workers as social and political actors, as well as with shifts in the intellectual perception of this presence.[5] In the most general sense, industrialization processes and the numerical increase of the group of industrial workers stood at the beginning of this story. Similar to most other countries, labour history in Brazil initially was not an academic practice but tied to labour movements and thus a "collateral" consequence of the

4. For a view of Brazilian labour history as embedded in a continental landscape of research efforts and traditions see: John D. French, "The Laboring and Middle-Class Peoples of Latin America and the Caribbean: Historical Trajectories and New Research Directions", in Jan Lucassen (ed.), *Global Labour History. A State of the Art* (Bern, 2006), pp. 289–333; James P. Brennan, "Latin American Labor History", in Jose C. Moya (ed.), *The Oxford Handbook of Latin American History* (Oxford, 2011), pp. 342–366; Rossana Barragán and David Mayer, "Latin America and the Caribbean", in Karin Hofmeester and Marcel van der Linden (eds), *Handbook Global History of Work* (Berlin [etc.], 2017), pp. 95–121.
5. In this sketch, we will limit the account to the interrelation between labour historiography as an academic field and the country's general history. This is, of course, a reduction of complexity for the sake of brevity. A fuller picture would include the entangled history of Brazilian and international historiographies in that field (as well as relevant political, social, and economic processes involved), i.e. analysing the ways in which Brazilian labour historiography has influenced developments in Latin America and other world regions, and vice versa. Painting such a fuller picture would, however, require a research effort in its own right and thus go beyond the scope of this introduction. More detailed accounts of the history of labour historiography in Brazil can be found in: Michael Hall and Paulo Sérgio Pinheiro, "Alargando a história da classe operária. Organização, lutas e controle", *Revista Remate de Males*, 5 (1985), pp. 95–119; Maria Célia Paoli, Eder Sader, and Vera Silva Telles, "Pensando a classe operária. Sujeitos ao imaginário acadêmico", *Revista Brasileira de História*, 6 (1983), pp. 129–149; Claudio Batalha, "Os Desafios Atuais da História do Trabalho", *Anos 90*, 13:23/24 (2006), pp. 87–104.

emergence of labour organisations since the late nineteenth century. Up to the late 1950s, the most important works on the subject were mostly descriptive narratives by activists, inspired both by the need to preserve the legacy of past struggles and by the interest of the different political currents inside the workers movement in diffusing their particular versions of crucial events.[6]

It was only in the early 1960s, particularly in the state of São Paulo, that an academic interest in labour-related topics arose, mainly in sociology (at that moment itself an incipient discipline in Brazil), which focused on three main issues: First, the quickly growing factory proletariat and the origins and composition of this "young" working class; second, the proclivity of this growing working class to being integrated into the corporatist arrangements offered by populism; third, the "legacy" of slavery, which was seen as a system that prevented any possibility of agency and self-consciousness by the slaves, as well as a historical burden causing enormous difficulties for the integration of black people in the capitalist labour market. These works were generally marked by a peculiar combination of Marxism and modernization theories. Their authors deplored the absence of a "strong" and "mature" working class in Brazil, which was attributed to the fact that most industrial workers were recent migrants from rural areas. Migration to the major urban areas was understood as upward social mobility, resulting in a degree of well-being and, at the same time, a series of yet unsatisfied demands, thereby creating the basis for mass manipulation by populist leaders.[7]

This metanarrative, based on a selective and frequently biased reading of scarce empirical data, has sunk deep roots not only in the academic universe, but also among a broader Brazilian public, especially "opinion makers". In the 1970s, it was further developed by contributions from the political sciences, especially those who accused the Brazilian Communist Party

---

6. The role of those pioneering militant narratives for the development of Brazilian labour history is examined in Claudio Batalha, "A historiografia da classe operária no Brasil. Trajetórias e tendências", in Marcos C. de Freitas (ed.), *Historiografia brasileira em perspectiva* (São Paulo, 1998), pp. 145–168. For a communist perspective, see Edgard Carone, *Movimento operário no Brasil. Vol. 1: 1877–1944* (São Paulo, 1979). A classic anarchist account is offered in Edgar Rodrigues, *Socialismo e Sindicalismo no Brasil. 1675–1913* (Rio de Janeiro, 1969).
7. Some classical sociological works are: Juarez R.B. Lopes, *Sociedade industrial no Brasil* (São Paulo, 1964), particularly ch. 1 entitled "O ajustamento do trabalhador à indústria. Mobilidade social e motivação"; Octavio Ianni, *O colapso do populismo no Brasil* (Rio de Janeiro, 1968); Leôncio M. Rodrigues, *Industrialização e atitudes operárias. Estudo de um grupo de trabalhadores* (São Paulo, 1970); Florestan Fernandes, *A integração do negro na sociedade de classes* (São Paulo, 1964); Fernando Henrique Cardoso, *Capitalismo e Escravidão no brasil Meridional. O negro na sociedade escravocrata do Rio Grande do Sul* (São Paulo, 1962). A good summary of this first moment of academic research on labour in Brazil is offered in Kenneth P. Erickson, Patrick V. Peppe, and Hobart A. Spalding Jr., "Research on the Urban Working Class and Organized Labor in Argentina, Brazil, and Chile: What is Left to be Done?", *Latin American Research Review*, 9:2 (1974), pp. 115–142.

(Partido Comunista do Brasil, PCB) and its moderate political strategy in the immediate post-war period of having enabled the survival of the state-controlled union system: Having been illegal during the corporatist dictatorship of the *Estado Novo* (1937–1945), the PCB was able to quickly gain ground in the unions which had become more independent of state control with the regime's end. Although the PCB was banned again in 1947, it continued to exert major influence over the union movement until the beginning of military dictatorship in 1964.[8]

In the late 1970s, however, a new wave of industrial conflict and union organizing (still under the conditions of a dictatorship) led to the emergence of "new unionism", a phenomenon that was more participatory and social-movement-oriented than previous experiences, and which played a major role both in Brazil's re-democratization process and the formation of the Partido dos Trabalhadores (PT) in 1980.[9] This scenario has greatly contributed to radical changes in Brazil's labour historiography. A group of historians at the new and innovative University of Campinas (Universidade Estadual de Campinas, UNICAMP) became the epicentre of initiatives as well as academic and political discussions that led to a much more sophisticated approach to labour history, resulting in more academic respectability and an increasing institutionalization of the field.[10] This group strongly emphasized the need for dense and strong empirical research, challenging a long-standing essayistic academic tradition in Brazil, not least in historical studies. It is thus no coincidence that, in the context of these new initiatives, the Edgard Leuenroth Archive was established at the UNICAMP, named after an important early twentieth-century labour leader; it became one of the main archives specialized in labour history in Latin America.[11]

---

8. For example: Francisco Weffort, "Origens do sindicalismo populista no Brasil (A conjuntura do Após-guerra)", *Estudos Cebrap*, 4 (1973), pp. 66–105; Luiz W. Vianna, *Liberalismo e sindicato no Brasil* (Rio de Janeiro, 1976); Ricardo Maranhão, *Sindicatos e democratização (Brasil, 1945/ 1950)* (São Paulo, 1979); Arnaldo Spindel, *O partido comunista na genese do populismo. Analise da conjuntura da redemocratização no apos guerra* (São Paulo, 1980).
9. On New Unionism see, for instance, Margareth Keck, "The New Unionism in the Brazilian Transition", in Alfred Stepan (ed.), *Democratizing Brazil: Problems of Transition and Consolidation* (New York, 1989), pp. 252–296; Maurício Rands Barros, *Labour Relations and The New Unionism in Contemporary Brazil* (London [etc.], 1999); Francisco Barbosa de Macedo, "Social Networks and Urban Space: Worker Mobilization in the First Years of 'New' Unionism in Brazil", *International Review of Social History*, 60:1 (2015), pp. 33–71.
10. Not long after that, labour historians in the states of Rio Grande do Sul (based at the Federal University of Rio Grande do Sul) and Rio de Janeiro (based mainly at Federal Fluminense University) also started to play an important role in the further the development of the field.
11. On the early days of the History Department at Unicamp and the creation of the Edgard Leuenroth Archive, see an interview with Michael M. Hall conducted by Paulo Fontes and Francisco Barbosa de Macedo, published in the journal *Estudos Históricos*, 29:59 (2016), pp. 813–846.

Closely connected with the political re-democratization since the late 1970s, this new historiography on labour shifted its focus away from the populism of the Vargas years (1930–1945; 1950–1954), and the ambiguous role of the communists therein, and back to the First Republic (1888–1930). Based on the primary sources available at the time, anarchist and syndicalist experiences were reconstructed in the light of recent political events, which witnessed inter alia a sensible call for "autonomy" among organized workers.[12] Moreover, a strong interest in working-class everyday life, communities, and experiences beyond the workplaces and political organizations started to take centre stage, particularly among historians interested in the late nineteenth and early twentieth centuries.[13]

Simultaneously, the well-established field of history of slavery engaged in a dialogue with these major changes on more traditional aspects of labour history. The history of slavery was a field that, due to the transcontinental characteristics of both the slave trade and slave-based production, had been well-connected to international debates ever since Gilberto Freyre's *Casa-Grande & Senzala* (*The Masters and the Slaves*) from 1933. In the 1980s, the international turn towards "agency" was translated into a renewed emphasis on the actions, culture, and experiences of slaves. This revealed "customs in common" between different groups of workers, which shaped not only the political arena of Brazil during the nineteenth century, but also the fundamental configurations in the state-building process. Among the main achievements of this historiography were its highlighting of the ways in which slaves and freed Afro-Brazilian actively used the laws and the courts, and of the way in which enslaved workers were able to imbue their experiences with political meanings.[14]

These shared perspectives, approaches, and historiographical problems helped to shape a common academic tradition. In 2009, historians Sidney

12. That parallel between the new unionism of the late 1970s and the early struggles of the first decades of the twentieth century was made explicit in works such as: Kazumi Munakata, "O lugar do movimento operário", in *Anais do IV Encontro Regional de História de São Paulo* (Araraquara, 1980), republished in *Revista História e Perspectivas*, 23:43 (2010), pp. 9–40; Amnéris Maroni, *A estratégia da recusa. Análise das greves de maio/78* (São Paulo, 1982); Edgar S. de Decca, *O silêncio dos vencidos* (São Paulo, 1981).

13. Sidney Chalhoub, *Trabalho, Lar e Botequim. O Cotidiano dos Trabalhadores do Rio de Janeiro da Belle Epoque* (São Paulo, 1986) is probably the most influential work in this perspective.

14. See, among others, João José Reis, "A greve negra de 1857 na Bahia", *Revista USP*, 18 (1993), pp. 6–29; Sidney Chalhoub, *Visões da Liberdade. Uma história das últimas décadas da escravidão na Corte* (São Paulo, 1990); Robert Slenes, *Na senzala, uma flor, esperanças e recordações na formação da família escrava (Brasil, sudeste, século XIX)* (Rio de Janeiro, 1999); Silvia Lara and Joseli Mendonça (eds), *Direitos e Justiças no Brasil. Ensaios de História Social* (Campinas, 2006). For an appreciative critique of this perspective see Emília Viotti da Costa, "Experience versus Structures: New Tendencies in the History of Labor and the Working Class in Latin America: What Do We Gain? What Do We Lose?", *International Labor and Working Class History*, 36 (1989), pp. 3–24.

Chalhoub and Fernando Teixeira da Silva would summarize its main targets as the demolition of "the Brazilian historiographical Berlin wall".[15] While the metaphor seems a little clumsy, what they meant was the need to study and analyse the history and experiences of slaves and "double-free" wage workers as part of the same historical process of working-class formation. They not only rejected the artificial boundaries and chronologies that divided the academic fields, but also envisioned an enlarged conception of "work" and "workers" themselves.[16]

A major point of reference in these studies was E.P. Thompson's work on the relationship between the exercise of hegemony through the law and the subaltern agency based on cultural notions about rights and justice.[17] The signature of Thompsonian labour history was also visible in a series of studies focused on the often regionally and locally specific forms of paternalistic domination that had existed in Brazil since slavery.[18]

As is well known, New Unionism and the PT rose successively to become an alternative political project for Brazil. In 1994, Eric Hobsbawm had already identified Brazil not only as an example among the "newly industrializing countries" that had developed "industrial working classes who demanded workers' rights", but also as one of the few cases that had given birth to "political labour-cum-people's parties reminiscent of the mass social

15. Sidney Chalhoub and Fernando Teixeira da Silva, "Sujeitos *no* imaginário acadêmico. Escravos e trabalhadores na historiografia brasileira desde os anos 1980", *Cadernos AEL*, 14:26 (2009), pp. 11–49, 44. These ideas had been developed previously by Silvia H. Lara, "*Blowin' in the wind*. Thompson e a experiência negra no Brasil", *Projeto História* 12, (1995), pp. 43–56. See also Antonio Luigi Negro and Flávio Gomes, "Além de senzalas e fábricas. Uma história social do trabalho", *Tempo Social. Revista de sociologia da USP*, 18:1 (2006), pp. 217–240.
16. Nevertheless, this perspective is far from unanimous among historians of slavery in Brazil, and many of them would not consider their field as part of labour history or even see the latter as connected to the former.
17. The section on "The rule of law" in Thompson's *Whigs and Hunters* had a particularly strong impact on Brazilian labour historians doing research on the Vargas era, as well as in the debates regarding the long process of emancipation of slaves in the nineteenth century. See. E.P. Thompson, *Whigs and Hunters. The Origin of the Black Act* (New York, 1975). Thompson's work has constituted a major influence on Brazilian historiography and the study of its reception has itself become a recurrent topic of enquiry. See, for instance: Marcelo Badaró Mattos, *E. P. Thompson e a tradiçao de crítica ativa do materialismo histórico* (Rio de Janeiro, 2012); Antonio Luigi Negro, "E.P. Thompson no Brasil. Recepção e usos", *Crítica Marxista*, 39 (2014), pp. 151–161; Francisco Barbosa de Macedo, "O (re)fazer-se da historiografia. A obra de E.P. Thompson na produção discente do Programa de Pós-Graduação em História da Unicamp (1982–2002)" (Ph.D., Universidade de São Paulo, 2017).
18. José S.L. Lopes, *A tecelagem dos conflitos de classe na 'cidade das chaminés'* (São Paulo/ Brasília, 1988); José R. Ramalho, *Estado-patrão e luta operária. O caso FNM* (São Paulo, 1989); Paulo Fontes, *Trabalhadores e cidadãos. Nitro Química: a fábrica e as lutas operárias nos anos 50* (São Paulo, 1997); Alexandre Fortes, *Nós do quarto distrito. A classe trabalhadora porto-alegrense e a Era Vargas* (Rio de Janeiro [etc.], 2004); João José Reis and Eduardo Silva, *Negociação e Conflito. A resistência negra no Brasil escravista* (São Paulo, 1989); and Sidney Chalhoub *Machado de Assis, Historiador* (São Paulo, 2003).

democratic movements of pre-1914 Europe". In this regard, the agenda of Brazilian labour history has also undergone important transformations.[19]

The political success of this new generation of activists – both from unions and from other social movements – turned them increasingly into officials of sizeable organizations, as well as members of legislative bodies and governments, initially at the local and state levels. In dialogue with those contemporary experiences, historical research started to re-examine processes of institutionalization of the labour movement in the past, thereby directing attention again to the years between 1930 and 1964, i.e. the Vargas era and its aftermath.[20] The huge presence of migrants from the countryside in this new industrial working class inspired historians to challenge traditional views of rural backwardness and those academic analyses, which had emphasised internal migration as an obstacle to working-class formation.[21] The struggles for the enforcement of the new social rights established by the 1988 Constitution gave another impulse to study this period and the similar experiences of conflicts surrounding the compliance with labour laws.[22] Although the 1990s brought a deeply changed political and economic environment with the neoliberal presidencies of Fernando Collor de Mello (1990–1992) and Fernando Henrique Cardoso (1995–2002), the focus of Brazil's (by now academically institutionalized) labour history remained on the populist experience, further deepening the revisionist view of populism, which had already begun in the 1980s and which offered readings that were both more nuanced and appreciative of the corporatist system established by the Getúlio Vargas governments (1930–1945; 1950–1954).[23]

19. Eric J. Hobsbawm, *The Age of Extremes. The Short Twentieth Century, 1914–1991* (London [etc.], 1994), p. 370.

20. Alexandre Fortes, "Revendo a legalização dos sindicatos. Metalúrgicos de Porto Alegre (1931–1945)", in Alexandre Fortes *et al.*, *Na luta por direitos. Estudos recentes em história social do trabalho* (Campinas, 1999), pp. 19–49; Angela M.C. Araújo, "Estado e trabalhadores. A montagem da estrutura sindical corporativista no Brasil", in *idem, Do corporativismo ao neoliberalismo. Estado e trabalhadores no Brasil e na Inglaterra* (São Paulo, 2002), pp. 29–57.

21. Paulo Fontes, *Migration and the Making of Industrial São Paulo* (Durham, NC, 2016); Antonio Luigi Negro, *Linhas de montagem. O industrialismo nacional-desenvolvimentista e a sindicalização dos trabalhadores, 1945–1978* (São Paulo, 2004); Murilo Leal, *A Reinvenção da Classe Trabalhadora, 1953–1964* (Campinas, 2011).

22. Maria Celia Paoli, "Trabalhadores e cidadania. Experiência do mundo público na história do Brasil moderno", *Estudos Avançados*, 3:7 (1989), pp. 40–66; John D. French, *The Brazilian Workers' ABC. Class Conflict and Alliances in Modern São Paulo* (Chapel Hill, NC, 1992); Hélio da Costa, *Em busca da memória (Comissão de Fábrica, Partido e Sindicato no Pós-guerra)* (São Paulo, 1995); Fernando Teixeira da Silva, *A carga e a culpa. Os operários das docas de Santos. Direitos e cultura de solidariedade, 1937–1968* (São Paulo/Santos, 1995); and *idem, Trabalhadores no Tribunal. Conflitos e Justiça do Trabalho em São Paulo no Contexto do Golpe de 1964* (São Paulo, 2016).

23. Ângela de Castro Gomes, *A invenção do trabalhismo* (Rio de Janeiro [etc.], 1988); John D. French, *Drowning in Laws. Labor Law and Brazilian Political Culture* (Chapel Hill, NC, 2004);

2000–2016: *MUNDOS DO TRABALHO* ON THE UPSWING

Around 2000, the political pendulum in Brazil, just as in many other Latin American countries, was veering to the left. The celebration in 2001 in Porto Alegre of the first edition of the World Social Forum gave the movements against neoliberal globalization, which had become visible during the previous years, a (however vague) political platform. The venue Porto Alegre was not a coincidence, as the city had, under the aegis of the PT, implemented a series of quite challenging social and political reforms, including the famous "participatory budget". More importantly, in 2002, Luiz Inácio Lula da Silva, the former north-eastern migrant and historical leader of the metalworkers, was elected as president. In this general context, Brazilian labour history further consolidated as a specialized historiographical field. A year earlier Mundos do Trabalho, a network of labour historians within the Brazilian Historical association ANPUH (Associação Nacional de História) was established.[24] It was, from the beginning, not only marked by the spirit of political opening experienced at that moment in Brazil, yet also by a broadened and inclusive definition of the concerns of labour history: historians working on all periods (including before 1900) and all regions (not only the centres of industries) were invited to participate. In addition, both urban and rural, formal and informal, as well as free and unfree labour were included. As a result of this "ecumenical perspective",[25] in the last twelve years this workgroup has organized a series of national and international conferences in which hundreds of researchers, many of them graduate students or young professors, take part on a regular basis.

Such a broadened outlook on labour was very much in tune with the politics of inclusion of the PT, which did not limit its social policies to industrial workers, particularly those organized and represented by unions. There is no space here to give a detailed assessment of the thirteen years of Workers Party rule in Brazil and all its contradictions and achievements. While it seemed clear from early on that the political and economic orientation of Lula's government would be definitely among the "pinker" streams of the new "red wave" in Latin America, its actions called the attention of many observers worldwide, not least because of the size of the

---

Barbara Weinstein, *For Social Peace in Brazil: Industrialists and the Remaking of the Working Class in São Paulo, 1920–1964* (Chapel Hill, NC, 1996).

24. See: https://gtmundosdotrabalho.org; last accessed 7 November 2017. Apart from regular academic gatherings and congresses, since 2009 it publishes an academic journal with the same name. See: https://periodicos.ufsc.br/index.php/mundosdotrabalho/index; last accessed 7 November 2017.

25. As mentioned before, this integration of different research fields is an ongoing quest that, despite its numerous successes, has not undone the existence of separate research communities – something that is well reflected in the number and names of working groups within ANPUH.

country (which is not only quasi-continental in territory, but the sixth in population) as well as the fact that it is one of the most industrialized countries in the Global South. Among the undeniable successes of the Lula years are the effective measures adopted to face the most dramatic results of the abysmal social inequalities in Brazil, seeing millions of households overcoming hunger and poverty. Furthermore, several years of economic growth and low unemployment rates in a political environment favourable to union activity and the effects of substantial rises in the national minimum wage increased workers' share in national income and their collective bargaining power.[26] On a different plane, Brazil was also able to attain a new position geopolitically, playing a central role among the BRICS countries and contributing to the weakening of the hegemony of the US over Latin America and the Caribbean.

New laws extended labour rights to categories historically kept in the informal sector, such as domestic workers. A series of measures were adopted to address the pervasive racial inequalities in Brazil (including affirmative action policies and quotas for public universities), thus abolishing not only the myth of Brazil as a harmonious "racial democracy", but giving the historical legacy of slavery a new relevance in public discourse. The acknowledgement of the continuing presence of unfree labour (called "contemporary slavery") led to improved laws to combat it; similar measures were taken against child labour. In the same vein, issues of gender were addressed in various ways. These outstanding achievements created a dynamic dialogue as well as many instances of cooperation between, on the one hand, a state that experienced a partial elite change with many former activists now in official positions, and, on the other hand, organizations from both the labour and "new" social movements. At the same time, this relationship was contentious from the outset (and increasingly so over the years), with many moments of conflict and alienation between movements and the government.

---

26. The literature analysing Brazil's recent development and the PT government, of course, fills libraries. For interventions from a labour history and labour studies perspective, see Alexandre Fortes and John D. French, "Another World Is Possible: The Rise of the Brazilian Workers' Party and the Prospects for Lula's Government", *Labor: Studies in Working-Class History*, 2:3 (2005), pp. 13–31; André Singer, "Raízes sociais e ideológicas do lulismo", *Novos Estudos – CEBRAP*, 85 (2009), pp. 85–102; Alexandre Fortes, "In Search of a Post-Neoliberal Paradigm: The Brazilian Left and Lula's Government", *International Labor and Working-Class History*, 75:1 (2009), pp. 109–125; André Singer, "A segunda alma do Partido dos Trabalhadores", *Novos Estudos – CEBRAP*, 88 (2010), pp. 89–111; Perry Anderson, "Lula's Brazil", *London Review of Books*, 33:7 (2011), pp. 3–12; John D. French and Alexandre Fortes, "Nurturing Hope, Deepening Democracy, and Combating Inequalities in Brazil: Lula, the Workers' Party, and Dilma Rousseff's 2010 Election as President", *Labor: Studies in Working-Class History*, 9:1 (2012), pp. 7–28; André Singer, *Os sentidos do lulismo. Reforma gradual e pacto conservador* (São Paulo, 2012).

The economic and political foundations on which that progressive moment of Brazilian history rested, however, had built-in contradictions that began to gradually exacerbate, eventually erupting into a crisis that led to the judiciary-parliamentary coup of 2016. On one hand, the political system of coalitional presidentialism led to the formation of highly contradictory alliances between the Workers Party and sectors of the political right, for the sake of governability.[27] On the other hand, the dependency on the commodities boom as a source of economic prosperity also implied a coexistence, if not cooperation, with an agribusiness that was responsible for great environmental destruction and involved in the most degrading forms of labour exploitation. The growth of such giant state-owned companies as Petrobras as well as major investments in infrastructure for the 2014 World Cup and the 2016 Olympic Games at the same time created the opportunity for large-scale corruption.

As tensions on all those fronts mounted, the second term of former guerrilla fighter Dilma Rousseff, Brazil's first female president, was increasingly confronted with attacks by a powerful alliance of the police-judiciary apparatus, media groups, and new right-wing groups active in social networks and street demonstrations. Meanwhile, the PT had gradually lost the support of many who were disenchanted with the *Realpolitik* associated with government politics. More importantly, the PT, which had once been held up as a "new type of party" due to its ability to give social movements ample space,[28] had been drained of most of its previous movement components. When it came under attack, there was not enough "movement" left to defend it.[29]

It seems evident that labour history in Brazil during the last fifteen years has been related, to a high degree, to the particular conjuncture the country has gone through – the articles assembled in this Special Issue bear witness to an atmosphere, both intellectually and politically, in which concerns of inclusion, participation, and social justice were given ample space. At the same time, labour historians in Brazil responded to a series of internal dynamics specific to academia in general and historiography in particular, both originating in the country itself and in international debates. Indeed, Brazilian labour historians have become increasingly internationalized since 2000. They have started to attend international conferences and

27. On the peculiarities of Brazilian presidentialism, see Fernando Limongi, "Democracy in Brazil: Presidentialism, Party Coalitions and the Decision Making Process", *Novos Estudos – CEBRAP*, 3 (selected edition) (2007), available at: http://socialsciences.scielo.org/scielo.php?script=sci_arttext& pid=S0101-33002007000100001&lng=en&tlng=en; last accessed 7 November 2017.
28. Michael Löwy, "A New Type of Party: The Brazilian PT", *Latin American Perspectives*, 14:4 (1987), pp. 453–464.
29. Alexandre Fortes, "Brazil's Neoconservative Offensive", *NACLA Report on the Americas*, 48:3 (2016), pp. 217–220; Perry Anderson, "Crisis in Brazil", *London Review of Books*, 38:8 (2016), pp. 15–22.

seminars more frequently, and to publish in some of the major academic journals of the field.[30] Their academic connections and networks have expanded beyond the traditional links with the US and Europe. There has been a growing presence of scholars from all over Latin America, as well as from India and Africa in the biannual conferences organized by Mundos do Trabalho. Its electronic journal, publishing articles in Portuguese and Spanish, is probably now the most important in the field in Latin America. In recent years, a growing number of Brazilian scholars are getting involved in research projects with comparative, transnational, and connected approaches, and interest in methodological and theoretical discussions on Global Labour History has risen.[31]

In spite of all these developments and achievements, Brazilian labour history remains, to a great extent, parochial and self-centred. There are many reasons for that, among them, language insularism and a resilient methodological nationalism. For instance, the fact that, for many decades, most of the scholarship was limited to the two most important states in economic and political terms (São Paulo and Rio de Janeiro) has engendered a huge demand for research on other regions within the borders of Brazil rather than a thrust to go *extra muros*. The international diffusion of the

---

30. Some recent and representative examples are Fernando Teixeira da Silva, "The Brazilian and Italian Labor Courts: Comparative Notes", *International Review of Social History*, 55:3 (2010), pp. 381–412; Marcelo Badaró Mattos, "Experiences in Common: Slavery and 'Freedom' in the Process of Rio de Janeiro's Working-Class Formation (1850–1910)", *International Review of Social History*, 55:2 (2010), pp. 193–213; Sidney Chalhoub, "The Precariousness of Freedom in a Slave Society (Brazil in the Nineteenth Century)", *International Review of Social History*, 56:3 (2011), pp. 405–439; Leonardo Pereira, "The Flower of the Union: Leisure, Race, and Social Identity in Bangu, Rio de Janeiro (1904–1933)", *Journal of Social History*, 46:1 (2012), pp. 154–169; Cristiana Schettini, "South American Tours: Work Relations in the Entertainment Market in South America", in Ulbe Bosma *et al.* (eds), "Mediating Labour: Worldwide Labour Intermediation in the Nineteenth and Twentieth Centuries", Special Issue 20 of *International Review of Social History*, 57 (2012), pp. 129–160; Paulo Fontes and Francisco B. Macedo, "Strikes and Pickets in Brazil: Worker Mobilization in the 'Old' and 'New' Unionism, the Strikes of 1957 and 1980", *International Labor and Working Class History*, 83 (2013), pp. 86–111; Henrique Espada Lima, "Wages of Intimacy: Domestic Workers Disputing Wages in the Higher Courts of Nineteenth-Century Brazil", *International Labor and Working Class History*, 88 (2015), pp. 11–29; Clarice Speranza, "European Workers in Brazilian Coalmining, Rio Grande do Sul, 1850–1950", in Ad Knotter and David Mayer (eds), "Migration and Ethnicity in Coalfield History: Global Perspectives", Special Issue 23 of *International Review of Social History*, 60 (2015), pp. 165–183; Fernando Teixeira da Silva and Larissa Rosa Corrêa, "The Politics of Justice: Rethinking Brazil's Corporatist Labor Movement", *Labor: Studies in Working-Class History*, 13:2 (2016), pp. 11–31. Also see the contributions to Paulo Fontes and Alexandre Fortes (eds), "Space, Culture and Labour: Brazilian Urban Workers in the Twentieth Century", Special Issue of *Moving the Social: Journal of Social History and the History of Social Movements*, 49 (2013).
31. An overview of recent trends and their connections to the political context is provided in John D. French and Alexandre Fortes, "When the Plumber(s) Come to Fix a Country: Doing Labor History in Brazil", *International Labor and Working-Class History*, 82 (2012), pp. 117–126.

scholarly works and of the rich debates that characterize the field of labour history in Brazil is thus still relatively timid, and, consequently, their contribution to the international historiographical debates until this point, has fallen short of its potential.

At the same time, this situation is not only a result of "shortcomings" and "deficiencies", but also of a degree of hesitancy, if not resistance: It is important to bear in mind that many Brazilian historians (like their colleagues in other Latin American countries) have received the "global turn" announced for historiography with some scepticism and mistrust. Labour history is no exception in this regard. The proclaimed newness of Global Labour History has been disputed and is considered by many as a typical exaggeration of international academic vogue. Some, indeed, see it as just another hegemonic Western academic project, pointing to the continuing asymmetries and hierarchies (both academically as well as in relation to the working and living conditions of historians), the dominance of English as lingua franca, etc. The agenda of Global Labour History still seems mainly set by the North, its academia, institutions, and journals. In addition, there are concerns that the current debates in Global Labour History tend to neglect power relations, potentially resulting in a "depoliticization" of the field, an issue particularly sensitive in Brazil and Latin America in general.[32] Scepticism is also voiced vis-à-vis those approaches that seem to privilege a return to macro-narratives with an emphasis on economic processes on a global scale. Many historians fear that their focus on local and micro scales could be buried by the global "wave". More importantly, many argue that these sort of global approaches risk erasing working-class experiences from the labour history narrative, something that is considered one of the most important gains of the field in the last three decades.[33]

---

32. See, for instance, a comment by Peter Winn, who asserts this political dimension and argues that labour history in Latin America remains, due to this political urgency, mostly centred on each national society and is thus not easily compatible with the enterprise of Global Labour History: Peter Winn, "Global Labour History: The Future of the Field?", *International Labor and Working-Class History*, 82 (2012), pp. 85–91.

33. These sceptical views persist despite the fact that most of the concerns summed up here have been repeatedly and self-critically addressed in the conceptual propositions about Global Labour History that insist on both a continued focus on agency and the open and collaborative character of Global Labour History as a "field of concerns" rather than a "paradigm". A proper debate about why these proclamations have not succeeded so far in fully convincing the sceptics would be worthwhile. Among the numerous propositions in that vein, see, for instance: Marcel van der Linden, "Labour History: The Old, the New and the Global", *African Studies*, 66:2–3 (2007), pp. 169–180; Leo Lucassen, "Working Together: New Directions in Global Labour History", *Journal of Global History*, 11:1 (2016), pp. 66–87. For Anglophone critical interventions that echo the concerns of many Brazilian and Latin American labour historians listed above, see, for instance, Dorothy Sue Cobble, "The Promise and Peril of New Global Labor History", *International Labor and Working-Class History*, 82 (2012), pp. 99–107; Fred Cooper, "What Is the Concept of Globalization Good For? An African Historian's Perspective", *African Affairs*, 100 (2001), pp. 189–213,

The interrelation between labour history in Brazil and Global Labour History is thus not a readily smooth or congenial one, but a dialogue that must be constructed. Consequently, the main aims of this Special Issue are to strengthen the links and to improve this dialogue. We wanted to ensure that the contributions by Brazilian labour historians go beyond "interesting" cases and examples in an otherwise well-contoured intellectual project, and aspire to co-shape the core discussions in Global Labour History. The nine articles assembled here offer a rich sample of the current state of the field in Brazil and certainly the most comprehensive compilation on Brazilian labour history ever published in English. They encompass a wide geographical scope, with studies ranging from the Amazon region to the extreme South, through the north-east and the central areas of São Paulo and Rio de Janeiro. In chronological terms, the articles brought together in this Special Issue also express the recent trend of integrating studies on periods before 1900 into labour history.[34] A broad array of workers (slaves, maids, prostitutes, industrial workers, rural workers, etc.) is covered. At the same time, this volume also presents a renewed historiography of movements and organizations, offering insights both on workers' collective actions and everyday life experiences, as well as on the workers' relations to institutions, the state, and politics. The topics explored by the authors resonate deeply with some of the central debates in Global Labour History, such as free and unfree labour; labour in "frontier" environments; the transnational circulation of militants and ideas; gender, race, and class; labour laws and the State; labour and space; populism, patronage, and workers; labour movements in an international perspective; or experiences of labour under dictatorships. Research problems are addressed through a diversity of methodologies, with the employment of a broad range of sources, producing innovative approaches and results. As non-familiar readers will notice when reading the articles in this Special Issue, Brazilian labour historians share numerous concerns with their counterparts in other countries; at the same time, there are some issues and perspectives that are quite specific to them. In the following, we will highlight some of these commonalities and specificities by introducing the contributions to this Special Issue along certain larger themes, such as "free/unfree" labour; the use of judiciary sources; the interlocking identities of "gender", "race", and "class"; the continuing currency of topics of political history and the history of movements; transnational and comparative perspectives; and the

and Neville Kirk, "Transnational Labor History: Promises and Perils", in Leon Fink (ed.), *Workers across the Americas: The Transnational Turn in Labor History* (Oxford, 2011), pp. 18–22.
34. Earlier periods have not yet tended to be in the focus of Brazilian labour history, although it seems evident that studies on the colonial period – again, taking the example of the historiography on slavery – should be integrated in the debates. This remains one of the main challenges for Brazilian labour history.

necessary integration of labour history with the history of New social movements.[35]

FLUID BOUNDARIES AND INTERLOCKING IDENTITIES – "FREE/UNFREE", "GENDER", AND "RACE"

One of the perennial topics in the current international debate is the inter-relation of free and unfree labour (and the manifold transitions between them), a debate to which Brazilian labour history has already made important contributions and which, indeed, has been one of the central concerns of the events of the ANPUH working group Mundos do Trabalho.[36] In this Special Issue, this tradition is further enhanced: In "Free and Unfree Labor in the Nineteenth-Century Brazilian Amazon", Adalberto Paz presents important findings on the still little-known characteristics of compulsory labour in the Northern areas of Brazil and its complex relations to the legal status of different ethno-racial groups. Paz analyses the different legal regulations vis-à-vis those coloured population groups who were not enslaved – indigenous, *mestiços, libertos*, etc. – and focuses on the ambiguities of the official claims that granted freedom to the indigenous population. While several attempts to introduce African slave labour as a replacement failed, the authorities resorted to changing, but continuous strategies to install regimes of forced labour (for both public and private work assignments) during the eighteenth and nineteenth centuries. Finally, adding a component of transnational history, Paz points to the strong connection between this kind of forced labour and the strategic operations implemented by the postcolonial Brazilian Empire (1822–1889) in order to defend its territorial control of the Amazon against French claims.

Fabiane Popinigis and Henrique Espada Lima further advance the current debate about the blurred boundaries not only of "free" and "unfree" labour", but also between the "domestic" and "non-domestic" spheres. In "Maids, Clerks, and the Shifting Landscape of Labor Relations in Rio de Janeiro (1830s–1880s)", they explore the connections between class, gender, and race during the last decades of legal slavery and the onset of European

---

35. A caveat should be added at this point: This introduction claims the contributions to the present Special Issue as "players" of a larger "team", namely Brazilian labour historiography. It goes without saying that such an engrossing attribution is debatable and that each article can be read as part of other intellectual or geographical affiliations.

36. As has been recently shown in a detailed analysis of the meetings and conferences of Mundos do Trabalho, papers related to topics of "free/unfree labour" (including "slavery") made up about one third of all papers presented between 2001 and 2015 at the groups' symposia. See Paulo Cruz Terra and Fabiane Popinigis, "As diversas formas de exploração do trabalho e de organização dos trabalhadores no âmbito da produção do GT Mundos do Trabalho", paper presented at the Congreso Latinoamericano y del Caribe de Trabajo y Trabajadores, 2–8 May 2017, La Paz.

mass immigration to Brazil. Making ample use of judicial sources, they highlight, through a number of vivid accounts of workers' experiences, important shifts during those years: Women, especially of Afro-Brazilian descent, were pushed out of small commercial establishments and street vending, turning the work of "clerks" into the domain of male, non-slave labourers, while domestic labour at the same time became more precarious and female.

Issues of "free" and "unfree" labour are further addressed in the article by Christine Rufino Dabat and Thomas Rogers about a group of workers that has, for most of Brazil's history, constituted the majority of workers, but which has often been neglected as a topic in labour history: rural workers. In their article about "Sugarcane Workers in Search of Justice: Rural Labour through the Lens of the State", they analyse two locations during the 1960s–1980s in the cane zone of Pernambuco, historically one of the centres of slave-based plantation production. At the beginning of the 1960s, these workers got access to the Brazilian system of labour courts (Juntas de Conciliação e Julgamento, JCJs). Using files from these courts both for an aggregate analysis of the situation of this group and for reconstructing some individual cases, it becomes clear that these workers were exposed to a number of onslaughts and impositions that placed them outside a "normal" labour relationship. The collusion of propertied groups and judiciary elites played an important role in enabling this situation, which persisted despite the existence of such regulatory bodies as the labour courts. By referring to a number of current studies on different world regions about the precariousness of workers, especially in contexts in which, historically, unfree labour has set the frame for labour exploitation and in which the access to land, education, etc. continues to be extremely limited, Dabat and Rogers highlight the degree to which violence and dynamics of exclusion have characterized the life of these workers. This is reinforced by a symbolical exclusion that came with condescending elite views about the rural as "backward" and "archaic".

Both the contributions by Fabiane Popinigis and Henrique Espada Lima as well as the one by Thomas Rogers and Christine R. Dabat point readers to a peculiarity of Brazilian labour history: the extensive use of judicial sources as a way to reconstruct not only aggregate social realities, but also the voices of individual workers. This methodological predilection (which indeed sets an important example for labour historians in other countries) has a strong tradition in Brazil and might be attributed to a number of factors: While Brazil was the last country in the Americas to abolish slavery, it has seen more freed slaves and free people of colour than any other of America's slave-based societies. This combination of "free" and "unfree" favoured that, in the long, drawn out process of the abolition of slavery during the years of the Empire (1822–1888), both enslaved and free Afro-Brazilians submitted cases to the courts, thereby leaving unique written traces of their claims and doings. Still more importantly, there is a powerful tradition of labour law in Brazil. As Aldrin Castellucci and Benito Bisso Schmidt point out in their article "From the Streets to the Government: Socialist Militants and Labour Law in Brazil", leading socialists of the Frist Republic (1889–1930), many of whom rose socially by studying in one of the country's law schools, shared a strong orientation towards a legal regulation of the labour–capital relation. Yet, it was especially since the "Revolution of 1930" and the beginning of the corporatist era of Getúlio Vargas (1930–1945; 1951–1954) that "labour law" became a central prism through which pro-worker policies were formulated and the relationship between labour, capital, and the state has been regulated. This culminated, in 1943, in the Consolidated Labour Laws (Consolidação das Leis do Trabalho, CLT), probably the most comprehensive and systematic legal body of labour regulation on the subcontinent. It has led historians to read the history of labour through the evolution of this body and to a keen sensitivity for the documentary potentials of one of its major institutions, the labour courts.[37] The records of these courts are not universally available, with many documents lost; yet, in a number of states (Rio Grande do Sul, Pernambuco, São Paulo, Bahia, among others) these have been preserved, at least partially, often with the help of attentive historians, and are explored today for a number of research questions.

Cristiana Schettini's contribution to the Special Issue brings in a group that has long been completely neglected by labour historians: sex workers. Focusing on the labour relations in the Mangue, one of Rio de Janeiro's red light districts in the 1920s, she combines a variety of sources to follow different trajectories: League of Nation's investigators (some of them undercover), local Brazilian authorities, particularly the police, and Fanny Galper, a former prostitute and madam. "Between Rio's Red-Light district and the League of Nations: Immigrants and Sex Work in 1920s Rio de Janeiro" integrates concerns of gender, race, urban history, social thought, and policymaking in order to gain a fuller understanding of the (highly racialized) work relations in sex work at the time, the forms of transnational mobility involved, Rio's specific policy of surveillance, and the international circulation of policies to regulate prostitution. Meanwhile, by focusing on one actor, the doings and voice of one of these women is partly preserved, allowing fascinating insights in the trajectory of a sex worker ascending to become a relatively well-to-do entrepreneur.

Cristiana Schettini's article also points to the interlocking identifications of gender, class, and race: She makes clear that the relation between such

---

37. For a general historical analysis of these labour courts, see the contributions to Ângela de Castro Gomes and Fernando Teixeira da Silva (eds), *A Justiça do Trabalho e sua história. Os direitos dos trabalhadores no Brasil* (Campinas, 2013).

prostitutes-turned-madams of European Jewish origin like Fanny Galper and the Afro-Brazilian sex workers who toiled for her was marked by inequality and exploitation. Racialized social hierarchies as mechanisms for defining different groups of workers (and their legal status) have played a fundamental role in Brazilian society, and they are also highlighted by Adalberto Paz for the Amazon, by Fabiane Popinigis and Henrique Lima for nineteenth-century Rio, and by Christine Dabat and Thomas Rogers for the mostly Afro-Brazilian cane workers in Pernmabuco. Also among the six biographies of socialists analysed by Aldrin Castellucci and Benito Bisso Schmidt (a political group that many would associate with "European immigrants"), two were of "mixed" Afro-Brazilian descent. Questions of race have recently gained increasing importance among Brazilian labour historians, thus breaking the previous tendencies of giving attention to Afro-Brazilians as slaves only, while "invisibilizing" their presence in the worlds of labour in the periods after abolition.[38] Such tendencies have echoed one of Brazil's central myths since the late 1940s, namely that it is a country of "racial democracy" in which all groups live in "harmony" thus making issues of race obsolete. Brazilian labour history (as well as many other fields of scholarly enquiry) is currently contributing to a deconstruction of this myth.

POLITICAL HISTORY REVISITED

As mentioned before, one of the specific characteristics of labour history in Brazil (and in Latin America in general) is the continuing currency of political history as well as the history of labour movements and organizations. This is a sensible difference to the debates about Global Labour History in Europe, which, in recent years, have tended to focus on social histories of work and labour relations (no wonder, one of the major critiques of Latin American labour historians vis-à-vis certain approaches of Global Labour History is its "depoliticization" and supposed lack of attention to asymmetric power relations). Such "traditionalism", however, should not be equated with "conventionalism", and several contributions to this Special Issue illustrate how questions of political history can be enhanced by a number of fresh perspectives – often using comparisons or transnational connections to revisit certain issues. In "Revolutionary Syndicalism and Reformism in Rio de Janeiro's Labour Movement (1906–1920)", Claudio Batalha provides an updated panorama of the differences and commonalities that characterized the most important

---

38. See, for instance, several of the contribution to: Alexandre Fortes and Habe Mattos, "Post- Abolition in the Atlantic World", Dossier of the *Revista Brasileira de História*, 35:69 (2015), available at: http://www.scielo.br/scielo.php?script=sci_issuetoc&pid=0102-01882015000l&lng=en& nrm=iso; last accessed 7 November 2017.

political currents inside Rio's unionism during the Brazilian First Republic. He not only proceeds to question a number of established myths (for instance, about a supposed "anarchist hegemony" at that moment), more importantly he shows how apparently stable attributes such as "reformist" or "revolutionary syndicalist" were much more fluid and porous than usually admitted. Contrasting Rio with both the European "models" of each of these currents (and their associated practices and positions) and the sometimes markedly different outlook of corresponding currents in Brazil's other industrial centre at the time, São Paulo, Batalha proceeds to show that "revolutionary syndicalism" in Rio was never very "revolutionary" (curiously, in contrast to the city's rebellious traditions), and that, despite the sometimes bitter struggles with "reformists", collaboration between the two currents was common. Furthermore, he shows that the "revolutionary syndicalists" pushed for (and actually gained) a number of reforms during the years 1917–1919, i.e. during a cycle of struggles that has often been associated with "revolution". Through a detailed analysis of local activities and sources as well as by comparing them to similar practices in other places (both in Brazil and internationally), Batalha achieves important nuances for a field of political action that previously was often depicted as organized in clear-cut blocks.

In a similar vein, Aldrin Castelucci's and Benito Bisso Schmidt's article "From the Streets to the Government: Socialist Militants and Labour Law in Brazil" uses a comparative biographical analysis of a group of socialists to highlight nuances, contradictions, and counterintuitive facts about a political current whose "performance" had long been viewed as unequivocally negative and problematic in terms of "selling out", first, to the oligarchic block predominating during the First Republic, then to the corporatist regime emerging after 1930 under Getúlio Vargas. Yet, the important and usually overlooked continuities between the experiences of the labour movement in the early twentieth century and the Vargas era is precisely the point of Castelucci's and Schmidt's argument: Older readings of a straightforward "cooptation" of these actors into the new regime are too simple, they say. They assert that the six individuals analysed did not experience too much of a rupture between their earlier (sometimes surprisingly militant) activities and their later role as legal advisors and officials to the Vargas regime. They also argue that they succeeded in actually connecting the struggles of the workers during the first three decades of the twentieth century to the reforms and legal provisions in favour of workers since 1930.

The transnational "lens" has, without doubt, been a powerful enhancement in labour history during the last decades. It has allowed for both the breaking of new ground and the re-interpreting of old questions. Christina Schettini's story about sex workers in Rio points to the potential of this "lens" for a social history of labour, allowing the movements of workers whose lives are marked by migration and diverse cross-border contacts to be traced. The political history of labour and its movements has equally benefitted from such transnational perspectives. As Alexandre Fortes illustrates in his article, they enable new interpretations of one of the most perennial topics of Latin American labour history: to understand the origins and the rise of populism in general, and the allegiance of workers to it in particular. The literature on populism, especially on the trinity of Argentinian Peronism (1943/45–1955), Mexican Cardenism (1934–1940), and Brazilian *Varguismo* (after the reign of Getúlio Vargas, 1930–1945; 1951–1954) fills libraries; yet, in Brazil, as elsewhere, it is largely dominated by approaches that see each of these phenomena as nationally isolated and idiosyncratic, to a point where the category of "populism" itself is rejected as too generic. However, there is a noticeable new interest in more comparative and transnational views in the study of Latin American populisms.[39] Adding to this fresh departure, Alexandre Fortes, in "World War II and Brazilian Workers: Populism at the Intersections of National and Global Histories", argues that the connections between total war on the one hand, and changes in labour relations and social rights on the other (otherwise a well-established topic in the international historiography), have been largely ignored in Brazil as a result of these limitations. In dialogue with other historiographies, particularly on foreign relations, economic development, and military history, the author emphasizes how Brazil's involvement in World War II reinforced or even enabled a series of transformations within *Varguismo*, among them the further inclusion of workers through a series of social reforms and the emergence of mass nationalism with a considerable mobilizational component – something that the Vargas regime, untypically for Latin American populisms, had previously been lacking. During and through its involvement in World War II, *Varguismo* thus evolved into a regime more akin to the political systems discussed under the label "populism".

Combining both comparative and transnational perspectives, Larissa Corrêa's article "Looking at the Southern Cone: American Trade Unionism

---

39. For a comparative advance on historical populisms published before 2000, i.e. before "populism" made a spectacular comeback in Latin America; see María Moira Mackinnon and Mario Alberto Petrone (eds), *Populismo y neopopulismo en America Latina. El problema de la Cenicienta* (Buenos Aires, 1998). More recent suggestions for a comparative and transnational reinterpretation are offered, for instance in: Matthew B. Karaush, "Populism as an Identity: Four Propositions on Peronism", in John Abromeit *et al.* (eds), *Transformations of Populism in Europe and the Americas. History and Recent Tendencies* (London, 2016), pp. 197–211. Interestingly, the Argentinian Network for the study of Peronism has, for the first time, included a stream on "comparative, regional, and transnational studies" for its next conference. See Call for Papers, 6th Conference on the Study of Peronism, University of Buenos Aires, 29-31 August 2018, available at: http://redesperonismo.org/wp-content/uploads/2017/10/First-Annoucement_6th-Conference-on-the-Study-of-Peronism.pdf; last accessed 7 November 2017.

in the Cold War Military Dictatorships of Brazil and Argentina" analyses the views and actions of AFL-CIO-affiliated organizations active in Latin America. Focusing on the American Institute for Free Labor Development (AIFLD) and comparing its activities in Brazil and Argentina during the 1960s and 1970s, she shows the degree to which the policies developed vis-à-vis Brazil – especially during and after the military coup of 1964 – served as a model for their actions in Argentina and other countries. While its outlook remained fully formatted by a Cold War rationale, they found it difficult to find interlocutors in the two countries as the local union movements were either under a left-wing or nationalist (or a left-nationalist) hegemony. A more favourable environment only emerged during the dictatorships, which saw the South American unions assaulted in many ways. While AIFLD directly and indirectly supported these dictatorships, a sensible shift occurred during the last Argentine dictatorship (1976–1983) with its no-holds-barred, genocidal form of repression, which also affected local contacts and allies of AIFLD. Taking up the "human rights turn" in international politics, the organization now (albeit timidly) confronted these regimes.

What, meanwhile, is a "movement"? Global Labour History aspires to break the divisions between historians of labour movements (however broadly defined) and the so-called New Social Movements. This division echoes some of the political struggles of the 1970s and after, when New Social Movements claimed to be wholly novel due to their non-affiliation with "labour" as well as its emphasis on other social identifications than "worker" (alternative identifications based particularly on local community and "citizenship", but also on race, gender, or ethnicity). However, as Paulo Fontes points out in his article about the "The Local and the Global: Neighborhoods, Workers and Associations in São Paulo (1945–1964)", such separations are artificial and should be overcome. Analysing with new archival material a series of mobilizations[40] in early post-war neighbour-hoods in São Paulo, he shows the degree to which being a "worker" and a neighbourhood "resident" were interwoven and resulted in processes that combined class formation, political participation, and the building of local community. In order to overcome this disjunction between "workers" and

---

40. For his research, Fontes strongly relies on records of the Department of Political and Social Order (Departamento Estadual de Ordem Política e Social – DEOPS), founded in the 1920s and of central importance in surveilling all activities of political and social movements both during the Vargas years and the military dictatorship from 1964 on. In the context of the re-democratization process the DEOPS was dissolved in 1983, its records being preserved and made publicly available in a number of Brazil's states. Today, these archives offer unique insights into the activities of a series of movements, often including otherwise unavailable original documents produced by the movements themselves. For more on DEOPS archives, see Paulo Fontes and Antonio Luigi Negro, "Using Police Records in Labor History: A Case Study of the Brazilian DEOPS", *Labor: Studies in Working-Class History*, 5:1 (2008), pp. 15–22.

"neighbours" and the corresponding division between labour history, on the one hand, and social movement studies, on the other, Fontes argues that Global Labour History should also attend more seriously to the "local": it is on the micro-level of neighbourhoods, etc. where such experiences of overlapping identifications and their effects for class formation and political participation can be observed best.

It was our aim to offer readers of this Special Issue more than a showcase of Brazilian labour history and to let the contributions engage with current debates in Global Labour History. In connecting with these ongoing debates in the international field, several contributions break new ground, others revisit topics and cases about which knowledge seemed deceptively final. In order to achieve such dialogue, we have aimed to produce articles that are as comprehensible as possible for all potential readers, including those unfamiliar with Brazil. We hope that colleagues from Brazil or scholars who belong to what, in Europe, is still sometimes called "lusitanistics" will be patient with the repetitive explicitness that this inevitably involves. More than an exchange within a small community, this Special Issue is thus intended as an exercise in the art of "translation": This relates, primarily, to the work of the translators, particularly Amy Chazkel and Bryan Pitts, who have rendered the manuscripts for this Special Issue in English and to whom we owe our gratitude. Translating these manuscripts was a huge effort that went beyond a technical task and involved a myriad of intellectually demanding decisions about notions, idioms, localisms, etc. The task of translation, meanwhile, also involved the authors and ourselves: In two workshops in October 2015 and December 2016 held at The School of Social Sciences of the Fundação Getulio Vargas (CPDOC/FGV) in Rio de Janeiro previous versions of the articles were discussed not only in relation to their actual content, but also to how such content can be communicated with an audience not familiar with Brazil. We hope that this sample of the ongoing research in Brazilian labour history can serve as both suggestion and inspiration for readers in other parts of the world, helping to further enable a multilateral dialogue in Global Labour History. Such a multilateral dialogue is necessary in order to achieve both a truly global perspective in historical labour studies and, at the same time, to avoid the pitfalls of a closed paradigm under which labour historians in all parts of the world are supposed to follow one single trail. The ongoing task thus remains to build Global Labour History as a pluralistic sphere of scholars who, in the first place, constitute local and macro-regional circuits of debate – each with its own concerns and dynamic, yet interconnected in manifold ways with discussions elsewhere.

IRSH 62 (2017), Special Issue, pp. 23–43 doi:10.1017/S0020859017000426
© 2018 Internationaal Instituut voor Sociale Geschiedenis

Free and Unfree Labor in the Nineteenth-Century Brazilian Amazon

ADALBERTO PAZ

Department of History, Federal University of Amapá, Brazil Rodovia Juscelino Kubitschek, KM-02, Jardim Marco Zero, CEP 68.903–419, Macapá/AP, Brazil

E-mail: adalbertopaz@unifap.br

ABSTRACT: The nineteenth-century Brazilian Amazon was characterized by a wide variety of unfree labor performed by Indians, *mestiços*, free blacks, freedpersons, and slaves. Since the mid-eighteenth century, the Portuguese Crown's failure to promote the mass influx of enslaved Africans resulted in legislation that successively institutionalized and regularized coerced labor, limiting the mobility of individuals in the lower classes and obligating them to work against their will. Initially, this was restricted to Indians, but the measures were eventually applied to the entire free population of color. This article discusses the conditions under which these laws emerged and their impact on the living conditions of the population subject to them, placing the nineteenth-century Amazonian experience within wider historiographical debates about free and unfree labor.

Just as in other colonial societies, the authorities in the Amazon were constantly concerned with finding viable methods of economic exploitation, combined with maximum possible control over those they saw as their labor source.[1] The abundance of land and confidence in the soil's fertility sustained the idea that, at some point, the plantation system based on African slave labor, which had long dominated several coastal regions of Brazil, would also succeed in this region. As long as this was not the case, however, the focus remained on indigenous labor and the extraction of natural resources from the forests and rivers.

Circumstances, however, repeatedly frustrated official dreams of an Amazon that specialized in export agriculture. Meanwhile, other goals and struggles surrounding the defense of this vast territory and the tensions

---

1. From the seventeenth century, the region today known as *"Amazônia"* has been given a variety of administrative names. After Brazilian independence in 1822, the province of Grão-Pará was created. It was divided into the provinces of Pará and Amazonas in 1850. After the fall of the Empire and proclamation of the Republic in 1889, these became the states of Pará and Amazonas and, in turn, were later subdivided into still more territories and eventually states. While the term *"Amazônia"* has only been disseminated since the nineteenth century, various studies have used it for earlier periods, including the colonial era.

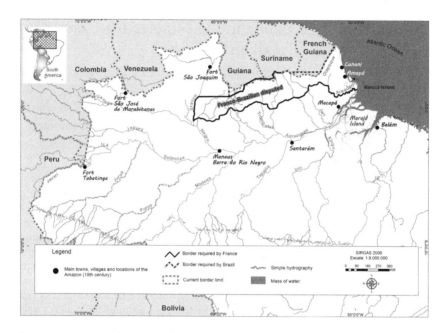

Figure 1. *Amazônia* in the nineteenth century.
Cartography by Luís Augusto Pereira Lima based upon *Karte vom Amazonen-Strome 1831*
and *Carte de la Guayana* as well as maps by the Instituto Brasileiro de Geografia e Estatística
(2016) and the Agência Nacional de Águas (2015).

between state planning and the actions of public and private actors on the
ground also shaped the local reality. Similarly, over the course of the
centuries, this society became more demographically diverse, composed
primarily of Indians,[2] blacks, and *mestiços* (people of mixed ethno-racial
descent) who often refused to submit to the will of their governors, owners,
lords, and bosses.

Labor, approached from a variety of angles, has often held a privileged
place among studies of the Amazon. For those who emphasized the role of
the Portuguese – usually reaffirming the discourses of the colonizers – work
and labor relations were "a problem to be solved", in which nothing that
was tried appeared to fit the civilizing project. In these analyses, the state
and its administrators occupied a central position, and everything and
everyone else, including other social actors and their material and symbolic
ways of life, were seen in the light of government decisions.

---

2. Contrary to North America and most countries in Spanish-speaking Latin America, in Brazil,
the use of the notion "*índios*" to denominate "indigenous peoples" is still common, including in
historical studies. Despite this apparent lack of terminological considerateness, Brazil has
experienced the same debates as other countries about the constructedness of ethno-racial attributions as well as a critique of their problematic connotations.

Over the last three decades, however, the analytic scope of studies about the Amazon has broadened significantly by accessing individual and collective experiences that earlier studies, focused on macroeconomic and political structures, had not examined. Methodologies from social history, in dialogue with anthropology and other disciplines, have not only offered important revisions to conventional views, but also expanded the range of subjects and sources and offered new interpretations.

This shift in the historiography has sparked interest in Amazonian workers themselves, an interest that extends beyond the study of the type of worker considered "typical" for each period. Initially, in the case of Indians, scholars focused on the long history of legal devices employed by the state to justify and regulate access to the indigenous labor force. Regarding Africans, scholars sought to determine the importance of enslaved labor in an economy that was primarily centered on extraction.[3] In recent years, they have emphasized resistance to black slavery through flight and the establishment of maroon communities (*mocambos* and *quilombos*), while still accounting for the various compromises that might be reached between slaves, masters, and the wider Brazilian society that was fundamentally built on slavery.[4]

Still, notwithstanding the important contributions made by studies of indigenous and African workers and the peculiarities of black slavery in the Amazon, much less attention has been paid to the forms, meanings, and conditions of freedom for the free and freed population in general. As most analyses point out, starting in the eighteenth century, the Portuguese Crown assigned distinct roles to Indians and blacks in that society. They granted the former a fragile and conditional freedom, while expecting that the latter would become the "hands and feet" of the region's elite – something that may have

---

3. "Extraction" here is defined as economic activities different from plantation agriculture (such as sugar or coffee) or animal husbandry and denotes the direct, non-cultivating exploitation of the natural resources of the forests and rivers.

4. The first great work about black slavery in the Amazon was published in the early 1970s. See Vicente Salles, *O Negro no Pará sob o regime da escravidão* (Rio de Janeiro, 1971). Since the 1990s, some of the most important works have included the analysis of documents published in the collection of sources edited by Anaíza Vergolino-Henry and Arthur Napoleão Figueiredo, *A presença africana na Amazônia Colonial. Uma notícia histórica* (Belém, 1990), and works influenced by the theoretical approaches of the social history of slavery. See Eurípedes Funes, "Nasci nas matas, nunca tive senhor. História e memória dos mocambos do Baixo Amazonas" (Ph.D., Universidade de São Paulo, 1995); Flávio dos Santos Gomes, *A hidra e os pântanos. Mocambos, quilombos e comunidades de fugitivos no Brasil (séculos XVII–XIX)* (São Paulo, 2005); and José Maia Bezerra Neto, "Fugindo, sempre fugindo. Escravidão, fugas escravas e fugitivos no Grão Pará (1840–1888)" (Ph.D., Universidade Estadual de Campinas, 2000). These studies, for the most part, focus on Pará. For studies of Africans in the Amazon that focus on flight from slavery, see Patrícia Melo Sampaio (ed.), *O fim do silêncio. Presença negra na Amazônia* (Belém, 2011), and Ygor Olinto Rocha Cavalcante, "'Uma viva e permanente ameaça'. Resistência, rebeldia e fugas de escravos no Amazonas Provincial (c.1850–c.1880)" (M.Sc., Universidade Federal do Amazonas, 2013).

become true in certain locales, but never materialized in the Brazilian Amazon as a whole.[5]

This article analyzes how the actions, conflicts, and setbacks in the process of political, economic, and socio-cultural domination of the late eighteenth- and nineteenth-century Amazon resulted in the subjugation of most of the region's inhabitants to coerced forms of labor. A central argument is that, despite the use of enslaved African labor and the official prohibition of capturing and enslaving indigenous people, successive laws and the authorities' interference with daily life deliberately muddled the boundaries between so-called free and unfree labor. Once instituted, such practices opened the way for establishing the legal foundations for coerced labor in the Amazon, which officially lasted into the mid-nineteenth century.

UNFREE INDIAN LABOR AND AFRICAN SLAVERY IN THE AMAZON

With the rise to power in 1750 of Sebastião José de Carvalho e Melo, Marquis of Pombal, as the leading minister to the king, indigenous freedom, African slavery, and export-oriented monoculture came to constitute the core of Portuguese planning for the Amazon.[6] In light of these new priorities, the Portuguese Crown took three closely connected measures. On 6 June 1755, all forms of indigenous slavery were abolished, and the next day orders were decreed revoking the temporal power of religious orders over the natives and creating the Grão-Pará And Maranhão General Trading Company (*Companhia Geral de Comércio do Grão-Pará e Maranhão*), whose goals were, amongst others, to promote the importation of enslaved Africans to the Amazon.[7]

Hoping to diminish the economic impact generated by the end of indigenous slavery and, at the same time, to increase colonists' access to this

---

5. The notion of "hands and feet" (*as mãos e os pés*) was coined by a Jesuit priest in the early eighteenth century and referred to the importance of enslaved labor in colonial Brazil as a whole. See André João Antonil, *Cultura e opulência do Brasil* (Rio de Janeiro, 1837), p. 31.

6. On Portuguese colonial policies during the period dominated by the Marquis of Pombal, see Marcos Carneiro de Mendonça, *A Amazônia na era pombalina*, 3 vols (Rio de Janeiro, 1963); Francisco José Calazans Falcon, *A época pombalina* (São Paulo, 1982).

7. On the Pombaline period and Indians in the Amazon, see Maria Regina Celestino de Almeida, "Os vassalos d'El Rey nos confins da Amazônia. A colonização da Amazônia ocidental (1750–1798)" (M.Sc., Universidade Federal Fluminense, 1990); Ângela Domingues, *Quando os índios eram vassalos. Colonização e relações de poder no Norte do Brasil na segunda metade do século XVIII* (Lisbon, 2000); Patrícia Maria Melo Sampaio, *Espelhos partidos. Etnia, legislação e desigualdade na colônia* (Manaus, 2011); Mauro Cezar Coelho, "Do sertão para o mar. Um estudo sobre a experiência portuguesa na América, a partir da colônia. O caso do Diretório dos Índios (1751–1798)" (Ph.D., Universidade de São Paulo, 2005). On the Grão-Pará And Maranhão Company, see Antônio Carreira, *As companhias pombalinas. De Grão-Pará e Maranhão e Pernambuco e Paraíba* (Lisbon, 1982); Manuel Nunes Dias, *Fomento e mercantilismo. A companhia geral do Grão-Pará e Maranhão, 1755–1778* (Belém, 1970).

workforce, however, the governor of Grão-Pará, Francisco Xavier de Mendonça Furtado, drafted a set of instructions that would become the *Directorio* in 1757, a collection of laws composed of ninety-five paragraphs.[8] In addition to its preoccupation with work, this *Directorio* was to serve as a civilizing manual that would ensure the "dilution" of the indigenous element into colonial society.

Although its emphasis on incorporating indigenous people into the colonial project was far from novel, the *Directorio* created an intentionally ambiguous legal precedent as a response to the ceaseless complaints of colonists about the scarcity of manual labor.[9] While the prohibition of indigenous slavery was reaffirmed, indigenous people residing in religious missions were nevertheless offered as a workforce, their labor to be divided between the state and private demands. Organized into "corporations", the natives were compulsorily drafted to work in private service and public works alike, often in places distant from their homes.[10]

Freedom, then, was not the freedom to come and go as one pleased, but was rather more akin to a limited concession that could be curtailed and conditioned at any time. To exercise it, the *Directorio* argued, Indians needed to learn to be "useful to themselves, to residents, and to the state".[11] To resort to this work force, it was enough that colonists, and even indigenous village leaders (called *principais*), argued that the coerced indigenous labor was "indispensable" to them. Of course, in practice, everything happened far more arbitrarily, especially when we observe the relationship between the Indians, on the one hand, and the public authorities and colonists on the other.

However, even if this limited indigenous freedom was to become effective, it was necessary that black slavery was broadly established in the productive realm, thus creating new and potent hierarchical distinctions between slaves and Indians. Thus, African slavery came to be seen as much more than just one of the pillars supporting export-oriented monoculture and

---

8. *Directorio que se deve observar nas Povoações dos Índios do Pará e Maranhão em quanto Sua Magestade não mandar o contrário* [*Legal Instructions to Be Observed in the Indian Villages of Pará and Maranhão as Long as His Majesty Does Not Order the Contrary*] [hereafter, *Directorio*], available at: http://bd.camara.gov.br/bd/handle/bdcamara/1929; last accessed 20 August 2017.

9. For an analysis of the similarities and differences between legislation regarding indigenous people in Portuguese America, see Beatriz Perrone-Moisés, "Índios livres e índios escravos. Os princípios da legislação indigenista do período colonial (séculos XVI a XVIII)", in Manuela Carneiro da Cunha (ed.), *História dos índios no Brasil* (São Paulo, 1992), pp. 115–132. See also Nádia Farage, *As muralhas dos sertões. A colonização e os povos indígenas do Rio Branco* (Rio de Janeiro, 1991), pp. 26–53.

10. Cecília Maria Chaves Brito, "Índios das 'corporações'. Trabalho compulsório no Grão-Pará no século XVIII", in Rosa Acevedo Marin (ed.), *A escrita da história paraense* (Belém, 1998), pp. 115–137, 125. Mauro Coelho argues that the *Directorio* was created because of resistance to the Pombaline reforms in Grão-Pará and Maranhão, since such legislation never appears to have been considered before Mendonça Furtado's arrival. See Coelho, "Do sertão para o mar", pp. 132–173.

11. *Directorio*, Third paragraph.

was considered as a counterpoint to and essential precondition for indigenous freedom.[12] Yet, as would become clear by the end of the eighteenth century, the Grão-Pará and Maranhão Company did not exactly achieve its goals.[13]

In August of 1797, Governor Francisco de Sousa Coutinho estimated that there were approximately 30,000 slaves of African origins in Grão-Pará.[14] This number was far higher than the estimates of historiographic studies realized in 1960s and 1970s which calculated a number of 15,000–18,000 enslaved people imported by the Grão-Pará And Maranhão Company between its founding and 1778, the year in which its trade monopoly expired.[15] However, the fact that the company still remained active for a few decades, along with the existence of private slave trafficking routes, suggests that Sousa Coutinho's estimate might have some validity for the number of enslaved Africans who entered Pará, even if they did not remain in the colony long term.[16] Still, the governor asserted that for the trade to recover from the "deplorable state of abandonment to which it has been reduced these last three years", it would be "urgently" necessary to double the number of slaves, something that would also enable continuity in their transfer from Pará, southward to Mato Grosso and Goiás.[17]

Thus, at the end of the eighteenth century, Indians remained the primary workforce available in *Amazônia*. And all the abuses historically related to forced indigenous labor, rather than being eliminated by the regulations of the *Directorio* and the incentives for the African slave trade, ultimately persisted. In the face of this, in 1797, Governor Sousa Coutinho abolished

---

12. On the debate among Portuguese authorities surrounding Indian freedom and the transfer of Africans to the Amazon, see Farage, *As muralhas dos sertões*, pp. 36–44.

13. On the failure of the African slave trade in the Amazon, see Colin M. Maclachlan, "African Slave Trade and Economic Development in Amazonia, 1700–1800", in Robert Brent Toplin (ed.), *Slavery and Race Relations in Latin America* (Westport, CT, 1974), pp. 112–145.

14. "Ofícios das Contas e Respostas dadas a Sua Majestade pela sua Secretaria de Estado de Ultramar pelo Conselho Ultramarino pelo Conselho d'Almirantado Pelo Real Erário", Pará, 21 August 1797, Arquivo Público do Estado do Pará, Correspondência dos governadores com a metrópole, Document 89. Transcribed in Vergolino-Henry e Figueiredo, *A presença africana na Amazônia colonial*, pp. 238–248.

15. There is no consensus about the total number enslaved between 1755 and 1778, and various estimates exist in addition to the range given here. See, for example, Vicente Salles, *O Negro no Pará sob o regime da escravidão* (Rio de Janeiro, 1971), p. 32; Antônio Carreira, *As companhias pombalinas de navegação comércio e tráfico de escravos entre a costa africana e o nordeste brasileiro* (Lisbon, 1969), p. 91; Dias, *Fomento e mercantilismo*, pp. 468–469; Maclachlan, "African Slave Trade and Economic Development in Amazonia, 1700–1800", in Toplin, *Slavery and Race Relations in Latin America*, p. 137.

16. On this basis, as well as sources gathered by Projeto Resgate (an online collection of historical documents related to Brazilian history originating from non-Brazilian archives) and statistics from the site *Voyages – Trans-Atlantic Slave Trade Database*, Bezerra Neto proposes a total of 35,597 slaves brought to Pará between 1756 and 1800. See José Maia Bezerra Neto, *Escravidão negra no Grão-Pará (séculos XVII–XVIII)* (Belém, 2012), pp. 63–64, 201–202.

17. "Ofícios das Contas e Respostas", cited from Vergolino-Henry e Figueiredo, *A presença africana na Amazônia colonial*, p. 247.

the *Directorio* under the allegation that the greed and corruption of the so-called directors of indigenous settlements (*diretores de aldeamento*) had spoiled the assimilationist ambitions of the reformist political project undertaken under the Marquis de Pombal.[18] Coutinho proposed new mechanisms for incorporating indigenous people into colonial society, through his "Plan for the Civilization of the Indians of Pará", in which their freedom was reaffirmed even as their obligations were expanded.[19]

UNFREE LABOR AND MILITARISM IN THE EARLY NINETEENTH CENTURY

Governor Coutinho's proposals would become law in the *Carta Régia* of 1798, a document most known for replacing the *Directorio*, although it has also been recognized for its attempts to accelerate the transformation of Indians into colonists, assigning them specific positions in the world of labor and the military hierarchy.[20] Indeed, the *Carta* makes this association between labor and military service explicit from the beginning, when it orders that all Indians living in colonial cities, towns, and indigenous settlements be enlisted into "Militia Corps" (*Corpos de Milícias*). Some of these would be selected for the "Effective Corps of Indians" (*Corpos Efetivos de Índios*), which would be dedicated preferentially to royal service; others would be assigned "agreed upon" work for public service contractors or other private parties; and still others would be destined for a "Company of Fishermen".[21] Moreover, the *Carta* added a fundamental innovation to previous indigenous policy by imposing compulsory service on the entire free, non-white population, including blacks, *mamelucos*, and *cafuzos*.[22]

---

18. These *diretores de aldeamento* were almost always non-indigenous persons.
19. Francisco de Sousa Coutinho to Rodrigo de Sousa Coutinho, 2 August 1797, Arquivo Nacional do Rio de Janeiro, Códice 101, II, fos 54–82.
20. For an analysis of the *Carta Régia* of 1798 in the context of indigenous policy in the Amazon, see Patrícia Melo Sampaio, "Administração colonial e legislação indigenista na Amazônia portuguesa", in Mary Del Priore and Flávio Gomes (eds), *Os senhores dos rios* (Rio de Janeiro, 2003), pp. 123–139; and Colin M. Maclachlan, "The Indian Labor Structure in the Portuguese Amazon, 1700–1800", in Dauril Alden (ed.), *Colonial Roots of Modern Brazil: Papers of the Newberry Library Conference* (Berkeley, CA, 1973), pp. 199–230.
21. "Carta Régia ao Capitão-General do Pará acerca da emancipação e civilisação dos índios; e resposta do mesmo acerca da sua execução", 12 May 1798 [hereafter, *Carta Régia*], *Revista do Instituto Histórico e Geographico Brazileiro* [RIHGB], 20 (1857), pp. 433–445. This article uses this published version of the law, which is the same as the one reproduced in Carlos de Araújo Moreira Neto, *Índios da Amazônia. De maioria a minoria (1750–1850)* (Petrópolis, 1988), pp. 220–247. Notwithstanding the existence of other royal decrees of the same date, this article refers exclusively to the one that abolished the *Directorio*.
22. *Mameluco* is a historical term for individuals viewed as being of mixed European and indigenous ancestry, while *cafuzo* refers to people of mixed African and indigenous descent.

All this was to be made possible through a complete census of the inhabitants of each town and city. Thus, on 6 January 1799, Sousa Coutinho issued the "Instructions to Be Circulated Concerning the Formation of New Militia Corps", through which he fulfilled the royal order that all Indians living "promiscuously with other [vassals]" in Pará be organized into militias, called the Light Troops (*tropa Ligeira*).[23] After the militias, the *Carta Régia* ordered the creation of the "Effective Corps of Indians", which, despite the name, would preferably enlist "the freed blacks and *mestiços* while they are available, as [they are] the most robust and capable of tolerating work". The corps would use as their model the auxiliary Infantry Companies (*Companhias de Pedestres*) established in Mato Grosso and Goiás.[24]

To avoid conflicts over the distribution of this labor force, the *Carta* defined priorities. Recruitment should avoid hampering the "transport of wood and other services in which the Indians are usefully employed". This exception aside, the Effective Corps of royal service could use men from the militias at their discretion to carry out its tasks. In exchange, Indians – most notably the oarsmen working on the numerous river boats – engaged by public contractors could not be drafted for any other public works, or to serve in the militias. Yet, this rule applied only to a limited number of indigenous persons, to be decided by the *Juntas da Fazenda* (administrative councils from the era of Pombal responsible for overseeing public expenditures, contracts, and works) or by the *Câmaras* (town councils).[25] If needed, a limited number of Indians could be recruited by judges at the request of public contractors who had not managed to hire oarsmen of their own. Finally, any person – especially colonists and property owners – had a right to the labor of those natives who they managed to "take out of the forest", with the only condition being that they educate them and instruct them in the Christian faith.[26]

The *Carta Régia* delegated powers to civil authorities (city councils and judges) and to military officials alike. In so doing, it set the stage for disputes over who ultimately commanded the conscripted workers and militiamen.[27] Similarly, the Crown incentivized direct agreements between private individuals, public contractors, and Indians without prior authorization.

---

23. "Instrução circular sobre a formatura de novos Corpos de Milícias", *RIHGB*, 20 (1857), p. 450.
24. *Carta Régia*, p. 434.
25. *Ibid.*, p. 436.
26. Indians brought by private individuals were baptized and received the legal status of orphans. They were required to work for a set number of years to repay the costs of their forced resettlement. *Ibid.*, p. 442.
27. See Sampaio, *Espelhos partidos*, pp. 236, 268, 291–295; André Roberto de A. Machado, "O fiel da balança. O papel do parlamento brasileiro nos desdobramentos do golpe de 1831 no Grão-Pará", *Revista de História*, 164 (2011), pp. 195–241.

The document thus expressed the ambition that no poor man, free or freed and physically capable of work, could escape the control of the state or remain "unemployed".

For a majority of the Amazon's population, the *Carta Régia* did not simply maintain the old practices of unfree labor that the *Directorio* had supposedly regulated. Rather, it represented a virtually unlimited expansion of the right of any civilian, military, or state-sanctioned private authority to exploit the involuntary labor of Indians, blacks, and *mestiços*. By leaving undefined the "concepts of freedom and servitude, free will and dependence", [28] the *Carta Régia* institutionalized an era of rampant coerced labor for the impoverished free and freed people of the Brazilian Amazon. Although the needs of the military offered the initial legal reasoning, over the course of the nineteenth century, this would be replaced by openly socioeconomic and racist justifications.

Thus, the combination of socioeconomic criteria – like type of property, income, and type of work – and socio-racial designations as established by the *Carta Régia*, cleared the way for an interlocking set of qualifications that made the forced use of people for labor tasks unquestionable. In the case of the Indians, the idea was to punish "their natural inclination to sloth and inaction", but also to provide "justice" to those who settled down to farm on their own. In this case, the natives would only be "exempt from all personal work, once the value of the tithe paid on the crops cultivated exceeds the wages they would receive".[29]

Such measures consolidated the modern basis for widespread coercive labor in the Amazon, whether for public or private ends. This system served both the military interests and the territorial aspirations of the Portuguese Crown, but it also provided ways to organize and gather a labor force at strategic points throughout the Amazon Basin. Thus, at the start of the nineteenth century, the region had become a place where any type of unauthorized free labor could be officially denounced and punished.[30]

In the years 1819 and 1820, shortly before the "peculiar" independence of Brazil in the form of the Brazilian Empire, the Bavarian naturalists Johann Baptist von Spix and Karl von Martius spent eight months traveling inland

---

28. Rita Heloísa de Almeida, "A Carta Régia de 12 de maio de 1798 e outros documentos sobre índios no códice 807", *RIHGB*, 163 (2002), pp. 171–180, 179.

29. *Carta Régia*, p. 439.

30. Such broad-based coercion, combined with an emphasis on military service, stands out from other types of unfree labor in Latin America, like the Spanish *mita* in colonial Peru. See Rossana Barragán Romano, "Dynamics of Continuity and Change: Shifts in Labour Relations in the Potosí Mines (1680–1812)", in Karin Hofmeester, Gijs Kessler, and Christine Moll-Murata (eds), "Conquerors, Employers, and Arbiters: States and Shifts in Labour Relations 1500–2000", Special Issue 24 of *International Review of Social History*, 61 (2016), pp. 93–114.

from Belém, the port city that was Grão-Pará's capital, to the present-day border with Colombia.[31] By then, they reported, recruitment for involuntary labor was being carried out throughout the Amazon. "Several times each year", they wrote, "entire bands of young Indians were removed from their villages in the interior and on Marajó Island and sent to Belém, where they received a daily wage of three *vinténs*,[32] in addition to food and lodging". They were employed in fisheries, public works, shipyards, and arsenals, in addition to serving as porters and, most often, oarsmen, which required vigilance and patience, because they frequently fled, "leaving the boat and its passengers in quite a predicament".[33]

When passing through Barra do Rio Negro (today Manaus), in the western Amazon, Spix and Martius again observed the use of forced recruitment for a wide variety of tasks. In addition to "policing and guarding public buildings" in town and serving in the forts at Tabatinga, São José de Marabitanas, and São Joaquim, the recruits were required to carry out tasks that facilitated trade and other economic activities. Among these were "patrols against hostile Indians" and the supervision of areas where turtles were found.[34] They also carried out "expeditions with the goal of bringing Indians to the towns"; that is, forced resettlements, and they accompanied travelers to the interior in search of "natural products". Others worked on government-owned livestock ranches along the Rio Branco, and any recruit could be requested and "paid separately" for private services.[35]

In the 1830s, however, the royal government of the postcolonial Empire decided to drastically reduce the size of the military throughout the country in response to the instability that occurred after Pedro I's abdication, a step that directly affected recruitment for regular and auxiliary troops throughout Brazil.[36] On 22 August 1831, the Regency dissolved the Light

---

31. The account of their journey was published in three volumes between 1823 and 1831. See Karen Macknow Lisboa, *A Nova Atlântida de Spix e Martius. Natureza e civilização na Viagem pelo Brasil (1817–1820)* (São Paulo, 1997). Their difficulties in obtaining crewmen in some respects resembled those faced by the British in India. See Nitin Sinha, "Contract, Work, and Resistance: Boatmen in Early Colonial Eastern India, 1760s–1850s", in Stefano Bellucci *et al.* (eds), "Labour in Transport: Histories from the Global South, c.1750–1950", Special Issue 22 of *International Review of Social History*, 59 (2014), pp. 11–43.

32. *Vintém de ouro* was a coin denomination introduced in late colonial Brazil with the peculiar value of 37.5 *réis*.

33. Johann B. von Spix and Karl Friedrich P. von Martius, *Viagem pelo Brasil, 1817–1820*, 3 vols (Belo Horizonte, 1981), III, pp. 26–28.

34. *Ibid.*, pp. 162–167, 177. The collection of turtle eggs for making oil and butter was one of the most important activities in the entire Amazon.

35. *Ibid.*, p. 143.

36. Pedro I, son of João VI of Portugal, was Emperor of Brazil from independence in 1822 until his abdication in 1831. His fifteen-year-old son, Pedro II, would only take the throne in 1840 (from 1831–1840, Brazil was ruled by regents); the Empire of Brazil lasted until 1889.

Militia Corps, which had been created by the *Carta Régia* of 1798 and had served as one of the main sources of coerced labor in Grão-Pará.[37] Nonetheless, the situation of Indians, blacks, and *mestiços* did not improve. The continuation of various forms of oppression along with other political and social conflicts, would combine to create the largest popular revolt the region had ever seen – an event that had direct and profound effects upon Amazonian worlds of labor.

THE WORKERS' CORPS AND WIDESPREAD COERCED LABOR

The 1835–1840 Cabanagem Revolt, a mass uprising with widespread popular support that challenged both local elite and Brazilian imperial rule in Grão-Pará, would have long-lasting effects on local society, including labor relations. A sizeable literature exists on the multiple causes, the protracted course, and the varied social actors involved in the revolt.[38] In this context, it seems important to reiterate that its human and material costs fell disproportionately upon people of color.[39] In the short term, imprisonment and execution killed tens of thousands, but the revolt's effects on the

37. *Collecção das Leis do Império do Brazil de 1831. Actos do Poder Legislativo de 1831* (Rio de Janeiro, 1875), I, p. 76. Also see Machado, "O fiel da balança", p. 213.

38. On the Cabanagem Revolt and other social and political unrest in the early nineteenth century, see Domingos Antônio Raiol, *Motins Políticos ou História dos principais acontecimentos políticos da província do Pará desde o ano de 1821 até 1835*, 3 vols (Belém, 1970). The early twentieth century saw renewed interest in the revolt, particularly among authors connected to the Instituto Histórico e Geográfico do Pará. See Henrique Jorge Hurley, *A Cabanagem* (Belém, 1936); Hurley, "Traços cabanos", *Revista do Instituto Histórico e Geográfico do Pará*, 10 (1936), pp. 3–284; and Ernesto Cruz, *Nos bastidores da Cabanagem* (Belém, 1942). From the 1980s onward, a new wave of interpretations appeared, including Julio José Chiavenato, *Cabanagem. O povo no poder* (São Paulo, 1984); Carlos Rocque, *Cabanagem. Epopéia de um povo*, 2 vols (Belém, 1984); Pasquale di Paolo, *Cabanagem. A revolução popular na Amazônia* (Belém, 1985); Vicente Salles, *Memorial da Cabanagem. Esboço do pensamento político-revolucionário no Grão-Pará* (Belém, 1992); Ítala Bezerra da Silveira, *Cabanagem. Uma luta perdida* (Belém, 1994); Luís Balkar Sá Peixoto Pinheiro, "Nos subterrâneos da Revolta. Trajetórias, lutas e tensões na Cabanagem" (Ph.D., Pontifícia Universidade Católica de São Paulo, 1998); Peixoto, *Visões da Cabanagem. Uma revolta popular e suas representações na historiografia* (Manaus, 2001); Magda Ricci, "Do sentido aos significados da Cabanagem. Percursos historiográficos", *Anais do Arquivo Público do Pará*, 4 (2001), pp. 241–274; Ana Renata do Rosário de Lima, *Revoltas camponesas no vale do Acará 1822–1840* (Belém, 2004); Mário Médice Costa Barbosa, "O povo cabano no poder. Memória, cultura e imprensa em Belém-PA (1982–2004)" (M.Sc., Pontifícia Universidade Católica de São Paulo, 2004); and Mark Harris, *Rebellion on the Amazon: The Cabanagem, Race and Popular Culture in the North of Brazil, 1798–1840* (New York, 2010). In 2002, the Arquivo Público do Estado do Pará and the Secretaria de Cultura do Pará published a primary source collection put together by anthropologist David Cleary. See David Cleary, *Cabanagem. Documentos ingleses* (Belém, 2002).

39. On race in the Amazon and its importance in the Cabanagem and its interpretations, see David Cleary, "'Lost Altogether to the Civilized World': Race and the *Cabanagem* in

lower classes would last far longer, particularly through a restructuring of the mechanisms through which elites ordered society and compelled the population of color to work. Some of the most important of these mechanisms were the so-called Workers' Corps (*Corpos de Trabalhadores*).

Created by Provincial Law 2 of 25 April 1838, under the provincial president (the equivalent of a governor), Francisco Jozé de Souza Soares de Andrea, the corps brought together Indians, *mestiços*, and free and freed blacks who did not own property or have full-time employment.[40] At the same time, "all white men capable of bearing arms" between fifteen and fifty were to be drafted for police service, as well as the "men of color" who owned property that could be used to supply them and their families during their absence.[41] Once these socioeconomic and racial exceptions and preferences had been observed, "all men of color age 10 and up" could then be drafted to form the Workers' Corps.[42]

The Workers' Corps were explicitly conceived as a measure taken by a militarized state to contain and restrict the classes it considered responsible for the "anarchy" and "harm" of the Cabanagem, and several of the scholars who studied the revolt would later reaffirm this dimension.[43] More recently, however, other analyses have highlighted the connections between the nineteenth-century Amazonian context and the institution created by Soares de Andrea with the national issues of the same period, including the debates about initiating the

Northern Brazil, 1750 to 1850", *Comparative Studies in Society and History*, 40 (1998), pp. 109–135.
40. *Collecção das Leis da Província do Gram-Pará*, 51 vols (Pará, 1854), I, pp. 3–5. This printed collection of laws is available at the Instituto Histórico e Geográfico Brasileiro.
41. "Instrucçoes para a organização dos Corpos de Trabalhadores e regulamento dos mesmos Corpos", in *Esposição do estado e andamento dos negócios da província do Pará no Acto da entrega que fez da prezidencia o Exmo Marechal Francisco Jozé de Souza Soares d'Andrea, ao Exmo doutor Bernardo de Souza Franco, no dia 8 de abril de 1839* (Pará, 1839), p. 24–28. All reports from the provincial presidents of Pará cited in this article are available at: http://www-apps.crl.edu/brazil/provincia; last accessed 20 August 2017. On the role of the police (*Guarda Policial*) and the reorganization of the Army during the administration of Soares de Andrea and after, see Carlos Augusto de Castro Bastos, "Os braços da (des)ordem. Indisciplina militar na província do Grão-Pará (meados do século XIX)" (M.Sc, Universidade Federal Fluminense, 2004), pp. 40–70.
42. Report of Andrea to Franco in 1839, p. 24. On 24 October 1840, the original law creating the Workers' Corps would be amended by Law 84, which changed the minimum enlistment age to fourteen and authorized the exemption of officials, apprentices to craft trades, overseers on agricultural or livestock plantations (something already part of the 1838 law), and "men who have sole responsibility for a family". *Collecção das Leis da Província do Gram-Pará*, III, pp. 95–96.
43. See Domingos Antônio Raiol, *Motins Políticos*; Pasquale Di Paolo, *Cabanagem. A revolução popular na Amazônia*; Vicente Salles, *O Negro no Pará*; Salles, *Memorial da Cabanagem*; Ítala Bezerra da Silveira, *Cabanagem. Uma luta perdida*.

"transition from slave to free labor", discourses that valorized regular work as morally edifying, and official strategies designed to combat vagrancy (*vadiagem*).[44]

However, it is also possible to understand the Workers' Corps as the pinnacle of a century-long official policy of drawing on coerced labor, starting with the *Directorio* of the mid-eighteenth century, and instituted through both legislation and everyday practices created and perfected with this goal in mind. Since the mid-eighteenth-century Pombaline era, the idea of freedom conditioned by and for work shaped the policies of successive governments, who were not simply permissive with regard to various forms of slavery and coercion, but were effectively committed to guaranteeing a labor supply for public and private projects. Thus, various changes in society were reflected in laws governing coerced labor, always with a tendency to extending it to other groups beyond those defined as Indians.

The relationship between Francisco de Sousa Coutinho and the *Directorio* is clear, as the 1798 *Carta Régia* was the direct result of his attempt to substitute the former. However, the connections between the *Carta Régia* and the Workers' Corps are less obvious, due to the ruptures caused by the Cabanagem and the repressive fervor of Soares de Andrea as he pacified Grão-Pará. But, as can be clearly seen in Table I, neither Sousa Coutinho, nor Soares de Andrea truly broke with the fundamental principles of compulsion in the Amazon; rather, both affirmed them.[45]

But significant changes also occurred as a direct result of the peculiarities of Soares de Andrea's vision of militarization: One of the most important was the 1838 law's clear attempt to distinguish the "dignity" of the military corps from the ignominy now attributed to those subjected to coerced labor. Coerced labor, once justified as a due complement to the supposed equality of all the king's vassals, was ultimately turned into a dishonor and punishment, a suitable burden for the indolent, with their "miserable" racial and social characteristics.

The Cabanagem-era policies surrounding coerced labor also attempted to end disputes among the authorities over control of the pool of available labor. Indeed, Soares de Andrea stated as much in his final report at the conclusion of his time in office: "[A]ll the military

---

44. See Claudia Maria Fuller, "Os Corpos de Trabalhadores. Política de controle social no Grão-Pará", *Revista Estudos Amazônicos*, 3:1 (2008), pp. 93–115; Bastos, *Os braços da (des)ordem*, pp. 29–40.

45. Vicente Salles and Carlos de Araújo Moreira Neto emphasize similarities between the indigenous-focused legislation of the eighteenth century and the law of 1838. For the former, the *Directorio* "inspired" the Workers' Corps, while the latter argues that the Corps "reintroduced" recruitment along the lines of the *Carta Régia* of 1798. See Vicente Salles, *Memorial da Cabanagem*, p. 61; Carlos de Araújo Moreira Neto, *Índios da Amazônia*, p. 97; Moreira Neto, "Igreja e Cabanagem (1832–1849)", in Eduardo Hoornaert (ed.), *História da Igreja na Amazônia* (Petrópolis, 1992), pp. 262–295.

Table 1. *Comparison of the organization of coerced labor in the Brazilian Amazon between the eighteenth and nineteenth centuries*

	Directorio (1757)		Carta Régia (1798)			Workers' Corps (1838)
Administrative Organizations	"Corporations" of Indians	Light Troops	Effective Corps of Indians	Royal public contractors and private interests	Fishing Service	Squadrons, Companies, and Corps
Control of the Workforce	heads of settlements (*diretores*), judges, municipal councils, and indigenous leaders (*principais*)	Commanding officials (indigenous leaders and white residents)	Corporals, sergeants, field captains and those in charge of recapturing fugitive slaves (*capitães de campo e de mato*).	Municipal councils, ombudsmen, and district judges	Could work under their own direction or that of others	Commanders, sergeants, officers, and corporals; Justices of the peace approved contracts with private parties authorized by the commanders
Ethnic and Social Origin of Workers	Indigenous	Entire free, poor population, including whites and Indians	Indians and other people of color, but with "preference for free blacks and *mestiços* when they are available"[46]	"Pacified" Indians and Indians who had been recently resettled and reported to the authorities	Indigenous	"Indians, *mestiços* and blacks who are not slaves"[47]
Principal Occupations	Agriculture, extractive activities, river trade (*negócios das canoas*)	Any service for which they were called, including military defense	Royal service, especially the transport of wood	River navigation, fieldwork, and extractive activities	Exclusively fishing (exempt from militias and the Effective Corps)	Agriculture, trade, public works, and ship crews

[46] *Carta Régia*, p. 434.
[47] Law 2 of April 25, 1838, art. 2.

commanders are at the same time also commanders of the police and Workers' Corps."[48] The third article of the law creating the Workers' Corps also ordered that its commanders and officials be the same as in the "old Light Corps", and, if these were not available, then it should be "the most qualified citizens" of each district, who would be nominated and receive charters to exercise this position.[49] In practice, this meant that Justices of the Peace could no longer deploy workers – even in cases in which the *Carta Régia* of 1798 had permitted them to do so. Instead, they were to restrict themselves to recording and validating the contracts authorized by commanders between private individuals and enlisted workers.[50]

In 1846, traveler William H. Edwards noted a great fear amongst the riverine communities near Belém that especially the men were likely to be drafted for coerced labor into the military and police forces.

> During the last few years, the enrollment of Indians has been carried to an unprecedented extent [...]. Since 1836, ten thousand young men are said to have been carried to the south, to the incalculable injury of the agricultural interests. As might be supposed, all this enlistment has not been voluntary. The police are constantly upon the alert for recruits, and, the instant that a poor fellow sets foot within the city, he is spirited away, unless some protecting white is there to intercede in his behalf. We frequently fell in with cottages in the vicinity of the city, whose only occupants were women and children, the men having, in this way, disappeared. Most of the market boats, also, are managed by women, the men often stopping at some convenient place above, and there [hiding and] awaiting the boat's return.[51]

The "free negroes", according to Edwards, were also "very apt to be caught in the same trap" of recruitment. After they were caught, the daily lives of recently recruited Indians and blacks were divided between training and imprisonment until, "the principles of honor therein imbibed, and the ardor of military glory excited", they became sufficiently trustworthy to be let loose, or too worn down and exhausted to desert. Edwards added that "most free negroes" resorted to becoming or pretending to be property, to escape what they saw as a worse fate. Thus, many continued "*nominally* still belonging to their old master, or some other willing protector".[52] The consent, however, which Edwards observed among black workers might actually point to the opposite: perhaps enslaved, free, and freed blacks were being forced to work under the threat that refusal would result in their being handed over to the recruiters.

---

48. Report of Andrea to Franco in 1839, p. 6.
49. Law 2 of April 25, 1838, art. 3.
50. *Ibid.*, art. 4.
51. William H. Edwards, *A Voyage up the River Amazon Including a Residence at Pará* (New York, 1847), p. 35.
52. *Ibid.*, emphasis in original.

In the Lower Amazon, prison and violence were used in areas where black slaves were scarce, and Indians were "difficult to catch" and "slippery when caught". Desertions, Edwards thought, were treated too harshly by the authorities, and the punishments for captured fugitives might include up to 300 lashes, with a whip known as "cat".[53] Still, flights continued. This often affected travelers, for it was common for the Indians forced to accompany them to escape as soon as they could, even leaving behind their personal belongings.

Forced recruitment led to significant criticism in the press and in sections of the middle and upper classes. It was also overwhelmingly rejected by the free and freed poor population. All these factors, combined with the insufficiency of voluntary enlistment, deeply concerned the authorities, who were most interested in forming well-trained, specialized, and professional troops. As a result, the solution they found was the Empire's extension of military recruitment to children and young men from ten to seventeen, through the creation of Navy Apprentice Companies (*Companhias de Aprendizes Marinheiros*) in most of the provincial capitals.[54]

Concomitant with the search for alternatives given the scarcity of new recruits in both the Navy and the Army, the authorities were also interested in keeping the sons of the popular classes occupied, arguing that this would prevent vagrancy and crime and instill in them discipline, morality, and a strong work ethic. Therefore, although minors could be placed in the Apprentice Companies by their parents or a legal guardian, most of them were recruited in a similar way to the adults: that is, after being "gathered up" by inspectors and officials. If they passed the aptitude tests, they were required to serve twelve years before becoming eligible for discharge, and only after sixteen could they receive a conditional discharge, with a right to a pension paying half the salary they had last received, although they could be called back to active duty if the need arose.[55]

---

53. Edwards, *A Voyage up the River Amazon*, pp. 131–132. The whip Edwards referred to was the cat-o'-nine-tails, commonly abbreviated to the "cat". It was used around the world, not only to punish sailors, but also as an instrument of torture in prisons.

54. The first was founded in Rio de Janeiro in 1840, followed by Pará and Bahia (1855) and extended in the following twenty years to most provinces. Álvaro Pereira do Nascimento, "Marinheiros em revolta. Recrutamento e disciplina na Marinha de Guerra (1880–1910)" (M.Sc., Universidade Estadual de Campinas, 1997), p. 51. See also Rozenilda Maria de Castro Silva, "Do suprimento humano para a Marinha de Guerra nacional à escola para a infância pobre: interesses recíprocos no surgimento da Companhia de Aprendizes Marinheiros do Piauí", paper presented at VI Congresso Luso-brasileiro de História da Educação, Universidade Federal de Uberlândia, 2006, pp. 5336–5346.

55. On the implications of the relationship between the Apprentice Companies (in the War Arsenals of the Army they were initially called Minor Apprentice Companies [*Companhias de Aprendizes Menores*], and after 1872, Journeymen Apprentice Companies [*Companhia de Aprendizes Artífices*]), efforts to combat vagrancy (*vadiagem*), and education towards being incorporated in the labor process in Brazil, in addition to the references cited above, see

There were intrinsic relationships, both direct and indirect, between the various types of forced recruitment and the worlds of labor all over Brazil. Independent of the immediate motives of the authorities – filling the ranks, discouraging laziness, increasing social control, or punishing crime – the accusation that someone was resisting work was enough to make freedom precarious for the "free", especially when combined with poverty and ethno-racial distinctions. This could happen in many ways, one of the most important being through laws and practices that maintained most of the free and freed population permanently eligible for recruitment. In many cases, the simple threat of forced service was enough to blackmail and intimidate the less fortunate. At the same time, for those for whom flight was not an option, many of the personal arrangements formed under such pressures could have a certain protective effect, even if they were manifestly unequal: They enabled workers to gain allies against the more aggressive and abusive "recruiters" roaming the country.[56]

Although it was in perfect keeping with nineteenth-century Brazilian principles of compulsory military service and labor, the Workers' Corps quickly became a target for criticism due to the excesses committed by its commanders, including using the workforce to serve themselves and their friends. Others argued that the institution incentivized flight and desertion among the free and freed population. In September 1858, ten deputies from the Pará Legislative Assembly introduced a bill to abolish the Workers' Corps. Their proposal, however, was rejected.[57] The next year, the provincial president, Manoel de Frias e Vasconcellos, submitted a plan to the Assembly to completely reform the Corps and create municipal police forces.[58] However, a surprising turn of events came barely two weeks later: On 18 October 1859, twelve deputies proposed another bill to abolish the Workers' Corps in all of Pará.[59] Three days later, the Assembly issued a

Walter Fraga Filho, *Mendigos, moleques e vadios na Bahia do século XIX* (São Paulo, 1996), pp. 128–130; Matilde Araki Crudo, "Infância, trabalho e educação. Os aprendizes do Arsenal de Guerra de Mato Grosso (Cuiabá, 1842–1899)" (Ph.D., Universidade Estadual de Campinas, 2005).

56. See, for instance, Richard Graham who precisely argues that clientelistic relationships could protect the poor from recruitment, even as it reinforced their dependence on the well-to-do. See Richard Graham, *Patronage and Politics in Nineteenth-Century Brazil* (Stanford, CA, 1990), pp. 27–29.

57. *Gazeta Official*, Belém, 11 September 1858, p. 2. *Gazeta Official*, Belém, 21 September 1858, p. 2. This and other official organs for the whole country and Brazil's provinces, are available at the Biblioteca Nacional do Rio de Janeiro.

58. *Falla dirigida á Assembléa Legislativa da provincia do Pará na segunda sessão da XI legislatura pelo exm.o sr. tenente coronel Manoel de Frias e Vasconcellos, presidente da mesma provincia, em 1 de outubro de 1859* (Pará, 1859), pp. 49–52.

59. Parte Official, Assembléa Legislativa Provincial, Sessão ordinária em 18 de outubro de 1859, *A Epocha*, Belém, 3 November 1859, p. 1. This newspaper published in Belém defined itself as a

highly critical brief on the reforms proposed by Vasconcellos, calling them "an attack on the inviolability of the citizen's civil and political rights", and concluding that Law 2 of 1838, which had introduced the Workers' Corps, should be "repealed as soon as possible".[60]

Over the following sessions, the deputies exchanged accusations over what might have led some of them to change their minds about the Workers' Corps, since many who supported this new abolition bill had just voted against an identical one a year before.[61] Nonetheless, the bill proceeded rapidly through the Assembly, and in less than one month it was sent to the provincial president, Antonio Coelho de Sá e Albuquerque, who signed it as Law 330 of 15 November 1859. Its single article ordered that "the Workers' Corps be abolished, with all laws and orders to the contrary repealed".[62]

In an official communiqué to the Minister of Foreign Affairs, Albuquerque put himself at the center of this turn of events reporting that, since taking office, he had pressured the Assembly to repeal the Workers' Corps law. According to the president, the enlistments caused so many "clamorous complaints from the less civilized and well-to-do population", that they chose to abandon "the capital and nearby towns in favor of the [northern] region of Amapá, thus preferring to serve the interests of the French and harm those of the Brazilians".[63] This geopolitical dimension was indeed an important additional factor and the abolition of the Workers' Corps was a decision taken between the provincial president, the deputies, and the Ministry of Foreign Affairs of the Empire to counter French interests in the long-standing dispute over the border between Brazil and French Guiana.[64] As the authorities came to realize the

publication dedicated to "political, trade and news". It is available at the Biblioteca Nacional do Rio de Janeiro.

60. Parte Official, Assembléa Legislativa Provincial, Sessão ordinária em 21 de outubro de 1859, *A Epocha*, Belém, 24 October 1859, p. 1.

61. Parte Official, Assembléa Legislativa Provincial, Sessão ordinária em 27 de outubro de 1859, *A Epocha*, Belém, 17 November 1859, p. 1.

62. *Collecção das Leis da Província do Gram-Pará*, XXI, pp. 12–13. See also Parte Official, *Gazeta Official*, Belém, 19 November 1859, p. 1.

63. "Ofício confidencial do presidente da província do Pará, Antonio Coelho de Sá e Albuquerque, ao secretário de Estado dos Negócios Estrangeiros, João Lins de Vieira Cansanção de Sinimbu", 23 November 1859, Arquivo Histórico do Itamaraty (Rio de Janeiro), Governo do Pará (Ofícios), Códice 308–4-4.

64. The Franco-Brazilian dispute dated from the colonial period and centered on a region in the far north of the Amazon, between the Araguari and Oiapoque Rivers. The disagreement would only be resolved in 1900, in Brazil's favor. In the nineteenth century, the term "Amapá" was already commonly used in newspapers and correspondence for both the settlement of the same name, a few miles from the Ilha de Maracá, and the disputed region as a whole. Once the region was awarded to Brazil, it would be separated from Pará to form the territory of Amapá in 1943 and state of Amapá in 1988.

considerable disadvantage at which they were placed in attempting to gain the trust and sympathy of escaped slaves, deserters, and others in the disputed region, they decided to give in. Shortly after the abolition of the Workers' Corps, Albuquerque published in the press the repeal of the law of 1838.

While the abolition of the Workers' Corps applied to the whole of Pará, the article came together with a letter that was exclusively addressed to the population of the contested region, in which he guaranteed the right to free movement to everyone coming from Amapá. The article, published in the *Gazeta Official* newspaper, said that the authorities of the cities of Macapá and Belém were flatly prohibited from recruiting any "individual who comes from the northern coasts", as long as he came to trade, or if he was employed "in fish salting, in the extraction of rubber and oil, or in the gathering of cacao, Brazil nuts, etc". To qualify for this exemption, residents of Amapá needed only to present themselves in either of these cities, where they would receive a guide, with whom they could "enter and exit at any port, river, or lake, with no further requirements and with no fear of difficulties".[65] The only exception was for smugglers, who would continue to be subject to punishment. Furthermore, the article emphasized that Amapá's workers and merchants would increase their profits and benefits by negotiating directly with Belém, while this city and its surrounding area would be able to obtain more merchandise at lower prices.

Thus, the conjunction of two factors led to an acute crisis that resulted in the rapid disappearance of the Workers' Corps: Firstly, there was Brazil and France's diplomatic quarrels over a vast area in the far north of the Amazon. Secondly, and more importantly, the constant flights, desertions, and several forms of political, social, and economic mobilization involving the free poor, indigenous, and enslaved population. The authorities had been constrained, pressured, and certainly surprised by the actions of subaltern people in such a way that, when the representatives of the Brazilian state realized what was at stake in 1859, the result was the collapse of the last official tool for recruiting forced labor in the Amazon.

CONCLUSION

The debates over free and unfree labor have sought to problematize the epistemological boundaries that separate these categories, as well as the chronological divisions that such boundaries have generated. According to older interpretations, slavery and other forms of unfree labor disappeared or diminished in importance in the wake of capitalism's ascendance as the globally dominant economic system. This article, however, by

65. *Gazeta Official*, 22 November 1859, pp. 2–3.

demonstrating the coexistence of and even interdependency between freedom, slavery, and coerced labor in the nineteenth-century Amazon, adds to the growing body of literature that points out that these categories are not quite as opposed, schematic, or exclusive as has been previously assumed.[66]

Within this larger picture, however, the conditions in the nineteenth-century Amazon were specific, as the dilemmas between free and unfree labor were related to two of the most long-standing problems for elites – the difficulties in accessing enslaved African labor and the supposed scarcity and excessive autonomy of the "free" workforce. As this article has shown, once the enslavement of indigenous peoples was terminated, the expectation was that this would lead to an increase in the number of African slaves whose labor would then allow for the remaining subjects to help occupy the vast territory of the Amazon. However, this move towards incorporating the Indians into Luso-Brazilian society did not signify that pressures to carry out labor tasks for the colonial economy abated. Over the course of centuries, one way or another, whether legal or illegal, unfree indigenous labor became established as a rule and indeed a fundamental part of the regions' economy.

In the nineteenth century, this was aggravated by a political project full of ideological vigor: The focus on repressing vagrancy and using work as a tool of social control had profound implications not only for the type of freedom that Indians supposedly enjoyed, but also for poor freemen, freedmen, and *mestiços*. For those who were not enslaved, freedom was threateningly precarious.[67] The effective possibility that the poor might reject economic dependency, choosing to survive from the resources of the forests and rivers or banding together to deny or elude a status quo based on domination and exploitation, exerted a profound influence on laws permitting coerced labor.[68] To prevent or defeat alternatives for the lower

---

66. See Tom Brass and Marcel van der Linden (eds), *Free and Unfree Labour: The Debate Continues* (Bern, 1997); Robert Steinfeld, *Coercion, Contract, and Free Labor in the Nineteenth Century* (Cambridge, 2001); Frederick Cooper, Thomas C. Holt, and Rebecca J. Scott, *Beyond Slavery: Explorations of Race, Labor, and Citizenship in Postemancipation Societies* (Chapel Hill, NC, 2000); Marcel van der Linden and Magaly Rodríguez García (eds), *On Coerced Labor: Work and Compulsion after Chattel Slavery* (Leiden [etc.], 2016).

67. The theme of "precarious freedom" has been introduced for free and freed blacks during the nineteenth century. It seems, however, equally useful for considering the situation of other groups in Brazil as well. See Sidney Chalhoub, "The Precariousness of Freedom in a Slave Society (Brazil in the Nineteenth Century)", *International Review of Social History*, 56:3 (2011), pp. 405–439. For an analysis of the impact these issues had on Brazil's legal and prison system, see Peter M. Beattie, *Punishment in Paradise: Race, Slavery, Human Rights, and a Nineteenth-century Brazilian Penal Colony* (Durham, NC, 2015).

68. The interrelation between abundant natural resources (especially land) for market-oriented agricultural exploitation, scarcity of labour, the effective possibility of the poor to retreat into remote and inaccessible areas, and the installment of regimes of unfree labor has been a central

classes, the Amazon's economic and political elites reinforced mechanisms of immobilization and compulsion.

The 1859 repeal of the Workers' Corps law in Pará offered hope for an enormous segment of the population that had been submitted to a long tradition of coerced labor. However, during the rise of the Amazonian rubber boom in the second half of the nineteenth century, other forms of unfree labor would develop in the far reaches of the forest, based on debt peonage, intimidation, and other mechanisms for "retaining" labor.[69] Free and unfree labor in the Brazilian Amazon were reinvented yet again, this time to meet modern capitalist industries' demands for primary resources.

Translation: Bryan Pitts

---

theme in the literature about unfree labor (and the resistance to it): See, for instance, Herman Nieboer, *Slavery as an Industrial System: Ethnological Researches* (The Hague, 1910); Evsey D. Domar "The Causes of Slavery or Serfdom: A Hypothesis", *The Journal of Economic History*, 30:1 (1970), pp. 18–32; James C. Scott, *The Art of Not Being Governed. An Anarchist History of Upland Southeast Asia* (New Haven, CT, 2009).
69. See João Pacheco de Oliveira Filho, "O Caboclo e o Brabo. Notas sobre duas modalidades de força de trabalho na expansão da fronteira amazônica no século XIX", *Encontros com a Civilização Brasileira*, 11 (1979), pp. 101–140, 131–135; and, more generally, Barbara Weinstein, *The Amazon Rubber Boom, 1850–1920* (Stanford, CA, 1983).

IRSH 62 (2017), Special Issue, pp. 45–73 doi:10.1017/S002085901700061X
© 2018 Internationaal Instituut voor Sociale Geschiedenis

Maids, Clerks, and the Shifting Landscape of Labor Relations in Rio de Janeiro, 1830s–1880s

HENRIQUE ESPADA LIMA

Departamento de História, Universidade Federal de Santa Catarina – UFSC, CEP: 88040–900, Florianópolis Santa Catarina, Brazil

E-mail: henrique.espada@ufsc.br

FABIANE POPINIGIS

Departamento de História, Universidade Federal Rural do Rio de Janeiro – UFFRJ, CEP: 23890–000, Seropédica Rio de Janeiro, Brazil

E-mail: fpopinigis@gmail.com

ABSTRACT: This article focuses on the lives of workers in small commerce and in domestic service in nineteenth-century Rio de Janeiro. It seeks to understand both what united and what differentiated maids (*criadas*) and clerks (*caixeiros*), two types of laborers whose lives and work had much in common, and two categories of labor that, although ubiquitous, are frequently overlooked in Brazilian labor history. We consider how, together, class, gender, and race shaped the divergent trajectories of *criadas* and *caixeiros* over the course of the nineteenth century, and what the legal disputes in which they were involved during that period can teach us about the shifting dynamics in labor relations in a society marked by both slavery and labor dependency more broadly. As sources for this analysis, we draw on documents produced by legal proceedings from the 1830s through the 1880s, in which men and women involved in petty commerce and domestic service presented their cases before the courts to claim their unpaid wages.

In recent years, Brazilian labor history has shown how the study of urban, non-industrial activities provides us with a privileged vantage from which to consider the connections between economic relations, the social and occupational structure of cities, and the ways in which workers have intervened in political life. New studies of urban labor have contributed significantly to an effort to re-think both the range of research questions and the general explanatory framework through which we have considered workers' experiences. This effort has been carried out through the intense analysis of a variety of types of primary sources and, at the same time, has gained theoretical and methodological inspiration from microhistory, from English social history, and, more recently, from international debates concerning the intersection of class, gender, and race.[1]

This article focuses on the lives of workers in small commerce and in domestic service in nineteenth-century Rio de Janeiro, and thus it is indebted to the debate concerning the social history of urban labor in Brazil. At the same time, this study contributes to this debate by focusing on two types of workers who, although among the most ubiquitous in the city, have been overlooked as a source of insight on how urban laborers confronted the era's transformations. Concentrating on Rio de Janeiro during the Brazilian post-independence period of constitutional monarchy known as the Empire (1822–1889), in which it functioned as the country's capital, this article places at the center of its analysis a city that experienced the economic, sociopolitical, institutional, and legal changes that characterized both Brazil and the broader Atlantic world in the nineteenth century in an almost emblematic way. As the main commercial and political center of the country and a space for the circulation of people and goods that connected at least three continents, the city of Rio was a site of experimentation for legal and institutional innovations. Rio de Janeiro was one of the most important slave-holding cities in the Americas and also the destination of thousands of immigrants of various nationalities. Nineteenth-century Brazil's capital city thus provides a privileged point of view from which to consider the changing urban social structure, as well as the ambiguous dividing lines between enslaved, dependent, and free labor, and the transformations to the social composition of the laboring classes.

Recent studies of social stratification in cities have primarily focused their attention on the lives and social and economic strategies of the intermediate social sectors, which fit poorly within the dichotomy so central to nineteenth-century Brazil between the propertied elites, on the one hand, and the enslaved persons subordinated to those elites on the other. Such studies demonstrate that the numerically significant presence of these

---

1. An incomplete list of these studies includes: Maria Odila Dias, *Power and Everyday Life. The Lives of Working Women in Nineteenth-Century Brazil* (New Brunswick, NJ, 1995); Sidney Chalhoub, *Trabalho, lar e botequim. O cotidiano dos trabalhadores no Rio de Janeiro da Belle Époque* (São Paulo, 1986); Sheila Faria, "Sinhás Pretas, Damas Mercadoras: as pretas minas nas cidades do Rio de Janeiro e São João del Rei (1700–1850)" (Tese de Titular, Universidade Federal Fluminense, 2004); Elciene Azevedo, J. Cano, Maria Cunha, and Sidney Chalhoub (eds), *Trabalhadores na Cidade. Cotidiano e Cultura no Rio de Janeiro e São Paulo, séculos XIX e XX* (Campinas, 2009); Fabiane Popinigis, "'Aos pés dos pretos e pretas quitandeiras'. Experiências de trabalho e estratégias de vida em torno do primeiro Mercado Público do Desterro, 1840–1890", *Afro-Asia*, 46 (2012), pp. 193–226; Juliana Farias, *Mercados Minas. Africanos ocidentais na Praça do Mercado do Rio de Janeiro (1830–1900)* (Rio de Janeiro, 2015).

workers in Brazilian cities has garnered far less scholarly attention than they deserved.[2] It was precisely from this heterogeneous social stratum, which consists of free men and women, freedpersons of African origin, and the Luso-Brazilian poor and working classes, in addition to foreign immigrants of various nationalities and legal statuses, that some of the century's most important social actors in Brazilian political and social life emerged. These men and women made up the urban middle classes as well as a large part of the urban laboring sectors, which were the socioeconomic sectors best positioned to aspire to upward social mobility and most able to organize themselves to fight for the recognition of the dignity of their work and of their political rights.[3]

At the fringes of this intermediary social group were those more or less impoverished (but not necessarily miserable) workers who were involved in a myriad of urban activities that were connected to the infrastructure that kept the city functioning. They were the less skilled civil construction workers, those who worked in various forms of urban transportation, the non-proprietary laborers in small commercial establishments, and the men and women involved in various types of domestic labor who were free, but often worked side by side with the enslaved.

This article seeks to understand both what united and differentiated one group of domestic laborers (female maids, or *criadas*), on the one hand, and one group of workers in small commerce (male clerks, or *caixeiros*) on the other, two types of non-enslaved laborers whose lives and work had much in common, and two categories of labor that are frequently overlooked in Brazilian labor history. We will consider what their divergent trajectories over the course of the nineteenth century can teach us about the shifting dynamics in labor relations in a society marked by both slavery and labor dependency more broadly. As sources for this analysis, we will draw on documents produced by legal proceedings from the 1830s through the 1880s in which men and women involved in petty commerce and domestic service presented their cases before the courts to claim their unpaid wages.

The principal objective here is to relate the ways in which, in the course of the nineteenth century, these workers' experiences in "serving" both approximated and diverged from each other as they lived through the social

2. Zephyr Frank, "Layers, Flows and Intersections: Jeronymo José de Mello and Artisan Life in Rio de Janeiro, 1840s–1880s", *Journal of Social History*, 41:2 (2007), pp. 307–328; Zephyr Frank, *Dutra's World: Wealth and Family in Nineteenth-Century Rio de Janeiro* (Albuquerque, NM, 2004).
3. Fabiane Popinigis, *Proletários de Casaca. Trabalhadores do comércio carioca (1850–1911)* (Campinas, 2007); Osvaldo Maciel, *A Persistência dos Caixeiros. O mutualismo dos trabalhadores do comércio em Maceió* (Recife, 2011); Artur Vitorino, *Máquinas e Operários. Mudança técnica e sindicalismo gráfico (São Paulo e Rio de Janeiro, 1858–1912)* (São Paulo, 2000); Marcelo MacCord, *Artífices da Cidadania. Mutualismo, educação e trabalho no Recife Oitocentista* (Campinas, 2012).

processes that profoundly altered the history of labor in Brazil: the transformation of the legal paradigms that had been developing to regulate and
organize contracts and commercial relationships; the imposition of new
forms of control over urban labor; the slow decline and eventual abolition
of slavery; and the social reconfiguration of the urban working classes and
the means by which they might claim their rights.

CRIADAS AND CAIXEIROS IN THE EXPANSION OF URBAN
SERVICES: UNSTABLE BOUNDARIES

The extraordinary development of the city of Rio de Janeiro in the first
decades of the nineteenth century was marked by two politically fundamental events: first, the transfer of the Portuguese royal court to the colonial
city in 1808; and second, the political independence of the colony and its
transformation into the Brazilian Empire in 1822, with the city serving as
the site of the nation's capital and the headquarters of the royal court. Rio
thus consolidated its role as the most important link connecting the country
with Atlantic markets, which brought about an increase in commercial
activity and allowed for an impressive accumulation of wealth.[4] Rio's new-
found economic strength affected urban life in many ways, but what
interests us here, in particular, is the resulting expansion of consumption
and the exponential growth of services and of all types of trade. The demand
for a variegated labor force made the city a major center for the importation
of both enslaved and contract immigrant workers, with profound consequences for its social dynamics.

Demographic data gives us a clear idea of the extent of the impact of this
process on the city. Its population in 1821 was approximately 112,000, half
of whom were enslaved. In 1849, around 110,000 enslaved workers lived in
Rio de Janeiro's parishes, out of a total population of approximately 226,000
inhabitants, a third of whom had been born in Africa.[5] Immigrant workers,
primarily Portuguese ones, made up a considerable part of the remaining
free population: in 1846, a representative of the Portuguese Crown estimated that between 20,000 and 30,000 of their compatriots lived in the city.[6]

4. Lyman L. Johnson and Zephyr Frank, "Cities and Wealth in the South Atlantic: Buenos Aires
and Rio de Janeiro before 1860", *Comparative Studies in Society and History*, 48:3 (2006), pp.
634–668. See also: Zephyr Frank, "Wealth Holding in Southeastern Brazil, 1815–60", *Hispanic
American Historical Review*, 85:2 (2005), pp. 223–258.
5. Jeffrey D. Needell, *A Tropical Belle Époque. Elite Culture and Society in Turn-of-the-century
Rio de Janeiro* (Cambridge, 1987), p. 22; Luís Felipe Alencastro, "Vida privada e ordem privada no
Império", in L. Alencastro (ed.), *História da vida privada no Brasil – Império. A corte e a modernidade
nacional* (São Paulo, 1997), p. 25.
6. Rosana Barbosa Nunes, "Imigração portuguesa para o Rio de Janeiro na primeira metade do
século XIX", *Historia & Ensino*, 6 (2000), pp. 163–177, 170.

Among the poor free laborers, whether immigrants or native-born, a sizeable portion worked in either commerce or domestic service.

The proliferation of both *caixeiros* and *criadas* resulted from this same growing demand for urban services in nineteenth-century Rio de Janeiro. These two groups' life experiences also converged in the particularities of their daily labor in private homes and commercial establishments, where work and life were elaborately intertwined. Most of these individuals resided in the homes and commercial establishments in which they worked, having neither accommodation of their own, nor any defined work schedule, carrying out an innumerable array of subaltern tasks. These two categories of workers thus shared a high level of domesticity and participation in the lives of their employers, with various levels of intimacy, and, relatedly, few opportunities for privacy and time to attend to their personal lives. This characteristic of their work and personal lives was intensified by the fact that both *caixeiros* and *criadas* were often recruited from the ranks of the city's youth, who had dependent relationships with and sometimes even family ties to their bosses.[7] The particular type of dependency that characterized these relationships was sometimes reflected in the forms of remuneration that they were offered for their work, where it was difficult to draw a clear line between an employer's obligation to provide training and sustenance on the one hand, and payment for services rendered on the other.

Criado and *caixeiro* do not describe stable and well-defined occupations and statuses inside private homes or businesses. Each of these words is a superficially straightforward, but essentially untranslatable term that denote a common occupation in nineteenth-century Rio; in English they roughly translate as, respectively, "maid" and "clerk". Yet, as this article will show, the words *criado* and *caixeiro* carry with them a cloud of contextual assumptions that make these terms, themselves, precious historical artifacts. For this reason, they appear throughout this article in their original Portuguese form.[8] The levels of responsibility and trust that these laborers

---

7. Lenira Martinho shows that, from a sample of documents mentioning the ages of Portuguese immigrants who were employed as *caixeiros* in the late 1820s, almost three quarters of them were between ten and nineteen years old. Lenira Menezes Martinho and Riva Gorenstein, *Negociantes e Caixeiros na Sociedade da Independência* (Rio de Janeiro, 1993), p. 80. On the relationship between paternalism and domestic labor, see Sandra Lauderdale Graham, *House and Street: The Domestic World of Servants and Masters in Nineteenth-Century Brazil* (Austin, TX, 1992).

8. *Caixeiro* directly translates into the English word "cashier" and is still in use today in the generic sense of someone who is in charge of the cash register in retail business. It derives from the Portuguese word *caixa*, which generally denotes a "box", but also refers to both a "cash register" and the person who operates it. In nineteenth-century Brazil, the word took on a broader meaning and was used to describe any clerk or servant working in any capacity in a commercial establishment. The word *criado*, and its feminine form *criada*, have more obviously domestic connotations, meaning someone who, not being part of the family, was created or educated within the household. (The word *criar* means "to raise", including to raise a child.) The word *criado* has long

enjoyed, as well as the type of activities they carried out, shaped hierarchical relationships within the workplace, which, in turn, were reflected in their levels of autonomy and their expectations concerning their remuneration. These hierarchies also grew out of discrimination based on gender, skin color, age and nationality, and they occupied a central place in these workers' lives. The problem of confronting these hierarchies was made even more dramatic for Rio's workers because they lived in a society where most manual labor was, in fact, carried out by enslaved persons, who were expected to be submissive and subservient.

This overview of the relative position of *criadas* and *caixeiros* gives us a useful point of departure, but it is not sufficient to elucidate either the specificities of the work and pay arrangements that involved these two categories of workers, or the tensions that beset their daily lives. In the pages to follow, we will thus subject a selection of legal cases involving labor arrangements worked out within private homes and businesses to detailed analysis, allowing us a closer view of the transformations these types of workers experienced and their relationship to the law over the course of the nineteenth century.

One of these legal cases is from April 1833, when Jacintho Almeida sued his former employer, Francisco da Costa, for wages he had never received. According to Almeida, his boss owed him for the final three years during which he had worked in Costa's small grocery store in Rio de Janeiro's port district.[9] Almeida further explained that he had only received part of his total annual wages of 300$000 *réis*,[10] and that his former boss owed him a debt of 758$620 *réis*, the payment of which he sought in court.

been generalized in Portuguese to describe any servant or personal assistant and extended to all adults working in a household, to which the person did not necessarily have any previous connection. The word was already employed in that sense in the *Ordenações Filipinas*, a corpus of Early Modern Portuguese laws: "Título XXIX. Do criado, que vive com o senhor a bem-fazer, e como se lhe pagará", in *Ordenações Filipinas*, 5 vols (Rio de Janeiro, 1870), Livro IV, p. 807. Note that the English "maid" has a clear gender connotation, whereas *criado* and *criada* are two separate words that specifically refer to a male or female domestic worker, respectively. While shifts in the gender composition of both "clerks" and "domestic workers/maids" in nineteenth-century Rio are at the heart of this article, for reasons of readability and in keeping with common usage in nineteenth-century Brazil, in this article we mostly use the female form in the case of "maids" (*criadas*) and the male for "clerks" (*caixeiros*). One important exception is the use of *criado* in legal texts, which only takes the generic masculine form.

9. "Apelação Cível. Apelante: Francisco José da Costa. Apelado: Jacintho Ignacio de Almeida, 1834", Arquivo Nacional do Rio de Janeiro [hereafter, ANRJ], Fundo: *Tribunal da Relação do Rio de Janeiro* (84), n. 664, Maço 167, All judicial cases discussed in this article came before the courts of appeal in the Brazilian capital city of Rio de Janeiro and were selected from a larger sample of court cases that are held at the ANRJ and catalogued under the title "disputes over salaries".

10. Brazil's basic currency unit in the nineteenth century was the *real*, but its basic denomination came to be considered the *mil réis* (one thousand *réis*), written as 1$000. One thousand *mil réis* was called one *conto de réis*, written as 1:000$000. Almeida's monthly stipend as *caixeiro* can be

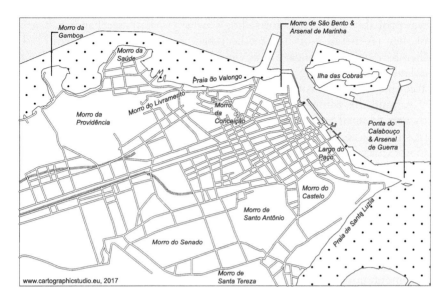

Figure 1. Map of Rio de Janeiro.

In his own version of the facts, Costa affirmed having put the management of his grocery store in Almeida's hands not just as a simple *caixeiro*, but instead as a "true administrator" (*administrador*) when he left for Portugal in May 1831. Costa may have made this trip to avoid the effects of the resurgence of anti-Portuguese sentiments that marked that year. These conflicts dealt a powerful blow to the Portuguese small business owners who dominated Rio's petty commerce and provided most of the few work opportunities available for the city's free poor.[11] In his testimony, Costa not only stated that he owed nothing to Almeida, but he also asserted that, when returning to Rio in 1833 and taking an inventory of his store, he discovered that, in his absence, his former employee had sold merchandise on credit without his permission. Worse still, he claimed that Almeida "came to enjoy [his] establishment, taking from it both merchandise and money, and in this way Almeida was able to set up his brother with his own small shop, which

---

estimated at 25$000 *réis* in the early 1830s. For purposes of comparison, an enslaved man who worked as a cook was advertised in the pages of one of Rio's newspapers in 1830 for rental for a monthly fee of 12$000 (twelve-thousand *réis*), *Correio Mercantil*, 1:12 (1 September 1830), p. 47.
11. On 7 April 1831 Pedro I, the Emperor of independent Brazil, born in Portugal, abdicated the Brazilian throne, thus allowing his son, Pedro II, who had been born on American soil, to take over as the new Emperor. The conflicts between the *pés-de-chumbo* (literally "lead-foots", as the Portuguese immigrants were called) and *cabras* ("goats", the nickname for poor, mixed-race Brazilians) took over the streets of the city of Rio de Janeiro as well as other Brazilian provinces. See Gladys Sabina Ribeiro, *A liberdade em construção. Identidade nacional e conflitos antilusi-tanos no Primeiro Reinado* (Rio de Janeiro, 2002).

was probably just a front for selling Costa's [stolen] merchandise, because neither [Almeida, nor his brother] had anything of their own."[12] He therefore refused to engage in any negotiation with Almeida concerning his delayed wages as long as his former *caixeiro* failed to "produce an exact accounting of the business".

Among the witnesses called to testify were other shop employees and owners of small businesses established on nearby streets. All attested to the trusting relationship between Costa and his primary shop employee before Costa's trip. Witnesses on both sides also affirmed the difficulty of establishing the kind of commitment that existed between a boss and an employee, providing information that corroborated the two conflicting versions of the dispute. On the one hand, Almeida argued that he had been Costa's *caixeiro*, and therefore his employee and subordinate, who should be payed a wage (*soldada*).[13] On the other hand, Costa affirmed that he had placed Almeida in the position of "administrator", but that Almeida had not carried out his obligations in accordance with that position. In his line of argumentation, which was ultimately successful in winning this case, Almeida's attorney recurred to the Philippine Ordinances (*Ordenações Filipinas*), a compilation of Portuguese laws that had been in effect since the end of the sixteenth century and continued to be used in independent Brazil until the first decade of the twentieth century. The argument directly cited the conditions under which bosses could demand reparations for damages done by *criados* to their *amos* (a word that means "master", without necessarily implying that the subordinate person is a slave), affirming, in Almeida's case, not just that the "damage" had not been proven, but also that the demand had been made too late to have had any legal effect.[14]

Almeida won his case before the trial court judge, a decision that was later confirmed by the final judgment (*acórdão*) rendered by the panel of magistrates of the appellate court (*Tribunal da Relação do Rio de Janeiro*). The judges ruled that Costa, the employer, had never established the terms under which Almeida should carry out the administration of his business affairs, which reinforced Almeida's position as *caixeiro* rather than as an actual business partner. In basing his legal defense on the difference between an "administrator" and a "*caixeiro*", Costa made a distinction that the law

---

12. "Apelação Cível. Apelante: Francisco José da Costa", fo. 12 reverse side.
13. The notion of *soldada*, which we chose to translate as "wage", is part of the legal vocabulary used in the *Ordenações Filipinas* to describe financial compensation for work in different capacities. According to Raphael Bluteau's eighteenth-century Portuguese dictionary, *soldada* comes from the word *soldo*, meaning "the payment or stipend paid to a soldier, [and now] used to describe the salary of anyone who serves". R. Bluteau, *Vocabulario Portuguez e Latino*, 10 vols (Coimbra, 1728), VII, pp. 699–700. All court cases discussed in this article refer to the chapters in the *Ordenações Filipinas* that concern wages (*soldadas*): Libro IV, titles 29 to 34.
14. "Título XXXV: Do que demanda ao criado o dano, que lhe fez", in *Ordenações Filipinas*, Livro IV, p. 841–842.

did not recognize and followed a model of commercial law that would only be established in Brazil two decades later. The provisions in the Philippine Ordinances that required the boss to provide evidence of any complaint against subordinate workers and to prove that he did not owe them wages, ultimately strengthened Almeida's case. The relationship between Jacintho de Almeida and José da Costa certainly did not represent the average labor dispute that developed in many businesses in Rio de Janeiro. In this particular case, there was an evident level of proximity and trust between the *caixeiro* and his employer, and Almeida's position as the "first caixeiro" and eventual administrator of his boss's business placed him in a privileged position to negotiate his wages. Disputes involving subaltern *caixeiros* only rarely found their way into the courts and were seldom as well received when they did.

An eloquent contrast with the case brought by Almeida can be found in a civil case that took place at a similar time in the courts of Rio de Janeiro, involving Francisca de Azevedo, a white woman from the neighboring state of Minas Gerais. In 1835, she presented a "compensation suit" (*ação de soldadas*) against the assets of her former employer, Valentim dos Santos. Santos was the owner of a commercial enterprise near the Valongo quay, a central area next to the city's port. His activities certainly placed him in a high social position, since his business served as the depository for the city's judicial courts.[15] According to Francisca, she had been employed in Valentim's shop and in his home as a *criada* since "more than twenty years ago, taking care of his house, overseeing the slaves, and carrying out all of the tasks inside the house that are the proper work of *criada*".[16] Since they had not made any specific agreement about her wages, she expected that her accumulated earnings would be paid to her once her services were no longer needed, as was customary in Rio de Janeiro. When her boss died without leaving a will or an account of his assets, Francisca sought recourse in the justice system, requesting the payment of her overdue wages, which she determined to be the modest sum of 12$000 *réis* per month.

15. The General Public Depository was a judicial institution that held chattels whose possession was under dispute, or which were being held as collateral in a judicial contest over money or property in the city of Rio de Janeiro. It was managed by a private citizen performing public duties. Occupying this position, Valentim dos Santos was responsible for the money, merchandise, real estate, animals, and even slaves that were held in the Public Depository. He was responsible for overseeing and maintaining these items until their eventual restitution to a legitimate owner or sale at a public auction.

16. "Apelação Cível. Soldadas. Apelante: Damazo da Costa Pacheco. Apelada: Francisca Perpétua Bernardina de Azevedo, 1835", ANRJ Fundo: *Tribunal da Relação do Rio de Janeiro* (84), n. 2899, Maço 218, Galeria C, fo. 5. All information concerning the case described here come from this file. About this case, see also: Henrique Espada Lima, "Wages of Intimacy: Domestic Workers Disputing Wages in the Higher Courts of Nineteenth-Century Brazil', *International Labor and Working-Class History*, 88 (2015), pp. 11–29, 15–17.

Damazo Pacheco, the executor of Valentim Santos's will, argued that Francisca de Azevedo had never been his *criada*, but rather his concubine for twenty years; she had been, Santos stated, *teúda e manteúda*, a typical expression of the day that unmistakably alluded to a consensual but highly asymmetrical sexual relationship outside of wedlock, "a kept woman". To prove his argument, Pacheco affirmed that Francisca, during the time when she lived in the General Depository (*Depósito Geral*), had built up her own business by selling groceries and even acquiring her own slaves to that end. Furthermore, according to Pacheco and several of the witnesses he called to testify about the relationship between the two, Valentim and Francisca had such a close, personal relationship that he entrusted her with the task of managing his paperwork and promissory notes. In one of his most striking arguments, Pacheco's lawyer insisted that he could only imagine Francisca as Valentim Santos's lover, given her role in his house and store: "Because it is not customary in this city to put pretty, young white women into service in the kitchen and the living room [...]; [they are], conventionally, limited to being a concubine and to being well treated."[17]

Francisca never accepted the version of this story that portrayed her as her boss's lover, nor did she admit in the court documents to having had any relationship with him that did not derive from her position as a *criada da casa*, a domestic servant. She was, nonetheless, unable to prove her case either through documentary evidence, or by offering witness testimony attesting to the fact that she had been employed by Valentim, or that she had made some arrangement with him concerning her remuneration. Francisca lost the case; the judge denied her demand for her back pay.

By closely examining those details of the case on which both Francisca de Azevedo and the witnesses agreed, however, we can extract a great deal of information both about her daily work life and the ambiguous space she occupied within Valentim dos Santos's house and store where her employer lived and conducted his business. The "General Warehouse labyrinth"[18] was how Francisca's lawyer, Antônio Picanço, described this space where the boundaries between house and place of business were impossible to establish. Francisca gave orders to the many household slaves charged with maintaining her employer's home, attended to the needs of the clerks who worked in her boss's store, as well as bearing direct responsibility for Valentim's documents. She also appears to have taken care of the enslaved workers who remained in the General Warehouse pending the resolution of legal disputes over them, and their masters appear to have paid her for this task. Just as significantly, Francisca also attended personally to Valentim, even caring for him when he became ill.

17. "Apelação Cível. Soldadas. Apelante: Damazo da Costa Pacheco", fo. 89.
18. *Ibid.*, fo. 89, reverse side.

The difficulties in defining the limits between *criada* and *senhora* (mistress) – in the vocabulary used by the witnesses to describe the ties between Francisca and Valentim's household – leave no doubt that she was essential to the day-to-day functioning of the warehouse, whether as a dwelling or as a business. Yet, Francisca did not demand her wages as a shop *caixeira*, but rather as a personal *criada*. Because of the evident social difference between boss and employee, it is unlikely that anyone would have believed them to be business partners. Francisca herself presented the fact that she did business at the fringes of the operation of the warehouse making and selling food as evidence of her boss's "liberal" nature and not as proof of her independence. In asking for "payment" as Valentim's *criada*, she used the legal language available to describe a complex relationship. This relationship involved not only work, but also the intimacy of close coexistence for over two decades and the mutual trust in conducting daily household and business affairs. Although the justice system did not agree with her vision of the facts, Francisca nonetheless had no doubt that hers was a relationship that merited compensation for services rendered.

The cases of the *caixeiro* Jacintho Almeida and of the *criada* Francisca de Azevedo raise numerous questions that cannot be explored in detail here, but their stories illuminate the contradictory situations that could arise in places of business and in homes in Rio de Janeiro in the 1830s. The contrast between the outcomes of these two cases is striking, as are the differences between what the parties in each case felt they needed to bring to light before the court. We learn little about the personal relationship between Almeida and his former boss, since the lawyers in this case only saw fit to present evidence concerning Almeida's wages and witnesses' testimony about the nature of the two men's business relations. By contrast, the other case contains both abundant information concerning the roles that Francisca played in her boss's life and often contradictory references to the real or alleged intimacy between her and Valentim. Both Jacintho and Francisca held central importance in the daily operation of their respective bosses' homes and businesses, and both held publically recognized responsibilities. Yet, the ways in which these cases were presented, argued, and adjudicated could not have been more different.

Jacintho and Francisca fought for their wages, which should have been paid to them for their work, dedication, and trustworthiness. These two litigants, however, were confronted with different strategies to deny them what they sought. Costa, Jacintho Almeida's boss, attempted to prove that Jacintho was not just any employee, but rather was someone whose position as an "administrator" imposed responsibilities that were not met. Therefore, he argued, Jacintho was not owed wages. Unable to prove his accusations, Costa was obliged to pay the wages due to Almeida. Francisca was met with entirely different arguments to counter her demands: she was forced to defend her position within her boss's home against attacks that called into question her morality. Her boss's trust in her ability to carry out her tasks, instead of having served as proof of her qualities as a worker, were used to attest to the type of intimacy that was judged incompatible with remunerated labor. In a slave society in which subaltern work was powerfully racialized, even Francisca's skin color was used as evidence against her; her "whiteness" indicated that she was not sufficiently subaltern to have been considered a paid domestic worker. As a laborer, Francisca was disqualified from being Valentim's business partner or his employee; as a woman, her connection with the household had not been formalized by marriage. Thus, the only possible place left for her in Valentim's home was that of a concubine, a position that neither conferred any rights on her except the generosity of her protector, nor gave her any grounds for demanding compensation as a "true" *criada*.

THE ARBITRARINESS OF THE LAW AND VULNERABILITY: HOW CAN ONE PROVE LABOR?

The legal actions described here so far were initiated at the beginning of the 1830s, a decade that witnessed the consolidation of political and legal institutions that formed the contours of the monarchy in post-independence Brazil. Among the legal transformations during the period after the passing of a constitution that was considered to be liberal (1824), Brazil also passed the first of a series of laws aimed at making the Atlantic slave trade illegal in 1831, as well as the promulgation of the Criminal Code (1830) and the Code of Criminal Procedure (1832). More specific legislation was introduced establishing the legal basis for labor contracts for free urban and rural workers in 1830 and 1837. These laws regulating "service rental" were, above all, motivated by the widespread anxiety among planters, still profoundly dependent on slavery, about the supply of available farm labor. It is no coincidence that, in the 1830s, the number of immigrants also increased exponentially, especially those coming from Portugal, who established themselves not only in rural areas, but above all in Brazil's major cities, where they had to compete with and find a space among other poor, free, or freed workers.[19]

These transformations in the legal context only partially affected the labor disputes discussed here. These laws had no measureable effect on the proximity and, indeed, the overlapping nature of *caixeiros'* and *criadas'* work; nor did these codes and statutes passed in the 1830s and 1840s, mitigate the ambiguity that marked *caixeiros'* and *criadas'* laboring lives,

---

19. Beatriz Mamigonian, "Revisitando a 'transição para o trabalho livre'. A experiência dos africanos livres", in Manolo Florentino (ed.), *Tráfico, Cativeiro e Liberdade. Rio de Janeiro, Séculos XVII–XIX* (Rio de Janeiro, 2005), pp. 389–417; Michael Hall and Verena Stolcke, "The Introduction of Free Labour on São Paulo Coffee Plantations", *The Journal of Peasant Studies*, 10 (1983), pp. 170–200; Joseli Mendonça, "Sobre cadeias e coerção. Experiências de trabalho no Centro-Sul do Brasil do século XIX", *Revista Brasileira de História*, 32 (2012), pp. 45–60.

Figure 2. This plate, entitled "Slave Market" was originally painted by the British officer Henry Chamberlain (1796–1843), who visited Rio de Janeiro in 1819 and 1820. It depicts the surroundings of the Valongo, the famous docks were the Africans who survived the Middle Passage were sold in the markets as slaves. Around the commercial area of the Valongo and Rio's waterfront, many of the stories discussed in this article unfolded. Chamberlain's description reads: "The Plate represents an elderly Brazilian examining the Teeth of a Negress previous to purchase, whilst the Dealer, a Cigano, is vehemently exercising his oratory in praise of her perfections. The Woman looking on is the Purchaser's Servant Maid, who is most frequently consulted on such occasions."
Views and Costumes of the City and Neighbourhood of Rio de Janeiro, Brazil, from Drawings taken by Lieutenant Chamberlain, Royal Artillery, during the years 1819 and 1820, with descriptive explanations (London, 1822).

which had for centuries been codified in the Philippine Ordinances still being cited in the cases examined in this article. The Ordinances established the conditions under which one could request wages for services rendered as a *criado*, a generic category that could have included *caixeiros*.[20] The legal uncertainty about how to treat these categories of workers persisted throughout much of the nineteenth century, even with the restructuring of the legal institutions and paradigms that shaped the administration of justice in post-independence Brazil. In the three versions of the laws promulgated

---

20. "Título XXIX. Do criado, que vive com o senhor a bemfazer, e como se lhe pagará o serviço" and "Título XXXI. Como se pagarão os serviços e soldadas dos criados, que não entraram a partido certo", in *Ordenações Filipinas*, Livro IV, pp. 807 and 808–810.

to regulate the "service rental contracts" (*contratos de locação de serviços*) for free persons, passed in 1830, 1837, and 1879, there were no references either to the work of *caixeiros* or of *criados*.[21] This interest in regulation was, above all, the product of anxieties about the labor supply and was part of the process of seeking alternatives to slave labor. The continuity of Brazil's socioeconomic system that depended on captive labor was under threat due to the attempts to abolish the Atlantic slave trade (which had been legally challenged since 1831, until it was finally abolished in 1850)[22] and to widespread expectations that slavery was about to end (which would only occur in 1888). Initially conceived in the context of this substitution of free for enslaved labor, above all on farms, the laws regulating "service rental" ended up indirectly providing a legal horizon that was also applicable, theoretically, to urban labor, even though the legislation did not touch on wage labor relations that potentially involved *caixeiros* or *criadas*.

It was not, however, the letter of the law that decided on the duties, rights, and limitations that applied to *caixeiros* and *criadas*, but rather, social and legal practices influenced the decisions and the differential results that each legal case produced. One can argue that this legal ambiguity implied that judicial cases involving unpaid wages proceeded in a particularly arbitrary manner, especially those whose results might have been influenced – directly or indirectly – by the litigants' gender, skin color, or nationality.

Another example of this legal ambiguity put into practice can be found in a case initiated in the Third Civil District (*3ª Vara Cível*) of Rio de Janeiro in 1842. On 25 May of that year, the lawyer Antonio Carneiro da Cunha, as legal representative of Francisca do Sacramento, filed a complaint demanding the payment of wages for work that had been carried out but never remunerated.[23] By way of her attorney, Francisca affirmed that on 1 September 1823 she had moved into the small grocery store (*casa de quitanda*) that José da Silva had established that year on a square called the Largo de Santa Rita, to "serve him receiving a salary of ten thousand per month". She continued working for Silva until his death on 2 April 1842. According to Francisca, in the nearly nineteen years during which she had worked in that house, she had never received "even one single *real* in wages" and Silva had died without having settled his debt to her.

---

21. The law of 13 September, 1830, which regulates written contracts of labor leasing made by Brazilians and foreigners, within or beyond the Brazilian Empire, Law no. 108, from 11 October 1837, and *Decreto* n. 2827, from 15 March, 1879. Cf. Henrique Espada Lima, "Trabalho e Lei para os Libertos na Ilha de Santa Catarina no Século XIX. Arranjos e contratos entre a autonomia e a domesticidade", *Cadernos AEL*, 14 (2010), pp. 135–75.
22. For the most recent and thorough treatment of this topic, see: Beatriz G. Mamigonian, *Africanos Livres. A abolição do tráfico de escravos no Brasil* (São Paulo, 2017).
23. "Apelação Cível. Apelante: José de Moraes Silva, curador a herança jacente do finado José João da Silva. Apelada: Francisca Maria do Sacramento, 1842", ANRJ, Fundo: *Tribunal da Relação do Rio de Janeiro* (84), n. 7064, Caixa 374, Galeria C, fo. 1 and the following pages.

Both José and Francisca were identified as "freed blacks" (*pretos forros*), indicating their past as enslaved persons. Three witnesses were called for Francisca to testify about the nature of her professional relations with Silva. Summoned to speak of Francisca's honesty, the witnesses described her in the following manner: a "rustic black woman, very hardworking and God-fearing [...] incapable of asking for what is not rightly hers". No one came forward to contest these witnesses' accounts of Francisca's character, and through them we can understand something about the importance of Francisca's work for her boss's business.[24] The testimony reveals that, from 1835 on, Francisca also worked in another business that Silva opened on the same street, the Rua do Valongo, which sold roasted coffee beans. This was a lucrative operation, and all of the witnesses in this case attributed Silva's financial success to this new business. According to Joaquim de Seixas, a forty-eight-year-old artisan who lived in the center of the city on the Rua do Sabão, Francisca's work involved activities inside the two places, but in this second store in Valongo, she "also occupied herself doing manual labor in addition to working in the kitchen, due to the fact that the most important part of this store was the sale of roasted coffee, which, because of the excellent way in which it was prepared, was in high demand among buyers", and it was, in fact, Francisca "who ground the coffee as well as operating the roaster, with whose business the late owner [Silva] had acquired a sufficient livelihood, and in fact a real fortune". Another witness, Xavier de Oliveira, was a man of more than fifty years of age of African descent but born in Rio de Janeiro, who sustained himself by working for the Ordem Terceira de São Domingos, a Catholic religious order. Oliveira confirmed that Francisca do Sacramento had worked as a *caixeira*, also "carrying out all types of work inside the house" where she lived and "rented" out her services and, above all, had worked on the Rua do Valongo "where she was continually grinding roasted coffee". Finally, José da Fonseca, a twenty-eight-year-old white man and a business owner and neighbor of Silva's with whom he was said to have made "commercial deals", recalled that six years earlier he had asked the late Silva why he had not purchased a slave, "given the great amount of work he always required". According to Fonseca, Silva's response was that he "had rented [Francisca] for a long time, and that it made the most business sense to have her as such, rather than to buy a slave and run the risk of losing her, and that in addition to that he was very used to the work that she did". At least implicitly, all of the witnesses appear to corroborate the statement that had been made in her petition to the court: "everything that [the late Silva] had acquired in his life" had been "at the cost" of Francisca's labor.

---

24. The testimony analyzed here can be found between pages 17 and 20 (reverse side) of the appelate case. Cf. "Apelação Cível. Apelante: José de Moraes Silva".

The trustee appointed by the court to oversee the distribution of the freedman José da Silva's inheritance did not call any witnesses to contest the facts presented by Francisca do Sacramento. Indeed, he even resisted responding to the official summons calling for arbitration to determine her wages, only asking his attorney, Caetano Alberto Soares, briefly to contest the validity of the entire procedure. Soares wrote his response to this request directly on the pages of the official court documents, in which he delegitimized Francisca's demand, saying that she had not "proven any one of the points in her lawsuit": neither the time that she had served, nor the price that she had arranged, nor even whether she had, in fact, performed any service for him at all. Once again, to build his case, Soares drew on the articles in the Philippine Ordinances that dealt with the conditions for paying *criados*.[25] With no written contract, and with nothing written in Silva's will that might confirm his debt to Francisca, Soares did not even bother to call the witnesses' validity into question, simply requesting that the court "not allow the estate to be held in abeyance" – in other words, that the court prevent the late Silva's property from becoming available to creditors.[26]

The lower court judge deciding this case summoned appraisers to arbitrate the wages owed to Francisca do Sacramento, and both agreed on a requested monthly sum of 10$000 *réis*, a modest amount of money. In his written decision, the judge affirmed that the facts presented by the witnesses had proven the case, awarding her a total of two *contos* and 230$,000 *réis*. The trustee of the estate, however, appealed the case to the Tribunal da Relação do Rio de Janeiro, where the appellate court judge (*desembargador*) Francisco de Campos overturned the decision. Campos considered the entire case, in his words, as "irremediable invalidity", since it had not been sent to the Juizado de Órfãos, the special court dedicated to the adjudication of family matters, and, according to this judge, the appropriate forum for disputes concerning post-mortem property inventories. Judging null and void the entire case because of this technicality, he ordered Francisca to pay the costs of the judicial procedings.[27]

We know no further details of this story other than those found in the petition that was submitted to the court in Francisca do Sacramento's name. The outcome here was similar to that suffered by other poor women who tried their luck in court requesting the unpaid wages that they had earned as *criadas*. Like Francisca, other women not only had their pleas denied, but also had to shoulder the financial burden of having dared to bring their cases to court and being ordered to pay the costs of their court proceedings.[28] Gender and skin color certainly played a role in these cases, although these

25. See particularly the aforementioned Títulos XXIX–XXXV, in *Ordenações Filipinas,* Livro IV.
26. "Apelação Cível. Apelante: José de Moraes Silva", fos 23–24.
27. *Ibid.,* fo. 47.
28. For more cases and their outcomes, see Lima, *Wages of Intimacy,* pp. 11-29.

factors do not appear explicitly in the official court documents. Francisca's vulnerability becomes visible, however, as this case unfolds. First, it is revealed in the basic fact of her subaltern position. Multiple witnesses' descriptions of Francisca as a "rustic" and uncultured woman, although uttered with discernable tones of condescension and undoubtedly colored with class and racial prejudice, allow us a glimpse of her genuine state of destitution. Second, it is apparent in the difficulties she experienced in trying to represent herself legally; as a woman, as a freedperson, and as someone who was illiterate, any access she had to the law depended on such male intermediaries as Manoel Pereira, the solicitor (*solicitador de causas*) whom she initially sought out to bring her case to court, or Antônio Carneiro da Cunha, the modest attorney who unsuccessfully presented her case to the appellate judge. Neither of these men showed themselves able to confront the opponent representing the other side of this case, *Doutor* Caetano Alberto Soares, a distinguished member of the capital city's judicial elite. The following year, Soares would be one of the founders of the Brazilian Institute of Lawyers, an important national professional organization.[29]

Caixeira was how Francisca do Sacramento's witnesses described the position that she occupied in João José da Silva's store. Under this label, however, fell an extensive set of responsibilities that included the care of Silva's home and his store, a range of kitchen duties, and other forms of "manual labor", menial tasks that under other circumstances at least one witness considered could have been carried out by a domestic slave. This description of her role as a *caixeira* effectively erases the limits between household tasks, on the one hand, and those to be carried out in public on the other: in other words, the limits between the supposedly reproductive activities carried out in the domestic sphere and the productive, commercial activities that defined the operation of a small coffee roasting and sales business.

NEITHER *CAIXEIRA*, NOR *CRIADA*: THE LEGAL LIMBO OF FEMALE LABOR

Payment agreements that went unfulfilled provided both male and female workers with the rare opportunity to express to judicial authorities their expectations about how their labor should be treated and remunerated. In a world where the notion of work as a source of specific rights had yet to take root, these judicial conflicts raised expectations about rights that the law, in general, rarely even contemplated.

---

29. The *Instituto dos Advogados Brasileiros* (IAB) was founded in 1843 and was one of the most important juridical institutions during the Empire. For a historical analysis of this institution, see Eduardo Pena, *Pajens da Casa Imperial. Jurisconsultos e escravidão e a Lei de 1871* (Campinas, 2001). The participation of Caetano Soares in the founding of the IAB is registered in the *Gazeta dos Tribunaes*, 1:58, 18 August (1843), p. 4.

As the cases that this article has presented so far demonstrate, despite the existence of a few juridical positions taken concerning *caixeiros* and of laws governing "service rental", the juridical language employed in disputes over the wages of *caixeiros* and *criadas* still came exclusively from the centuries-old "Philippine" Luso-Brazilian body of laws.

The great legal innovation that had the potential to change this situation was the Commercial Code of the Empire (*Código Comercial do Império*), which became law in June 1850.[30] This code established the legal parameters for the exercise of commercial activity in the country. The Commercial Code did not directly address the conditions of wage laborers, but, in its article 226, it defined a broad range of commercial leasing, which included the rental of "something" or of a person's labor, for a specific amount of time and price. Thus, what this law covered was piecework and not, properly speaking, wage labor. In November of that same year, however, the introduction of the Procedural Commercial Code included, within the realm of commercial law, "questions concerning the setting of payments, and of wages, rights, obligations, [and] responsibilities of auxiliary commercial agents".[31] Thus, at least theoretically, disputes involving *caixeiros* who, to the degree that their "persons and acts" could be defined as strictly commercial, now fell within the purview of Brazilian national commercial law.

The legal foundation of labor contracts in general, and above all those in Brazil, remained the object of controversy, as a query made by the Emperor to the Justice Section of the Council of State in 1860 suggests.[32] In their officially published response to the question about which legislation was in force to regulate the work performed by Brazilian (as opposed to immigrant) laborers, the Council pointed to the Commercial Code of the Empire. Domestic labor was, however, explicitly left out.[33]

There is no doubt that the passing of the Code intensified the distinction between the work of *caixeiros* and that of other types of workers before the law.

---

30. Low no. 556, from 25 June 1850. See: *Código Commercial do Império do Brasil.* Annotado com toda a legislação que lhe é referente [...], pelo bacharel Salustianno Orlando de Araujo Costa, 3rd edn (Rio de Janeiro, 1878).

31. See article 14, second paragraph of *Decreto* no. 737, 25 November 1850, "Determina a ordem do Juizo no Processo Commercial", *Collecção de Leis do Império do Brazil*, Tomo XIII, Parte II, 1850 (Rio de Janeiro, 1851), pp. 271–370, 273.

32. The Council of State (*Conselho de Estado*) was an institution introduced by the 1824 Brazilian Constitution after Independence and survived until the end of the regime, in 1889. Composed by notable polititians and jurists chosen by the Emperor, the function of the *Conselho* was to advise the monarch on political and administrative issues, as well as on diplomacy and the interpretation of the law. On the *Conselho de Estado* see Maria F. Martins, "A Velha Arte de Governar: o Conselho de Estado no Brasil Imperial", *Topoi*, 7:12 (2006), pp. 178–221.

33. Henrique Espada Lima, "Trabalho e Lei para os Libertos na Ilha de Santa Catarina no Século XIX. Arranjos e contratos a entre a autonomia e a domesticidade", *Cadernos AEL*, 14 (2010), pp. 135–175, 149.

The Code required that "owners of businesses in any kind of commerce", maintain "uniform order in accounting and bookkeeping, and have books for these necessary purposes".[34] This provision accentuated the formalization of *caixeiros'* labor arrangements, to the extent that it was expected that wages and money paid and owed would be registered in the accounting books. Thus, the Commercial Code had the effect of reinforcing the contractual character of labor relations in wholesale and retail stores, favoring formalized relations to the detriment of the informal and sometimes familial arrangements that were so common both in domestic labor and in the relationships between bosses and their apprentices in commercial establishments.

Once again, the letter of the law did not directly discriminate with respect to the sex of the workers, and it would, at least in theory, have been possible to imagine the existence of women in the ranks of the *caixeiros*. Yet, as the cases of Francisca de Azevedo and Francisca do Sacramento in the preceding decades already signaled, it was not so easy to establish clear boundaries between the work assigned to *criados* and that of *caixeiros*, much less in the case of a woman. And for those women whose work was simultaneously domestic and commercial, the difficulty of proving an employment relationship shows that theirs was a type of domesticity that the law and its agents failed to recognize as a source of rights.

Thus, it is not surprising that, after 1850, all of the judicial cases in Rio de Janeiro that included the demand for the payment of wages on the part of *caixeiros*, who were invariably male, were only heard in the Commercial Court. Similar demands for wages made by women presenting themselves as *criadas*, for their part, were still directed to the Civil Court Judge (*Juízo Civil*), a jurisdiction that continued to function according to a body of laws that remained contaminated by the same legal ambiguity which had characterized the earlier decades. The last case we will analyze powerfully reveals how the legal ambiguities confronted by women who worked in homes and commercial establishments persisted in the following decades, a period marked by major socio-political transformations.

In May 1878, by way of a solicitor named Antônio Carvalho Guimarães, Anna Maria de Jesus presented a petition to the Judge of the First Civil District of Rio de Janeiro, to force her former boss, José Gonçalves Maia, to pay a debt of back pay she said was owed to her.[35] Anna affirmed that she had been José Maia's *criada* since October 1870, when she was invited to live and work as a servant in his home in Rio's Santa Teresa neighborhood, where he also operated a small tavern in the same building. She worked there until 14 February 1878 when, dissatisfied with her job, she decided to

---

34. *Código Commercial do Império do Brazil*, Capítulo II, art. 10, p. 11.
35. "Apelação Cível. 1º Apelante: José Joaquim Gonçalves Maia Apelante: Anna Maria de Jesus, 1879", ANRJ Fundo: *Tribunal da Relação do Rio de Janeiro* (84), n. 2587, Caixa 157, Galeria C, fo. 4 and the ones to follow. All subsequent references to this case come from this file.

collect the money owed to her. Anna affirmed that, in the seven years during which she had worked for José, he had never paid her any wages, which she calculated as amounting to a sum of 30$000 réis per month.

In the year in which she brought her case to court, Anna was fifty-two years old and José was thirty-two. Both were Portuguese immigrants of limited means, who had gone to Rio de Janeiro to make a life for themselves. José Maia, following the example of the many other young immigrants who were his compatriots, was a subaltern *caixeiro* working for other Portuguese shopkeepers before he was able to save enough money to acquire an establishment of his own. Anna worked as a wage-earning maid in a familial household. Once José had accumulated enough money to buy what the archival documents describe as an "insignificant tavern", he invited Anna to join him there. Despite the modest accommodation – the structure was no more than a "shack made of wooden slabs and zinc" – Anna accepted the offer, perhaps seeing it as an opportunity to have a more independent life and work arrangement. At a certain moment during this period, Anna not only worked in his home and his tavern, but she also shared "a common bed" with José. From the moment when they began to live together, despite their obvious proximity, the parallel lives of these two Portuguese immigrants began to diverge in important respects. José Maia had opened his business as a small tavern, but a few years later he was able to acquire another similar establishment, in addition to other real estate in the Santa Teresa neighborhood. And in May 1878, José got married, but not to Anna. By then, he had trodden the well-worn path traveled by many young Portuguese immigrants in Rio de Janeiro: ascending the social ladder by working in petty commerce, going from being *caixeiro* to being a boss.

While living under the same roof as José, however, Anna's life took a different turn. The various witnesses in this legal case agreed that her work had extended to all aspects of José Maia's life and business: she performed housekeeping tasks and cooked, as well as washing and ironing his clothes and those of his shop employees. In his taverns, she cooked, carried firewood, and made deliveries, and she sometimes oversaw the work of his *caixeiros*. Finally, she also raised animals on a small scale and provided services for other people, cleaning, cooking, and taking care of clothing for young, unmarried men, and in this manner she was able to put aside some extra money. The more José prospered, the more intense Anna's workload became. When she decided to leave José's home, the man for whom she was, in her own words, a *criada*, her decision was based on the excessive work, which was ruining her health. She was, she said, "disgusted" with the excess of tasks for which she was responsible, and she resented José's decision to marry. At the time she presented her case, she had fallen ill and was interned in the Hospital da Ordem do Carmo, a charity hospital that was part of a Catholic religious order with which she was associated. She did not appear to have many resources and, in addition to the wages she never received, she also demanded that José Maia return the money she had loaned to him – money that she had been able to save from earnings from her work "outside".

The dispute around this case was intense, carrying it to the appellate court. Although she did not deny her sexual relationship with José during the time when she worked in his home, Anna argued that her recognized personal sacrifice from when she worked in both his home and his businesses had conferred on her certain rights, which had not been respected. Although she had labored without making a previous arrangement for receiving wages, she was convinced that her efforts merited compensation since, in her lawyer's words, "to work without pay is against justice". But the response from José Maia and his lawyers contested the logic of the entire case, which, they said, was "unproven" and groundless and constituted a "false, imaginary, and impertinent story". The nature of the relationship between José and Anna was at the center of the argument:

> Because the plaintiff and the defendant cohabited, she as his lover, [...]; she gave orders to his *caixeiros*, raised chickens, sold eggs, washed and pressed clothes, provided food for his customers, [...], but all of this on her own account and without the defendant having received for himself any payment for these small jobs – she did not carry out, in the end, the work of a paid *criada* for the defendant but rather *only those [tasks] compatible* with communion between her and the defendant, compensated for with a roof over her head, food, friendship, *a shared bed, and caresses.*[36]

José Maia's formal reply to Anna's petition to the court left no doubt about the extent of Anna's activities and the diligence with which she had carried them out, or even the fact that on more than one occasion she had lent José money. What he contested, however, was the significance of these activities and her description of them as "work" that deserved remuneration. In the "communion" that constituted a relationship with a concubine, the question of its morality aside, there was no place for monetary compensation, since it was a voluntary relationship between two parties founded on an entirely different type of compensation. If Anna actually carried out all of the activities she described, she had done so out of gratitude for being José's "dependent" and his "lover", compensating him with her work in exchange for medical treatment and the other forms of care that he provided. Finally, in another strategy that he used to argue this case, José also tried to delegitimize Anna's demands by questioning her case's standing in that court. Since Anna was a foreign national demanding wages, she should have pursued her case before the Justice of the Peace (*Juiz de Paz*) and not in the civil

---

36. "Apelação Cível. 1° Apelante: José Joaquim Gonçalves Maia", fo. 13. Emphasis in original.

court, according to the legal guidelines laid out in legislation passed in 1837, which dealt with the rental of the services of foreign workers.[37]

Witnesses on both sides of this case corroborated the extensive range of tasks that were part of Anna's work, although the doubt concerning whether she was in fact a *criada* or a *amásia* (lover) appeared, to most of the parties involved, to be an especially difficult question to resolve. The Judge of the First Civil District of the city, Caetano Andrade Pinto, analyzed the case in an exceptionally long, seven-page decision. After carefully describing the arguments one by one, his decision began by contesting the validity of applying laws that regulate service rental of foreign workers to questions related to domestic service, affirming his jurisdiction over this case. He proceeded by stating that he did not see any contradiction between the fact that the plaintiff in this case was both "the defendant's lover" and his *criada*. Thus, if Anna "performed her own services [...] as a *criada* and not as a lover", she would have the right to compensation for her work, "being that", the judge continued, "the law does not recognize the communion resulting from a romantic relationship as having the civil effect of formal marriage uniting the couple's property, and in this latter case [the defendant] would have to share this joint married property with the plaintiff; not even the fact of not having agreed upon the price of rental [of her services] takes away from the plaintiff the right to have her work paid at the price that shall be [determined by the court]."[38]

Andrade Pinto only partially awarded Anna what she sought in this case, taking into account the lack of a written agreement concerning her wages and the fact that José was poor and "allowed her time to perform other types of service [outside his home]". Both parties appealed the decision, and the case was then brought to the appellate court, the Tribunal da Relação. In December 1879, after reviewing the case, citing a lack of proof, the judge Luis Carlos de Paiva Teixeira decided against Anna's demand for unpaid wage and, in addition, ordered her to pay the legal costs that the state had incurred. She unsuccessfully attempted to stay the decision, and the case was closed.

In light of the cases discussed above that had unfolded in previous decades, the outcome of this long process of litigation between Anna and José Maia is not surprising. The lack of a legal framework that made it

37. *Idem*, fls. 23 and 23 reverse side. Law no. 108, passed on 11 October 1837 specified that the Justice of the Peace (*Juizado de Paz*) for the municipality where the renter resides shall be the jurisdiction where any legal action that came out of service rental contracts for foreigners shall be brought. See: Joseli Mendonça. "Os Juizes de Paz e o Mercado de Trabalho – Brasil, Século XIX", in Gladys S. Ribeiro *et al.* (eds), *Diálogos entre Direito e História. Cidadania e Justiça* (Niterói, 2009), pp. 238–255.

38. The sentence is dated 27 August 1879. Cf. "Apelação Cível. 1° Apelante: José Joaquim Gonçalves Maia", fls. 92 reverse side and 93.

possible to recognize unequivocally the labor relationship between these two people exacerbated the arbitrary nature of the judicial decision for this case. Once again, personal details concerning both parties abounded throughout the legal battle, as did the moral debate on the nature of their relationship. One of the elements of this ambiguity was precisely the difficulty of establishing with any precision which body of laws could provide the foundation for a judicial decision. The Philippine Ordinances were not directly cited, nor is there any mention of the Commercial Code. Laws regulating service rentals are mentioned, but the judges never actually considered them. In the lower courts, the case was decided favorably for Anna, but the decision makes no mention of any particular statute. The basis for the lower-court judge's decision points toward a contrast that Brazilian law in the nineteenth century did not recognize: that a concubine relationship was not the same as a marriage and did not produce the "civil effect of formal marriage uniting the couple's property", and that must therefore be treated as a work relationship like any other. The appellate judge disagreed with this interpretation and dismissed the case rather than even rendering a decision on it.

Women who worked in Rio's small commercial establishments and brought lawsuits demanding their unpaid wages only stood a chance of winning if they could present material evidence. They bore the burden of proof, a demand that was often impossible to meet. The expectation that a wage labor relationship could be proven by written documentation was at the center of these suits. As Brazil experienced a series of legal transformations over the course of the mid-nineteenth century, this expectation only gained importance in determining the outcome of similar legal disputes. The Commercial Code was only one of the laws that reinforced this dependency on written evidence and, therefore, on the public registry of contracts: a growing demand in commercial and civil relationships, but one that directly contrasted with the characteristic informality of domestic labor arrangements of that period.

If we think of these legal cases and their outcomes as indicators of the place women who labored in private houses and businesses had in nineteenth-century Brazil's legal culture of work, we might say that the invisibility of female labor was its most apparent feature. These women engaged in extraordinarily difficult legal battles to demonstrate that they had performed genuine work; these battles mirrored their disputes over the definition of the real place they occupied in the homes where they lived. Their ultimately fruitless struggles to defend their personal respectability effectively rendered invisible both their productive labor and their role in the economic success of the men for whom they worked. And just as the value generated by domestic labor was obscured behind a haze of the legal ambiguity, as we shall see, women and their labor came to occupy a marginal place in the urban public sphere.

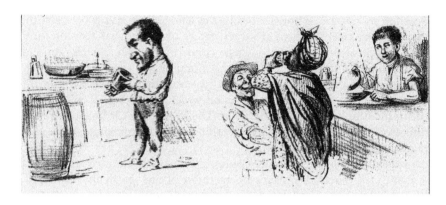

Figure 3. This cartoon, drawn by Angelo Agostini (1843–1910), is originally from *Revista Illustrada*, a magazine printed by the famous illustrator and publisher in Rio de Janeiro between 1876 and 1898. The image's original context is a series of ironic cartoons about the reaction of Rio's small business owners to the introduction of a "Consumer's Cooperative" in the city. It depicts an everyday scene from inside a small dry goods store: on the left, the shop owner, very likely Portuguese, ponders the profits that he could have made by using tempered weights in his shop scales. On the right, a young *caixeiro* weights some flour or sugar while a woman drinks a glass of spirit (*cachaça*). Another patron watches the scene and laughs. She is wearing a piece of fabric tied around her head in a fashion that was common among *quitandeiras*, women of African descent (both free and enslaved) who used to work selling prepared food and vegetables in the city's streets. Both pictures repeat common stereotypes about the habits and mores of Portuguese shop-owners and black women.
Revista Illustrada, *Anno I, n. 20, Rio de Janeiro, May 27, 1876. p. 8.*

CONCLUSION: DIVERGENT TRAJECTORIES OF *CAIXEIROS* AND *CRIADAS*

The cases explored in this article present eloquent evidence of the trajectories – both interwoven and diverging – of *caixeiros* and *criadas* in the course of the nineteenth century in Rio de Janeiro. Although it would be impossible to discuss all the dimensions of these cases, we can reflect on some possible ways to understand this process as connected to the dynamics of labor relations in Rio, on the one hand, and to national politics on the other.

First, it is important to note that labor relations were inseparable from the social and demographic reorganization of the city, above all in the second half of the century. In the 1850s, with the freeing of capital after the end of the Atlantic slave trade, business owners began to invest in hiring European immigrants.[39] These were, in general, poor workers, both individuals and families, who made the journey to Brazil to do farm labor there in the hope

---

39. Luís Felipe Alencastro, "Proletários e escravos. Imigrantes portugueses e cativos africanos no Rio de Janeiro, 1850–1872", *Novos Estudos*, 21 (1988), pp. 30–56.

of buying a piece of land and improving their lives. Whereas in other regions of the country immigrants moved to rural areas, including the recently created "colonies" that were organized to bring groups of foreign immigrants to establish agrarian settlements, recently arrived unmarried Portuguese often settled in the capital city, finding work in petty commerce or other forms of urban labor. Together with enslaved day laborers and freedpersons of African descent, these immigrants formed the basis of a heterogeneous proletariat and a large reserve of available, cheap labor.

In the two subsequent decades, the social and ethnic composition of Rio de Janeiro changed significantly. According to the census carried out in 1872, among the city's population of 274,972 persons, 49,939 were still enslaved. The number of immigrant inhabitants of the city was 73,311, among them 55,938 Portuguese, of whom over eighty per cent were men. Whereas in 1849 out of every ten inhabitants of Rio only four were considered as white, in 1872, reflecting above all the large influx of Portuguese immigrants and the sale of many urban slaves into rural labor in the provinces, this proportion was inverted: for every ten inhabitants of the city, six were white.[40]

This demographic shift is intertwined with other transformations in the organization of urban labor. The growing presence of Portuguese immigrants had a direct impact not only on the composition of the male working class, but also on the female labor market. As the historiography on urban commerce in Rio de Janeiro in the first half of the nineteenth century shows, the participation of African and Afro-descended women in retail commerce and in street vending was quite significant. Once the Atlantic slave trade definitively ended in 1850, however, this presence diminished markedly, and workers in commerce came to be recruited, albeit not exclusively, from the ranks of the city's young, white men, primarily Portuguese and Luso-Brazilian men, often hired by their own compatriots.[41]

The world of domestic labor offers a contrasting image. In 1872, 55,011 of the city's workers were occupied in domestic service, of whom 41.52 per cent were enslaved and 58.47 per cent were free. This occupational category, the single largest listed in the census, accounted for seventy-two per cent of the 48,558 female workers in the city of Rio de Janeiro.[42] The end of slavery

40. Alencastro, "Vida privada e ordem privada no Império", p. 30; Luiz Carlos Soares, *O 'Povo de Cam' na Capital do Brasil. A Escravidão Urbana no Rio de Janeiro do Século XIX* (Rio de Janeiro, 2007), pp. 376 and 379.
41. Alencastro, "Proletários e Escravos", p. 41; Faria, "Sinhás Pretas, Damas Mercadoras", p. 75; Farias, *Mercados Minas*, pp. 23–24.
42. Sandra Lauderdale Graham, *House and Street: The Domestic World of Servants and Masters in Nineteenth-Century Brazil* (Austin, TX, 1992), p. 6; Flávia Souza, "Criados ou empregados? Sobre o trabalho doméstico na cidade do Rio de Janeiro no antes e no depois da abolição da escravidão", paper presented at XXVII Simpósio Nacional De História, ANPUH, Natal, July 2013, p. 7, available at: http://www.snh2013.anpuh.org/resources/anais/27/1371332466_ARQUIVO_Texto_versaofinal_-FlaviaFernandesdeSouza.pdf; last accessed: 24 September 2017. The "domestic service"

reinforced the feminization of domestic labor, because the labor market for men emerging from captivity gave them more opportunities to escape from the often oppressive circumstances inherent in domestic work, some of which this article has examined. With this, emancipated men turned out to be better positioned than women under the same conditions to strive for and to attain, however limitedly, those ideals of both freedom and masculine respectability that entailed the expectation of removing one's self from the bonds of personal dependency that were inevitable in domestic labor.[43]

The gradual exclusion of women, particularly those of African descent, from commercial occupations in Rio de Janeiro reinforced the place of domestic labor as a primordial space of work for poor women during this moment of massive immigration around the time of abolition. Freed women, who had found more opportunities for gaining access to urban occupations during earlier periods, appear to have seen these opportunities diminishing, not only due to competition in the commercial realm as it became an increasingly masculine and "whitened" space, but also because of the emergence of models of female respectability that cast negative judgment on their public sociability and marginalized their independent labor arrangements.

The difficulty of making a clear distinction between women's work as *criadas* in the private, domestic territory of homes, on the one hand, and as *caixeiras* in small businesses on the other, recalls another characteristically indistinct feature of women's working lives in nineteenth-century Brazil: the ambiguities female laborers confronted as women sought their place in the public sphere of collective politics, the space where people constructed a "working-class" identity. Through studying the legal cases presented here, we can draw connections between this private sphere of residential homes and commercial establishments on the one hand and the public sphere mediated by an institutionalized justice system on the other. The cases examined here and others like them allow us to think about how, as they traversed these two spheres, people constructed and transformed the relationships between *caixeiros* and *criados* and the law, between these types of workers and political and judicial institutions, and between these and other types of workers. Thus, through these cases, we can investigate the

category can also be broken down by gender: Among the 20,801 Brazilian-born free workers occupied in domestic labor, 16,683 were women. Among the free, foreign domestic workers, 7,595 out of a total of 11,367 were women. Of the 22,842 enslaved workers in domestic service, 14,184 were women. See: "Município Neutro. População considerada em relação às profissões", in *Recenseamento do Brazil Império em 1872* (Rio de Janeiro, 1874).

43. For an analysis of how notions of liberty and citizenship interacted with ideas about gender, see Diana Paton and Pamela Scully, "Introduction: Gender and Slave Emancipation in Comparative Perspective", in Pamela Scully and Diana Paton (eds), *Gender and Slave Emancipation in the Atlantic World* (Durham, NC, 2005), pp. 1–37.

process through which certain categories of workers managed to distinguish themselves from the rest, mobilizing the meaning of respectability and citizenship and fighting for political and social rights.

The Brazilian Constitution passed in 1824, two years after independence had established the right to vote as a constituent element of male citizenship. All male "Brazilian citizens in enjoying their political rights" and "naturalized foreigners" could vote and run for public office, as long as they met the minimum income requirements. Even male former slaves could vote in local elections, as long as they were Brazilian-born and fulfilled the rather restrictive income requirements. The Constitution excluded from the electorate not only non-citizens (foreigners and slaves), but also women, minors, and *criados de servir* (a disenfranchised category of *criados* that explicitly excluded the more respected *primeiros-caixeiros* and *guarda-livros* or bookkeepers).[44] Yet, in contrast with *criados* and male freedpersons, and even male foreigners who could acquire at least some of the attributes of male citizenship, being a woman was an insuperable barrier to active citizenship for maids, women shop workers, and elite women alike. Thus, it is not surprising that this gender distinction played a fundamental role when *caixeiros* and *criadas* tried to find or to transform the place they occupied in the political world as well as public recognition of their work.

From the 1870s on, *caixeiros'* struggles for regulation of the operating hours of commercial establishments, as well as the articulation of these struggles with both the republican and the workers' movements to abolish slavery, turned on these workers' efforts to distinguish themselves from the indistinct universe of servile labor that brought them closer to *criados* and domestic maids.[45] The personal and collective affirmation of the dignity of work and of the "clerking" class – *a classe caixeiral* – expressed itself in the language of male citizenship and public rights, distancing themselves from the subaltern (and emasculating) character of personal servitude and domesticity. These gendered and class dynamics fueled the divergent trajectories of *caixeiros* and *criadas* and made this divergence into an entrenched reality.

Meanwhile, in the final decade of slavery and the years immediately after abolition in 1888, municipal authorities became especially interested in regulating and controlling domestic work. The government proposed legislation that attempted to establish a *caderneta*, a logbook in which to register labor contracts and the professional histories of domestic *criadas*

---

44. "Art. 92", *Constituição Política do Império do Brasil (de 25 de março de 1824)*, available at: http://www.planalt.gov.br/ccivil_03/Constituicao/Constituicao24.htm; last accessed: 24 September 2017.
45. Cf. Fabiane Popinigis, "'Todas as liberdades são irmãs'. Os caixeiros e as lutas dos trabalhadores por direitos entre o Império e a República", *Revista Estudos Históricos*, 29:59 (2016), pp. 647–666.

and *criados*, under the control of the police. Once these regulations were finally approved in the early 1890s, their enforcement met with resistance from the very group for which the law had been passed, and it was never implemented.[46] Municipal power thus functioned in strikingly different ways for these two types of workers. For *caixeiros*, the proposals for regulation came out of their political intervention and from the pressure they exerted on legislators and other public authorities. In contrast, the various proposals presented in the Municipal Chamber, the local governing body, in the course of the 1880s to regulate *criados* of both sexes, resulted from legislators' concerns about the need to control this mass of workers who, soon to be removed from any of the ties that bound them to slavery, continued to occupy domestic spaces and, dangerously, to share the intimacy of their bosses. In their various versions, however, legislative bills that aimed to regulate domestic service managed to displease both employers and workers. The employers because they objected to the interference of public authorities in private business (who to hire to work in one's own home, and how) and they opposed the limitations on their freedom to hire. The workers because they saw it as an attempt to control them and limit their freedom in general, subjecting them to the strict vigilance of the police authorities and uncomfortably reminding them of the final years of slavery.

José do Patrocínio and Machado de Assis, two of the era's most important commentators and both Afro-Brazilian, had telling reactions to the laws governing these prevalent forms of urban labor. The important abolitionist politician José do Patrocínio (1853–1905), writing about a proposal to regulate the service of *criados*, affirmed that it was a "new law of dissimulated slavery", and for that reason was rejected by "public opinion". [47] For his part, in the same year and just months after the abolition of slavery, the renowned writer Machado de Assis (1839–1908) argued that "all liberties are siblings" in voicing his support for a movement by *caixeiros* to pass legislation that regulated the working hours in commerce.[48]

Thus, as we have sought to demonstrate in this article, female domestic workers' aspirations for citizenship and for public recognition of their work ran aground in the emerging definition of male citizenship, which stood in explicit contrast to domesticity. Public space and politics actively excluded women, whose difficulty in having their labor valued and their rights recognized in the public and legal spheres both antedated and resulted from this exclusion.

---

46. Graham, *House and Street*, p. 123; Souza, "Criados ou empregados", p. 9.
47. Flávia Fernandes de Souza, "'Entre nós, nunca se cogitou de uma tal necessidade'. O poder municipal da Capital e o projeto de regulamentação do serviço doméstico de 1888", *Revista do Arquivo Geral da Cidade*, 5 (2011), pp. 29–48, 37.
48. Popinigis, "Todas as liberdades são irmãs", p. 658.

At the end of the nineteenth century, *caixeiros* made up a respectable part of the urban working class of Rio de Janeiro, organized in associations and capable of having their demands for improved working conditions recognized by municipal authorities and in legislation. In contrast, during the same period, the professional reality of female domestic workers looked very different: placed at the margin of the organized working class, confined to labor arrangements marked by domesticity and paternalism, the law only saw them as objects of political and sanitary regulation, with little or no recognition of any direct link to their condition as workers.

Translation: Amy Chazkel

IRSH 62 (2017), Special Issue, pp. 75–103 doi:10.1017/S002085901700044X
© 2018 Internationaal Instituut voor Sociale Geschiedenis

Revolutionary Syndicalism and Reformism in Rio de Janeiro's Labour Movement (1906–1920)

CLAUDIO BATALHA

State University of Campinas (UNICAMP)
Rua Cora Coralina, 100
13083-896 Campinas, SP, Brazil

E-mail: batalha@unicamp.br

ABSTRACT: Divided between revolutionary syndicalism and reformist unions, Rio de Janeiro's labour movement represented one of the most complex local cases during the Brazilian First Republic. This article intends to show how relations between these two currents were far from clear cut, and that, despite the confrontational discourse they adopted and the disputes over labour unions they were involved in, they eventually shared common practices and, to some degree, a common culture.

To most observers, Rio de Janeiro's labour movement after 1906 appeared clearly divided into two antagonistic factions: "revolutionary syndicalism" or followers of "direct action", on the one hand, and "reformist" trade unions on the other. This division persisted at least up to the 1920s, when a third competing force, the Communist Party, entered the dispute. However, like in many other countries, these two currents continued to be major referents in the subsequent political disputes within the labour movement. Until today, these labels are among the best known in the history of labour movements: They are firmly established, even iconic attributions, apparently valid all around the world with a stable meaning. Furthermore, they have been perpetuated by historians, who use them to make sense of different actors and currents in the history of labour. Of course, to a high degree these labels refer to differences that were real (both in the sense of stemming from realities and of creating these realities through their discursive power), and such differences are most commonly defined along a spectrum of certain programmatic and strategic orientations. Yet, as has repeatedly been pointed out by both activists and academics, they are also deeply problematic: their meaning shifts over time and, within one period, is not the same in different locations; their boundaries are not clear cut, sometimes even fluid, even within or in relation to the same organizational and individual actors (especially over the course of a lifespan). In addition, this division, to the degree that it was real, was rendered in different terms.

In the case of Rio's labour movement, for instance, an observer in 1913 spoke of a dispute between "legalists", i.e. all "movements submitted to political discipline – parliamentarism – organized in a great political party" and the "revolutionary column, which knows no political discipline and uses direct action as its sole means".[1]

The unclear boundaries between the "reformist" and "revolutionary syndicalist" spheres are further complicated by the fact that all labels involved are controversial in their own right, denoting more a spectrum of positions and practices than a stable phenomenon. Especially the interrelation (or not) between "syndicalism" *sans phrase*, "revolutionary syndicalism", and "anarchism" haven been debated vigorously among scholars: Sometimes an identity is presupposed ("revolutionary syndicalism" being a specifically anarchist form of unionism), sometimes a much looser and often discontinuous affinity is envisioned, sometimes an independence of each current is insisted upon.[2] As this article will make clear, the case of Rio de Janeiro gives credence to those positions that see "anarchism" and "revolutionary syndicalism" as often interrelated, though not at all moments and under all circumstances.

The aim of this article is thus to explore how the boundaries between "reformist" and "revolutionary syndicalist" ideological currents and union practices were drawn in the case of Rio de Janeiro, and the way in which these were, at the same time, blurred from the beginning, becoming even more fluid over time, especially in the context of the long strike waves between 1917 and 1919.[3] The particularities of Rio de Janeiro (the capital of Brazil during this period) are highlighted by pointing to some differences with international trends and by comparison to other locations and regions in Brazil, especially São Paulo, where a different constellation of forces led to a different outcome. The argument is based on the research conducted in Brazil on the trajectories of revolutionary syndicalism and anarchism,[4]

---

1. Rozendo dos Santos, "A ação operaria", *A Voz do Trabalhador*, 6:23, 15 January 1913, pp. 1–2.
2. For examples of the former see Max Nettlau, *Histoire de l'anarchie* (Paris, 1983); James Joll, *The Anarchists* (London, 1970); Nildo Viana, "Aurora do anarquismo", in Rafael Borges Deminicis and Daniel Aarão Reis Filho (eds), *História do anarquismo no Brasil* (Niterói, 2006), pp. 23–43; and Tiago Bernardon de Oliveira, "Anarquismo, sindicatos e revolução no Brasil (1906–1936)" (Ph.D, Universidade Federal Fluminense, 2009); for the latter see Jacques Julliard, *Autonomie ouvrière. Études sur le syndicalisme d'action directe* (Paris, 1988); Edilene Toledo, *Travessias revolucionárias. Ideias e militantes sindicalistas em São Paulo e na Itália (1890–1945)* (Campinas, 2004).
3. From now on "reformism", "anarchism", and "revolutionary syndicalism" are used without quotation marks.
4. There are three main approaches concerning the relation between revolutionary syndicalism and anarchism among Brazilian scholars: those who see them as inseparable and make no distinction between the two currents; those who consider them as separate and clearly different currents; and, finally, those that view revolutionary syndicalism, although distinct from anarchism, mainly as a practice adopted by anarchists in the trade union movement.

as well as on recent international debates, which both stress their transnational connectedness and their remarkable changeability according to different contexts and circumstances.[5]

WHO WERE THE WORKING CLASSES IN RIO DE JANEIRO?

According to the 1920 Census of the Federal District, which encompassed the city of Rio de Janeiro and its environs, the city had 1,157,873 inhabitants, representing an increase of forty-three per cent over the 811,443 found in the previous Census of 1906.[6] Men formed 51.8 per cent of the population in 1920, slightly outnumbering women (48.2 per cent).[7] The preponderance of men in the population was attributed to mostly male immigration. Foreigners represented 20.6 per cent of the population (of which only thirty-five per cent were women), a proportion that had been rapidly decreasing since the beginning of the century.[8]

Foreigners represented an important part of Rio de Janeiro's population and of its workforce but, unlike in southern Brazil, Rio's immigrant population was composed primarily of adult males. Hence, the formation of relatively closed immigrant communities was less frequent and integration easier ("integration" here meaning a more regular contact between the immigrant communities as well as between these and the wider Brazilian society). Another aspect of Rio's particular demographics, which, in comparison with other Brazilian cities, smoothed over differences within the capital, was the fact that the Portuguese were by far the largest immigrant group (followed by Italians and Spanish), so language was no barrier between them and Brazilian-born workers. Despite their relatively limited participation in the total workforce, foreign-born workers formed the majority in certain trades, industries, and even whole sectors, such as wood processing (slightly over 50 per cent), the food industry (52 per cent), land and (curiously) air transportation (51 per cent) and commerce (57 per cent).[9] Women represented about 27 per cent of the industrial workforce, while they formed a clear majority of workers in the garment industry (62 per cent) and, as elsewhere, in domestic

5. For this topic, see Neville Kirk, *Comrades and Cousins: Globalization, Workers and Labour Movements in Britain, the USA and Australia from the 1880s to 1914* (London, 2003); Jonathan Hyslop, *A Notorious Syndicalist. J.T. Bain: A Scottish Rebel in Colonial South Africa* (Johannesburg, 2004); Steven Hirsch and Lucien van der Walt (eds), *Anarchism and Syndicalism in the Colonial and Postcolonial World, 1870–1940: The Praxis of National Liberation, Internationalism, and Social Revolution* (Leiden [etc.], 2010).
6. Directoria Geral de Estatística (Ministerio da Agricultura, Industria e Commercio), *Recenseamento do Brazil. Realizado em 1° setembro de 1920*, Rio de Janeiro, 1923, vol. 2 (1st part), p. XXII.
7. *Ibid.*, p. XXXVII.
8. *Ibid.*, pp. 11 and 13.
9. *Ibid.*, pp. 514–515.

service (82 per cent). In comparison, the share of women among all industrial workers was slightly higher in the city of São Paulo (29 per cent), but there they made up 58 per cent of the workers in the textile industry (production of yarn and cloth), while in Rio women comprised no more than 39 per cent of this sector, for reasons that are not entirely clear.

Until the 1920s, Rio de Janeiro was the country's principal industrial city. Of the ten most important cotton mills of Brazil in 1915, six were installed in the Federal District,[10] and textile mills were by far the most mechanized and employed one of the largest workforces. But other branches of industry and services exceeded the workforce employed in the production of yarn and cloth, such as construction, transportation, the garment industry, wood processing, and even metal works. Industries were, in general, predominated by small-size establishments with a mostly low level of mechanization. For instance, one post-World War I observer commented on the shoe industry:

> The manufacture of shoes has been greatly stimulated by the war, although the industry has been well established for some time. There are over 4,000 shoe factories in Brazil, including the home industries, but there are only 116 establishments which employ more than twelve people, and only sixty-one have between six and twelve employees. The modern factory system, the piecework system, and the home industry are all competitors.[11]

Of the 116 plants mentioned above, fifty-five were located in the Federal District. Although the shoe industry is an extreme case, this excerpt illustrates vividly the coexistence of different "stages" of production in Brazilian industry. Even the textile industry, in which, according to the aforementioned report, "many of the plants are equipped with the most modern machinery and are run by electricity, comparing favourably with the great New England mills",[12] had a broad range of technological levels. In the Federal District, alongside the cotton mills employing thousands of workers, a wool manufacturing facility had only thirty employees.[13] The contrast was even more accentuated in the city of São Paulo, with numerous manufacturing facilities not having more than two to five workers.[14]

The censuses show a significant number of adults (twenty-two per cent of the total population in 1920) classified under categories such as "ill-defined professions" or "undeclared professions", which certainly encompassed

---

10. Centro Industrial do Brasil, *Relatorio da diretoria do Centro Industrial do Brasil para ser apresentado à Assemblea Geral Ordinaria do anno de 1915* (Rio de Janeiro, 1915), pp. 239–253.
11. Arthur H. Redfield, *Brazil: A Study of Economic Conditions since 1913* (Department of Commerce/Bureau of Foreign and Domestic Commerce, Miscellaneous Series, No. 86) (Washington, DC, 1920), pp. 63–65.
12. *Ibid.*, p. 58.
13. Centro Industrial do Brasil, *Relatorio da diretoria*, p. 244.
14. *Ibid.*, pp. 252–253.

not only the "dangerous classes" of vagrants, beggars, criminals, sex workers, etc., but also the casual labour force that was essential to the operation of the city's port and various other activities.

During the 1980s, scholarly works, especially those influenced by sociology, typically tried to establish a correlation between nationality, profession, and ideological choices. In short, this scholarship implied that immigrant industrial workers were more likely to turn to direct action,[15] while Brazilian port or transportation workers would choose reformism. Workers employed in strategic sectors of a commodity-export economy would undeniably have more leverage to negotiate and to have their demands met. The exact opposite would happen to industrial workers who produced mainly consumer goods.[16] Nevertheless, there is substantial evidence that supplies counter-examples to this kind of premise, thus any automatic correlation between structural circumstances and ideological choices impedes our understanding of the multiple and complex factors, many of them conjunctural, that lead people to take a particular political stand.

THE 1906 LABOUR CONGRESS

The First Brazilian Workers Congress, which met in Rio de Janeiro from 15 to 20 April 1906, only became possible after a long organizing process in which different groups proposing the congress finally managed to agree. Despite all the effort and the twenty-eight delegates present (sixteen of which were from the Federal District, that is, the city of Rio de Janeiro), in fact they represented only five states. Nonetheless, this congress attempted to bring together different currents – in itself a remarkable fact in view of the already clearly established separation between anarchism (and its numerous tendencies) and socialists in many European countries at the time. The congress confronted a series of classical issues of political and strategical orientation (formation of a political party, participation in elections, relations between trade unions and political organizations, forms of struggle, etc.), and it established the defining characteristics of the labour movement for the next two decades.

Edgard Leuenroth (1881–1968), one of the main leaders of São Paulo's anarchists, cunningly eliminated any discussion about the possible creation

15. "Direct action", it should be remembered, has experienced a shift in its meaning during the last decades. Whereas at the turn of the twentieth century, especially in the context of French revolutionary syndicalism, the emphasis was on direct *economic* action without institutional intermediation and in relation to sites of productions, through strikes, factory occupations, etc., since the 1970s, the meaning has shifted towards the contestation of public space, acts of civil disobience, or the disruption of symbols of power and order.
16. On this subject, see for example, Fernando Teixeira da Silva and Maria Lucia Gitahy, "The Presence of Labour in the Urban Culture of Santos", *Moving the Social*, 49 (2013), pp. 11–29, 25.

of a working-class political party, a point scheduled for debate by the congress, by proposing a resolution establishing that "the congress was composed of working-class associations organized on economic grounds, and it was not intended to discuss political opinions and actions of the members of those associations".[17] Thus, the approval of Leuenroth's resolution by a majority of delegates rendered any further discussion of political action meaningless. The congress decided to found the Confederação Operária Brasileira (COB; Brazilian Workers Confederation) as an umbrella organization, inspired by the French General Confederation of Labour (CGT) and thus of clearly syndicalist orientation. Years later, a report by the COB presented to the 1913 workers' congress described what happened in 1906 in a way that is worth quoting at length as it makes clear how the identifications of "reformist" and "revolutionary syndicalist" were clearly becoming discernible, although not necessarily with these labels:

> If it were not for the combative temperament of the delegates representing São Paulo's workers, united with the representatives of Rio de Janeiro, already seasoned by previous fights, the 1906 Congress would have been useless for the working class of Brazil, since its main promoters were committed to extract from that magnificent clash of ideas a *strong political party* to serve the interests of the bourgeoisie.
>
> [...] The struggle sustained in that memorable encounter of two currents of action, until then unknown, was one of the most exciting we have witnessed. On the one hand – the majority – highly organized in their efforts to make a compromised set of ideas prevail, a real denial of common interests; on the other hand – the minority – a phalanx of brave companions who are propagators of new ideals, tired of promises, full of ardour, bearing the torch of solidarity, fighting against prejudice, snatching the naïve worker from the darkness of ignorance, illuminating our camp with the light of their knowledge on the question that concerns us and that will inevitably lead us to the final destination of our aspirations, which is the abolition of this iniquitous regime, this dammed institution.
>
> Reason, thus, has won against ignorance and wickedness.[18]

It is remarkable how this quote presents those who, after all, managed to convince the majority to vote for this resolution as a struggling and somewhat heroic minority, and those defeated as an oppressive majority. Furthermore, it is striking how the partisans of direct action here consider their political project as one of "illumination" and education.

Whatever the numeric correlation of forces at the beginning of the congress (when it seemed that the reformist side had a majority), in its main

---

17. The resolution was reprinted as "Os operarios – O Congresso Operario Regional", *Correio da Manhã*, 16 April 1906, pp. 1–2.
18. Quoted from an extract of the congress' report reprinted in a compilation of documents by the Brazilian labour movement: "O Segundo Congresso Operário (1913)", in Paulo Sérgio Pinheiro and Michael M. Hall (eds), *A classe operária no Brasil. Documentos 1889 a 1930*, vol. 1, *O movimento operário* (São Paulo, 1979), pp. 172–223, 207–208. Emphasis in the original.

resolutions the principles of revolutionary syndicalism held sway, especially in relation to two issues: the forms of action to be adopted and the way trade unions should be structured. Under the general principle of direct action, the resolutions prescribed that workers themselves should take action against employers without help from outsiders (such as politicians, government officials, lawyers), by means such as boycotts, sabotage, and strikes. For its part, the trade union organization had to be autonomous and as unbureaucratic as possible, with no paid officials, directed by an executive committee with no hierarchical distinction between its members, and dedicated exclusively to "economic" struggle, that is, to improving wages and working conditions. Activities such as cooperatives and those related to mutual aid, which where common in most Brazilian working-class associations by that period, were considered undesirable and should be avoided by unions. A number of trade unions based on these principles were founded in the aftermath of the congress, but very few survived the industrial crisis that bore a powerful impact on employment and working-class organization between 1908 and 1911.

CONGENIAL NON-IDENTITY: REVOLUTIONARY SYNDICALISM AND ANARCHISM

Revolutionary syndicalism was an international current in the labour movement, although it could assume quite different characteristics in the various national contexts in which it was present. In its original French version, revolutionary syndicalism was formed by labour activists, many of whom were former anarchists or socialists, into a third and quite distinct ideological current.[19] In Italy, it was the offspring of the anti-parliamentary left wing of the Socialist Party. A similar process occurred in the Argentinian case, where also it emerged from socialist ranks.[20] In the USA, and to a lesser degree in Canada, it can be associated with the organization of the Industrial Workers of the World (IWW), which had its own particularities.[21]

19. It should be added that "syndicalism" and "revolutionary syndicalism" have mostly been used synonymously (both by contemporary activists and subsequent historians) although there are instances of a syndicalism that did not identify itself as "revolutionary", but as "gradualist" or "reformist".
20. On Argentina, see for instance, Hugo del Campo, *El "sindicalismo revolucionário" (1905–1945). Selección de textos* (Buenos Aires, 1986), pp. 9–10; Alejandro Belkin, *Sobre los orígenes del sindicalismo revolucionario en Argentina* (Cuadernos de Trabajo Nr. 74) (Buenos Aires, 2007). On France, see Julliard, *Autonomie ouvrière*; Marco Gervasoni, "L'invention du syndicalisme révolutionnaire en France (1903–1907)", *Mil neuf cent*, 24 (2006), pp. 57–71. On Italy, see Alceo Riosa, *Il sindacalismo rivoluzionario in Italia e la lotta politica nel Partito socialista dell'età giolittiana* (Bari, 1976); Willy Gianinazzi, "Le syndicalisme révolutionnaire en Italie (1904–1925). Les hommes et les luttes", *Mil neuf cent*, 24 (2006), pp. 95–121.
21. Among these particularities are that the IWW was based on industrial unions, an organizing method that, although it also existed in other contexts, gained pre-eminence among the Wobblies.

It is doubtful whether revolutionary syndicalism ever represented a consolidated political current in Rio de Janeiro. It was, rather, an ideological reference point and a conception of how trade unions should be organized, and it was a set of ideas adopted by anarchists in the trade union movement. In this sense, Rio de Janeiro was quite different from São Paulo, where in addition to anarchists adopting revolutionary syndicalist practices, a distinct revolutionary syndicalist current emerged under the leadership of Italian socialist militants such as Alceste De Ambris.[22] Other major differences between the two cities, which may help to understand certain political choices, are that the Brazilian capital had a middle-class opposition that eventually established alliances with the working class, while nothing of the sort existed in São Paulo. Also, repression of the labour movement in São Paulo tended to be far more brutal than in Rio. Nevertheless, it is quite likely that, in Rio, a number of trade union officials were more attracted to a revolutionary syndicalist stance than to an anarchist ideology proper.

Whether or not Brazilian revolutionary syndicalism ever became a coherent political project, one thing is certain: theirs was a moderate version of its European counterpart. The resolutions passed by the First Workers Congress in 1906, which endorsed direct action and other revolutionary syndicalist conceptions, never used the word revolutionary either as an adjective or as a noun.[23] This can be attributed, at least in part, to the need for partisans of revolutionary syndicalism to convince delegates of that congress to adopt their approach to labour organizing; in other words, to the fact that the results of the congress were a compromise. Yet, despite such constellations of opportunity and necessary compromise, Brazilian revolutionary syndicalism was certainly more syndicalist than revolutionary on its own terms, precisely because it had less affinity to the ideological horizon of a larger project ("revolution") and more to the cornerstone of syndicalism, the limitation to the "economic" struggle. This does not mean the ideas of French or Italian revolutionary-syndicalists were unfamiliar to Brazilian activists: For instance, as advertised in the COB newspaper, *A Voz do Trabalhador*, the writings by the following were found on sale at the federation's offices: Émile Pouget, Victor Griffuelhes, Marc Pierrot, Aristide Briand, Enrico Leone, alongside Marx and anarchists such as

---

Another characteristic was the One Big Union concept, i.e. the demand for a united union organization for all workers, which was unfamiliar to most revolutionary syndicalists elsewhere.
22. Toledo, *Travessias revolucion*árias, ch. 2; Edilene Tolede and Luigi Biondi, "Constructing Syndicalism and Anarchism Globally: The Transnational Making of the Syndicalist Movement in São Paulo, Brazil, 1895–1935", in Hirsch and Van der Walt (eds), *Anarchism and Syndicalism in the Colonial and Postcolonial World, 1870–1940*, pp. 363–393.
23. "O Primeiro Congresso Operário (1906)", in Pinheiro and Hall, *A classe operário no Brasil*, vol. 1, *O movimento operário*, pp. 42–49.

Malatesta, Kropotkine, Réclus, or Grave.[24] And translated articles written by Pelloutier, Pouget, Lagardelle, Yvetot, or Gustave Hervé (or at least quotes from them), were published not only by *A Voz do Trabalhador*, but also other papers of the labour press.[25]

Whatever the proximity of the unions of syndicalist orientation and anarchist groups, as far as the leading persons promoting revolutionary-syndicalist principles in labour unions (which included philosophical, political and religious neutrality) were concerned, these were, in most cases, outspoken anarcho-communists – in other words, followers of the international anarchist current whose most famous representatives included Kropotkin in Russia and Malatesta in Italy. In Brazil, the principal theoretical defence of anarchists' adoption of revolutionary-syndicalist practice within unions came from the São Paulo-based, Portuguese-born journalist, Gregorio Nazianzeno de Vasconcelos (1878–1920), better known as Neno Vasco.[26] Although this position managed, until 1920, to assure a solid majority among anarchists who supported participation in the trade union movement, it had to deal with contestation both from anarcho-communists who opposed trade union action altogether and from those who, in an opposite but similarly radical stance, sustained that unions should adopt anarchism in their programmes. Both views had some currency in the state of São Paulo, less so in Rio de Janeiro.

The historiography concerning the Brazilian labour movement, especially up to the 1990s, tended to use the term "anarcho-syndicalism" to designate anarchists acting in trade unions, despite the fact that this term did not appear in Brazilian labour vocabulary before mid-1920s, and even then usually with pejorative connotations. The term only began to appear more frequently in documents produced by the Communist Party (PCB) from 1928 onwards.[27] The popularization of this designation in labour history reaches back to the writings in the post-war years of militant historians, many of whom were members or former members of the PCB.[28] The use of

---

24. "Livros à venda", *A Voz do Trabalhador*, VII (71), 8 June 1915, p. 4.

25. For Rio de Janeiro, see for example *O Marmorista*, 1907; *O Baluarte*, 1907; *Novo Rumo*, 1906, 1910.

26. Neno Vasco arrived in São Paulo, as a child along with his father and stepmother. Some years later, he returned to Portugal to complete his studies and attend the Law School of the University of Coimbra. On returning to Brazil in 1901, he became an active anarchist, publishing a number of newspapers, as well as a prolific political writer, playwright, and translator. In 1910, with the establishment of the Portuguese Republic he returned to his homeland, where he continued his anarchist engagement until the time of his death. The most complete study on Neno Vasco is Alexandre Samis, *Minha Pátria é o Mundo Inteiro. Neno Vasco, o anarquismo e o sindicalismo revolucionário em dois mundos* (Lisboa, 2009).

27. For some of the first mentionings of this term, see "Para Genebra", *O Alfaiate*, VI (25), 13 May 1926, p. 4; "O III Congresso (dezembro de 1928–janeiro de 1929)" in Edgard Carone (ed.), *O P.C.B. –Vol. 1: (1922–1943)* (São Paulo, 1982), p. 73.

28. See for example, Astrojildo Pereira, *Formação do PCB. 1922–1928, notas e documentos.* (Rio de Janeiro, 1962).

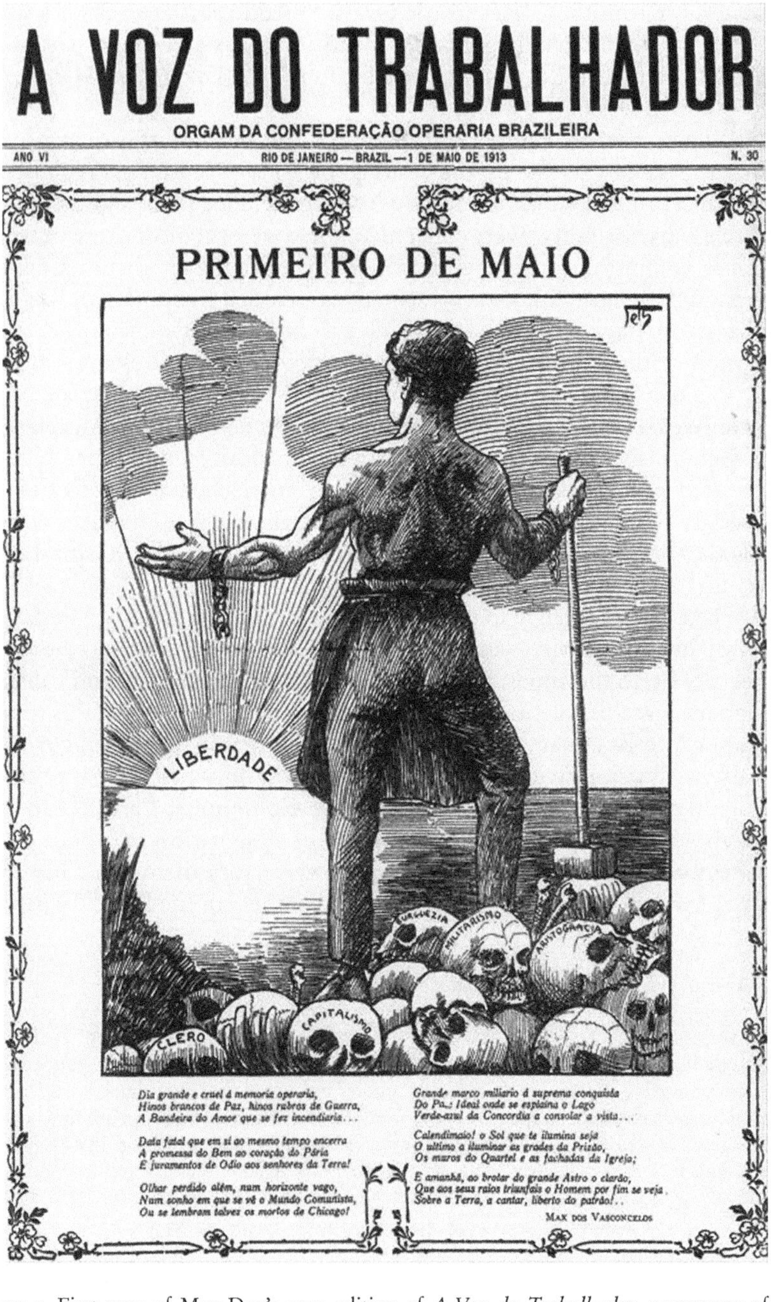

A VOZ DO TRABALHADOR

ORGAM DA CONFEDERAÇÃO OPERARIA BRAZILEIRA

ANO VI — RIO DE JANEIRO — BRAZIL — 1 DE MAIO DE 1913 — N. 30

PRIMEIRO DE MAIO

Dia grande e cruel á memoria operaria,
Hinos brancos de Paz, hinos rubros de Guerra,
A Bandeira do Amor que se fez incendiaria...

Data fatal que em si ao mesmo tempo encerra
A promessa do Bem ao coração do Pária
E juramentos de Odio aos senhores da Terra!

Olhar perdido além, num horizonte vago,
Num sonho em que se vê o Mundo Comunista,
Ou se lembram talvez os mortos de Chicago!

Grande marco miliario á suprema conquista
Do Pa..: Ideal onde se espraina o Lago
Verde-azul da Concordia a consolar a vista...

Calendimaio! o Sol que te ilumina seja
O ultimo a iluminar as grades da Prizão,
Os muros do Quartel e as fachadas da Igreja;

E amanhã, ao brotar do grande Astro o clarão,
Que aos seus raios triunfais o Homem por fim se veja
Sobre a Terra, a cantar, liberto do patrão!..

MAX DOS VASCONCELLOS

Figure 1. First page of May Day's 1913 edition of *A Voz do Trabalhador*, newspaper of the revolutionary syndicalist Confederação Operária Brasileira [Brazilian Workers' Confederation]. *A Voz do Trabalhador, Rio de Janeiro, 1st May 1913, p. 1. Collection Arquivo Edgard Leuenroth/IFCH/UNICAMP, J/0013.*

this term, however, is by no means a Brazilian peculiarity. Such English-speaking historians as George Woodcock use it as a synonym for "revolutionary syndicalism" when speaking of France.[29] But this designation, as more recent labour history has shown, is both imprecise and problematic:[30] If the designation is controversial for the French case, where not all revolutionary syndicalists came from anarchism, it is completely pre-posterous when speaking of the Italian or the Argentinian case, where they came mostly from socialist ranks. In the Brazilian case, with its considerable regional differences in almost all matters related to the labour movement, at least until the mid-twentieth century, such an approach certainly does not aid understanding of the complex relationship between anarchism and revolutionary syndicalism, nor does it illuminate the specific contours that this relationship acquires in different places, such as Rio de Janeiro and São Paulo.

One final aspect to be considered are the individuals – more than one anarcho-communist changed position concerning trade union activity according to the shifting historical circumstances. José Elias da Silva, for instance, one of the future founders of the PCB, in 1913 served as the Secretary General of the Federação Operária do Rio de Janeiro – FORJ (Rio de Janeiro's Workers Federation), the city's most important revolutionary syndicalist organization. Three years later, at a moment when labour associations were experiencing a major crisis, he published, together with two other disillusioned anarchists, a pamphlet that harshly criticized the participation of anarchists in trade unions.[31] As the labour movement regained force in 1917, Silva returned to the syndicalist ranks. In other words, for many, revolutionary syndicalism was not a matter of principle, but rather a form of action to be adopted under favourable circumstances.

THE CURRENCY OF REFORMISM AND THE ABSENCE OF A SOCIALIST PARTY

Reformists in the labour movement were a similarly heterogeneous sphere of different positions, ranging from trade unionists seeking concrete

29. George Woodcock, *Anarchism: A History of Libertarian Ideas and Movements* (Harmondsworth [etc.], 1983), pp. 277; 303–304.

30. A critique of this term in Brazilian context first came from Adhemar Lourenço da Silva Jr., "O anarco-sindicalismo no Brasil. Notas sobre a produção de um mito histórico-historiográfico", in Ana Lúcia Velhinho D'Angelo (ed.), *Histórias de trabalho* (Porto Alegre, 1995), pp. 151–159. It was further developed in Claudio Batalha, *O movimento operário na Primeira República* (Rio de Janeiro, 2000); and figures as one of the central arguments in Edilene Toledo, *Anarquismo e sindicalismo revolucionário. Trabalhadores e militantes em São Paulo na Primeira República* (São Paulo, 2004).

31. José Elias da Silva, Manoel Campos, and Antonio Moutinho, *O anarquismo perante a organização sindical. Para desfazer mal entendidos* (Rio de Janeiro, 1916).

improvements for their specific crafts or industries to socialists trying to establish links between unions and working-class parties; a number of other ideological orientations inhabited the wide space between these two extremes. Craft or class, political activism or neutrality, cooperation resp. negotiation or class confrontation were some of the issues that divided the heterogeneous reformist camp. In addition to socialism, other tendencies were present, one of the more significant being positivism. Positivism (in a local and, again, heterogeneous adoption of the French version) had been a guiding ideology for Brazil's First Republic (1889–1930), informing various sectors of the state, the military and middle-class professionals, while also having some currency among wider layers of the population. One of the tenets of this positivism was to acknowledge and address the "social question". Its adherents within the labour movement proposed that workers participate in elections and present their own candidates.[32]

Unlike other South American cases, including Argentina, Uruguay, and Chile, no enduring, unified, and nationwide socialist party was established in Brazil before the 1940s, something that should be seen as one the main determinants of the country's political history and which poses a major challenge for labour historians to explain.[33] One must recall that all Brazilian politics during the First Republic (1889–1930) was based on single states, thus political parties had a state and not a national organization (the first important exception would be the 1922 Communist Party). Even the few attempts to create ruling-class national parties failed. Furthermore, Brazilian socialists never had any solid connection with the Socialist International, among other reasons, because the many labour and socialist parties created from the 1890s to the 1930s did not last long enough for this connection to be established. All formal contact with the International was limited to two reports sent by German-speaking workers, members of São Paulo's Allgemeiner Arbeiterverein (General Workers' Association), in 1893 and 1896.[34] Nevertheless, the lack of organic links with the International did not mean other forms of contact with international socialism did not exist, such as correspondence, the exchange of periodicals, migrational links, occasional visits by militants, and so forth. Italo-Argentinian José Ingenieros and Portuguese social-republican Sebastião Magalhães Lima played a major role in the 1890s as correspondents of Brazilian socialist newspapers and in introducing various works

---

32. Adalmir Leonidio, "Saint-simonismo e positivismo nos primórdios do movimento operário no Brasil", *Mediações*, 10 (Jan.–Jun. 2005), pp. 165–183; Teresa A. Meade, *"Civilizing" Rio: Reform and Resistance in a Brazilian City, 1889–1930* (University Park, PA, 1997), pp. 95–101.
33. On the repeated attempts to found such a party and on the trajectories of a group of leading socialists, see the contribution by Aldrin Castellucci and Benito B. Schmidt in this Special Issue.
34. Georges Haupt, "Militants sociaux-democrates allemands au Brésil (1893–1896)", *Le Mouvement Social*, 84 (July–August 1973), pp. 47–61.

and their authors to local socialists.[35] The works known to Brazilian socialists, mostly through French, Italian, and Argentinian editions, reflect an eclectic, mainly reform-oriented socialism. Authors made known to Brazilian activists in this way included Benoît Malon, Gabriel Deville, Filippo Turati, Enrico Ferri, Ferdinand Lassalle, August Bebel, or Friedrich Engels. Marx, although frequently quoted, was mainly known through the interpretations and didactic syntheses of his work then in circulation.[36]

Local socialists not only mixed different authors, in a practice that was not uncommon in many parts of the world during the Second International, but also proposed a selective reading of these authors. For instance, Benoît Malon, who was one of the most popular among Brazilian socialists, was stripped of an essential aspect of his thinking, his defence of federalism. Likewise, Brazilian socialists' selective reading of Malon disregarded his anti-Semitism (something many French socialists had also turned a blind eye to before the Dreyfus Affair).

The positivists or followers of what was known as the "Labour Cult" (*Culto do Trabalho*), under the leadership of Francisco Juvêncio Sadock de Sá, a mechanic who worked as a foreman at Rio de Janeiro's Army Arsenal, were an ideological phenomenon that was specific to Rio de Janeiro (with limited presence in some other cities) and, although based on an interpretation of Auguste Comte's writings, with no apparent links with international tendencies. Initially, during the early years of the twentieth century, Sadock de Sá and his followers held positions similar to those of other reform-oriented groups promoting working-class candidates in local and federal elections, demanding labour laws, supporting strikes (but only under certain circumstances), and making vague references to socialism.[37] By the end of the first decade of the century, with the creation in 1909 of the Círculo dos Operários da União (Federal Government's Workers Circle), however, followers of this ideological tendency became a pressure group that primarily recruited its followers from the ranks of workers employed in state-owned firms. With their stance towards the state significantly softened, they proposed collaboration with government, "social harmony", the adoption of an anti-strike stand, withdrawal from collective action with

35. Among the more important of the numerous newspapers of this orientation were *A Questão Social*, Santos, 1895–1896; *Echo Operario*, Rio Grande, 1896–1898; *O Socialista*, São Paulo, 1896–1898; *Primeiro de Maio*, Rio de Janeiro, 1898; *Aurora Social*, Recife, 1901–1902.
36. See Claudio H. M. Batalha, "A difusão do marxismo e os socialistas brasileiros na virada do século XIX", in João Quartim de Moraes (ed.), *História do marxismo no Brasil. Os influxos teóricos*, 1st repr., (Campinas, 2007), vol. 2, pp. 9–41; Benito Bisso Schmidt, "Os partidos socialistas na nascente República", in Jorge Ferreira and Daniel Aarão Reis (eds), *As esquerdas no Brasil*, vol. 1, *A formação das tradições (1889–1945)* (Rio de Janeiro, 2007), pp. 131–183.
37. See, especially, Sadock de Sá's contributions during these years, written under the pseudonym of François Seul, in the fortnightly newspaper *Brazil Operario*, published from 1903 to 1904 under the direction of a group of printing workers.

other workers, and a new focus on getting favourable laws passed by means of petitions and other forms of pressure on the National Congress as well as the government. It is thus not surprising that the associations that followed this tendency refused to participate in any of the working-class congresses after 1906.[38]

A number of reform-oriented unions – probably the majority of them – had no particular ideological affiliation; they were "reformist" by default and aimed to obtain gains for the particular crafts and sectors they represented by whatever means they found suitable. This trend was particularly present among Rio's dockworkers' and stevedores' unions, in which semi-professionalized and clientelistic leaders known as the "Colonels of the Port" (*Coronéis do Porto*) dominated for a long period.[39] In many respects, these unions had positions similar to those of the American Federation of Labor under Samuel Gompers, with its epitomized mix of confrontational action when necessary and negotiation whenever possible. Similarly, Rio's port strikes were among the most violent during the period, and these unions did not hesitate to strike when necessary. At the same time, these unions and their leaders were often especially supportive of authorities and rushed to endorse government policies during World War I.[40]

Regardless of their differences, the diverse reformist tendencies had much in common. Firstly, all conceived strikes were to be a last resort, used only when all other means of pressure had failed. In contrast with revolutionary syndicalism, any help to obtain their demands was welcome, so during labour conflicts they would frequently appeal to lawyers, politicians, government officials, the Chief of Police, ministers, and even the president of the Republic seeking mediation. Another distinctive quality of reformist unions was their view of working-class associations: to be strong, even during periods of crisis, they should be able to offer their associates modes of support beyond fighting for their labour demands, such as providing mutual aid and cooperatives. Furthermore, trade unions should be institutionally efficient and effective, for which hierarchical boards of directors and headquarters in the union's own premises were required. In other

---

38. Claudio H. de Moraes Batalha, "Le syndicalisme 'amarelo' à Rio de Janeiro (1906–1930)" (Ph.D., Université de Paris I – Panthéon-Sorbonne, 1986), pp. 176–177.

39. The exact origin of the designation is unknown, but, most likely, it is a reference to the "colonels", a group who, being mostly landowners, held military ranks in the National Guard and who dominated politics during the Brazilian First Republic (1889–1930).

40. See Michel Zaidan Filho, "Pão e Pau. Política de governo e sindicalismo reformista no Rio de Janeiro (1923–1926)" (MA, Universidade Estadual de Campinas – UNICAMP, 1981), ch. 3; Maria Cecília Velasco e Cruz, "Amarelo e negro: matizes do comportamento operário na República Velha" (MA, Instituto de Universitário de Pesquisa do Rio de Janeiro – IUPERJ, 1981); Marli B.M. Albuquerque, "Trabalho e conflito no porto do Rio de Janeiro (1904–1920)", (MA, Universidade Federal do Rio de Janeiro – UFRJ, 1983); Batalha, "Le syndicalisme "amarelo".

words, institutional and financial stability were seen as essential for trade unions to reach their objectives.

Until the 1980s, "reformism" was completely misunderstood by Brazilian labour history. Based on their fundamental belief in liberal or orthodox Marxist presuppositions, historians tended, first, to conflate the broad and shifting spectrum of reform-oriented unions, non-confrontational currents, and socialist activism under one label and, second, to view reformists as manipulated either by the state or by employers, denying them any agency. At least in part, this view was inherited from Astrojildo Pereira, a former anarchist who later became Secretary General of the PCB and, later, one of the main exponents of militant labour history.[41] In the mid-1910s, still in his anarchist years, Pereira began to refer to reformists using the term *sindicalismo amarelo* (yellow unionism), which explicitly established a parallel with the French *syndicalism jaune*, a conservative, Catholic, and anti-socialist labour ideology sponsored by employers. The obvious differences between this French approach and the Brazilian reformists mattered little, what mattered was the political impact of such labelling. The relative success of this denunciation can be gauged by the long shadow this label was able to cast, including on historiographical assessments. Until recently, reformism, whatever terms it was described in, was either seen as negligibly small or altogether suspicious: While for some it was a phenomenon limited to Rio de Janeiro, for many others it was an early manifestation of the state-controlled unionism that existed from the 1930s onwards under the corporatist regime of Getúlio Vargas. A series of recent studies has revisited these received wisdoms, making clear that reformists had agency both during the First Republic and after, and that their role during the 1930s and under the Estado Novo (1937–1945) dictatorship was more complex than previously thought. Furthermore, these studies have also revealed that it was a much more widespread phenomenon, both numerically and regionally, that was present, in one way or another, in most of Brazil.[42]

LABOUR DIVISION BETWEEN TWO CONGRESSES

The number of trade unions and of the workers they organized grew steadily between 1902 and 1908, in particular in the aftermath of the 1906 congress, which was accompanied by victorious strikes. Unionized workers at this time remained mostly male and belonged to the skilled trades.

41. Pereira, *Formação*.
42. Joan L. Bak, "Labor, Community, and the Making of a Cross-Class Alliance in Brazil: The 1917 Railroad Strikes in Rio Grande do Sul", *Hispanic American Historical Review*, 78 (1998), pp. 179–227; Osvaldo B.A. Maciel, *A perseverança dos o mutualismo dos trabalhadores do comércio em Maceió (1879–1917)* (Recife, 2011); Aldrin A.S. Castellucci, *Trabalhadores e política no Brasil. Do aprendizado do Império aos sucessos da Primeira República* (Salvador, 2015).

From 1907 onwards, the tide turned in Rio and wages, which had continuously increased since the earliest years of the century, began to decrease in some industrial sectors, while food and housing became more expensive. Government monetary and taxing policies benefitted the importation of manufactured goods, leading industries to slow down production and to fire their workers. To render the situation even worse for organized labour, in 1909 a number of important strikes were defeated. Under these circumstances, not surprisingly, many working-class societies ceased to exist or, at least, closed down temporarily.

By 1911, the labour movement began a slow recovery as old associations were reactivated and new ones created, while strikes increased once again. One year later, some of the reformist unions decided to organize their own congress, which they called the Fourth Brazilian Workers' Congress (4° Congresso Operário Brasileiro). The organizers of this gathering considered the 1906 Congress as the third of its sort and counted the socialist congresses of 1892 in Rio de Janeiro and of 1902 in São Paulo as the first two events.

At that time, Brazil's president was Field Marshal Hermes da Fonseca (1910–1914), whose election has resulted from an alliance between the oligarchies of a number of states that had previously had relatively little power in national politics and the military. Hermes da Fonseca was one of the first presidential candidates to mention the existence of a social problem and, consequently, he received support from part of the labour movement. Thanks to these circumstances, the Congress managed to obtain some support from the government, such as free train tickets and the use of a government venue, the Monroe Palace in Rio, then the seat of the Brazilian Senate. The Congress was held from 7 to 15 November 1912 and was composed of seventy-four delegates (sixteen of whom were from Rio), representing thirteen different states.[43] Some of the resolutions approved did not differ greatly from the type of demands usually presented by the partisans of direct action, such as the eight-hour work day, weekly rest, indemnities for work accidents, regulation of women's and child labour, and so forth. Yet, other proposals would immediately be met with opposition from revolutionary syndicalists, such as the approval of the creation of an umbrella organization named the Confederação Brasileira do Trabalho (Brazilian Confederation of Labour), which was simultaneously a political party and a confederation of trade unions. Following the contemporary critics of this Congress in the labour movement, especially anarchists who were excluded (with very few exceptions) from participation, the historiography has tended to view the Congress as an early expression of *peleguismo*.[44]

---

43. Confederação Brazileira do Trabalho (Partido Político), *Conclusões do 4° Congresso Operario Brazileiro. Realizado no Palacio Monroe no Rio de Janeiro de 7 a 15 de novembro de 1912* (Rio de Janeiro, 1913).
44. The term derives from *pelego* (a lambskin used between the saddle and the horse's back in Southern Brazil) and is used to designate state-controlled unionism after 1930.

Figure 2. Members of reformist trade-unions on their way to the May Day 1913 demonstration. *Fon-fon*, *Rio de Janeiro, 10 May 1913 [no page number]. Collection Arquivo Edgard Leuenroth/IFCH/UNICAMP, R/0359.*

It took the adherents of revolutionary syndicalism a little longer to give an appropriate response to the challenge represented by the reformists, because its main organization, the COB, founded in 1906 yet hibernating since 1909 (when a congress was supposed to take place but never actually happened), was only reorganized at the beginning of 1913. By September of this year, the confederation finally managed to hold a new congress. In comparison to the competing congress, the COB event had fewer delegates (sixty-two), but a superior number of states were represented (nineteen). At the same time, the Second Brazilian Workers' Congress (whose very name showed their disregard for the reformist view of the legitimate lineage of congresses) had to deal with several problems: in addition to having to face a reinvigorated reformist camp, it saw an urgent need to launch campaigns to confront the growing increase in the cost of living and to oppose a new law mandating the expulsion of foreigners. As part of its mobilization against the law, the COB sent representatives to Europe to campaign against emigration.[45] Interestingly, the resolutions passed at this congress were largely similar to those approved in the one held in 1906. The main difference in 1913 was that the rhetoric of revolutionary syndicalism finally came to the fore; indeed, unlike in 1906, when the word "revolutionary" was

---

45. In this remarkable campaign, COB representatives tried to convince those willing to emigrate that working conditions in Brazil were worse than in Europe and that promises made to emigrants were not fulfilled.

never uttered, participants in this later gathering explicitly discussed the possibility of a "revolutionary general strike".[46]

The 1912 and the 1913 congresses where held at a moment when unions had just begun to reorganize, but instead of contributing to unity these events exacerbated division. This was a period that witnessed the brief rebirth of the labour movement, which soon after plunged into a new crisis that grew in intensity as World War I began. By mid-1915, the COB stopped the publication of its newspaper, *A Voz do Trabalhador*, and vanished from the scene shortly thereafter.

THE GROWTH OF LABOUR PROTEST IN 1917–1919

As World War I proceeded, industrial activity regained momentum, while competition from foreign industrial goods diminished with the sharp decrease in imports. The cost of living, however, kept rising as industrialists maintained wages at a stagnant level, a combination of factors that created favourable conditions for labour protest. From 1916 onwards, Rio de Janeiro's labour movement began to reorganize itself as old unions reopened and new ones were created. One major change during the period was the creation of local industrial unions in sectors of production that, until then, had been divided into various craft unions, such as among metal and construction workers. This change also allowed for greater participation of unskilled workers in unions, where their presence had previously been quite limited. Another change was the creation of two federations that were less based on sectors than on similar jobs and activities: one was the Brazilian Maritime Federation (Federação Marítima Brasileira – FMB), combining port and maritime workers' unions; the other was the Vehicle Drivers' Federation, which gathered the land transportation unions. Both of these federations were considered as reformist, although, again, this meant quite different orientations and practices in each case.[47] By 1917, labour had regained and surpassed the force it had during the period from 1912 to 1913. As workers from various sectors of the economy went on strike, in particular to demand better wages and working conditions, they initiated a prolonged cycle of struggles that lasted until 1919. This cycle had its own local backgrounds (often greatly varying between its numerous locales in Brazil); yet, it was also connected to the international wave of labour, often revolutionary unrest at the end of World War I and in the wake of the Russian Revolution. In international comparison, it is a relatively sustained series of mobilizations, lasting much longer than in many

46. See the partial reprint of the congress' report in "O Segundo Congresso Operário (1913)".
47. While the FMB was more willing to compromise with government representatives and even sustained government policies, the federation of land transportation unions was less inclined to such a collaboration.

other countries. At the same time, the mobilization's ability to shatter the whole of society remained more limited in Brazil than in other places.[48]

Although general strikes took place in 1917 in Rio and in other major Brazilian cities like São Paulo and Porto Alegre, each movement had a distinct dynamic. In Rio, strikes were carried out by trade unions and even if the Workers' Federation of Rio de Janeiro (the Federação Operária do Rio de Janeiro, FORJ), the city's major union federation of revolutionary syndicalist orientation, did present a common list of demands, negotiations with employers were conducted separately by individual unions, many of which did not recognize the Federation as their representative. Meanwhile, in São Paulo, where repression was more intense, the reorganization of unions did not occur as swiftly as in Rio, so strikes were not organized based on the workplaces or certain economic sectors, but through the workers' communities by neighbourhood associations. These were then brought together in a city-wide body called Comitê de Defesa Proletária (Committee of Proletarian Defence). This phenomenon probably contributed to the greater unity of São Paulo's strike movement. Thus, the negotiation of a common list of demands presented to employers and to the state administration by the Committee of Proletarian Defence led to strikers' collective acceptance of the final agreement with their employers and the government. Nevertheless, despite their differences, labour movements in both cities during this time experienced what may be seen as a more flexible and more pragmatic turn. This also applied to unions adhering to revolutionary syndicalism. The list of demands in São Paulo was a mix of labour, consumer, and political requests that was strikingly different from the usual agenda of direct action, a tendency that supposedly dominated organized labour in that city. At the same time, albeit indirectly, São Paulo's unions established channel of negotiation with the state government (something openly rejected in previous conflicts). As for Rio, trade unions affiliated to a revolutionary syndicalist tradition and their leadership also acted with a discernable degree of pragmatism. All this might seem, at first sight, paradoxical: Were these mobilizations, after all, not connected to the great, international wave of revolutionary unrest at the end of World War I and, subsequently, to "1917", with all the principles and high political stakes that it involved? Was this not an epoch of an abundance of "ideology" and a lack of "pragmatism"? However, as the Brazilian case illustrates, the ascendancy of "ideology" and "pragmatism" were not mutually exclusive: "Revolution", above all the fear of revolution by those in power, also bred opportunities for reform, while the momentum of the mobilizations led its

48. Cristina Hebling Campos, *O sonhar libertário. Movimento operário nos anos de 1917 a 1921* (Campinas, 1988); Aldrin A.S. Castellucci, *Industriais e operários baianos numa conjuntura de crise (1914–1921)* (Salvador, 2004); Isabel Bilhão, *Identidade e trabalho. Uma história do operariado porto-alegrense (1898–1920)* (Londrina, 2008).

Figure 3. Maritime workers demonstration called by the Brazilian Maritime Federation against the lease of Brazilian Merchant ships.
O Malho, *Rio de Janeiro, 24 March 1917 [no page number]. Collection Arquivo Edgard Leuenroth/IFCH/UNICAMP, R/0363.*

leaders to grasp these opportunities and seize the moment with whatever means seemed appropriate to achieve them.

During a strike in August 1917, as part of the ongoing dispute between direct action and pragmatic reformist unionism, the Shoemakers' Union, affiliated with the syndicalist FORJ, saw the birth of a dissident organization called the Shoe Workers' League, which included only industrial workers but omitted craftsmen.[49] While it officially professed a syndicalist allegiance, the League managed to reach an understanding with employers, with the mediation of the Chief of Police, which established higher wages, a fifty-two-hour work week, and a rule that employers should give workers two days' notice before their dismissal.[50] The most important part of the

49. "Rapido retrospectivo do movimento associativo: um ano de vida operaria", *A Razão*, 19 December 1917, p. 9.
50. The agreement and a later addition are documented in Liga dos Operarios em Calçado, "Accordo feito entre o Centro da Industria de Calçados e Commercio de Couros e a Liga dos

negotiation, and an entirely new consequence of these talks, was the intention to constitute a commission, composed in equal parts by employers and employees, to discuss ongoing and future industrial conflicts. But the correspondence that the League exchanged in the following months with the Chief of Police, who had been transformed into a kind of guarantor of the deal, shows that employers were not respecting the terms of the agreement.[51] Although the Chief of Police of the Federal District was occasionally called upon to mediate labour conflicts, this was probably the first time that he had taken on such an institutionalized role.

Pragmatism now not only reigned in matters of trade union work, it also started to characterize some of the more political interventions of the union's leaders. In April 1917, Pascoal Gravina, who had been a delegate to the 1913 Workers' Congress, became president of the newly created General Union of Metal Workers (União Geral dos Metalúrgicos – UGM), again, a union of revolutionary syndicalist orientation. A few months later, he publicly supported Evaristo de Moraes, a lawyer retained by several different labour unions, as a candidate for the Chamber of Deputies, running as part of the Brazilian Socialist Party (one of the many parties organized under this denomination during this period).[52] After the episode, however, the UGM published a note insisting on syndicalist principles and forbidding any of its members to speak on the union's behalf on such matters.[53]

Gravina, however, was not the only one to flirt with electoral politics. In October 1915, the Graphic Workers' Association of Rio de Janeiro (Associação Gráfica do Rio de Janeiro – AGRJ) was created after several years during which these workers were unorganized or were divided into different craft unions. The AGRJ originated from a coalition of direct action and reformist militants, with João Leuenroth, former member of the COB board and brother of the well-known anarchist Edgard Leuenroth, as its president until 1918. After a short interlude, in which the board was dominated by anarchists who, however, soon resigned, João Leuenroth once again became the association's president in 1919. In that same year, he failed to win a seat the City Council. Both João Leuenroth and the previously mentioned Gravina

Operarios de Calçado e a União dos Cortadores de Calçado da cidade do Rio de Janeiro", 26 July 1917, Arquivo Nacional (Rio de Janeiro) [henceforth, ANRJ], Secretaria de Policia do Distrito Federal, 1887–1930, 6 C–584 [old classification].

51. The agreement's aftermath is documented in the same file through letters of the Liga dos Operarios de Calçados to the Chief of Police, number 60, 22 January 1918 and number 63, 23 January 1918.

52. The UGM's support for Evaristo de Moraes is mentioned in "A candidatura do Dr. Evaristo de Moraes à deputação federal", *A Razão*, 10 December 1917, p. 5. On the trajectory of Evarista de Moraes see also the contribution by Aldrin A.S. Castellucci and Benito B. Schmidt in this Special Issue.

53. "Proletariado – União Geral dos Metalurgicos", *A Razão*, 16 December de 1917, p. 6.

had been known as anarchists until the late 1910s, and yet they turned to or at least flirted with electoral politics. In 1920, when anarchists decided to quit the association for good and create a competing union of their own,[54] Leuenroth remained.

Yet another piece of evidence demonstrating the flexible and pragmatic stance that unions tended to adopt during those years are the relations they cultivated with certain politicians, especially those who tried to pass laws regarding working conditions. Even during the preceding period, when anarchists and reformists still coexisted in the AGRJ, this association maintained close ties with city councillor Ernesto Garcez.[55] Thanks to Garcez, the AGRJ received a symbolic subvention from the city to aid the Professional School (Escola Profissional) it intended to establish and a gold medal to offer as a prize for "the most artistic work" in the Graphic Exhibition it organized.

One might argue, of course, that the AGRJ's relationship with Garcez can be understood in light of the composition of the Association's leadership, which included both reformists and anarchists. Nonetheless, Garcez also had relations with the Centro Cosmopolita (Cosmopolitan Centre), a union of workers in hotels, restaurants, and bars, which was affiliated with the FORJ and hence more clearly identified with syndicalism and direct action.[56] Acting with the agreement of the Centre, Garcez presented a bill establishing a twelve-hour workday (ten hours for those who worked in kitchens) with a weekly day off for workers in that sector. In December 1917, the bill was approved by the City Council and enacted in January of the following year.[57] Although the intransigent demand for an eight-hour workday was present in the resolutions of all workers' congresses and was part of various strikes, this episode shows that, under certain circumstances, unions, despite their revolutionary syndicalist rhetoric (which ruled out any compromise on such a central issue, especially when reached through outside intermediation), would pursue any possible gain, even if it meant settling for results that fell short of goals once considered indispensable.

---

54. Competing unions in the same trade or industry were rare during the Brazilian First Republic (1889–1930). Although there was no legal prohibition, such situations were usually short-lived. This was the case of the anarchist dissident graphic workers' union, which ceased to exist within a year of its creation.

55. Ernesto Garcez Caldas Barreto (1874–?), was a lawyer, who, after being state representative in the Northeastern State of Pernambuco, began a political career in Rio de Janeiro, where he was city councilor from 1907 to 1910 and from 1917 to 1925. He entertained close ties with certain unions and presented bills concerning work regulations for various occupations.

56. On the activity of the Centro Cosmopolita and the role of Garcez, see Adailton Pires Costa, "A história dos direitos trabalhistas vista a partir de baixo. A luta por direitos (e leis) dos trabalhadores em hotéis, restaurantes, cafés e bares no Rio de Janeiro da 1ª República (DF, 1917–1918)" (MA, Universidade Federal de Santa Catarina – UFSC, 2013).

57. *Ibid.*, pp. 180–190.

After the 1917 strike movement, which managed to attain a number of victories, repression became more intense, leading to the closure by police of the FORJ on the pretext of the need to preserve public order.[58] The following year, the number of strikes grew significantly again[59] and workers formed a new, equally revolutionary-syndicalist federation, the União Geral dos Trabalhadores (Workers' General Union, UGT). News from international news agencies and greatly distorted by the local mainstream press offered limited knowledge of what was going in Russia, yet, as in other parts of South America, the idea of a revolution in which workers had actually taken power was received enthusiastically by many activists.[60] Especially anarchists tended to see the Revolution as their own (and did so, in view of the deep chasm dividing Bolsheviks and Anarchists, at the latest from the civil war on, for a remarkably long time). The journalist Astrojildo Pereira, by then an anarchist with a particular interest in Russian events, wrote that the Russian Bolsheviks's programme, drafted already in 1905, was "in essence anarchist".[61] Nevertheless, to some degree inspired by the Russian Revolution, in November 1918 an unlikely alliance of anarchists (including Pereira), trade union leaders linked to the UGT, and dissident politicians planned an insurrection (to start in Rio, but which they would spread to the whole country). The plan was to launch a general strike that would receive the support of military units. Strikers mainly included metal workers, textile workers (who had their own specific demands and remained on strike despite repression, even after the attempted uprising had failed), and a limited number of construction workers. The Army lieutenant who was supposed to serve as a liaison between the striking workers and

58. Delegacia do 4° Districto Policial, 22 April 1918, ANRJ, Secretaria de Policia do Distrito Federal, 1887–1930, 6 C–602.

59. Different studies reach different conclusions concerning the number of strikes during the 1917–1919 period: 21, 33 and 26 are the numbers found by Eulalia Maria Lahmeyer Lobo and Eduardo Navarro Stotz, "Flutuações cíclicas da economia, condições de vida e movimento operário – 1890 a 1930, *Revista Rio de Janeiro*, 1:1 (December 1985), pp. 61–86, 86; while 13, 29 and 22 were those established by Branno Hocherman Costa and Francisco Josué Medeiros de Freitas, "Greves e polícia política nas décadas de 1920 e 1930", in Marcelo Badaró Mattos (ed.), *Trabalhadores em greve, polícia em guarda. Greves e repressão policial na formação da classe trabalhadora carioca* (Rio de Janeiro, 2004), pp. 137–160, 139.

60. For Argentina and the remarkably long-lasting group of "Anarcho-Bolsheviks" that had formed there, see Andreas L. Doeswijk, "Entre Camalões e Cristalizados: Os anarco-bolcheviques rioplatenses, 1917–1930" (Ph.D., Universidade Estadual de Campinas – UNICAMP, 1999); and Roberto Pittaluga, "Lecturas anarquistas de la revolución rusa", *Prismas. Revista de historia intelectual*, 6 (2002), pp. 179–188. Also see Pittaluga's much broader study about the Russian Revolution in Argentina (including the debates until the end of the 1920s), Roberto Pittaluga, *Soviets en Buenos Aires, la izquierda de la Argentina ante la revolución en Rusia* (Buenos Aires, 2015).

61. Astrojildo Pereira, "A Russia revolucionaria. Um ano depois", *O Cosmopolita*, 2:29, 25 March 1918, p. 1.

military units proved to be an agent of the police who had infiltrated the workers' movement. Consequently, the main leaders of the strike were arrested, the UGT and the three unions representing the sectors on strike were shut down, and the police applied further repressive measures to the entire labour movement.[62] For many labour activists, the insurrection was a government provocation to justify wide-scale repression.[63] Without doubt, several factors came together in this failed insurrection (which was partly planned as a *putsch*): Rio had a long tradition of popular revolts, the last one having taken place in 1904. At the same time, Brazilian anarchists had been rather reluctant to take up the local tradition and never assumed an insurrectionist stance (in sharp contrast with numerous partisans of Anarchism in Europe). Yet, the Russian experience and the powerful promises it seemed to carry might have led many of these activists to reconsider and see the moment come for such action.

Strikes were still numerous in 1919, but repression grew steadily and employers were more organized to resist workers' demands. In place of the UGT, a new syndicalist federation named Labour Federation of Rio de Janeiro (Federação dos Trabalhadores do Rio de Janeiro, FTRJ) emerged, which proved to be even more pragmatic than previous federations by accepting affiliations with such trade unions as the AGRJ. The FTRJ even managed to launch a daily newspaper the following year, *Voz do Povo*.

THE DECLINE OF REVOLUTIONARY SYNDICALISM

In March 1920, a strike broke out at the Leopoldina Railways,[64] a strike which was to become a particular challenge to labour in many ways. Syndicalist principles were once again combined with pragmatism, and the strike became an arena in which the dispute between different tendencies seeking to influence the movement played out fully.

Initially, a list of demands containing points that ranged from wage increases and better working conditions to union control over conditions in railroad workshops was presented to the company by a workers' association formed in the town of Além Paraíba (in the state of Minas Gerais), which was part of the railroad's network. The company did not bother to respond to these demands and, shortly thereafter, workers in Rio formed another organization, the Leopoldina Employees' Union (União dos

---

62. For a more detailed account on the insurrection see Carlos Augusto Addor, *A Insurreição Anarquista no Rio de Janeiro* (Rio de Janeiro, 1986), ch. 3.
63. For a typical example of this suspicion, see "Movimento operario", *O Graphico*, 4:74, 1 February 1919, p. 4.
64. The Leopoldina Railways (Estrada de Ferro Leopoldina), founded at the turn of the twentieth century under the auspices of British investors, was one of Brazil's major railway companies, its huge network covering mainly the states of Rio de Janeiro and Minas Gerais and thus playing an important role in the coffee economy.

Empregados da Leopoldina). The new union endorsed the existing list of demands and agreed on a date to strike. The resulting strike was not limited to the city of Rio de Janeiro, but rather reached the entire railroad network in different states. From the outset, the company refused to engage in direct talks with union representatives, so some kind of state mediation seemed inevitable, a task carried out by the Minister of Transportation and Public Works. Despite the minister's proclaimed intention of an negotiated ending of the conflict, the government provided the company with military personnel to operate the trains. As negotiations stalled, the strike took on a new dimension when an impressive number of other trades and industries entered into solidarity action, backed by the syndicalist FTRJ as well as the particularly reformist Vehicle Drivers' Federation. Rio was paralyzed as the strike extended from the city's transportation to its bakeries, restaurants, etc., even including the street cleaners. *Voz do Povo*, the FTRJ's daily, covered the events closely. After four days of what was nearly a general strike (and was the last great strike of the period), police and army launched a massive wave of repression, resulting in the arrests of over 2,000 strikers and the invasion of the headquarters of the unions involved. To justify the repression, the government alleged that a Bolshevik conspiracy lay behind the strike movement.[65]

In the meantime, the Leopoldina Employees Union reached an agreement with the company, with the mediation of the FMB that had abstained from joining the strike. This Federation had, by its own initiative, from the beginning tried to reach an agreement to end the strike, securing from the President of the Republic, Epitácio Lindolfo da Silva Pessoa (1919–1922), the release of some of the arrested strikers before the strike ended. The final agreement, concluded with the President of the Republic acting as guarantor, did not obtain the wage increase that had been the main reason for the strike, but even under these difficult circumstances the workers did gain some concessions, such as the release of all imprisoned strikers, the re-employment of fired strikers, and the promise that nobody would be subject to punishment. Both the Drivers' Federation and the FTRJ considered the agreement to be a form of treason and criticized the Leopoldina Employee's Union for negotiating and agreeing to it. On its part, the railroad company never complied entirely with the terms of the agreement.[66]

This strike not only represented a turning point in Rio de Janeiro's labour movement, just some weeks before a new workers' congress was held, but it also shows that reformist policies could present themselves in different

65. For an eyewitness account see Astrojildo Pereira, *A greve da Leopoldina* (Rio de Janeiro, 1920).
66. A historiographical analysis of the Leopoldina Railway strike is offered by Glaucia Fraccaro, "Morigerados e revoltados. Trabalho e organização de ferroviários da Central do Brasil e da Leopoldina (1889–1920)" (MA, Universidade Estadual de Campinas – UNICAMP, 2008).

ways and that certain groups, notwithstanding their identification with "revolutionary syndicalism" or "reformism", were more eager than others to compromise with the government. It is necessary to stress, nonetheless, that during the Brazilian First Republic regional differences played a central role with considerable variation in the conditions under which these unions acted. And in Rio de Janeiro, despite the repressive policies that were similar to those in the rest of Brazil, possibilities for negotiation and mediation were greater than those found in São Paulo, where the authorities followed a repressive approach much more consistently. In part, this can be explained by the fact that the national government was installed in a port city with a long tradition of unruliness and conflict that could not be managed exclusively through force.

When the Third Brazilian Workers' Congress met in April 1920 (here, again, the nomenclature followed the revolutionary syndicalist rather than the reformist mode of counting), participants had to deal with the changes that labour was undergoing during those years. Although reaffirming the resolutions passed at the two previous congresses, its own resolutions adopted a more pragmatic tone, recognizing the different situations encountered in various economic sectors. More remarkably, the Third Brazilian Workers' Congress, while sustaining the principles of direct action, saw the adjective "revolutionary" disappear from its documents yet again. This congress was the most representative of all up to that time, with seventy-two delegations present, thirty-two of which were from the Federal District.[67] The opening session was attended by 103 delegates.[68] For the first time, different ideological tendencies were present, from reformist through revolutionary syndicalist to anarchist, although in key areas such as the port, dock, and maritime workers, not all unions sent representatives.

The proposals presented tried to obtain a minimum agreement of the majority of the delegates, sometimes by simply adopting a rhetoric of the least common denominator that would seem acceptable for other delegates. The AGRJ, for instance, presented ideas that fell under the title "union neutrality", proposing that unions should avoid all involvement in politics, including ideologies such as anarchism (which at first sight seemed a proposition following the traditional stance of revolutionary syndicalism), while, at the same time, proposing that workers engage in politics outside the unions. Even the references used to give credence to this proposition were inaccurate: The authors attributed the endorsement of such a policy to Félicien Challaye, a French philosophy professor who wrote a book on revolutionary and reformist syndicalism, when, in fact, the quotations, cited

67. For a detailed account of the congress see Edgar Rodrigues, *Nacionalismo & cultura social (1913–1922)* (Rio de Janeiro, 1972), pp. 307–320.
68. "Terceiro Congresso – A imponente sessão de hontem", *Voz do Povo*, 1:77, 24 April 1920, p. 1.

in Challaye's work, came from a French socialist, Albert Thomas, who had been Minister of Armament during the war. Although Thomas's name is never mentioned in the congress proceedings, it was his works that Challaye used to illustrate the reformist position, in the same way as he quoted revolutionary syndicalists to illustrate theirs. Even the title of the proposal that called for "union neutrality" came from an article by Thomas.[69]

Apparently, the congress tried to carry out the impossible task of obtaining a minimum consensus among organized labour while reaffirming some of the main principles of revolutionary syndicalism, and while a pragmatic approach held sway in all major issues. The congress did not stop the erosion of the prestige that revolutionary syndicalism once had among anarchists. In the years that followed, they preferred to adopt the position that unions should assume an anarchist programme, a proposal that had been defeated in the past and which bore all the hallmarks of a self-isolating minority position. At the same time, those anarchists who had turned to other experiences, such as the Industrial Workers of the World (IWW) and particularly the Russian Revolution, ultimately formed the Communist Party (Partido Comunista do Brasil) in 1922.

A SHARED CULTURE?

At first glance, the orientations, which are conventionally labelled as direct action and reformism, appear to have been completely incompatible with and clearly opposed to each other. Yet, they did share some common ground, starting with a number of more obvious commonalities, such as the importance attributed to working-class education, temperance, the demand for an eight-hour work day, and the celebration of May Day.

The shared appreciation for certain symbolic practices could lead to surprising, even amusing episodes: In April 1913, for instance, a dozen working-class associations, representing both major ideological tendencies present in Rio de Janeiro's labour movement, sent a letter do the Chief of Police protesting against a carnival that the Club dos Fenianos (Fenians' Club)[70] planned to hold on May Day, an act that was supposed to honour the working classes. The authors of this letter judged the celebration an affront to the day universally dedicated to the struggle against exploitation. Some days after receiving the protest letter, the Chief of Police invited a delegation of workers to discuss the matter and assured them he would not

69. On this subject, see Claudio Batalha, "Syndicalisme révolutionnaire et syndicalisme réformiste. Les modèles européens dans le mouvement ouvrier brésilien (1906–1920)", in Tania Régin and Serge Wolikow (eds), *Les syndicalismes en Europe. À l'épreuve de l'international* (Paris, 2002), pp. 15–26.

70. The club's name originated from the fact that it was formed in 1869 at an Irishman's home. See Maria Clementina Pereira Cunha, *Ecos da folia. Uma história social do carnaval carioca entre 1880 e 1920* (São Paulo, 2001), p. 110.

authorize the carnival.[71] Under other circumstances, one could hardly imagine anarchists or revolutionary syndicalists seeking the Chief of Police's help; yet, this seemed a matter, despite its symbolical character, too important not to use all means at hand.

As this article has highlighted for Rio de Janeiro's labour movement between the beginning of the twentieth century and 1920, the boundaries between the revolutionary syndicalist, anarchist, and reformist orientations could be quite porous. This not only applied to symbolical matters and shared demands, but also held true for those issues seen as absolutely divisive, such as the question of negotiation with and the intermediation through the state, the involvement in electoral politics, the achievement of concrete gains falling short of long-held *sine qua non*-demands, or the building of a professionalized organization. Here, the history of the labour movement of countries seen as "typical" (and where a clear-cut separation into different spheres is supposed to have happened in the 1890s at the latest) can obfuscate the degree to which the different currents in other world regions were densely interwoven for much longer. In the case of Rio, there are manifold moments when the revolutionary syndicalist and reformist stances intermingled, and when leading individual activists or whole organizations proceeded to change their practices (while often maintaining the rhetorical claims). This intermingling has seen a certain development over time: While in the years from the Congress in 1906 positions seemed to be entrenched, the recovery of the movement from 1917 onwards and a subsequent three-year cycle of struggles have witnessed all currents acting under more pragmatic and flexible auspices, swiftly reacting to the opportunities offered. Not coincidentally, this turn towards pragmatism, especially among adherents of revolutionary syndicalism, happened in a period considered in more traditional accounts as being under the signature of "revolution". However, both dynamics – the revolutionary and the pragmatic – were not mutually exclusive, the former (or, more precisely, the threat of it) opening space for the latter. In Rio, it was those currents that had long borne the attribute "revolutionary" in their commitment as unionists that, in particular, grasped this accurately. This was favoured by a local version of revolutionary syndicalism that, in comparison to other Brazilian cities as well as internationally, had been relatively moderate from the beginning, and a political landscape that (compared to São Paulo) had always offered more opportunities for gradual gains.

Despite different interpretations, defenders of direct action could thus adopt reformist stances (and vice versa). Yet, the commonalities between the different currents had roots that were deeper than the issues of strategic orientation and political demands: Both currents shared certain beliefs and

---

71. "A festança dos fenianos", *A Voz do Trabalhador*, 8:70, 11 May 1915, p. 1.

practices – a common culture – that, in most cases, were older than the division between the two currents of labour activism. As early as the mid-nineteenth century, working-class associations supported the importance of workers' education, whether in the form of formal or professional education. Thus, it was quite common for trade unions, at least in their by-laws, to propose the creation of libraries, courses, and schools, as we have previously seen in the case of the AGRJ. In 1913, another union, the Sailors and Rowers' Association, declared in its by-laws that it should establish basic educational classes, a library and, eventually, professional training for its associates, all these proposals being subject to the availability of financial resources.[72]

May Day was a date that both direct action activists and partisans of reformism shared, and their speeches would refer to a common repertoire associated with the occasion: remembrance of the "Chicago martyrs", a universal stoppage of work, the fight for the eight-hour work day, and so forth. This occasion simultaneously reinforced unity and made important differences visible in the way the day should be observed. Direct action preferred sober and clearly class-oriented meetings, even if plays, poetry reading, and musical presentations did occur, while reformism tended to prefer larger-scale public demonstrations and parades with military fanfare and the presence of politicians. Yet, even at moments when relations between the two currents were particularly tense, gestures of conciliation were made: In 1913, during the period between the two competing workers' congresses, the socialist cigarette worker Mariano Garcia inaugurated a Workers' Column in the daily newspaper *A Epoca,* which, on the occasion of Mayday, he also opened for anarchists to set out their ideas about the date.[73] Conversely, two days later, in Rio, anarchist leader Edgard Leuenroth, taking part in FORJ's May Day activities, attended a session organized by the Workers' League of the Federal District, the association that was directly responsible for the 1912 Congress so bitterly criticized by anarchists.[74] Thus, even before revolutionary syndicalist practice became so pragmatic by the end of the 1910s that it could barely be distinguished from reformism, it did, ultimately, share a common culture with the other currents of the labour movement.

72. *Estatutos da Associação de Marinheiros e Remadores* (Rio de Janeiro, 1913), p. 7. It should be noted that with such concerns about stable finances these organizations already went beyond a "pure" revolutionary syndicalist orientation, according to which financial issues, etc. are secondary.
73. "Columna Operaria", *A Epoca,* 1 May 1913, pp. 5–8.
74. Antonio Mariano Garcia, "Liga do Operariado do Distrito Federal", *A Epoca,* 4 May 1913, p. 11.

IRSH 62 (2017), Special Issue, pp. 105–132 doi:10.1017/S0020859017000621
© 2018 Internationaal Instituut voor Sociale Geschiedenis

Between Rio's Red-Light District and the League of Nations: Immigrants and Sex Work in 1920s Rio de Janeiro

CRISTIANA SCHETTINI*

*National Scientific and Technical Research Council (CONICET),
National University of San Martín – Institute of Advanced Social
Studies (UNSAM – IDAES), Avenida Roque Saenz Peña, 832, piso 6
Ciudad Autónoma de Buenos Aires, 1035, Argentina*

E-mail: crischettini@gmail.com

ABSTRACT: This article focuses on sex work relations in the Mangue, one of Rio de Janeiro's red light districts in the 1920s. It follows multiple simultaneous trajectories that converge in Rio's changing urban landscape: League of Nation's investigators (some of them undercover), local Brazilian authorities, particularly the police, and Fanny Galper, a former prostitute and madam. It argues that the spatial mobility of the persons involved in sex work is part of broader debates: On the one hand, these experiences of mobility are closely connected to the variegated attempts at surveillance of sex work that characterized Rio de Janeiro in the 1920s and the specific racialized organization of the women's work as prostitutes. On the other hand, the actors analysed in this article also participated, in different ways, in the production of meanings in broader debates on the international circulation of policies intended to regulate and surveil prostitution. These encounters offer the opportunity to explore some of the intersections between this international circulation of policies, local social dynamics of European immigration, and the racialized history of labor relations in Brazil.

In 1923, Franklin Galvão, chief of the Ninth Police District of Rio de Janeiro, which included the area known as the Mangue (the Marsh), one of the city's two red-light districts, sent the city's chief of police a "Descriptive Map of the Prostitutes Who Live Beneath the Jurisdiction of the Ninth District". The "map" was actually a detailed list that in ten typed pages, identified, street by street and house by house, the landladies and tenants (as well as their nationalities) occupying the houses of prostitution that fell under his oversight. All told, 674 women occupied an area that covered only

* I would like to thank Paulo Fontes and Alexandre Fortes for the invitation to join this enterprise, as well as the participants of the two workshops dedicated to the discussion of previous versions of this article for their suggestions and comments. I am also grateful to Bryan Pitts, Amy Chazkel, and David Mayer for their patience and their efforts to make this text readable in English.

nine streets, a significantly higher concentration than in the more elegant neighborhood of Lapa.[1]

More than a mere description of a neighborhood, Galvão's list documented the results of an evolving set of policies that redefined *carioca* urban space.[2] These ten pages also offer insights into a consequence of the reorganization of prostitution during Rio de Janeiro since 1889, when the city became the capital of the newly established Brazilian Republic. Such reorganization above all involved a process of *concentration*, in at least two different ways:[3] First, there was the spatial concentration of the Mangue's houses of prostitution, due in large measure to the unprecedented expansion of the police's prerogative to surveil and supervise sex work in the early years of the Republic, but also the consequence of an adaptation by the sex business to shifting patterns of urban masculine sociability. Second, there was a concentration of African-descended women listed as "tenants", in contrast to the predominance of European women (particularly ones with Jewish surnames) on the list of "landladies". Among the seven women who owned two or more houses, only one was Brazilian. There was also one Portuguese woman, while the others were variously identified as "Austrians", "Poles", and "Russians". Lists like this one also had less evident meanings: for instance, they were useful for sustaining broader debates about the traffic in women. For many social reformers and private European and US organizations, the presence of European women in houses of prostitution in cities like Buenos Aires and Rio de Janeiro served as evidence of "the traffic in white women", a widely used notion at that time based on the belief that the mobility of a certain groups of sex workers was automatic proof of the forced nature of their labor.

Due to these simultaneous connotations, the list can serve as a point of departure from which to examine the connection between two broader issues. First, the Mangue and its prostitutes seen from a labor history point of view: what was their world of labor like in the 1920s? Second, how were

---

1. "Descriptive Map of the Prostitutes Who Live Beneath the Jurisdiction of the 9th District", Arquivo Nacional, Rio de Janeiro, GIFI (Grupo de Identificação de Fundos Interno), 6C–751A. For more on Lapa and the Mangue, see Sueann Caulfield, "The Birth of Mangue: Race, Nation, and the Politics of Prostitution in Rio de Janeiro, 1850–1942", in Daniel Balderston and Donna Guy (eds), *Sex and Sexuality in Latin America* (New York, 1997), pp. 86–100.

2. *Carioca* is a noun and adjective that refers to residents of the city of Rio de Janeiro.

3. See Cristiana Schettini, *Que tenhas teu corpo. Uma história social da prostituição no Rio de Janeiro das primeiras décadas republicanas* (Rio de Janeiro, 2006). Although it had also served as capital during Brazil's 1822–1889 Empire, after the establishment of a republic in 1889, elites sought to remake Rio as a modern capital modeled on a European ideal that would epitomize "order and progress", the central slogan of the positivist current then dominant among Brazilian elites and which also emblazoned the republican national flag. The result was radical urban reform and the persecution of some popular, especially Portuguese and African-descended, cultural practices. The creation of the Mangue in the 1910s should be seen in the context of this process.

their lives affected by both national and transnational debates about prostitution that were intensifying at the time through organizations like the
recently created League of Nations Committee on the Traffic of Women
and Children? Formed by representatives of various countries and private
organizations, in 1924 the Committee sent investigative agents to more than
100 cities, with a plan to interview both officials and representatives of the
"underworld" in order to discover the "truth" about the traffic in women
since World War I.[4] A few months after the Mangue's list was put together,
Rio de Janeiro was one of the cities to receive such a visit from three
American investigators, official and undercover, in the name of the League
of Nations. In 1927, the Committee released its final report, which became
known as the first document about the traffic in women produced from an
empirical, systematic study of intercontinental reach. In the following
decades, the report would help form the foundation of an "abolitionist"
paradigm that would come to dominate international discourse about
prostitution, especially after the creation of the United Nations.

   This article uses the League's investigators' visit to Rio de Janeiro as an
entry way through which to examine the local social relations surrounding
prostitution. It then contrasts their observations with the experiences of
Fanny Galper, a well-to-do owner of several houses in the Mangue, cited in
Galvão's list. The case of Galper, a native of Russia, is of special interest
because, contrary to other landladies and madams, it is possible to follow
her across time through a variety of sources. Some of the documents about
her reveal the police's attempts to surveil and control the movement of men
and women across international borders (through passports and entry and
exit registries), others reveal local authorities' attempts to control urban
space and its construction (through tax records and municipal registries),
while still others reveal Galper's desire to register some of her own decisions
(through contracts and deeds). Since some of these sources do not refer
directly to the world of prostitution, but rather to her own economic,
commercial, family, and affective relations, they go beyond the documents
usually consulted when women's lives in the sexual marketplace are studied.
Her life thus sheds light on labor relations in the world of prostitution,
immigrant trajectories, and strategies for accumulating wealth, all in the
context of changes in the 1910s and 1920s that shaped the neighborhood of
cheap prostitution known as the Mangue.

   Like the neighboring capitals Buenos Aires and Montevideo, Rio de
Janeiro was a point of entry for large numbers of immigrants and sex

---

4. Jean Michel Chaumont, *Le mythe de la traite des blanches. Enquête sur la fabrication d'un
fléau* (Paris, 2009); Paul Knepper, "The Investigation into the Traffic in Women by the League of
Nations: Sociological Jurisprudence as an International Social Project", *Law and History Review*,
34:1 (2016), pp. 45–73; Magaly Rodriguez García, "The League of Nations and the Moral
Recruitment of Women", *International Review of Social History*, 57:1 (2012), pp. 97–128.

workers and often served as a transit point between Europe and other South American cities. Since the 1870s, both Montevideo and Buenos Aires adopted a regulationist policy towards prostitution, employing a set of sanitary and municipal measures, which subjected prostitution to special state oversight. In contrast, Rio de Janeiro never adopted any kind of formal regulation. Instead, the 1890 Brazilian Penal Code followed a Germanic tradition by criminalizing diverse ways of inducing someone into prostitution and mediating access to it, in a broader fashion than Argentina's and Uruguay's penal codes.[5] Rio's legislation was closer to the abolitionist view, which criticized and denounced both the inefficacy and the double standard of regulation systems. By adopting a terminology from the British fight against the regulation of prostitution at home and its colonies, abolitionists in different parts of the world were also more willing to broaden the criminalization of pimping than to control prostitution itself.

In Rio, abolitionist legislation mixed with intense police vigilance over prostitution houses, resulting in an idiosyncratic practice that came to be known, around the 1920s, as "police regulation".[6] While the use of "regulation" signaled a degree of acceptance of prostitution in social life, it was the police who should be responsible for defining how and where prostitution was practiced in urban space. Police also played a central role in expelling women and suspected pimps from the downtown area (and also from the country, using the 1907 expulsion law). In the 1920s, prostitution houses would become concentrated in specific neighborhoods, like Lapa and the Mangue. Therefore, in Rio, medically-inspired educational and prophylactic initiatives directed at sex workers and their customers in order to prevent sexually transmitted diseases coexisted with broad police prerogatives to surveil prostitutes and to repress pimps.[7]

Rio de Janeiro was also unique compared to the nearby South American capitals in the way the internationally used expression "traffic in white women" acquired local meanings. This can be better understood in the light of previous histories of Brazilian race and labor relations: For most of the nineteenth century, slavery had been the habitual way to organize labor relations in Rio. Brazil was the last country on the continent to abolish it, only in 1888. In the last decades of that century, African-descended workers found themselves living and working in close proximity with new European immigrants, in a world shaped by the racialized logics of

---

5. For a comparative analysis of these cities see: Yvette Trochon, *Las rutas de Eros. La trata de blancas en el Atlántico Sur. Argentina, Brasil y Uruguay (1880–1932)* (Montevideo, 2006).
6. Caulfield, "The Birth of Mangue"; Schettini, *Que tenhas*, pp. 29–88. Police inspector Armando Pereira reinforced the idea of a peculiar police regulation within an abolitionist system in his 1967 book Armando Pereira, *Sexo e Prostituição* (Rio de Janeiro, 1967), p. 90.
7. Sergio Carrara, *Tributo a Vênus. A luta contra a sífilis no Brasil, da passagem do século aos anos 40* (Rio de Janeiro, 1996).

seigneurial domination in Brazil.[8] Thus, the vocabulary circulating in many of the world's cities, which used metaphors of racialized slavery to talk about forced prostitution, would gain a specific weight in Brazil. Based on these singular factors, this article argues that the Brazilian approach to regulating sex work was not the result of a misunderstanding of European tendencies, or of a "lack of a system", as some socialist opponents of the policing practices claimed at the time.[9] Rather, it was the product of a specific interaction between the international circulation of policies intended to regulate prostitution, the local social dynamics of European immigration, and the racialized history of labor relations in Brazil.[10]

In keeping with recent trends in the historiography, this article treats the history of prostitution as labor history.[11] Framing the analysis in this way draws on two scholarly trends in Brazil that have examined women's labor from a gendered perspective: First, the experiences of working-class urban women, which have received much attention in scholarship that has examined the social and cultural history of the First Republic (1889–1930). This literature has focused on daily life, urban history, and "popular culture" and so does not fall squarely within what has traditionally been understood as labor history. Yet, these studies have indeed allowed a rich and multilayered understanding of how women in early twentieth-century Rio lived and how they worked. Many authors have examined, for example, the various ways in which they earned a living or made use of the legal system. They have also explored the gendered and moral meanings of urban space.[12]

8. Sidney Chalhoub employs the notion of a "seigneurial domination logics" to describe the hegemonic way of reproducing social subordination in nineteenth-century Brazilian society, further discussing its changes in the face of the emergence of new forms of racial science. See Sidney Chalhoub, "What Are Noses For? Paternalism, Social Darwinism and Race Science in Machado de Assis", *Journal of Latin American Cultural Studies*, 10:2 (2001), pp. 172–191.

9. For the socialist lawyer Evaristo de Moraes, Rio's police could not be called regulationists, abolitionists, or hygienists, since, in his view, local police authorities simply did not have a system. Evaristo de Moraes, *Reminiscências de um rábula criminalista*. (Rio de Janeiro, 1989 [1922]), p. 84.

10. Racialized notions, meanwhile, were central in the whole international debate about sex work, as can be clearly seen in the trajectory of the term "white slavery": Gunther Peck, "White Slavery and Whiteness: A Transnational View of the Sources of Working-Class Radicalism and Racism", *Labour: Studies in Working-Class History of the Americas*, 1:2 (2004), pp. 41–63. Peck traces how this expression was feminized among North American and British workers during the nineteenth century, demonstrating the historical meanings of the connection between sex work and wage labor in denunciations of labor exploitation.

11. For entry points into this strand of research see Luise White, *The Comforts of Home. Prostitution in Colonial Nairobi* (Chicago, IL, 1990); and Lex Heerma van Voss, "The Worst Class of Workers: Migration, Labour Relations and Living Strategies of Prostitutes around 1900", in Marcel van der Linden and Leo Lucassen (eds), *Working on Labour. Essays in Honor of Jan Lucassen* (Leiden, 2012).

12. Martha Abreu, *Meninas perdidas. Os populares e o cotidiano do amor no Rio de Janeiro da belle époque* (Rio de Janeiro, 1989); Sueann Caulfield, *In Defense of Honor. Sexual Morality, Modernity, and Nation in Early Twentieth Century Brazil* (Durham, NC, 2000).

Second, the social history of slavery, which has produced some of the most exciting research in Brazilian labor history during the last decades, has recognized women's centrality in organizing labor tasks and family ties, in cultivating cultural ties between Africans and their descendants, and in developing strategies for accumulating property and gaining autonomy or freedom.[13] Together, both trends in the literature have repeatedly demonstrated that a gender perspective has much potential in terms of elucidating long-standing problems in social history, including the trajectories of immigrants, social mobility, and social networks.

UNDERCOVER IN RIO

The 1920s were a critical period for the emergence of a transnational framework to think about and political deal with sex work. One key moment in this was the establishment of League of Nations Advisory Committee on the Traffic of Women and Children in 1921. Although most members took an abolitionist stance and criticized measures that sought to regulate prostitution, the debates in the committee were intense, especially concerning licensed bordellos.[14] Its early years focused on keeping an eye on ports and employment agencies, persuading participating countries to approve anti-trafficking legislation, and on becoming familiar with how prostitution was regulated in various cities. The International Anti-Trafficking Convention of 1921, in addition to recommending the creation of the committee, also proposed substituting the expression "traffic in white slaves", widespread in the previous decade, for "traffic in women and children". Although the old label would continue to be popular in the following decades, the shift in terminology signaled an intention to construct a problem of global dimensions, not simply one of European women emigrating to other continents. It was in this context that a representative of the United States proposed an unprecedented "social research project", which would include sending several researchers to examine the situation on the ground, with financial assistance provided by the Rockefeller fortune, via the American Bureau of Social Hygiene.[15]

---

13. Particularly important are Maria Odila Dias, *Quotidiano e poder em São Paulo no século XIX* (São Paulo, 1984); and Flavio Gomes *et al.*, *Mulheres negras no Brasil escravista e do pós-emancipação* (São Paulo, 2012).
14. Jessica R. Pliley, "Claims to Protection: The Rise and Fall of Feminist Abolitionism in the League of Nations' Committee on the Traffic in Women and Children, 1919–1936", *Journal of Women's History*, 22:4 (2010), pp. 90–113; Rodriguez García, "The League of Nations and the Moral Recruitment of Women", p. 105; League of Nations, *Report of the Special Body of Experts on Traffic in Women and Children*, 2 vols (Geneva, 1927), League of Nations Archive [hereafter, LNA], C.52.M.52.1927.IV, vol. 1, p. 8.
15. Cf. League of Nations, *Report*, pp. 5–7.

That this proposal came from an US representative was no coincidence: In New York, the first decades of the twentieth century had been a heyday for local organizations promoting urban reform and social hygiene. John Rockefeller Jr. had funded new techniques for researching organized crime, corruption in municipal government, gambling, and prostitution. In Lower Manhattan, these private initiatives (which at the end of the nineteenth century had been dedicated to exposing ties between local authorities and organized crime) had begun to employ new strategies: the use of secret agents to infiltrate the criminal underworld and obtain valuable information for doctors, private detectives, social workers, scientists, and puritanical reformers.[16] In the US, these investigative initiatives had been associated, from the beginning, with efforts to combat the municipal regulation of prostitution. For many US reformers, "regulation" equaled "acceptance", while combatting the traffic in women was a central step on the road to abolishing not only regulation, but also virtually all types of sex business.

Although the members of the League of Nations Committee received the idea of "social research" with enthusiasm, not all of them agreed with the North American researchers premises. In Geneva, the proponents of local regulation of prostitution continued to believe that prostitutes should live in licensed bordellos, where they could be identified and subjected to periodic medical examinations. In fact, throughout the nineteenth century, a variety of measures were taken for protecting "public morality" and "health", all these converging in the creation of a separate legal status for prostitutes. In the cities that adopted this regulationist strategy, moral and hygienic arguments had the practical effect of placing a broad group of women under permanent suspicion and special police and medical control. The abolitionists, on the other hand, opposed regulation by denouncing its sanitary inefficiency, since it failed to prevent the spread of syphilis; its injustice, since it sanctioned what they saw as a sexual and moral double standard; and its immorality, since it led the state to tolerate, if not protect pimps (thus turning into a pimp itself), placing prostitutes at the mercy of unscrupulous exploiters.[17] Consequently, many abolitionists also urged the criminalization of a variety of intermediation activities in relation to sex work. Thus, in settings like the Anti-Trafficking Committee, the idea began to take hold that "abolition" was the most effective way to combat the exploitation of and traffic in women.[18]

---

16. Jennifer Fronc, *New York Undercover: Private Surveillance in the Progressive Era* (Chicago, IL, 2009), pp. 3–10; Maira Keire, *For Business and Pleasure. Red Light Districts and the Regulation of Vice in the United States, 1890–1933* (Baltimore, MD, 2010), pp. 69–88.

17. One of the paradigmatic cases was the scandal caused in the 1880s by the trafficking of young British prostitutes to Belgian (regulated) brothels, which helped abolitionist propaganda. See Chaumont, *Le Mythe*, pp. 24–27.

18. Rodríguez Garcia, "The League of Nations and the Moral Recruitment of Women", p. 105; Jessica Pliley, "Claims to Protection", pp. 90–113.

Drawing from these previous experiences, such as the North American social reform initiatives, and, more indirectly, from the European debates on regulation and abolitionist positions, three American researchers embarked on a long journey in 1924 with the goal of discovering first-hand, beyond "rumours" and "sensational stories", the "real facts of the situation" concerning the global traffic in women.[19] Significantly, the trip started in South America; for the first leg, between May and July 1924, Bascom Johnson, a major of the US Army, accompanied by Samuel Auerbach and Paul Kinsie (the undercover agent referred to as P.K. in the project's correspondence), visited Buenos Aires, Montevideo, the Argentine-Uruguayan border towns of Concordia and Salto, and finally arrived in Rio de Janeiro. They began in Buenos Aires precisely because they expected it would be an ideal place to demonstrate the harmful connection between systems of regulation and the traffic in women.[20]

In South America they faced a significant challenge. In contrast to the experiences they had made when doing similar research in New York, the three researchers were unable to communicate directly with locals, they were not familiar with the urban geography, and they knew nothing of the everyday contact between residents and the authorities. They had to take the word of their private informants from the "underworld" and use this information to evaluate and question information obtained through official channels.[21] Upon their arrival in Rio, the difficulties became even greater: they had to understand a system that, as opposed to Buenos Aires, did not allow them to confirm their previous assumptions that the regulation of prostitution was connected to sex trafficking. Even though Rio de Janeiro did not regulate prostitution (at least not in ways that, at the time, were seen as "regulation", such as a specific legal status for sex work and public health policies, for instance) it seemed to the researchers to be an important spot in the trafficking routes.

Paul Kinsie arrived at Rio ahead of the group in what was an exploratory trip. There, he met with Boris Thomashevsky, a well-known actor in the Yiddish theater scene of New York, who was in South America on tour with his troupe. Like P.K., Thomashevsky had previously lived in Manhattan's Lower East Side. He had been active in theatrical productions with social themes since the 1910s. While talking to P.K., Thomashevsky expressed an interest in gathering information for an article on the

---

19. League of Nations, *Report*, p. 9.
20. On this trip, see Cristiana Schettini, "Conexiones transnacionales. Agentes encubiertos y tráfico de mujeres en los años 1920", *Nuevo Mundo Mundos Nuevos* [Online], *Débats*, put on line on 28 November 2014, available at: http://nuevomundo.revues.org/67440; last accessed 15 October 2017.
21. This can be seen throughout the reports. Chaumont analyses this operation in the production of the Final Report by the Body of Experts: Chaumont, *Le Mythe*, pp. 88–102.

participation of "people of his race" in South American prostitution.[22] The two of them made a few visits to houses of prostitution in Rio. Their conversations with Jewish women revealed that they had chosen to come to Rio both because they had friends who were already there and in order to escape Europe's terrible post-war economic conditions.[23]

This first visit had a powerful impact on P.K., labeling what he saw as "truly beyond description". He was particularly struck by the "segregated districts" with up to 10,000 prostitutes, who were "clad in loose-fitting chemises and short dresses, with arms and legs exposed", as they stood at the doors of rooms that offered little in the way of privacy or health.[24] P.K. did not name the streets or the neighborhood, but it is likely that he was describing the Mangue. What he saw as a sordid geography was home to women whom he described as "some of the most depraved that can be imagined", prepared to offer such "perverted" sexual practices as the "Brazilian fashion", which P.K. explained was a local term for "sodomy". Despite the massive presence of Brazilian women working in the area, the two observers had the impression that foreign women predominated. The foreigners stood out from the locals due to both age and color. The Brazilians were "younger and the greater number [among them are] Portuguese negroes", an expression that focused on the two outstanding features of these women in P.K.'s perspective: their skin color and the language they spoke (most likely, they were looking at Afro-Brazilian women). They noted that in Rio there were neither obligatory medical

22. "Commercialized prostitution", Rio de Janeiro, Brazil, 18–19 May 1924, LNA, Fonds du Secretariat [hereafter, FS], S 172. On Boris Thomashewsky, see Zachary Baker, "G'vald, Yidn, Buena Gente: Jevel Katz, Yiddish Bard of the Rio de la Plata", in Joel Berkowitz and Barbara Henry (eds), *Inventing the Modern Yiddish Stage: Essays in Drama, Performance, and Show Business* (Detroit, MI, 2012), pp. 202–224, 222. One of the few announcements of the Thomashewsky troupe in Rio shows that they stayed at least until September: "Companhia israelita de operetas, dramas e comédias dirigidas pelo célebre ator sr. Boris Thomashewsky", *Jornal do Brasil*, 28 September 1924, p. 32.

23. "Commercialized prostitution", Rio de Janeiro, 18–19 May 1924, LNA, S 172. What follows in this section is based mostly on the field reports of the First Enquiry on Traffic in Women and Children produced by the three researchers in their official and undercover investigations, particularly the transcriptions of first-hand conversations and observations conducted by P.K. The same source also contains a collection of official and unofficial documents, letters and charts they gathered during their stay in Rio. Overall, this is the raw material from which the Body of Experts produced the Final Report published in 1927. Actual names were replaced by codes, which can be deciphered with a Code Book in box S 171. For a careful critique of the making of the final report, see Chaumont, *Le Mythe*. For an analysis of this material in its ethnographic dimension, see Jean-Michel Chaumont, Magaly Rodriguez García, and Paul Servais, "*Introduction*", in *idem* (eds), *Trafficking in Women, 1924–1926. The Paul Kinsie Reports for the League of Nations*, vol. I (Geneva, 2017), pp. 7–18. In the second volume, the authors have included a careful transcription of Paul Kinsie Reports and the Code Book.

24. "Commercialized Prostitution", Rio de Janeiro, 18–19 May, 1924, LNA, FS, S 172.

exams for sex workers, nor any restrictions on the women's movement throughout the city.[25]

Two months later, in July 1924, Kinsie returned to Rio, this time accompanied by Samuel Auerbach and Bascom Johnson, who devoted themselves to the official aspects of the study. During this second visit, P.K. established contact with the owner of an elegant house of prostitution in Lapa. He introduced himself as an envoy of his informant in Buenos Aires, who, he claimed, was interested in expanding his investments in the *carioca* market.[26] Sophie, anonymized as "7-M" in the report ("M" for madam), hoped to convince him to buy her boarding house for women in Lapa. It was in this way that she became one of P.K.'s most valuable informants; both talked in English, and in her attempts to close the sale she shared her understanding of the peculiarities of prostitution in Rio. Like P.K.'s informants in Buenos Aires, she believed that the market had become saturated with European women hoping to save money and return to Europe. But unlike in Buenos Aires, she highlighted the importance of avoiding any arrangement that might smack of pimping, since under Brazilian law, with its abolitionist undertones, a variety of ways of facilitating, intermediating, or profiting from prostitution were crimes.

This perspective was reiterated both by other madams and the men who lived with them, identified by P.K. as "T" (for "traffickers"). They explained to P.K. that, in Brazil, the "girls" were not allowed to have "managers", but only "suckers" (customers). It was thus necessary to take certain precautions. These men seemed to see themselves as associates of either the girls or madams, and they hoped that their partners would someday have their own houses of prostitution.[27] In the meantime, the "girl" would usually work in a house, while her "boy" looked for an "honest and legitimate job" to avoid police harassment or potential denunciations by previous and "vengeful" girlfriends. Although everyone involved expected social mobility, many things could go wrong along the way, and many couples and agreements ended badly. Indeed, almost twenty years before the League of Nations researchers' visit, many of the cases of expulsion of foreigners from Brazil recounted tales of relationships of this sort that had ended due to violence, pregnancy, or disease.[28] In Rio de Janeiro, unlike in Buenos Aires, 8-M, another anonymized madam, explained, with one quick complaint at a police station, a girl could "finish him". All the men and women with whom P.K. spoke during his July 1924 visit alerted him to the dangers of the police campaigns to find and expel pimps.

25. "Traffic in Women and Children", 11 July 1924, Rio de Janeiro, Brazil, LNA, FS, S 172.
26. Schettini, "Conexiones".
27. Rio de Janeiro, "Commercialized prostitution", 25 July 1924, LNA, FS, S 172.
28. For more details on South American sex work circuits through the lens of the expulsion of foreigners, see Cristiana Schettini, "Exploração, gênero e circuitos sul-americanos nos processos de expulsão de estrangeiros (1907–1920)", *Tempo*, 33 (2012), pp. 51–73.

Sophie and the other foreign madams of the more elegant Lapa boarding houses explained to P.K. that their main task, in addition to maintaining the house, was to serve as an intermediary in the oldest sense, by finding men willing to pay their girls' bills. This was a good business, according to Sophie, because for rich men in Rio de Janeiro, maintaining a young foreign woman was a sign of prestige.[29] When she spoke of her niece in Warsaw, who she hoped to introduce to a prosperous Brazilian merchant, Sophie explained that she considered herself more matchmaker than job intermediary. Her goal was not so much for her niece to start working in a house and to specialize in specific sexual services, but rather for her charms to attract the rich man in question and thus save her from the fate of a "beggar" in the streets of Warsaw.[30]

In their conversations with informants in both Rio de Janeiro and Buenos Aires, many of the perceptions of the men and women of the "underworld" clashed with the Americans' expectations about the work, commercial, and affective relations of the sex workers. In both cities, pimps and madams found it awkward when P.K. asked them about strategies to recruit and deceive victims, and were taken aback by his obsession with so-called greenies (the inexperienced young women who P.K. assumed would bring in the most profit).[31] In both places, the informants emphasized that there was a high turnover among the women, and, as P.K. observed in Rio, the younger ones were more likely to be Brazilian. In contrast to the tacit presumption by P.K., it seemed obvious to the informants that older women, who were more experienced at the sexual techniques in demand in each city, were always the best option for working in houses of prostitution. For his part, P.K. searched for anything that might look like a constraint on the freedom of European women among all their complex strategies geared to survival and mobility. Any trace of coercion, threat, or deception led him to characterize these relations as "slavery" – "white slavery", we might say, although the researchers did not use this expression anymore. After all, the way they ignored the plight of young Brazilian women, some of whom were children, who they saw in the houses they visited, indicated that exploitation required a certain type of victim, one that excluded Brazilians and non-whites.[32]

---

29. See also Margareth Rago, *Os Prazeres da Noite* (São Paulo, 1990), pp. 167–200.
30. Rio de Janeiro, Brazil, 17, July, 1924, LNA, FS, S 172.
31. For instance: "You're a mersugar (crazy)!", exclaimed his main informer in Buenos Aires, 1 – DH, when P.K. expressed his preference for a "green" woman. Buenos Aires, Argentina, 7–9 June 1924, LNA, FS, S 171. See also Cristiana Schettini, "Conexiones".
32. P.K. found two Brazilian girls at "10-M"'s house in Lapa; she told him they were fifteen and sixteen years old. He noticed that "both girls are Brazilians and appear very young". He refused to choose one of them when the Madam offered. As he was leaving, a police officer entered, as a "friend of the house", not finding anything wrong with the girls' presence there. Rio de Janeiro, Brazil, 11 July 1924, LNA, FS, S 172. A few days later, P.K. dropped by many houses looking for

The disconnect between the perspectives of researchers, madams, and "traffickers" illustrates different conceptions about what constituted exploitation and "white slavery". For the researchers (as well as for Brazilian lawmakers), deception, seduction, lack of autonomy, threats, and other forms of coercion were all components of a relation equivalent to slavery.[33] But for those who were directly involved in this business, what they did was more akin to "work placement", matchmaking, and other types of intermediary activities that were common at the time both among immigrants and in the domestic service sector, as well as in all sorts of commercial and artistic professions. This role was based on networks of friendship and kinship, both real and fictive, many founded upon common ethnic identities, which eased their departure from home and their arrival in a new country and culture.

Through these conversations, P.K. constructed a certain perspective on how prostitution worked in Rio de Janeiro. His view was strongly influenced by the racism and classism expressed by the European madams, who considered themselves far removed from the "window prostitutes" who filled various corners of the city center, many of them Brazilians whom they called "half niggers". As one of the "traffickers" explained, the Brazilian women were "dumb" and not suitable for men like them.[34] Comments like these show the ways in which the social organization of prostitution was predicated upon a combination of racist, ethnic, and age-based criteria.

SEX WORK IN RIO: THE VIEW OF LOCAL AUTHORITIES AND PROFESSIONALS

The risk of police harassment for the men who lived with prostitutes and madams was something raised not only by P.K.'s informants, but also by the Brazilian authorities in their meetings with the research team of the League of Nations. They emphasized their compliance with the new international norms, explaining to the foreign visitors that Rio de Janeiro had not adopted the much-criticized Buenos Aires model of officially regulating prostitution. They proudly pointed to their laws governing the expulsion of foreigners, especially the more recent 1921 law that barred foreign prostitutes from entering the country and restricted the international movement

---

"girls of foreign birth, under 21 years"; all the underage girls he met seemed to be Brazilian. Rio de Janeiro, Brazil, 22–23 July, 1924, LNA, FS, S 172.

33. Metaphors of slavery, beginning with the notion of "traffic", appeared everywhere. On their ubiquity as well as the local meanings of such conceptions, see Schettini, *Que tenhas*, ch. 2.

34. A madam explained to P.K. that men "who spend money" don't want these "half-niggers"; they would prefer European girls. Rio de Janeiro, Brazil, 11 July 1924, LNA, FS, S 172. A few days later, a pimp told him that he considered Brazilian women "dumbs", "not for us". Rio de Janeiro, Brazil, 15 July 1924, LNA, FS, S 172.

of both prostitutes and pimps, in accordance with the recommendations of the international convention from that very year.[35]

Still, the researchers had been trained to mistrust the authorities, and they suspected that the law was both poorly enforced and easy to evade; after all, the sex trade seemed to be functioning quite well. Indeed, P.K. had witnessed first-hand the cordial relations between the owners of the boarding houses in Lapa and the police, who ignored the presence of underage Brazilian girls and accepted bribes from the madams to protect their houses from troublesome clients.[36]

The researchers also spoke with other informants, such as "respectable" individuals and representatives of private groups like the lawyer Lourenço de Mattos Borges, of the Brazilian Council of Social Hygiene.[37] In an effort to explain Brazilian racial categories, Borges, who was more comfortable speaking French than English, classified the prostitutes as *blanches natives*, *blanches étrangères*, *mulâtres* (*café au lait*), and *noires*. The last two categories contained, in Borges' estimation, almost half of Rio's prostitutes. While the *noires* were predominantly to be found in the Mangue (ninety-one out of 143 in the whole city, according to his count), the *mulâtres* were divided fairly equally between Lapa (139) and the Mangue (174). These statistics were complemented with data provided by the American nurse Bertie Rice, who worked in the Prophylactic Inspectorate for Leprosy and Venereal Diseases (Inspetoria de Profilaxia da Lepra e Doenças Venéreas), created in 1921.[38] Through Rice, they gained access to the lists of houses in Lapa and the Mangue put together by visiting nurses, who tried to convince the women to get treated for sexually transmitted diseases.[39]

Consistent with the racially marked gaze of Lapa's madams and of P.K. himself in his initial excursions with Thomashevsky, Rice explained that the Mangue was a small neighborhood, made up of just seven streets between the Mangue Canal and Salvador de Sá Avenue and packed with houses of "the worst type of prostitution" to be found in the city. The conditions were cramped and unhealthy: two or three women shared one small room, with nothing better to do than stand "partly clothed" in their doorways, where they tried to attract the attention of passersby. They ate their few

---

35. The authorities' claims and positions are set out in the transcription of official interviews with the Committee researchers and in official questionnaires sent to all governments. The Final Report reproduces the Reply by the Brazilian Government to the Questionnaire issued by the Secretariat on 6 August 1921, from which researchers extracted the official position of Brazilian Government. League of Nations, *Report*, vol. 2, Appendix III, "Reply by the Brazilian Government", pp.39–40.
36. See note 34.
37. "Respectable individuals" was a particular classification in the Code Book. See LNA, FS, S 171.
38. On the Inspectorate, see Sergio Carrara, *Tributo a Vênus*, pp. 229–245.
39. "Relatorio Mensal para el Distrito de las Prostitutas", Rio de Janeiro, Brazil, LNA, FS, S 172.

meals of coffee and rolls in the area's cheap restaurants. According to the visiting nurses, of the 579 women who lived in those houses, the overwhelming majority (396) were Brazilian, followed by seventy-four "Russians" and forty-five "Poles". Of all the women, 174 were classified as "mulattos" and ninety-one as "blacks". According to Rice, the local government's complete lack of interest in this small area left the police as the only point of contact with the authorities and frequently gave way to fraternization with police officers who visited the women during their patrols.

To complement the knowledge they gained from both official and underworld informants, the researchers also had access to legal decisions and legislative debates, which might have offered further insight into local conceptions of prostitution and exploitation. For instance, the 1915 legislative debates – eventually resulting in revisions to the Penal Code that criminalized the "traffic in women" – clearly reveal that Brazilian parliamentarians were informed about debates taking place in France, Germany, and Italy about the definition of consent for adults, deception (both through informal promises and work agencies), and ways of intermediating and profiting from prostitution. Brazilian legislators were thus mindful of the international abolitionist trends, which they used to intensify the criminalization of relationships that involved prostitutes and their intermediaries. For them, the traffic in women was akin to slavery, "in which the poor victims completely lose their individuality and become subject to the vilest exploitations".[40]

As can be concluded from their reports, however, the League of Nations researchers were not very interested in the content of the cases that prosecuted pimps or the details of expulsion cases against pimps. Actually, both the Brazilian authorities and researchers from the League of Nations preferred to cite as their evidence the aggregate data from police stations and courts. For the Brazilians, lists of expelled foreigners offered proof that they were actually fighting human trafficking; for the researchers, lists of foreign prostitutes showed that victims of trafficking were living in the Brazilian capital. Since the way both groups conceived of prostitution was as if all were European women, it is easy to understand why the form of repression chosen was summary expulsion, carried out by the police, in accordance with the 1907 law of expulsion of foreigners, combined with more recent measures that sought to control who disembarked at the ports. The goal was to prevent foreign women from establishing a foothold to begin with.

The contrast between the documents produced by local authorities and the observations of the researchers from the Anti-Trafficking Committee

---

40. See the documentation of the Brazilian legislative debates gathered by the League of Nations Comittee research delegation in: "Câmara dos Deputados, Pareceres, 1908–1915", Rio de Janeiro, Brazil, LNA, FS, S 172.

offers a multifaceted view of the nature of sex work in Rio de Janeiro in the years after World War I. Despite language barriers and cultural mis-understandings, P.K.'s direct contact with the houses of prostitution in "elegant" Lapa and "depraved" Mangue shows, if only in an indirect and fragmented way, how the madams, pimps, and even sex workers themselves understood their experiences. It was more difficult for P.K. and his collea-gues to make sense of the actions of local authorities and the peculiar *carioca* system, which combined abolitionist legislation (not least through a crim-inalization of pimps) with semi-official toleration in zones like the Mangue. The researchers preferred to view the records and statistics they gathered as unequivocal proof that European prostitutes comprised a significant por-tion of the women working in Rio's brothels and that the city was thus a major destination in the international networks of trafficking.

THE LIFE OF FANNY GALPER IN RIO

Rio's specific combination of abolitionism and regulation (the latter in a rather repressive, police-mediated variant) formed the general framework for the city's world of prostitution and its sex workers. It is evident that such a framework did not function as a significant obstacle for those who acted as business people in the field, including the madams. At the same time, state practices influenced both the social mobility and race relations within the world of prostitution. Fanny Galper's life in Rio de Janeiro is a case in point. In Franklin Galvão's 1923 list, she was one of the few women who owned more than one house, both located in Rua Pinto de Azevedo (at numbers eighteen and twenty-three, see Figure 1). A Pole and a Brazilian lived in the first; two Russians and six Brazilians in the second.

Fanny Galper owned still more houses; notary books contain records of some of her economic and personal relations over a nearly fifteen-year period, between 1921 and the mid-1930s. In addition, in 1930, her ex-husband Solly Debrotiner was accused of being a pimp and subjected to expulsion pro-ceedings. Finally, entry and exit records from the United States reveal details of her life before she came to Brazil, which she deliberately omitted later on. Together, these documents form the pieces of a puzzle that hint at some of the strategies of a Russian immigrant whose life revolved around prostitution.

In 1930, when Fanny was fifty-two years old, an assistant police chief accused a fellow Russian, Solly Debrotiner, of having taken advantage of Fanny's "weakness" following an illness making her "fall into his clutches" and marry him. The marriage lasted only a few months, enough for him to extort a part of her fortune, under the pretense of investing it in business ventures. Called to testify, Fanny gave the police a most interesting narra-tive that partly went along with the authorities expectations, and partly presented a remarkable account of her life. Through stereotyped expres-sions characteristic of police allegations, she accused her husband of having

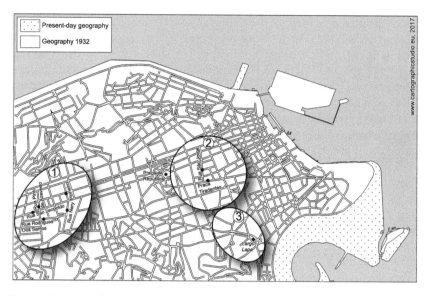

Figure 1. Rio de Janeiro's downtown area in the 1930s. From the last years of the nineteenth century up to the second decade of the twentieth century, prostitutes' houses converged in the area around Praça Tiradentes. They were part of an expansive nightlife area, together with its many theatres, restaurants, cafés-concert and pubs. São Jorge street is highlighted. Known for hosting "Polish" women at the turn of the twentieth century, it is believed to be the first place that Fanny Galper established herself in Rio (circle 2). During the 1910s, police actions resulted in a spatial concentration into two neighborhoods: in Lapa (circle 3), elegant houses, known as "pensions des artistes", whose residents were generally white, European women who identified themselves with a French style of prostitution; on the other hand, in the small group of streets around the Canal de Mangue, on the other side of the Praca da República, the Mangue neighborhood was associated with Russian and Polish house owners and Brazilian women. The picture (circle 1) also highlights the Mangue streets where Fanny Galper had her houses.

repeatedly asked her for money. When she got "tired" of this situation, she decided to ask for a divorce. The main lines of this accusation were the common point of many deportation trials for pimping, which con-temporaries accused of expressing inquisitorial police procedures. As can be seen from registers of her financial procedures in those months (further analysed below), her accusations were not the whole story.

The other part of her testimony, in which she recreates her life as a prostitute, is unique and revealing. She arrived in Rio in 1908 and began working as a prostitute on Rua São Jorge (see Figure 1).[41] Since the end of the nineteenth century, this area had housed prostitutes who had been

41. Her testimony forms part of the file on Solly Debrotiner's expulsion case: "Auto de declar-ações de Fanny Galper", 28 December 1929, in "Expulsão de Solly Debrotiner", Arquivo Nacional (Rio de Janeiro) [hereafter, AN], Fundo: Série Interior. Extrangeiros. Expulsão, IJJ7 – 148, 1930.

expelled from the houses located along busy tram lines, where they would post themselves in the ground floor windows. This highly visible "window prostitution" was antithetical to the authorities' efforts to "morally cleanse" the city center, and many of the prostitutes expelled by police wound up on Rua São Jorge. These included both Brazilians and foreigners, particularly women from the Azores. According to an official report from 1912, only four years after Fanny's arrival, forty-one houses of prostitution existed on Rua de São Jorge at the time.[42] The majority were home to only one to three tenants, most of whom were European women like Fanny: Persons identified as "Poles", "Russians", "Germans", or "Austrians" made up more than half; there were also eight Italians, six Brazilians, and one Portuguese woman. The street had long been known not only as a "stronghold of prostitution", but also as a place where sex was inexpensive, and the women who worked there, Brazilian and European, white and black, felt the force of police efforts to control both the location and nature of their activities.[43] Fanny Galper testified that she had moved away when "the police closed the houses in that [other] zone". She was most likely referring to the periodic expulsions that happened during the 1910s, which forced many prostitutes to relocate to the Mangue, further still from the city center. In 1916, a journalist interpreted this new displacement as a symptom of the police's lack of an effective plan, not as a conscious strategy to concentrate prostitution in a specific area: With this new wave of expulsions, the women began to "invade streets previously inhabited only by families", particularly in the area known as Cidade Nova, where the Mangue was located.[44] In this process, Fanny Galper moved to Rua Pinto de Azevedo, one of the areas that would become known for "Poles", a generic designation for cheap prostitutes from Eastern Europe. Although Fanny attributed her move to police measures, once established in the area, her life began to change radically. By 1930, she owned four buildings, whose rooms she rented or sub-rented to prostitutes, who paid 10 *mil-réis* per day.[45] All told, Fanny had four or five tenants per house.

42. The report was compiled by the police commissioner in response to an enquiry by the Dutch diplomatic mission about the measures taken by the Brazilian government to combat the traffic in white women. "Ofício do chefe de polícia ao subsecretário das Relações Exteriores", 3 January 1913, Arquivo Histórico do Itamaraty (Rio de Janeiro), Ministérios e Repartições Federais, Maço 303-3-6. The diplomatic query, in turn, is a graphic illustration of the degree to which the idea of "white slavery" had become an issue of international politics at the time.

43. The expression is from the socialst lawyer Evaristo de Moraes, in his *Ensaios de Patologia Social* (Rio de Janeiro, 1921), pp. 282–283. On Evaristo de Moraes, see Joseli Nunes de Mendonça, *Evaristo de Moraes. Tribuno da República* (Campinas, 2007). Also see the contribution by Aldrin A. S. Castellucci and Benito Bisso Schmidt in this Special Issue.

44. "O decoro da cidade. Ostentação cínica do vício", *A Noite*, 21 January 1916, p.1.

45. Until the beginning of the 1940s, Brazil's currency was based on the *real* (plural: *réis*), its basic denomination being *mil réis* (one thousand *réis*; written as 1$000). One thousand *mil réis* was

Fanny's situation and prosperity constitute a striking contrast to the image of a sordid and miserable Mangue that the League of Nations researchers had described. This image, on the one hand, was one of the results of a reorganization of the sex trade attempted to segregate the cheapest prostitutes; on the other hand, it also resulted from the researcher's informants who, being from Lapa, had looked down on the Mangue. At any rate, in the deportation case against Fanny's ex-husband, police were not interested in how she had become a madam or in explaining how she assembled so much property, but rather in presenting her as a victim, a (white) "slave". Perhaps because of the pressures of the interrogation, she abruptly stopped telling her life story and switched to a tale typical of deportation cases (a switch that comes across as sensible in the document): "About eleven months ago, she met Solly Debrotiner in her home. [...] He had no profession whatsoever." She was sick, and he proposed marriage. Soon after, he began to ask for money, to launch business ventures that failed, until, "tired of satisfying her husband's demands", she applied for an amicable legal separation.[46] Satisfying the then prevailing needs of a police investigation for the expulsion of foreigners, Fanny's case entered the annals of the "traffic in white women". Despite this apparent conformity, Fanny's testimony at the same time manifests how different her case was from what the League of Nations researchers considered as typical: Far from a young, recently arrived European, she was an experienced and prosperous woman. For police authorities, though, her age and illness had made her vulnerable to the shady interests of a man who the commissioner in charge of the case called a "rabbi of a society of Israelites, composed exclusively of prostitutes and pimps, charged with inspecting the bookkeeping for brothels".[47]

When Solly Debrotiner was in jail, and the authorities had already issued a decision for deportation, a request for habeas corpus to halt his expulsion reached the Supreme Court.[48] In addition to accusing the police of manipulating the accusations, the defense explained that Debrotiner and Galper's

called one *conto de réis*, written as 1:000$000. She leased one of her houses for 800$000 a month. If she had four tenants in another house, she would make around 1:200$000 a month. In 1930, the average monthly rent of a residential home (for a family of seven) was around 500$000. Therefore, she made almost the double of a regular rent. "Custo de vida na cidade do Rio de Janeiro. Orcamento mensal de uma familia segundo o 'Economical Data About Brasil, 1912–1930'", *Jornal do Commercio. Retrospecto commercial* (Rio de Janeiro, 1931), pp. 1–263, 153.

46. "Auto de declarações de Fanny Galper", 28 December 1929.

47. See the testimony of a police officer: "Auto de declarações de Eduardo Boselli", in "Expulsão de Solly".

48. A brief cronology would be: The police investigation started on 28 December 1929; he was in jail from 3 January 1930; the expulsion decree was issued on 22 January 1930; the habeas corpus request reached the Supreme Court on 24 January 1930; and he was finally released on 23 February 1930. "Expulsão de Solly".

separation had been friendly, seeking to prove that he was not a pimp, but rather a prosperous businessman and leather manufacturer.[49] Curiously, the defense did not mention his activity as a rabbi, although he had officiated a wedding at the "Beneficent and Recreational Society of the Sons of Israel", whose membership included the "most distinguished elements of the Israelite colony".[50] Thus, at least until his brief marriage to Fanny attracted the authorities' attention, Solly Debrotiner appears to have been seen as a respected businessman, both within and outside of the Jewish community.

At this point in Fanny's story, two questions still await an answer. First, how did she transform herself into a successful landlady in the Mangue, after starting out as a "Polish" and therefore rather marginal prostitute on Rua São Jorge? And second, why, as a successful landlady, did she marry a man who apparently was only after her money? The only way to answer these questions is to track her doings through other types of sources, in which she appears as neither prostitute, nor madam, and that shed light on a part of her life that she never revealed publicly. Particularly useful are the notary books of Rio de Janeiro, in which private individuals could record certain transaction and deeds. Fanny Galper made ample use of this instrument of legal certification having debts, purchases, leases of property, and even a will registered. Through these, it is possible to understand more fully some of her relations and decisions as well as fill some of the gaps in her life. Fanny Galper appears to have acquired her first property in the Mangue in 1921, when she purchased a building at 65 Rua Nery Pinheiro via a public auction of the estate of a Brazilian or Portuguese woman. Two years later, she bought her second property, at 250 Rua São Leopoldo, from an Italian couple.[51] Fanny's acquisition of these two properties shows how the expansion of the sex trade in the Mangue was closely tied to the dynamics of the real estate market, illustrating how the character of premises in the area changed from "residential" to being used in sex business.

The researchers from the League of Nations and other contemporaries searched at length for evidence of organized crime rings run by traffickers and pimps of Jewish origin. But the transactions that Fanny recorded over fifteen years depended on other people, particularly on a Portuguese man named Antônio Alves Dias Pereira. He signed, in her stead, all the transactions that she registered, since she always declared that she did not know how to read or write. She also leased to him the building on São Leopoldo

49. "Supremo Tribunal Federal – Habeas corpus", 24 January 1930, "Expulsão de Solly". Also see the mentions of his business activities in "À praça", *Correio da Manhã*, 22 June 1924, p. 9.

50. "Vários cultos – judaísmo", *Gazeta de Notícias*, 5 January 1927, p. 5.

51. Livro de Notas, Alves, Maria Luisa Ferreira (outorgante), Galper, Fanny (outorgada), AN, 50 Oficio de Notas do Rio de Janeiro, Livro 281, fs. 11v, 30 April 1921; Livro de Notas, "Venda", Lattari, Francisco (outorgante), Galper, Fanny (outorgada), AN, 10° Oficio de Notas do Rio de Janeiro, Livro 148, fs. 59, 15 March 1923.

Street between 1924 and 1931. Finally, the two of them formed a consortium to construct dwellings on Rua Rodrigues dos Santos. The consecutive numbering of the addresses (twenty-two to twenty-six) indicates that these were probably small houses or even single rooms to be rented to prostitutes.[52]

In addition to having been Fanny's business partner throughout the 1920s, Antônio also had an affective role in her life. In her 1925 will, she named him her sole heir, calling him "a person who holds her esteem and consideration, with whom the testator lived in a marital relationship since nearly two years, and from whom she has received much affection and demonstrations of consideration and esteem".[53] Antônio's presence, in both economic and affective terms, was in keeping with practices common in Rio de Janeiro since at least the end of the nineteenth century, when the houses of prostitution were still located in the city center: Older foreign women, some of them ex-prostitutes, became commercial and romantic partners of Portuguese or Brazilian men, with whom they opened or took over establishments combining bar and brothel. As we have seen, this was also an expectation of the young "traffickers" with whom P.K. spoke, who hoped that their "girls" might eventually become madams, thus ensuring a more peaceful life for both. Rio de Janeiro's legal strategy of targeting pimps placed these (as well as other persons who related to prostitutes) in the police's crosshairs. It is in this light that we might make sense of both Fanny's relationship with Antônio and her marriage to Solly. To understand why only the latter was prosecuted as a pimp, it may be relevant to consider that Antônio was a Portuguese merchant, far removed from the stereotype of the Jewish pimp, while Solly seemed to smoothly fit this image.

In contrast to both the expectations of the League of Nations researchers and the police about the "vile exploitation" of and the traffic in women, Fanny Galper's reasons for associating with both men were far more complex. One additional factor here was the debt that she incurred with Antônio to build the houses on Rua Rodrigues dos Santos in 1926. They borrowed 110 *contos de réis* from a Lapa merchant, a significant debt that would demand sacrifices from both. Two years later, construction was complete, and they divided the houses between them in accordance with the investment each had made. When the debt was due, they were only able to make a partial payment and obtain an extension on the remainder. In 1930, the loan repayment was demanded under the extended terms. At that point,

---

52. Livro de Notas, "Arrendamento", Galper, Fanny (outorgante), Pereira, Antonio Alves Dias (outorgado), AN, 10° Oficio de Notas do Rio de Janeiro, Livro 163, fs. 46, 12 May 1924; Livros de Notas, "Dissolução de condomínio", Pereira, Antonio Dias da Silva (outorgante), Galper, Fanny (outorgada), AN, 16° Oficio de Notas do Rio de Janeiro, Livro 122, fs. 2V, 25 May 1928.

53. Livro de Notas, "Testamento", Galper, Fanny, AN, 10° Oficio de Notas do Rio de Janeiro, Livro 183, fs. 40, 19 August 1925.

Fanny listed herself as Solly Debrotiner's wife, although they had already begun the process of obtaining an amicable legal separation. Not only did Fanny not make any reference to their separation vis-à-vis the merchant, she used their marriage, which was legally designated as including joint ownership of their possessions, to amortize the debt, which was reduced to thirty *contos de réis*. The next year she finally paid off the debt. Fanny's short marriage to Debrotiner thus might make more sense when we realize that it helped her reduce the debt she had incurred with Antônio.

Yet, there is another, even more surprising aspect of Fanny's life that is revealed through the records of her prior stops in the United States: In the US, Fanny Galper, at least since 1904, had been Fanny Debrotiner, wife to real estate agent Solly Debrotiner and mother to William Debrotiner. In 1912, Solly obtained permanent US residency, and in 1916 he moved to Rio de Janeiro, where he intended to dedicate himself to the leather business.[54] Meanwhile, Fanny, who had, according to her later testimony, arrived already in 1908, built her own life in Rio using her maiden name, first as prostitute, then as a landlady in the Mangue.

So, Fanny left the US as Fanny Debrotiner, wife of Solly and mother of William, and, according to US documentation, a literate resident of Peabody, Massachusetts, and disembarked as Fanny Galper, an illiterate Russian prostitute on Rua São Jorge. During her long relationship with Antônio in the 1920s, she always presented herself as a Russian and a widow. Not even in her will did she mention her son, although she wanted to leave some money to siblings back in Russia. Thus, both Fanny and Solly seem to have shared a preoccupation with keeping the two worlds, one associated with the US and the other with Brazil, separate, omitting mention of the former in the documents generated in the latter.

The evidence from Fanny Galper's actions and economic movements constitutes a context for the deportation trial against Solly Debrotiner in 1930. Although these documents do not offer a plausible explanation for many of her actions (why she remarried him, why she accused him) or a conclusive indication of the nature of her relationship with Antônio, they do help to see the "old, vulnerable" Fanny and the "evil pimp" Solly in a different light. Both of them handled substantial sums of money during their years in Brazil. Both of them agreed not to mention their previous family life and their son, whatever their conflicts were. Therefore, there might be a possibility that what the police in its 1930 investigation saw as Solly extorting the vulnerable Fanny could equally be interpreted as way

---

54. This information is gathered from "United States Passport Applications, 1795–1925", database with images, *FamilySearch*, available at: https://familysearch.org/ark:/61903/1:1:QKDF-CZMS; last accessed 15 October 2017; "United States Census, 1910", database with images, *FamilySearch*, available at: https://familysearch.org/ark:/61903/1:1:M2JN-LM3; last accessed 15 October 2017.

Figure 2. Pictures from passport applications submitted by the Debrotiner family. In October 1916, 47-year-old Solly Debrotiner (bottom right) applied for a passport to travel to Rio de Janeiro. He declared the purpose of his travel as starting a "leather business for himself". Five years later (29 September 1921), 42-year-old Fanny (top) and her son, 24-year-old William (bottom left), also applied for US passports to go to Rio de Janeiro. Both declared that the purpose of their travel was to join their father and husband Solly Debrotiner. Identified as a "housewife", Fanny signed her own application and countersigned that of her son, William. All three declared that they were from Russia, and submitted proof that Solly Debrotiner had been naturalized in 1912. Solly's 1916 passport picture was reprinted in a *carioca* newspaper during his deportation trial in early 1930. The report suggested that he was a victim of police persecution.
Solly's passport picture is reproduced in: "United States Passport Applications, 1795–1925", database with images, FamilySearch, available at: https://familysearch.org/ark:/61903/3:1:3QS7-99X7-CGNL?cc=2185145&wc=3XZ8-PTP%3A1056306501%2C1056640201; last accessed 15 October 2017. See also "A polícia e sua campanha contra os exploradores de lenocínio. Solly Debrotiner estará sendo vítima de perseguição?", Diário da Noite, 11 January 1930, p. 3. Fanny and William's application are in: "United States Passport Applications, 1795–1925", database with images, FamilySearch, available at: https://familysearch.org/ark:/61903/1:1:QKDF-CZMS; last accessed 15 October 2017.

for both to put their accounts in order at the end of their lives, thus formalizing a separation that dated from years earlier. In other words, Fanny Galper's actions during the brief time she was remarried to Solly Debrotiner suggest that this second marriage was, to a certain degree, economically convenient for her, at least inasmuch as it allowed her to amortize the debt she shared with Antônio – something that never came up in the trial. This hypothesis also offers plausible reasons for her to remarry for such a brief time. She thus may have acted on the grounds of previous agreements with Solly. In fact, after her second marriage to Debrotiner, Fanny continued to be in close contact with the Portuguese Antônio, with whom she invested in a bar in 1930.[55] Even if this was not the case, and there is no way to decipher the reasons and circumstances of many of her actions, the Fanny Galper that emerges from these fragmented references appears an attentive woman, prepared to take advantage of the few opportunities she had in order to build a life of wealth in Mangue, in the midst of police eviction orders and unequal partnerships conditions, among other constraints.

It is difficult to keep track of Fanny's subsequent activities. She had put money aside in 1925 for the Israelite Beneficent Funeral and Religious Association, an organization that congregated Jewish prostitutes, to bury her in Inhaúma Cemetery.[56] Her participation in this Association had multiple dimensions: first, the importance of her religious identity, especially when she thought she was going to die soon. Secondly, as historian Beatriz Kushnir has shown, religious associations were a fundamental way of maintaining connections of mutual aid in the world of sex work in order to deal with the multiple challenges individuals were facing, as women, as Jewish persons, as immigrants, and as prostitutes or madams. Although there were similar associations in many cities where there was a strong presence of Jewish European immigrants in the sex trade during the first half of the twentieth century, Kushnir remarks that Rio's association for many years was composed exclusively of women.[57] In this sense, Fanny Galper's life was hardly unique.

There are indications that there is a grave in New York of a person named Fanny Debrotiner who passed away in 1942. Whether this is the burial place of the Fanny who prospered as a madam in Rio de Janeiro is still to be conclusively established – like so many other aspects of her remarkable life.[58]

55. The registration of their new partnership in the Board of Trade on 30 June 1930 is referred in "Junta Comercial", *Diário de Notícias*, 4 July 1930, p.5.

56. Livro de Notas, "Testamento", Galper, Fanny, AN, 100 Oficio de Notas do Rio de Janeiro, Livro 183, fs. 40, 19 August 1925.

57. On the Israelite Beneficent Funeral and Religious Association, see Beatriz Kushnir, *Baile de máscaras. Mulheres judias e prostituição* (Rio de Janeiro, 1996), pp. 27–48; 95–160.

58. The burial place is cited as: "Fanny Debrotiner, 1942; Burial, Springfield Gardens, Queens, New York, Montefiore Cemetery", retrieved from "Find A Grave", available at: https://www.findagrave.com/cgi-bin/fg.cgi?page=gr&GRid=148970695; last accessed 15 October 2017.

EXPLOITATIVE RELATIONS IN RIO'S WORLD
OF SEX WORK

The League of Nations researchers were correct to stress the importance
they placed on listening to the voices of the men and women whom they
identified with the "underworld", in order to achieve some understanding
of the relations in and around prostitution in each place they visited.
Despite their cultural perspectives, language restrictions, and abolitionist
convictions, they established a dialogue that forced them to adapt their ideas
about sex trafficking to the evidence they found. The eventual adoption of
a broader and more malleable conception of trafficking demonstrates some
of the difficulties they and Brazilian authorities encountered in drawing
clearly marked lines between acceptable and unacceptable migrations.[59]

The journeys and choices of Fanny Galper/Debrotiner as well as the
relationship and agreements she entered allow us to see just how hard this
was. Although the accusation against her ex-husband Solly Debrotiner
portrayed Fanny as Solly's "slave", other records allow us to see her as a
wife and mother, as a madam and real estate entrepreneur in partnership
with Antônio, and as a Jewish immigrant concerned with guaranteeing a
burial in accordance with the rites of her faith. In light of Fanny's multiple
identities over the course of her life as an immigrant, we can observe how,
like many similar women in Buenos Aires and Rio de Janeiro, her economic
and personal relations overlapped.

Fanny's prosperity was partly built upon her ability to associate with and
dissociate herself from different men at different points in her life. Also, her
trajectory reflects a sense of opportunity in acquiring real estate property at
precisely the moment when police were pushing for a reorganization of
urban space and the creation a concentrated and segregated zones for sex
trade and sex work. Similar trajectories of other European women, particularly "Russians" and "Poles", such as those associated in the Israelite
Beneficent Funeral and Religious Association, together with the widespread expectations among Jewish men and women who P.K. met as an
undercover investigator, converge to suggest how widespread such stories
of upward mobility were among the sex workers during those years. This
does not mean that actual opportunities for such upward mobility were
abundant, rather it was the expectations and hopes connected to such stories
that counted. To follow Fanny Galper's steps thus not only sheds light on
her personal abilities and the particular circumstances of her life; it equally
reveals the broad historical constraints and contexts in which such a
biography became possible and in which her actions acquire meaning. These
contexts involve the impact of the *carioca* way of dealing with paid sex work
in the 1920s – in which regulation, abolition, and police repression were

---

59. Chaumont, *Le Mythe*, 2009, pp.87–90.

combined in a peculiar fashion, giving way to a specific social organization of prostitution. Under these circumstances, Fanny's dependence on different kinds of men (from her lovers to, very probably, police officers) and the risk of having to hand over her money to them were constant. In this sense, questions about exploitation, gender relations, family organization, friendship and love intertwine in her history.

Another crucial context for understanding Fanny's life is the racial dimension of this specific social organization of prostitution and its impact on the unequal production and distribution of wealth. Fanny Galper built her prosperity upon the exploitation of her tenants. By concentrating cheap prostitution in the Mangue, the police rendered these women vulnerable, nearly invisible, and potentially highly dependent on better positioned intermediaries such as Fanny. In other words, Fanny's prosperity was, to a high degree, the result of very unequal labor arrangements that she established with young prostitutes, who were mainly Brazilians and mostly black. All national and foreign observers from the 1920s agreed in recognizing the difficult conditions in which these young women lived, as they paid up to ten *mil-réis* per day to women like Fanny, ate precariously in places like the bar that she owned with Antônio, and had to confront the attempts by Bertie Rice and others to urge them to come for a stay in the new venereal disease dispensary. This appears to have been a direct effect of the spatial and social organization of prostitution in Rio de Janeiro in the 1920s, which could be defined as concentration-cum-marginalization: enhanced opportunities to accumulate wealth for white women, based on the sexual labor of black women, in conditions marked, if not ensured by police control. All these dimensions of the world of prostitution and its labor relations remained unacknowledged in the abolitionist thrust among the League of Nations observers and the Brazilian authorities.

While it is possible to trace at least some of the moments in the lives of individuals such as Fanny Galper, it is much more difficult to know further details about those mostly Afro-Brazilian women who worked for her. In a few exceptional cases, however, their tragic fate allows us to catch a glimpse of their lives. Such was the case of Brazilian Hercília Maria Luz (see Figure 3): Her name appears on the list compiled by Franklin Galvão's in 1923 as one of Fanny's tenants. Since 1926, Hercília had been living in a house on Rua Rodrigues dos Santos, which Fanny and Antônio had just built together.[60] She may have been one of those very young Brazilian girls who P.K. observed fraternizing with soldiers and sailors during his excursions to the Mangue. Women like her were described as part of a degraded milieu that only worsened the condition of the European women living there, the potential "white slaves", but their own work conditions and lives

---

60. "Matou a tiros a mulher que o repelia", *O Jornal*, 27 September 1927, p. 5.

were never an object of interest. In 1927, her lover, a young soldier, mur-
dered her, according to a newspaper.[61] The paper noted that she looked no
older than twenty and was originally from Bahia, while her murderer was
twenty-four, *pardo* (of "mixed" ethno-racial descent), and from the
northeastern state of Pernambuco. Upon her return from a dance ("by
automobile", as the newspaper noted), she found the soldier waiting for her
at the door of the house with his revolver. His motive, according to the
newspaper, was that he felt "rejected".

In addition to her tragic death, we know that, for at least four years, she
paid Fanny and thus contributed to her prosperity. Such a relationship
normally also included letting her "landlady" know about her comings and
goings, possibly also the night she went to a dance and was killed after-
wards. It is possible to imagine, then, how police measures to segregate
prostitution facilitated the dependence of women like Hercília on women
like Fanny. In spite of the fact that the sexual specializations associated with
African-descended women were more highly valued and thus commanded
higher rates, it was white women like Fanny who had more access to wealth
and the skills and networks necessary for negotiations with the police,
and who could even garner some kind of protection if they managed to be
considered (white) "slaves".

In the end, the *carioca* "system" was not the result of the distortion or
misreading of debates that occurred elsewhere, but rather of a confluence of
factors. To trace some of them shows the limitations of an approach that
sees "local" and "international" settings as neatly separate. Rather, it seems
more pertinent to follow the traces of human trajectories in the midst of an
"international traffic in prostitution policy" in order to describe what took
place in Rio.[62] In this way, "productive misunderstandings" between dis-
similar actors can be properly highlighted, such as those produced in 1924
between the North American League of Nations researchers, local authorities, private organizations, madams, pimps, and prostitutes. They were
"productive" in the sense that, from these encounters, the contested out-
lines of the very idea of "traffic in women" emerged. In the meantime, the
terms under which these encounters took place were deeply connected to
the partly unintended results of the city's peculiar system of police
surveillance of prostitution and the sex workers – a policy that, despite its
"abolitionist" overtones, had a peculiarly "regulationist" effect giving way

61. "Matou a tiros"; "Matara a tiros a mulher que o repelira", *O Jornal*, 28 September 1927, p. 11.
The photos are from "Uma cena de sangue na rua Rodrigo [sic] dos Santos", *Gazeta de Notícias*,
27 September 1927, p. 4, and "A cena de sangue da rua Rodrigo [sic] dos Santos", *Gazeta de
Notícias*, 28 September 1927, p. 4.
62. The notion of "international traffic in prostitution policy" is from Laura Briggs, *Reproducing
Empire. Race, sex, science and U.S. imperialism in Puerto Rico* (Berkeley, CA, [etc.] 2002),
pp. 21–45.

Figure 3. Pictures of Hercília Maria Luz, Fanny Galper's tenant at least since 1923, and of José Ribeiro do Nascimento, her lover and murderer, in 1927, in his Army uniform. Both pictures are from the police column of *Gazeta de Notícias*, one of the most important carioca's daily newspapers. They could have been one of the many couples formed by Brazilian military men and Brazilian young prostitutes that P.K. and other contemporary observers found in the streets, in windows, and in the doorways of the Mangue's brothels in the 1920s.
Hercília's picture is from: "Uma cena de sangue na rua Rodrigo [sic] dos Santos", Gazeta de Notícias, 27 September 1927, p. 4. José's picture is from: "A cena de sangue da rua Rodrigo [sic] dos Santos", Gazeta de Notícias, 28 September 1927, p. 4.

to a situation of repressive tolerance. All that became sharply visible in the more marginal red-light district of the Mangue, where the poverty and precariousness seen by P.K., Thomashevsky, Rice, and other contemporary observers, contrasted with the fact that the area was a source of wealth and prosperity for people such as Fanny Galper. Just as a Brazilian journalist observed in 1930, the Mangue's sordidness tended to obscure that it offered more possibilities for striking it rich than elegant Lapa.[63] But these new economic opportunities for some white women cannot be fully grasped without understanding the context of prostitutes' displacements in the urban landscape and across wider spaces. In this way, a focus on work relations is also a way to address the spatial mobility of the persons

63. Ricardo Pinto, *Tráfico das brancas. Observações em torno dos cáftens franceses que vivem no Rio de* Janeiro (s.l., 1930), pp. 43–47.

involved – within an urban area, within the country, yet also across national borders. These experiences of mobility were all bundled in the Mangue and the lives of those working there. At the same time, they are closely connected to the variegated attempts at surveillance of sex work that characterized Rio de Janeiro in the 1920s, and which had multiple effects on the organization of the women's work relations in prostitution.

Translation: Bryan Pitts

IRSH 62 (2017), Special Issue, pp. 133–164 doi:10.1017/S0020859017000438
© 2018 Internationaal Instituut voor Sociale Geschiedenis

From the Streets to the Government: Socialist Militants and Labour Law in Brazil

ALDRIN A.S. CASTELLUCCI

Universidade do Estado da Bahia (UNEB)
Rodovia, Alagoinhas-Salvador, BR 110, KM 03
48.040-201, Alagoinhas, Bahia, Brazil

E-mail: acastellucci@uneb.br

BENITO B. SCHMIDT

Universidade Federal do Rio Grande do Sul (UFRGS)
Avenida Bento Gonçalves, 9500, Prédio 4331, sala 116
91.509-900, Porto Alegre, Rio Grande do Sul, Brazil

E-mail: bbissos@yahoo.com

ABSTRACT: This article analyses and compares the careers of a group of socialist militants who were active in several regions of Brazil in the final decades of the nineteenth century and the early twentieth century. It underscores their similarities and differences with a view to understanding the various ways of being a socialist in that context. This includes examining their wide-ranging activities, the main ideas they upheld, and their role in the development of Brazilian labour laws in the 1930s and 1940s.[1]

On 4 February 1931, Minister Lindolfo Collor was honoured with a lunch commemorating his forty-first birthday. He was the head of the Ministry of Labour, Industry and Commerce (Ministério do Trabalho, Indústria e Comércio – MTIC), which had been formed a few months earlier. The creation of that Ministry was one of the first acts of the "Revolution of 1930", which, using an anti-oligarchic and nationalist discourse, overthrew Brazil's First Republic (1889–1930) and installed Getúlio Vargas as president. Due to its importance, it was known as the "Ministry of the Revolution", and its aim was to create laws that would solve the "social

1. The authors of this article are supported by National Council for Scientific and Technological Development (CNPq), Brazil.

Figure 1. Lindolfo Collor is honoured with a birthday lunch, 4 February 1931. From left (seated): Evaristo de Moraes, Mário Ramos (3rd), Hermínia Collor, Lindolfo Collor and B. de Mello (7th); (standing): Bruno Lobo, Nascimento and Silva, Carlos Cavaco (5th), Horácio Carter (7th), Heitor Muniz (9th), Joaquim Pimenta (12th) and Agripino Nazareth (13th). *CPDOC/FGV Archives, used by permission.*

question" as well as to pacify Brazil's labour unions by offering substantial concessions and, at the same time, bringing them under the control of the state, thus eliminating tendencies considered "subversive", such as anarchism or communism.

In the photograph documenting his birthday tribute, Collor appears beside his wife, Hermínia, and is surrounded by his Ministry staff, including a number of socialist militants who had played an important role in the workers' movement in the last decades of the nineteenth century and the first decades of the twentieth (Figure 1): Evaristo de Moraes, Carlos Cavaco, Joaquim Pimenta, and Agripino Nazareth. Born between 1871 and 1886, they came from different states in Brazil – Rio de Janeiro, Rio Grande do Sul, Ceará, and Bahia, respectively – each with its own socio-political characteristics. All four men had a biography that included not only militancy, but also active and leading participation in strikes, mobilizations, and even attempted uprisings. How did these figures, who had not hesitated at times to get involved in radical political action, come to be at this place, serving as high-ranking officials to the new Minister? Of course, a trajectory from "activist" or even "street fighter" to "government bureaucrat" is nothing unusual in the history of the labour movements throughout the world, especially in the period spanning the late nineteenth century and the first decades of the twentieth century. What is remarkable in this case, however, is that these socialists were involved in a regime that, although professing a rhetoric of "revolution" and engaging in a series of social reforms, eventually veered to the right (giving way, in 1937, to the Estado Novo with its openly fascist leanings). Furthermore, these actors saw their different roles not as contradictory but in harmony with each other. At the same time, as peculiar as these trajectories were, these men should not be seen as overly exotic converters: Activists and proponents from other political-ideological currents (reformist unions, cooperative unions, Catholic unions, nationalist military personnel) supported the new regime as well (at least initially), especially the new model of relations between the state and the unions introduced after 1930. In this article, we will examine the careers of six socialists who had leading roles in regional context during the first decades of the twentieth century and who became involved in national politics after 1930, underscoring their differences and similarities in order to better understand the various and changing ways of being a socialist: their varied "styles" of doing political work, the main ideas they upheld, as well as their role in the development of Brazilian labour laws (which was one of the most important outcomes of the changes ushered in by the 1930 "revolution").

According to their opponents, particularly those among anarchists and communists, as well as some historians, the leading socialists during the First Republic (1889–1930) and particularly especially those playing a role in the new regime after 1930 were "sell-outs"; that is, people who collaborated with bourgeois governments and betrayed the workers' cause, especially the cause of revolution, in exchange for favours from the state. Following that line of interpretation – which, obviously, was based on the assumption that the "true" workers' movement was intrinsically revolutionary – the socialists had failed to provide a solid, viable political alternative for Brazilian workers during the Republic and after. The fact that major socialist leaders signed onto Vargas's project after 1930[2] supposedly confirmed that view by revealing their ideological weakness and opportunism vis-à-vis a regime that, despite its apparent friendliness towards workers and their demands, was essentially alien to their cause.[3] More

---

2. It should be stressed, however, that the term "project" and the common notion of *Varguismo* (or *Getulismo*, after Vargas' first name) presuppose a coherent political and ideological platform that did not exist in the early 1930s. Emerging successively over the years, the *Varguismo* "project" contains a high degree of hindsight knowledge, which, of course, was not available to many of these leading socialists at the time.

3. Such a view is, for instance, posited in: José Albertino Rodrigues, *Sindicato e desenvolvimento no Brasil* (São Paulo, 1968); and Leôncio Martins Rodrigues, *Conflito industrial e sindicalismo no Brasil* (São Paulo, 1966).

recently, however, several authors have shown that this interpretation falls short of the mark, demonstrating that numerous workers followed and identified with the Brazilian socialists and their orientation towards reform. These authors point to the fact that socialist activists exerted a strong influence on several unions, led major strikes, sometimes even uprisings, published newspapers that were widely read among workers, and sought to form a workers' party.[4]

This article argues that, by following the careers of some of these militants, we can gain a better understanding of their experiences and expectations. Methodologically, it connects to a longer research tradition in labour history of biographical studies, emphasizing in particular one of the advantages that such an approach offers: It can serve as a means to break with some of the historical and political stereotypes that emerged from a political history of ideas and organizations by pointing to the nuances, contradictions, and counterintuitive facts that are frequently found in individual biographies. While biographical studies are realised in several ways – from individual biographies, to biographical dictionaries, to prosopographic studies[5] – this article is inspired by a tradition that both reconstructs biographies in their individual particularity and attempts to gain wider results by comparing the trajectories of several actors (albeit a qualitative comparison, as such groups of actors would be too small and varied to attempt any kind of quantifying prosopographic analysis).[6] Thus, we wish to advance the following arguments: Firstly, that "socialism" in the Brazilian context was a label that could claim a certain ideological-political coherence and function as a realm of manifold political practices, especially in the different regions of the country. There were several ways of being a

---

4. Benito B. Schmidt, "Os partidos socialistas na nascente república", in Jorge Ferreira and Daniel Aarão Reis (eds), *As esquerdas no Brasil. A formação das tradições (1889–1945)* (Rio de Janeiro, 2007), pp. 131–183; Claudio Henrique de Moraes Batalha, *Le syndicalisme "amarelo" à Rio de Janeiro, 1906–1930* (Ph.D., Paris, Université de Paris I, 1986); Maria Cecília Velasco e Cruz, "Amarelo e negro. Matizes do comportamento operário na República Velha" (M.A., Rio de Janeiro, IUPERJ, 1981).

5. Claude Pennetier, "L'expérience du Dictionnaire biographique du mouvement ouvrier el la mémoire ouvrière", in *Mémoires des solidarités* (Ramonville Saint-Agne, 1997); Michel Dreyfus, Claude Pennetier, and Nathalie Viet-Depaule (eds). *La part des militants* (Paris, 1996); Dossiê "De l'usage de la biographie", *Le Mouvement Social*, 186, 1999.

6. Benito B. Schmidt, "Trajetórias e vivências. As biografias na historiografia do movimento operário brasileiro", *Projeto História*, (16), 1998, pp. 233–259; Benito B. Schmidt, "Que diferença faz? Os estudos biográficos na história do trabalho brasileira" in: Alexandre Fortes *et al.*, *Cruzando fronteiras. Novos olhares sobre a história do trabalho* (São Paulo, 2013), pp. 61–76; Claudio Henrique de Moraes Batalha, *Dicionário do movimento operário. Rio de Janeiro, do século XIX aos anos 1920 – militantes e organizações* (São Paulo, 2009); Regina Xavier, "Biografando outros sujeitos, valorizando outra história. Estudos sobre a experiência dos escravos", in Benito B. Schmidt (ed.), *O biográfico. Perspectivas interdisciplinares* (Santa Cruz do Sul, 2000), pp. 97–130.

socialist during Brazil's First Republic. Secondly, despite that diversity, the militants analysed here shared a number of ideas and had certain forms of intervening in common. Thirdly, for these activists, joining the Vargas regime was a conscious political choice that was consistent with their previous careers, and not a moment of "conversion", "renunciation", or even a "betrayal".

SOCIALISTS OF THE FIRST REPUBLIC: A GENERATION?

Although they were born in different states, came from diverse social backgrounds, lived in different cities, studied at various institutions, and practised their professions in a variety of settings, the paths of the six individuals analysed in this article crossed on several occasions, either physically or at least through ideas published in newspapers. They shared certain ideas and nurtured common political concerns, even if they disagreed about the course they should take at certain times. They sometimes joined forces with or distanced themselves from other activists from a wide range of political-ideological currents, getting involved in a variety of movements and taking on different commitments and positions over the course of time. In the following pages, we will provide a brief overview of their social backgrounds, education, and professional and political activities. In doing so, we address one of the standard questions that arises during the analysis of any group of actors, namely whether they belonged to the same "generation".[7]

Francisco Xavier da Costa was born on 3 December in the early 1870s (exact year is unknown), in Porto Alegre, the state capital of Rio Grande do Sul, the southernmost state in Brazil. At that time, Rio Grande do Sul was characterized by cattle raising, a relatively small number of slaves, and a strong presence of European immigrants. His father seems to have been one of the poor free black men who had fought in the Paraguayan War (1864–1870), and all indications are that his mother worked all her life within the domestic sphere. Francisco was racially categorized as *pardo* (of mixed ethno-racial ancestry) and must have encountered the racial and social barriers that limited the lives of free but low-income people of colour at the time. When he was eleven, his father died, and he had to go to work to

---

7. "Generation" is used here as coined by Karl Mannheim in 1928 and taken up, in different ways, by many after him, i.e. denoting a social group that is less defined by its age cohort and more by the fact that its individuals share certain social and political experiences. See: Karl Mannheim, "The Problem of Generations", in *idem*, Essays on the Sociology of Knowledge (London, 1952), pp. 276–322. For the use of "generation" as a heuristic concept in labour history, see, for instance: Claudine Attias-Donfut, "La notion de génération. Usages sociaux et concept sociologique", *L'homme et la societé*, 90:4 (1988), pp. 36–50; Hans Jaeger, "Generations in History: Reflections on a Controversial concept", *History and Theory: Studies in the Philosophy of History*, 24:3 (1985), pp. 273–292.

support his mother and sisters. He found a job as a lithographer's apprentice in a German-owned printing shop in Porto Alegre. While there, he learned his employers' and co-workers' language, which facilitated his access to newspapers published in German both in Europe and in Rio Grande do Sul, where there were large numbers of German-speaking immigrants, including socialists.[8]

Antonio Evaristo de Moraes was born the son of Basílio Antonio and Elisa Augusta de Moraes on 26 October 1871, in Rio de Janeiro, then the capital of the Brazilian Empire. From 1883 to 1886, he received a grant to complete his secondary education at Colégio São Bento, to which he later returned as a history teacher. He also worked as a journalist for the *Gazeta Nacional* and *Correio do Povo* newspapers. Thanks to those activities, he managed to support himself and his mother after his father abandoned the family in 1887. He practised as a lay lawyer for many years and gained a reputation as a criminal defence attorney before obtaining a Law degree in 1916. A *mestiço* (another of the categories indicating mixed ethno-racial ancestry), he had already taken part in the campaigns to abolish slavery and establish the Republic. While facing colour and class prejudice similar to that experienced by Xavier da Costa, he made himself publicly visible as a defender of the socialist cause in the press and in trade unions as well as the interests of individual workers at the courts.[9]

Custódio Carlos de Araújo, whose childhood nickname was "Cavaco", was born on 18 September 1878, in Santana do Livramento, located on the Brazil-Uruguay border. His father was a decorated soldier and, according to documents, his mother was a "housewife", who, after her husband's death, started to work as a seamstress to support her children. Cavaco joined the military at a very young age, but was forced to quit due to what was seen as his unruly, bohemian behaviour. He also devoted himself to literature, influenced by the revolutionary romanticism of Victor Hugo and the regionalism of the Argentinian José Hernández, who had developed a style and a set of themes attuned to the idiosyncrasies of the Rio de la Plata basin. Cavaco had a reputation as a distinguished orator, which helped advance his career as a lawyer. He arrived in the state's capital, Porto Alegre, in 1904, seeking to join the social circles of the local literary scene. During that period, he published his writings in books and newspapers.[10]

Agripino Nazareth was born on 24 February 1886, in Salvador, the capital of Bahia, a state that was very different from the aforementioned

---

8. Extensive biographical information on Francisco Xavier da Costa and Carlos Cavaco can be found in Benito B. Schmidt, *Em busca da terra da promissão. A história de dois líderes socialistas* (Porto Alegre, 2004).
9. On Evaristo de Moraes, cf. Joseli Maria Nunes Mendonça, *Evaristo de Moraes, Tribuno da República* (Campinas, 2007).
10. On Carlos Cavaco, cf. Schmidt, *Em busca da terra da promissão*.

Rio Grande do Sul: Located in the tropical north-east, its coastal regions had long been one of the centres of the slave-based production of sugar cane and other cash crops. Agripino Nazareth, too, was the son of a decorated Brazilian Army officer, while his mother was listed as homemaker. He studied law at universities in Recife, Rio de Janeiro, and São Paulo. In May 1911, he was appointed Chief of Police for the Department of Alto Juruá, in the territory of Acre, located in the Amazon region. He achieved this position thanks to his friendship with Pedro Avelino, a politician originally from the state of Rio Grande do Norte (located in the north-east of Brazil), who had been appointed Mayor in Alto Juruá.[11] The following year, he returned to Rio de Janeiro, then the nation's capital, and began working for the newspaper *A Época*[12] and teaching at the Free School of Law, Pharmacy, and Dentistry. It was through his contributions to *A Época*, that he engaged in a vigorous struggle with the representatives of the dominant oligarchies of Brazil. Meanwhile, he also established close ties with figures linked to the dissident elites.[13]

Maurício Paiva de Lacerda was born in Vassouras, Rio de Janeiro on 1 June 1888. His mother worked within the domestic sphere and his father was a lawyer and politician, who held several elected posts after the early years of the Republic, and later became a magistrate. Lacerda graduated from the Rio de Janeiro Law School in 1909. He and Agripino Nazareth (who obtained his Law degree in São Paulo in 1909) had been classmates in Rio. Lacerda was elected state congressman in 1910 and federal congressman in 1912, 1915, and 1918 as a member of the Fluminense (Rio de Janeiro State) Republican Party (Partido Republicano Fluminense), a party professing republican ideals winning numerous votes from workers, but which was dominated by Rio's agrarian elites. He held three elected offices simultaneously – congressman as well as city councilman (1913–1923) and Mayor (1915–1920) of the municipality of Vassouras (located in the interior of the state of Rio de Janeiro and at the time dominated by coffee production). He served as an elected city councilman of the Federal District (then the city of Rio

11. For documentary traces of this connection see: Registro de Diploma e Histórico de Agripino Nazareth, Arquivo da Faculdade de Direito da Universidade de São Paulo (São Paulo), Prontuário n. 5266; Agripino Nazareth, "Ao Povo Baiano", *Jornal de Notícias*, Salvador, 15 June 1919, pp. 3 and 5.

12. A daily published in Rio de Janeiro from 1912 until 1919 with an explicitly anti-oligarchic orientation campaigning especially against the senator Pinheiro Machado (from Rio Grande do Sul) and President Wenceslau Braz of the Partido Republicano Conservador (PRC).

13. On Agripino Nazareth, cf. Aldrin Armstrong Silva Castellucci, "Agripino Nazareth and the Workers' Movement in the First Republic", *Revista Brasileira de História*, 32:64 (2012), pp. 77–99, available at: http://dx.doi.org/10.1590/S0102-01882012000200006; last accessed 19 August 2017.

de Janeiro) whilst in prison in 1926,[14] and he was re-elected to the same post in 1928.[15]

Joaquim Pimenta was born on 13 January 1886 in Tauá, in the state of Ceará (located further north-east, with a predominantly agrarian economy, though it had never been one of the centres of slave-based plantation labour). The son of a "housewife" and an impoverished pharmacist and merchant, he was a sexton and began his studies under a priest-tutor. He moved to Fortaleza, the state capital, where he made a living from various forms of manual labour and teaching in a primary school. While in that city, he enrolled in the Law School, where he first came into contact with socialist ideas, questioned elements of his Catholic upbringing, and worked for several newspapers as an editor and contributor. In 1909, he moved to Recife, the capital of Pernambuco (historically, one of the prototypical areas of sugar cane plantations and slave labour), enrolling in the Recife Law School, an institution where, as we have seen, Agripino Nazareth had been enrolled for the first years of the same course of study. Pimenta graduated in 1910 and worked as the public prosecutor in Recife in 1911. He had to quit due to the political conflicts involving the dominant oligarchy and the opposition, which he had joined. He was appointed Secretary of the Public Education Inspectorate in 1912, and was a professor at the Law School in 1915. In the 1910s, he helped found trade unions and socialist parties, and was the main leader of the 1919 general strike in Recife. In 1924, he moved to Rio de Janeiro and became a commissioned civil servant in the Ministry of Justice during Artur Bernardes's presidential term (1922–1926). Bernardes governed in a state of siege and launched several campaigns to persecute Lacerda, Nazareth, and other socialists, as well as communist and anarchist activists.[16]

The figures analysed here were all born within a period of a little less than twenty years (from the early 1870s to 1888). Despite the significant chronological difference, they all went through circumstances that the

---

14. Maurício de Lacerda was arrested for two years for taking part in the unsuccessful military rebellion on 5 July 1924, in São Paulo, which, in turn, was directly related to the previous "18 of the Copacabana Fort Revolt" (Revolta dos 18 do Forte de Copacabana) of July 1922. Both insurrections mark the beginnings of *tenetismo* (from: *tenentes*, lieutenants), a movement of younger army officers that attempted to overturn the oligarchic republic and aimed at a series of social reforms. It was an important forerunner of the 1930 "revolution". Lacerda offered an account of the 1924 events in two books: *Entre duas revoluções* (Rio de Janeiro, 1927) and *História de uma covardia* (Rio de Janeiro, 1927).
15. For more information see the entry on Lacerda in: Robert Pechman, "Maurício de Lacerda", in Alzira Alves de Abreu *et al.* (eds), *Dicionário histórico-biográfico brasileiro pós-1930*, vol. III, (Rio de Janeiro, 2001), pp. 2993–2995.
16. For more information on Pimenta's trajectory see his autobiography: Joaquim Pimenta, *Retalhos do passado. Episódios que vivi e fatos que testemunhei* (Rio de Janeiro, 1949). Also see Sílvia Pantoja, "Joaquim Pimenta", in Alzira Alves de Abreu *et al.* (eds), *Dicionário histórico-biográfico brasileiro pós-1930*, vol. IV, (Rio de Janeiro, 2001), pp. 4618–4619.

French historian Jean-François Sirinelli has labelled as "inaugural",[17] i.e. formative experiences shared by the actors in question or events that have a fundamental long-term impact, also on those who were born shortly after the events themselves, such as the abolition of slavery (1888) and the proclamation of the Brazilian Republic (1889). Xavier da Costa, Moraes, and Cavaco (either young men or coming of age in the early republic) had high hopes for the new regime. They all became labour activists in the late nineteenth century and the first decade of the twentieth. Nazareth, Pimenta, and Lacerda, the younger members of the group, who had been born shortly before the end of the old regime, played a leading role in the workers' struggles during the early twentieth century, when the Republic was increasingly controlled by the "oligarchies", a term that was widely used at the time as a political denunciation and indicates the stable alliance between state elites and varying groups of landed property (of different regional origin and competing among each other).

Apart from their similarities, however, it is also important to stress the differences among then, especially their different social origins. Xavier da Costa and Moraes came from working-class or poor backgrounds, while Cavaco, Nazareth, Pimenta, and Lacerda were from more-or-less well-off middle-class groups. For Moraes, Cavaco, Nazareth, Pimenta, and Lacerda, a legal education was a key to their upward social mobility, bringing them into contact with new social ideas, allowing them to make a living, and to participate in politics. Xavier da Costa represents something of an exception in this regard: in his case, it was the profession of lithographer that offered him access to other milieus and ideas. In the case of the poorer of six, the death or absence of their father forced them to seek ways of making a living while they were still young. In terms of gender roles, however, they all appear to have grown up in conventional families, their fathers regarded as "breadwinners", working in the public sphere, and their mothers as "homemakers", working most of the time in the private space of their homes (unless their husbands died or abandoned the families).

With regard to Xavier da Costa and Moraes, it is important to note that both were of African descent and born before the abolition of slavery. This must have had a significant impact on their lives, not least their careers, which were marked by serious limitations and racial prejudice, on the one hand, and strenuous efforts to improve their social status on the other. Whatever the similarities and differences in their backgrounds and trajectories, the common generational position of the six socialists and their

---

17. Jean-François Sirinelli, "A geração", in Marieta de Moraes Ferreira and Janaína Amado (eds), *Usos e abusos da história oral* (Rio de Janeiro, 1996), pp. 131–137, 133.

involvement with the emerging labour movements meant that they shared similar concerns and agendas, marked, in many ways, by the attempt to transform the variegated social struggles and localized, often small-scale organizations into larger political projects.

WORKING WITH UNIONS AND FORMING POLITICAL PARTIES

The figures analysed here were politically socialized in an epoch in which "labour" in Brazil had already begun to constitute an actor in its own right, but in which no larger political parties claiming to represent labour existed yet. They thus devoted a good part of their activism to working with labour unions and attempting to form workers' parties that could elect candidates who should be genuine representatives of workers, capable of fighting for a better living and working conditions, while advancing the gradual and peaceful introduction of socialism – though not all socialists (both among the six analysed here and in general) opted for such gradualism, especially in the earlier years. The degree of radicalism in their words and actions varied considerably, determined to a great extent by the circumstances, i.e. by the political environment in the region they were active in and the opposition they encountered from the dominant classes and the state. Therefore, on some occasions, they went so far as to support violence as a means of overthrowing capitalism. Until the mid-1920s, their main competitor within the labour movement were different currents of anarchism, which were also seeking to influence the unions, but which rejected party politics as a form of political struggle, preferring direct action, general strikes, and the (self-) education of workers in terms of a rationalist worldview.

The six protagonists thus acted in a world marked by a myriad of smaller organizations that had manifold overlaps among them, yet no central point of crystallization, despite some unsuccessful attempts to establish genuinely national organizations. Each region saw a specific "mix" of traditions and organizations, often greatly shaped by the presence of communities of European immigrants, but also the regional socioeconomic structure. Rio Grande do Sul was a typical case in this regard. Xavier da Costa, for example, from the last decade of the nineteenth century, took part in organizations representing typographers, as well as socialist-inspired associations such as the Liga Operária Internacional (International Workers' League, 1895) and the Partido Socialista do Rio Grande do Sul (Rio Grande do Sul Socialist Party, 1897). He was one of the leaders of the Congresso Operário do Rio Grande do Sul (Rio Grande do Sul Workers' Congress), which, for a limited time in 1898, and in a political project quite remarkable in comparison with the labour history of most other countries, brought together socialists and anarchists.[18] After a period of decline caused by internal disputes, the Porto Alegre workers' movement reorganized in 1905, through the formation of the Partido Operário Rio-Grandense (Rio Grande Workers' Party), of which Xavier da Costa was one of the leaders. The party's manifesto is a document of a continued (and quite intriguing) compromise between anarchist and socialist ideas: it did not advocate taking over the state, but it did call for the participation of "true" representatives of the workers in its operations and decisions. With such a strategy, the document explained, Brazil could avoid a violent solution to social problems, similar to what had taken place in Europe.[19] During that period, Xavier da Costa enjoyed much prestige among the city's numerous labour associations (including both union organizations and more political projects), such as the Confederação Obreira (Worker's Confederation), of which he was president, and the União dos Trabalhadores em Madeira (Wood Workers' Union) and the União dos Empregados em Padaria (Bakery Employees' Union), in which he was considered a "moral authority".[20] He was later involved in further (but, again, short-lived) attempts to launch higher-level and unifying workers' associations such as the Partido Socialista de Porto Alegre (Porto Alegre Socialist Party, 1908) and the Confederação Geral dos Trabalhadores (General Confederation of Workers, 1911).

Further north, in Rio de Janeiro, it was a similar story for Evaristo de Moraes. By 1890, he had helped found the Partido Operário Nacional (National Workers' Party), created in Rio de Janeiro under the leadership of the typographer Luiz da França e Silva. Since at least 1903, Moraes had used the pages of the *Correio da Manhã* newspaper to deliver a staunch defence of the right to strike and organize trade unions, as well as the need for labour laws in Brazil.[21] During that time, he also worked as a lawyer for unions of shoemakers, coachmen, and carters, and several categories of

18. The proximity between advocates of socialist and anarchist ideas during the congress in Porto Alegre in 1898 might be explained by the fact that the labour movement in general and the circulation of socialist and anarchist theoretical and programmatic texts in Brazil were still in their infancy at that time. There were some disagreements in the congress, yet they were resolved in its final resolutions. For instance, the socialists suggested the foundation of a socialist party, obviously refused by the anarchists. The congress, therefore, opted for a general formulation highlighting the event's "socialist nature". *Gazetinha*, Porto Alegre, 6 January 1898, p. 2. This shows the degree to which the word "socialism" had a broader meaning at that time, encompassing all trends in the local workers movement. In the first decades of the twentieth century, however, the relatively good relationship between the two political trends would come to an end, giving way to deep ruptures and harsh disputes.

19. "Manifesto do Partido Operário ao operariado do Rio Grande do Sul", *A Democracia*, Porto Alegre, 1 May 1905, pp. 2–3.

20. Schmidt, *Em busca da terra da promissão*, pp. 145–153.

21. His collected articles for the *Correio da Manhã*, a daily in Rio published since 1901 and known for its critical stance vis-à-vis presidential power, were republished in 1905 as: Evaristo de Moraes, *Apontamentos de direito operário* (São Paulo, 1998 [1905]).

workers in the Rio de Janeiro port complex, helping release several workers who had been arrested for taking part in mobilizations.[22]

Meanwhile, in Bahia, a Labour Party (Partido Operário da Bahia) was founded in 1890 which, having been renamed the Labour Centre of Bahia (Centro Operário da Bahia) in 1893, was able to gather thousands of workers; under its banner dozens of justices of the peace and councillors were elected in Salvador until 1919.[23] From 1919 on, Nazareth became the main socialist leader in the state and played a key role in the process of organizing labour unions and establishing more stable political representations among Bahian workers, particularly the Federação dos Trabalhadores Baianos (Federation of Bahian Workers) that was founded in 1920, an umbrella organization that included sixteen unions and over 25,000 members. Not untypically for labour movement organizations in different countries of Latin America in the years after 1917, both of anarchist and socialist orientation, one of the federation's documents demanded the recognition of the Soviet Union – serving as an indicator for the prestige that the "first proletarian state" enjoyed among organized workers of different persuasion during the 1920s.[24] That same year, Nazareth founded the Partido Socialista Baiano (Bahian Socialist Party) and ran for election as its candidate for the Federal House of Representatives, while Maurício de Lacerda was the same party's candidate for the Senate. The political platform of the Partido Socialista Baiano was similar to those of other labour movement organizations of that kind created during the First Republic, propagating a programme that was remarkably radical in comparison to similar documents by socialist parties in Europe or North America. It contained the following points, among others: the socialization of commerce, major industries, and all means of transportation; the introduction of a minimum wage; the abolition of all indirect taxes, and a progressive taxation on incomes of over six million *réis* per year; the right to vote for women and soldiers,[25] and a reform of the laws on tenancy and eviction.[26]

22. For his role in the activities of port workers see: Maria Cecília Velasco e Cruz, "Cor, etnicidade e formação de classe no porto do Rio de Janeiro. A Sociedade de Resistência dos Trabalhadores em Trapiche e Café e o conflito de 1908", in *Revista USP*, 68 (2005–2006), pp. 188–209, esp. pp. 197–201.

23. Aldrin A. S. Castellucci, "Política e cidadania operária em Salvador (1890–1919)", *Revista de História* (USP), 162 (2010), pp. 205–241, available at: http://dx.doi.org/10.11606/issn.2316-9141. v0i162p205-241; last accessed 19 August 2017.

24. "Coluna Operária", *A Tarde*, Salvador, 16 July 1920, p. 2.

25. A male universal suffrage was established in Brazil by 1890 for all men of twenty-one years and older. Any restrictions based on income were explicitly prohibited. However, certain, sometimes highly exclusionary restrictions applied. For instance, non-literate persons, soldiers, vagrants, convicts, or others who had been stripped of their personal freedoms were barred from political rights.

26. "Coluna Operária – As primeiras resoluções do Partido Socialista", A Tarde, Salvador, 24 August 1920, p. 3; "Coluna Operária – A segunda reunião do Partido Socialista", A Tarde, Salvador, 27 August 1920, p. 3.

Like Nazareth in Bahia, Pimenta was involved in the organization or reorganization of several labour unions, represented some as a lawyer, and founded short-lived socialist parties in the states of Pernambuco, Alagoas, and Paraíba (all located in the coastal north-east of Brazil). In 1921, intervening in a Rio newspaper about one of the pressing issues debated in the labour movement at the time (in favour of or against the formation of political parties and the participation in elections), Nazareth connected his pro-position with both an international comparison to Argentina and a regionalist stance accusing, from the point of view of a more advanced "periphery" (the northeastern states) the ignorance of the "centre" (Rio). Workers in the capital of the Republic, he wrote, would be making a serious mistake if they remained "indifferent" to the "advancing provincial proletariat", especially in the north-east, and continued to be "restricted to union activities, which are insufficient, in and of themselves, to benefit the surge of demands" that could "be addressed while the bourgeois regime is still in power". He said that it was essential for workers to participate in elections, because political activity made it possible to elect lawmakers who were committed to the workers' cause (as in the case of Argentina, he believed) and bring about social reforms within the capitalist regime without losing the prospect of building a socialist society.[27] This was, of course, an overt criticism of the anarchists and revolutionary syndicalists, who, at the time, had a dominant position in Rio's labour movement.[28]

In mid-1921, four of the six socialists analysed here – Nazareth, Moraes, Pimenta, and Lacerda – joined forces with Nicanor do Nascimento, Everardo Dias, and Afonso Schmidt to found the Brazilian Clarté Group, the "International of Thought" initiated in 1919 by Henri Barbusse as an anti-war organization of progressive intellectuals.[29] There is no space here to recount in detail how the trajectories of these four socialists crossed paths, but it is clear that their contact and collaboration had been going on for longer and was based on a shared inclination towards a rather left-wing socialist stance, above all advocating the foundation of parties. They saw themselves as "reformers" within the movement and their activities culminated on 1 May 1925, when Nazareth and Moraes spearheaded the founding in Rio de Janeiro of the Partido Socialista do Brasil (Socialist Party of Brazil, hereafter, PSB). Moraes was entrusted with writing the Manifesto-Programme, which was published in and commented on by virtually all of

---

27. Agripino Nazareth, "O Socialismo na Argentina. Necessidade da organização política do proletariado brasileiro", *Hoje*, Rio de Janeiro, 31 March 1921, pp. 1–2.
28. Also see Claudio Batalha's contribution in this Special Issue.
29. Michael Hall and Paulo Sérgio Pinheiro, "O grupo Clarté no Brasil. Da Revolução nos espíritos ao Ministério do Trabalho", in Antonio Arnoni Prado (ed.), *Libertários no Brasil. Memória, lutas, cultura* (São Paulo, 1986), pp. 251–287.

the country's major newspapers. The Manifesto appealed to the "living forces" of society, especially the "proletarian classes". The plural in "proletarian classes" is noteworthy as it indicates sensitivity among Brazilian socialists for the country's multi-layered and ethno-racially fragmented characteristic of the working class. The manifesto called on these "proletarian classes" to join a "party organization that, with frank socialist ideas", sought to "achieve true democracy", which, according to the document, the contemporary Republic was about to turn away from. The socialists advocated the need for a process of "administrative recentralization" with the aim of dissolving the oligarchies, attacking their control of public resources, and the "mockery of direct universal suffrage", which resulted in a regime that lacked "legitimate representatives" or "worthy representees".[30] Moreover, the Party stated that it was willing to obey the Constitution of 1891 regarding the separation of Church and State, in addition to promoting basic, vocational, and higher education. Within the sphere of "reforms of an essentially economic nature" that were achievable before the "radical transformation" of capitalism, the PSB undertook to fight for the "establishment of direct, sole, and progressive taxation of the incomes of all able-bodied individuals"; "the limitation, through indirect means, of large land ownership"; "the officialization of the banking industry[31] with a view to suppressing money-lending, the foreign exchange game, and an unconvertible currency"[32]; "restricting the right to property ownership by foreign collective persons" who were not committed to the "provision of services of public utility proportional to their possessions and profits in the country"; introducing a public "insurance against all social risks"; "limiting the profits of industry and commerce, with the consequent suppression of usury"; a state monopoly of land, sea, river, and air transport services, as well as the ports, roads, electric power, mines, etc., and encouraging and supporting cooperatives. In other words, both in political and economic terms, the new socialist party appeared to advocate a peculiar mix of demands for reform, many of them quite radical in their nature, and a revolutionary outlook (however attenuated in tone). As to the international arena, the PSB declared its commitment to combating "militarism" (*armamentismo*) in all its forms and fostering "sincere unity among all peoples" and the "solidarity of the South American Republics" with a view to forming a "Confederation" of those countries. It also promised to "advocate the recognition of the Soviet Republic", which,

---

30. These and the following quotes are taken from: "Um novo partido político. Como se apresenta à nação o Partido Socialista do Brasil", *O Brasil*, Rio de Janeiro, 1 May 1925, p. 7.

31. "Officialization" (*oficialização*) in the jargon of the time meant nationalization of the banking system.

32. Curiously, it is not clear, from this and other documents, whether the PSB was in favour of a convertible currency, or whether they wanted to suppress any attempt to have a convertible currency.

in 1925, when communists and socialists in other regions of the world had already parted ways, was a remarkable statement.

The Party also emphasized the need for "propaganda among unions", clearly stating that all its members should join "professional unions". In an argument that once again manifested the currency of anarchist and syndicalist ideas in the Brazilian labour movement, yet which also made the potentially corporatist leanings of syndicalism visible, the document stressed that unions were bodies that would produce the "elements for an electoral reform based on a representation by classes".[33] Later, in the 1930s, Vargas would – echoing similarly ambiguous overlapping zones between certain syndicalist concepts and fascists ideas, especially in Italy – selectively appropriate such arguments when establishing his explicitly corporatist regime and the labour laws that would be associated with it.

The PSB continued to disseminate its ideas through "Propaganda Lectures" held between October and December 1925 at the Free University of Rio de Janeiro. The speaker was Evaristo de Moraes, who explained that the PSB was not "exclusively a workers' party," but an organization aimed at the "solution of the problem of wage labour, without overlooking other social and economic problems". Furthermore, Moraes stressed his adherence to what he called, after the well-known current in late nineteenth-century France, "possibilist socialism", accepting "reforms and institutions" that could "improve the living conditions of the working classes" under capitalism, "raising them up on the material level and the intellectual level". Pointing to the importance that leading Brazilian socialists attributed to the law in general and labour laws in particular, he made clear that, unlike anarchism, his kind of socialism did not see anything "noxious" in "the so-called *labour laws*". He argued that state intervention in relations between capital and labour was positive and necessary as an antidote to the influence of "propagandists of violent action, which is not always advisable and does not always achieve appreciable results", and as an alternative to the economic damage caused by strikes and lockouts.[34]

These more moderate statements by Evaristo de Moraes contrast quite sharply with the radicalism of the party's foundational declarations. This might

---

33. *O Brasil*, Rio de Janeiro, 1 May 1925, p. 7.
34. "Partido Socialista. Conferências de Propaganda", *Correio da Manhã*, Rio de Janeiro, 7 October 1925, p. 3; "Conferências Socialistas", *Idem*, 8 October 1925, p. 7; "Terceira Conferência do Sr. Evaristo de Moraes", *Idem*, 22 October 1925, p. 6; "As conferências do Partido Socialista", *Idem*, 24 October 1925, p. 8; "As conferências do Partido Socialista", *Idem*, 25 October 1925, p. 2; "O curso público do Partido Socialista do Brasil", *Idem*, 26 November 1925, p. 5; "Partido Socialista do Brasil", *Idem*, 4 December 1925, p. 2; "As conferências públicas do Partido Socialista do Brasil", *Idem*, 23 December 1925, p. 5; "As conferências públicas do Partido Socialista do Brasil", *Idem*, p. 8; "A questão social no Brasil. O curso encetado pelo Partido Socialista na Universidade do Rio", *O Combate*, São Paulo, 14 October 1925, pp. 1 and 4.

be explained, on the one hand, with the need for the socialists to position themselves as more attuned to local realities than their new competitor, the Partido Comunista do Brasil (Communist Party of Brazil), created in 1922 by a group of former anarchists.[35] As was to be expected, the young communist party sharply criticised the socialists for what they considered a reformist accommodation with the political system and the existing socioeconomic regime. Confronted with this critique, Evaristo de Moraes highlighted his gradualism all the more, stating that he had always preferred "a peaceful solution, political intervention, slowly gaining positions or, at least, influence over legislative bodies and elections".[36] On the other hand, the moderation in tone as well as the emphasis on the need for political organization and to involve workers in the electoral process had a clear objective: the elections of the Rio de Janeiro City Council and, at the same time, the president and vice-president of Brazil, scheduled for 1 March 1926. Evaristo de Moraes and Maurício de Lacerda stood as candidates representing the working class for the first and second districts of Rio de Janeiro, respectively.[17] In the end, only Lacerda managed to get elected, not least due to the strong opposition by the established elites and the repressive behaviour by the authorities.

In 1927, pressurized by the Third International and trying to get around the ban on their party imposed by authorities, the PCB invited Maurício de Lacerda, Azevedo Lima, and the PSB to form a tactical alliance. The idea was to take part in the 1927 federal elections with a common platform that demanded laws protecting workers and the establishment of diplomatic relations with the Soviet Union. While the socialists rejected the communists' appeals to form a united front (which the latter took as an hostile act), the PCB candidates to the National Congress were João Batista de Azevedo Lima, a physician who managed to get elected as a federal congressman, and the printing industry worker João da Costa Pimenta, who failed to get enough votes.[37]

In relation to one of their main goals – forming a socialist party for the whole of Brazil – the socialists analysed in this article had, by the late 1920s, both succeeded and failed: A party of relevance had been founded, enabling the socialists to realize some of the ambitions related to it

---

35. On the PCB foundation and its early years, see Edgard Carone, *O P.C.B. –Vol. 1: 1922–1943* (São Paulo, 1982); Dulce Pandolfi, *Camaradas e companheiros. História e memória do PCB* (Rio de Janeiro, 1995), chs 3–4.

36. "A política e o operariado", *Correio da Manhã*, Rio de Janeiro, 29 January 1926, p. 4.

37. On the "united front" proposed by the communists and the elections see "Ensaios de frente única. Os blocos operários (1927, 1928, 1929)", in Paulo Sérgio Pinheiro and Michael Hall (eds), *A classe operária no Brasil. Documentos (1889–1930), vol. 1 – O movimento operário* (São Paulo, 1979), pp. 290-297; Also see the autobiographical memoirs of a central figure of Brazilian communism: Octavio Brandão, *Combates e batalhas, vol. 1 – Memórias* (São Paulo, 1978), pp. 319, 349–354.

(participating in elections, getting representatives voted, influencing the law-making process). Yet, this party had only been founded in 1925, relatively late in comparison to European developments, but also to other countries in Latin America, especially Argentina, and at a moment when, with the Communist Party, a small but relevant competitor had already arisen. At the same time, anarchist traditions remained strong among many workers. Moreover, the socialists faced multiple kinds of state repression as well as fraudulent practices in elections. These factors combined, on the one hand, to give the socialists a certain standing both in the labour movement and the mainstream political scene. On the other, they frustrated many of the hopes the leading figures had associated with the foundation of the party – which might explain why, only a few years later, they would become directly involved with the state in such a smooth way when the "revolution" of 1930 offered the opportunity to do so. However, this account of a swift integration and assimilation into the state's apparatus can eclipse the more contradictory earlier experience of radical interventions and direct activism that several of them shared.

STRIKES AND UPRISINGS

Before going into further detail about the doings of the six socialists after 1930, it is worth remembering some of their interventions and activities in an earlier period when they actively took part in several strikes and (attempted) uprisings, sometimes as leaders, and at others as mediators. Those experiences, particularly the mediation of conflicts between employers and workers, were key in building up a political capital that later was brought to bear, when, in the 1930s, Brazilian labour law was being formulated and several strikes erupted demanding the effective implementation of the rights achieved. It should also be stressed that each of the six socialists analysed here exhibited quite different degrees of radicalism in their statements and actions during these strikes and other mobilizations, something that was not only due to individual political "style", but also the regional context with its different levels of elite opposition and state repression.

In August 1906, thousands of workers staged the first general strike in Porto Alegre. Their main demand was an eight-hour work day. As the movement developed, the rivalries between anarchists and socialists, which had marked the local labour movement already for quite some time, grew even stronger, as both groups vied to lead the strike. During that conflict, the Federação Operária do Rio Grande do Sul (Workers' Federation of Rio Grande do Sul, FORGS) was initially led by the socialists (later it became dominated by supporters of revolutionary syndicalism). The strike ended in an agreement between the employers and some of the workers, mediated by Xavier da Costa, for a nine-hour work day.[38] As Da Costa had to admit later on in an article in *A Democracia*, the agreement was soon broken.[39]

The initiation of Custódio de Araújo ("Cavaco") into socialist activism probably took place through Xavier da Costa, who introduced him into the circle of those leading the 1906 strike. The press at the time stressed his fiery oratory, capable of mobilizing large crowds. At a rally, he advised them to put up physical resistance "[...] to the demands of the exploiting potentates", and "[...] if necessary, to set up barricades in the streets, [for] he was willing to die beside his rifle for the proletarian cause".[40]

For their parts, Agripino Nazareth and Maurício de Lacerda made their first major public appearances in Rio in late 1915 and early 1916 – much later than Xavier da Costa, Moraes, and Cavaco in Porto Alegre – when they took part in a thwarted mutiny of enlisted men and sergeants in the Army, Navy, Police, and Fire Brigade of Rio de Janeiro with the stated objective of deposing the president and establishing a parliamentary republic in Brazil. Workers were supposed to be mobilized as well to generate a broad uprising. *A Época*, the newspaper for which Nazareth had been a key player since 1912, was intended to be the main channel of communication with the workers. However, the conspiracy was discovered and foiled due to police infiltration.[41]

In 1917, a wave of strikes and mobilizations broke out in several Brazilian cities that would continue well into 1918 and 1919. It had its local backgrounds and reasons, but it was also clearly related to the international revolutionary wave triggered by the Russian Revolution.[42] Some of the common demands were the eight-hour work day, the abolition of child labour, equal pay for men and women performing the same jobs, and wage increases. Agripino Nazareth was deeply involved in these mobilizations (both as organizer and commenting journalist). However, while many

---

38. On the 1906 general strike, see Benito B. Schmidt, *De mármore e de flores. A primeira greve geral do Rio Grande do Sul (Porto Alegre, outubro de 1906)* (Porto Alegre, 2005).
39. "Operários, alerta! Querem anular a redução do labor diário à medida de nove horas! Preparemo-nos!", *A Democracia*, Porto Alegre, 15 December 1906, pp. 1–2.
40. *Petit Journal*, Porto Alegre, 24 September 1906, p. 2.
41. "Os sargentos do Exército e o general Bittencourt", *A Época*, Rio de Janeiro, 8 December 1915, p. 1; "O caso dos sargentos. O inquérito militar policial prossegue", *Idem*, 21 December 1915, p. 1; "Conspiração que fracassa", *A Notícia*, Rio de Janeiro, 6 April 1916, pp. 1–2; "O fato do dia. A conspiração", *Correio da Manhã*, Rio de Janeiro, 8 April 1916, pp. 3–4; "A conspiração", *Idem*, 12 April 1916, p. 3; "A conspiração", *Idem*, 27 April 1916, p. 3; "A última conspiração", *Idem*, 23 May 1916, p. 3.
42. Christina Roquette Lopreato, *O Espírito da revolta. A greve geral anarquista de 1917* (São Paulo, 2000); Luigi Biondi, "A greve geral de 1917 em São Paulo e a imigração italiana. Novas perspectivas", *Cadernos AEL*, 15:27 (2009), pp. 261–308; César Augusto Bubolz Queirós, "*Desvarios anarquistas na Rússia rio-grandense". As grandes greves na Primeira República (1917– 1919)* (Manaus, 2016).

activists fully embraced a revolutionary outlook during these feverish days, Nazareth was prone to point to the parliamentary level as well, for instance in an article in which he commented ironically on President Wenceslau Braz's (1914–1918) sudden interest in social issues; such novel curiosity, he declared, stood in flagrant contradiction to the opposition presented by the government and its allies to all of the bills on worker protection that Congressman Maurício de Lacerda had introduced to Congress that year.[43] In November 1918, Agripino Nazareth got involved in yet another conspiracy in Rio de Janeiro, joining forces with several libertarian leaders to establish a Republic of Workers and Soldiers in Brazil. However, once again due to infiltration, government forces disrupted the movement at an early stage, closed down some trade unions, arrested many workers, and prosecuted several anarchist and socialist leaders, including Agripino Nazareth.[44]

In June of the following year, Nazareth, who had moved back to his native state Bahia, fleeing the Rio de Janeiro police,[45] led approximately 50,000 artisans and workers, primarily Afro-descendants, in the state's first general strike. Virtually all the city's workshops, manufacturers, and factories shut down. Bakers, stevedores, dock porters, and transport, power, public lighting, and telephone workers also walked off the job. On behalf of the Central Strike Committee, Nazareth drafted a detailed memorandum for the government and employers, which basically contained the same demands as the previous wave of 1917 strikes.[46] This general strike was victorious in terms of the demands conceded by the government and employers. The momentum of the first general strike and the role Nazareth played in it were so powerful that as early as June 1919, thousands of workers from a wide range of sectors staged fresh strikes in the interior and capital of the state, reiterating the same demands. In September, 8,000 textile workers from Salvador rose up again under the leadership of Nazareth and the Sociedade União Geral dos Tecelões da Bahia (General Union Society of Textile Workers of Bahia, SUGTB), this time to maintain the achievements of the

---

43. Agripino Nazareth, "Aos operários", *O Debate*, Rio de Janeiro, 26 July 1917, p. 3.
44. Carlos Augusto Addor, *A Insurreição Anarquista no Rio de Janeiro* (Rio de Janeiro, 1986).
45. Agripino Nazareth was arrested at least three times: The first imprisonment occurred in January 1921, for leading workers strikes in a textile factory and a stevedores strike at the Salvador port. He was held incommunicado for two days and expelled from Bahia to Rio de Janeiro, where he immediately resumed his militancy. The other imprisonments were during the 5 July 1922 and 5 July 1924 military rebellions. An account of his arrests is given in: Agripino Nazareth, "Bolchevistas de ópera cômica (Resposta ao Partido Comunista do Brasil)", *Vanguarda*, Rio de Janeiro, 5 April 1926, p. 1.
46. On the 1919 general strike in Salvador, see Aldrin A.S. Castellucci, "Flutuações econômicas, crise política e greve geral na Bahia da Primeira República", *Revista Brasileira de História*, 25:50 (2005), pp. 131–166, available at: http://dx.doi.org/10.1590/S0102-01882005000200006; last accessed 19 August 2017.

general strike. It is interesting to note (and tells a lot about the limitations of insight and intellectual comprehension of the opponents of the left) that, in some press articles, Nazareth was accused of being influenced by the "subversive ideas" of the British writer William Godwin, as well as the Russian revolutionary theorists Mikhail Bakunin and Vladimir Ilyich Lenin.[47]

In another locale, Joaquim Pimenta led a successful general strike in Recife during that same period. This mobilization, however, had a different character, combining social issues with a nationalist stance: The walkout had been initiated by the union of employees of Pernambuco Tramways, a company that was in British possession. It responded to the workers' demands by sacking all the union leaders. Pimenta gave his speeches a strong anti-imperialist note, and won avowals of sympathy not only from the mainstream media, but the government itself, which did not order any police action to suppress the strike. Finding themselves isolated, the employers conceded to workers' demands for better working conditions and wages.[48]

These examples of the involvement of the six socialists in strikes and even uprisings highlight how pointedly militant their action could be under certain circumstances. When these leading socialists entered ministerial offices after 1930, those experiences were not undone or negated, but, at least from the point of view of the protagonists themselves, brought to bear in the context of elaborating the extensive (and, in international comparison, exceptional) body of Brazilian labour laws.

IN THE MINISTRY'S OFFICES WITHOUT LEAVING THE STREETS

Francisco Xavier da Costa, born already in the early 1870s and thus the oldest of the six socialists, constitutes a somewhat special case: He does not appear in the photograph mentioned at the beginning of this article depicting the Labour Minister Lindolfo Collor and his aides (among them several of the socialists at the centre of this article). The reason for this absence is that Francisco Xavier da Costa had already long been involved in what his opponents (and even he, for some time) called "bourgeois politics".

He seems to have become disenchanted with the political and organizational state of the labour movement at the end of the first decade of the twentieth century, especially the electoral failure of the numerous, but ephemeral attempts to found (local) socialist parties. In 1911, he therefore joined the Partido Republicano Rio-Grandense (Rio Grande Republican

---

47. "O maximalismo na Bahia", *Diário de Notícias*, Salvador, 5 September 1919, pp. 1 and 7.
48. See the description of the events by the rather controversial US-American historian John W.F. Dulles, *Anarquistas e comunistas no Brasil (1900–1935)* (São Paulo, 1977), pp. 81–82.

Party, PRR), which had been the dominant party in the state of Rio Grande do Sul since the beginning of the Republic, and he was elected city councilman in Porto Alegre. The PRR mostly adhered to positivism (in its Brazilian adoption),[49] the main ideological strand of some local elite sectors in the young republic who considered themselves "progressive". Following August Comte's call for an integration of the modern proletariat, the republicans gave increasing attention to the "social question" and sought support from the workers' and representatives of the emerging labour movement.[50] The other factor that drove a certain perceptiveness for workers' concerns, giving the socialists room to negotiate and bargain, was the competition between the two main parties in Rio Grande do Sul at the time, the republicans and the federalists (a constellation that could be found, *mutatis mutandis*, in several of the Brazilian states).

The social policy of the state's government, following the outlook of the republicans and their positivist ideals, was based on two complementary principles: support from the executive branch for certain demands from the workers' movement (shorter work days, wage increases, and so on) and state mediation of conflicts between employers and employees – principles that, as we will see, were also the basis of the official policies of the federal state after 1930.[51] Furthermore, both socialists and positivists drank from the font of the pseudo-scientific and evolutionist culture characteristic of the time, which emphasized the need for a "moral regeneration" of society.[52] These commonalities might have contributed to the "defection" of Xavier da Costa to the republicans; yet, all indications are that he was not fully co-opted by his new party or the state's government (at least not in terms of becoming ideologically entirely assimilated), but rather saw it as a continuation of his earlier activities by other, more official means. In that

49. Positivist ideas had a relatively strong following in Brazil since the last decades of the Empire of Brazil, when a republican movement was beginning to form, especially among some sectors of the intelligentsia and the Brazilian Army. The most valued positivist concepts among these groups were scientism, evolutionism, and the notion that progress should occur as a gradual process without social ruptures ("Order and progress" is the Brazilian flag's motto, designed and adopted at the beginning of the First Republic in 1889). However, positivism was not the official ideology in most of the states, except for Rio Grande do Sul, where it was the basis of a local Republican Party's project. For further information: Hélgio Trindade (ed.), *O Positivismo. Teoria e prática* (Porto Alegre, 2007), pp. 193–227; and Céli Pinto, *Positivismo. Um projeto político alternativo (RS 1889–1930)* (Porto Alegre, 1986).
50. Nelson Boeira, "O Rio Grande de Augusto Comte", in José Hildebrando Dacanal and Sergius Gonzaga (eds), *RS. Cultura e ideologia* (Porto Alegre, 1993), pp. 34–59.
51. On the genealogy of social policies in Brazil and its origins in Rio Grande do Sul, see Alfredo Bosi, "A arqueologia do Estado-providência: sobre um enxerto de ideias de longa duração", in Hélgio Trindade (ed.), *O Positivismo. Teoria e prática*, pp. 193–227.
52. Benito B. Schmidt, "O Deus do progresso. A difusão do cientificismo no movimento operário gaúcho da I República", *Revista Brasileira de História*, 21:41 (2001), pp. 113–126, available at: http://dx.doi.org/10.1590/S0102-01882001000200006; last accessed 19 August 2017.

sense, his trajectory is less of an exception compared to the other five socialists analysed here than it might appear at first sight, as they saw their own biographical turns in a similar way. Moreover, Da Costa, like the other protagonists in this story, combined his government activities with activism in the streets, in the press, and in conjunction with workers' associations. For instance, he directed the *Gazeta do Povo* and *O Inflexível* newspapers, in which he both defended the PRR interests and demanded rights for workers. He was also a "union columnist" for *Correio do Povo*, then the most important newspaper in Rio Grande do Sul. In these years, he also acted as of co-founder of numerous unions and played an active role in several mutual aid organizations, cooperatives, etc.[53] These activities reveal the degree of Xavier da Costa's continuing connections to and influence on the local labour movement.

The Aliança Liberal (Liberal Alliance), the political front for which Getúlio Vargas ran as a candidate for the presidency of Brazil in 1930 (an electoral contention that led to the "revolution" of 1930), had a platform that included several proposals aimed at improving workers' living and working conditions, which led some of the protagonists of this article to give it their support. For example, Xavier da Costa saw the victory of that group as a means of achieving the ideal nurtured by Brazilian socialists since the end of the nineteenth century: the construction of a "true" Republic that was to be very different from the disappointing regime installed in 1889, one that was aware of the labour question and willing to bring the interests of employers into "harmony" with those of the workers. Agripino Nazareth also joined the Aliança Liberal's campaign. At one point, the newspaper *Correio da Manhã* reported him as arguing in one of his speeches that workers "from all categories" should vote for Vargas because his programme "offers the material improvements that the working classes will obtain from his government".[54] In fact, not only Nazareth, but also Moraes, Lacerda, and Pimenta spoke at rallies of the Aliança Liberal's rallies in as many as nine different states (Alagoas, Amazonas, Bahia, Ceará, Minas Gerais, Pará, Pernambuco, Rio Grande do Norte, and Rio de Janeiro).[55]

---

53. He co-founded the União dos Operários Estivadores (Stevedores Trade Union), in 1919, the União dos Trabalhadores em Trapiches de Porto Alegre (Warehouse Workers Trade Union of Porto Alegre), in 1922, the Centro dos Chauffeurs (Chauffeurs Trade Union), in 1928, and, A Cosmopolita (Hotel Labours Trade Union), in 1929. In 1921, he became a member of Cooperativa de Consumo dos Operários (Workers Consumption Cooperative), an organization linked with PRR; a supporting member of Sociedade Beneficente União e Progresso (Union and Progress Friendly Society); a representative of Associação dos Foguistas (Stokers Trade Union); and a member of the technical committee of União Tipográfica (Typographers Trade Union). Schmidt, *Em busca da terra da promissão*, pp. 342–344.
54. "A sucessão presidencial", *Correio da Manhã*, Rio de Janeiro, 12 February 1930, p. 1.
55. These appearances are recorded in the following newspapers notes: *Correio da Manhã*, Rio de Janeiro, 18 September 1929, pp. 3 and 6; 19 September 1929, p. 6; 20 September 1929, p. 3;

On 1 March, the Aliança Liberal was defeated in an election characterized by widespread fraud and previous violence on both sides. That marked the beginning of an armed movement (supported by a sector of military officers), which tried to put Vargas into power. It eventually succeeded with an uprising (or, for the revolution's opponents, a "coup"), beginning on 3 October, that wanted to stop the officially elected candidate from assuming office.[56] Nazareth, then editor-in-chief of the *Diário de Notícias*, made good use of that newspaper's pages to support the 1930 movement, and the "New Brazil" and "Ministry of the Revolution" that were born from it.[57] Cavaco fought at Vargas's side in the armed uprisings. Xavier da Costa, on 15 October 1930, introduced a motion of "solidarity for the current movement" in the Porto Alegre City Council.[58]

While the events of 1930 have been assessed very differently, it is clear that a genuine mobilization arose in that year, one which was, in multiple ways, related to the labour movements, which saw leading socialists as it protagonists, and which was accompanied by a language of social change, if not transformation. Thus, the protagonists in this story entered the 1930s full of hopes and plans and saw the new regime, at least at the beginning, as a means to carry on their struggle for the workers' cause. In contrast to the fascist leanings of the subsequently installed Estado Novo under Vargas (1937–1945), it is remarkable the degree to which the politics of the regime immediately after 1930 was rendered, including by the protagonists of this

3 October 1929, p. 2; 6 February 1930, p. 2; 15 February 1930, p. 2; 22 February 1930, pp. 3–4; 26 February 1930, p. 3; *A Província*, Recife, 26 October 1929, p. 2; 28 January 1930, p. 3; *A Batalha*, Rio de Janeiro, 19 January 1930, p. 2; 28 January 1930, p. 2; 4 February 1930, p. 3; 6 February 1930, p. 3; 8 February 1930, p. 3; 11 February 1930, p. 3; 12 February 1930, p. 1; 14 February 1930, p. 3; 20 February 1930, p. 3; 23 February 1930, p. 1; 26 February 1930, p. 1.
56. "The Revolution of 1930" was an armed movement, led by Minas Gerais, Paraíba, and Rio Grande do Sul states, which resulted in a coup d'état that overthrew Washington Luís, the Republic's president, on 24 October 1930, prevented the elected president Júlio Prestes's inauguration, and ended a period called "Old Republic". The rebels' main reason was their refusal to accept the outcome of the earlier presidential elections in which the Aliança Liberal (Liberal Alliance), led by Getúlio Vargas, governor of Rio Grande do Sul, had been officially defeated by Júlio Prestes, representative of São Paulo oligarchies. The Aliança Liberal assembled oligarchical sectors that were not sympathetic to São Paulo's political and economic hegemony, lower-rank Army officers (lieutenants), bourgeoisie sectors, as well as part of the class and workers. Its programme had "modernizing" proposals such as incentives for industry and the resolution of "social problem", by implementing a social legislation, which reflected directly upon the working class. Boris Fausto, *A revolução de 1930. História e historiografia* (São Paulo's, 1997); Cláudia Viscardi, *O teatro das oligarquias. Uma revisão da "política do café com leite"* (Belo Horizonte, 2012); Edgar de Decca, *1930. O silêncio dos vencidos* (São Paulo, 1988).
57. *A Batalha*, Rio de Janeiro, 6 March 1930, p. 3; 7 March 1930, p. 3; 18 March 1930, p. 3; *Diário de Notícias*, Rio de Janeiro, 18 November 1930, p. 8.
58. *Correio do Povo*, Porto Alegre, 16 October 1930, p. 1.

article, in a language of socialism. For example, about one year after the
"Revolution", Xavier da Costa gave a speech before the general assembly of
the Sociedade União dos Trapicheiros (Warehouse Workers Trade Union),
at the port in Porto Alegre, in which he declared:

> In the Government, the eminent young man who ennobles the ministerial
> portfolio to which the interests of the proletariat are attached, the great worker for
> good, namely Dr. Lindolfo Collor, is paving the way to solve the great problems
> associated with the social question. Let us make the best of his meritorious efforts;
> let us take the open road, through which we will reach the promised land that
> Karl Marx spoke of, the emancipation of the proletarian class.[59]

This statement is noteworthy for two reasons: First, it symbolically links
the new Minister Lindolfo Collor (who had never been a socialist, but
rather saw himself as a progressive in the positivist tradition) to Karl Marx,
the "promised land", and the emancipation of the working class. Second,
these words carried some of Xavier da Costa's own contradictions: While at
the beginning of his political career he was a professed socialist (declaring
himself a follower of Karl Marx after being voted first into the city council,
running for the ruling PRR)[60], he had stopped adhering to socialist ideas,
yet took them up again in the context of the 1930 events. Xavier da Costa
died a few years later, on 11 May 1934, and it must be left to psychological
speculation whether he had come full circle, returning to ideas once shed, or,
alternatively, had never actually left his initial views, only to come out of the
"closet" again when circumstances seemed appropriate.

The other figures analysed here (with the exception of Lacerda) joined the
MTIC's diverse team, which included socialists, liberals, conservatives,
technicians, and industrialists, whose task was to produce social legislation
that was supposed to rise above class antagonisms. Cavaco was initially
appointed to the post of First Officer of the General Directorate of Records
and Accounts (Diretoria Geral de Expediente e Contabilidade). Shortly
thereafter, Collor, who wanted to surround himself with people he could
trust, invited Cavaco to become his Chief of Staff.[61] Nazareth was hired as a
technical consultant at the MTIC. His discourse soon took on explicitly
anti-communist tones, increasingly rejecting the validity of the liberal tenets
of democratic politics in the face of the communist "threat". He was not
alone in this anti-liberal turn with several of his former comrades in the
socialist struggles undergoing the same transformation. In a lengthy missive
published in the *Diário de Notícias* newspaper in the city of Salvador on
8 January 1931, he explained that he had accepted Collor's "honourable

---

59. *Ibid.*, 5 September 1931, p. 2.
60. Schmidt, *Em busca da terra da promissão*, pp. 323–338.
61. Rosa Maria Barboza Araújo, *O batismo do trabalho. A experiência de Lindolfo Collor* (Rio de
Janeiro, 1981), p. 66.

invitation" because he was imbued with the "conviction" that Collor, this "eminent fellow countryman", was "firmly disposed to include the Brazilian proletariat in the rights they were due", and for which he had always fought. In his words, "the Brazilian Revolution created for the workers, until very recently exposed to police brutality, an environment conducive to fulfilling necessary demands". Every day, with every act of the Ministry, he was more convinced that Collor had not spoken "mere words" when he acceded to his post, and "declared that the Labour Ministry would be the Specific [sic] Ministry of the Revolution". He pointed to the "keen and discriminating sense of values" that Vargas had recognized in Collor. He also said that Evaristo de Moraes and Joaquim Pimenta shared that belief, otherwise they would not "cooperate" with the Provisional Government as he did.[62]

As soon as they took their new posts, the three socialists – Moraes (until 1932), Nazareth, and Pimenta – became responsible for a range of administrative and supervisory roles at the MTIC and were involved in drafting labour and union laws as well as the creation and recognition of trade unions. In May 1931, they were invited to participate in a task that was, in every way, more important than any of their previous activities: They became part of a new commission made up of MTIC representatives, employers, employees in commerce, and workers, which was commissioned to study draft legislation on individual and collective work contracts and on the establishment of reconciliation and judgement councils. The activities of this commission and the documents elaborated by it greatly contributed to what would become the impressive body of Brazilian labour laws and labour regulation – a system of rules and institutions that, at least in intra-Latin American comparison, is both extensive and comprehensive.[63] Topics discussed in this commission included "certain and determined economic and social conditions of labour" in Brazil, regardless of agreements between employers and workers; they covered the "nationalization of labour, establishing measures on the percentage of Brazilian workers that each company should have"; they also established working hours, weekly periods of rest, guarantees for workers with illnesses, the restriction of child labour, equal pay for men and women performing the same jobs, and six weeks of maternity leave for female workers (before and after childbirth), with two thirds of their original pay.[64]

---

62. "As reivindicações operárias", *Diário de Notícias*, Salvador, 8 January 1931, p. 1.
63. On the history of labour law in Brazil, see: Ângela de Castro Gomes and Fernando Teixeira da Silva (eds), *A Justiça do Trabalho e sua história* (Campinas, 2013); Magda Barros Biavaschi, *O Direito do Trabalho no Brasil 1930–1942: A construção do sujeito de direitos trabalhistas* (São Paulo, 2007).
64. "Está sendo elaborada a nova legislação sobre o trabalho", *A Batalha*, Rio de Janeiro, 16 May 1931, p. 1.

As we have seen, these measures had long been part of the socialist agenda, and experienced leading activists like Moraes, Nazareth, or Pimenta were of fundamental importance to the new MTIC, not only because they were familiar with the inner workings of the labour movement and its struggles, but because they had the legal backgrounds necessary for participating in the elaboration of a new legal framework to regulate labour relations.

During his relatively short time in office (he was dismissed in early 1932), Collor and his social policies came under pressure from several sides: from those lieutenants of anti-oligarchic orientation who had played a central role in the mobilizations to bring Vargas to power and who demanded more radical reforms for the workers; from employers who were opposed to state intervention in relations between them and the workers; and from the regional oligarchies, such as the one in Rio Grande do Sul, Collor's main base of support, for which the presence of such figures as Cavaco, Moraes, Nazareth, and Pimenta in the MTIC sounded alarming. Vargas sought to conciliate the interests of these various groups, but rising tensions (which, again, had a strong component of intra-regional conflict) led to the collective dismissal of all ministers from Rio Grande do Sul, including Collor, in March 1932.

Cavaco, Nazareth, and Pimenta carried on working for the Ministry after Collor's departure;[65] yet, the euphoric and pioneering mood of the first months started to vanish when Joaquim Pedro Salgado Filho, formerly the chief of the political police, took charge of the MTIC. It should not be forgotten, however, that most of the social legislation that regulated labour relations in Brazil were enacted during his time in office. At the same time, the thrust for integration-cum-control of the labour movement, a hallmark of the Vargas era, became increasingly noticeable with closer ties between the trade unions and the state being established and the repression of the independent union movement becoming more intense.[66]

The protagonists analysed in this article were certainly not "innocent" in this process and merely "used" by those in power. They knew that they were working in a minefield, cooperated with the new Minister, and, at the same time, strove to see their political and personal projects prevail. Sometimes they succeeded, sometimes they did not. In any event, once Collor left the Ministry, they had to re-assess and re-direct their plans: Cavaco held onto his government office and continued to express his loyalty to Vargas until the latter's suicide during his second (and democratically legitimized) presidency (1951–1954). At the same time, he carried on with his socialist activism, having participated on 15 November 1932 in the First Brazilian Revolutionary Congress (Primeiro Congresso

---

65. Evaristo de Moraes also left the MTIC in 1932, declaring his loyalty to Collor.
66. Angela de Castro Gomes, *A invenção do trabalhismo* (Rio de Janeiro, 2005), pp. 175–182.

Revolucionário Brasileiro) in Rio de Janeiro, which re-founded the Partido Socialista Brasileiro (PSB), an umbrella group representing the "left" of the Provisional Government (lieutenants and socialists), with Evaristo de Moraes at its head.[67] Cavaco died on 22 December 1961.

Nazareth and Pimenta also stayed on at the MTIC, rising to the post of legal counsel for the National Labour Department (Departamento Nacional do Trabalho).[68] In 1941, the Labour Court, a cornerstone of the labour regime under the Estado Novo of Vargas, was officially established and Nazareth became the legal counsel of its supreme entity, the National Labour Council (Conselho Nacional do Trabalho, CNT), holding that post until the end of the Estado Novo in 1945. The 1946 Constitution shifted the Labour Court from the sphere of the Executive Branch to the Judiciary, and the CNT gave way to the Superior Labour Court (Tribunal Superior do Trabalho). Then, Nazareth joined the office of the Labour Public Prosecutor, retiring on 25 February 1959, and passing away on 1 August 1961.[69] Pimenta did not stay on long enough to experience many of these changes first-hand: In 1937, he was barred from holding two posts simultaneously – labour attorney and professor at the National Law School – and, with the signs of the coming dictatorship of the Estado Novo already visible, opted for the teaching position.[70]

Major segments of the labour movement were euphoric at the prospect of seeing long-demanded social welfare laws enacted during the 1930s and 1940s. As is well known from a series of historical studies revising older views of the period after the "revolution" and of the Estado Novo dictatorship, these years were not (or not only) characterized by a top-down process of integration, co-optation, or repression in relation to workers and the labour movement, they also saw support for and

---

67. The first PSB, founded in 1925, was never formally dissvoled. There is also no detailed information about the dissolution of the second PSB, founded in 1932. Both parties, however, shared an explicit commitment to adapting socialist ideas to the Brazilian realities. Meanwhile, the third PSB, founded in 1947, did not refer itself officially to the previous organizations of the same name. The manifestos and programmes of the Brazilian socialist parties of 1932 and 1947 are reprinted in: Evaristo Moraes Filho (ed.), *O socialismo no Brasil* (Brasília, 1979), pp. 262–265; 272–278.

68. Nazareth acted as general legal counsel of the National Labour Department on an interim basis from 1936 to 1941 until the death of office holder, Deodato da Silva Maia Junior (1875–1941).

69. For these institutional changes and career steps and see the following notes from both internal and public periodicals: *Boletim do Ministério do Trabalho, Indústria e Comércio*, Rio de Janeiro, n. 3, November 1934, p. 305; *Revista do Conselho Nacional do Trabalho*, Rio de Janeiro, n. 9, June 1941, p. 26; "Ministério do Trabalho, Indústria e Comércio", *Diário Oficial da União*, Rio de Janeiro, 12 March 1936, Section 1, p. 4; "Procuradoria da Justiça do Trabalho", 5 August 1960, pp. 38-39; *Idem*, 3 January 1961, p. 7; "Agripino Nazareth", *A Noite*, Rio de Janeiro, 2 August 1961, p. 7; "Fundador do MTPS", *Idem*, 3 August 1961, p. 7.

70. See his autobiographical account: Joaquim Pimenta, *Retalhos do passado. Episódios que vivi e fatos que testemunhei* (Rio de Janeiro, 1949), p. 424.

considerable active involvement by workers in the new regime as well as numerous social conflicts.[71] These conflicts were partly sparked by the employers' resistance to the enforcement of the new labour and welfare laws. As they already had experience with strikes during the First Republic, the figures analysed here played a key role in mediating those conflicts, both following their self-image as movement activists and the maxim of the new regime of the state as "arbiter" in clashes between capital and labour. As early as 1931, for example, Nazareth, Moraes, and Pimenta successfully intervened as mediators in a conflict involving thousands of dissatisfied textile workers in the states of Rio de Janeiro and São Paulo, who complained to the MTIC about cuts and squeezes on wages and the sacking of strikers and union leaders.[72] Furthermore, the three protagonists were playing an active role in the creation and organization of trade unions (something expressly fostered, even initiated by the state) as well as in adapting them, from the start, to the new corporatist structure established by the regime.

Thus, whilst handling routine administrative duties at the MTIC and belonging to the group of intellectuals that was drafting labour laws, the three protagonists also maintained a more direct involvement with the unions and the labour movement. Such involvement, however, was frowned upon, if not openly condemned by major sectors of organized workers. The fiercest resistance to the new corporatist relationship between the state and organized labour, established after 1930, came from the long-standing supporters of revolutionary syndicalism, particularly in those urban centres where it had its traditional strongholds, like São Paulo. However, the corporatist structure of unions was widely accepted in the areas dominated by practitioners of a reform-oriented unionism, which had had much currency in several regions already during the First Republic, such as in Rio de Janeiro (both the federal capital and the state), Bahia, and Pernambuco. Many of the leaders of these reform-oriented unions, generally influenced by socialist ideas, did not necessarily adhere to corporatism in an uncritical and submissive way, trying to maintain a modicum of independence from

---

71. These revisionist interpretations started to emerge in the 1990s and include, for instance, John D. French: *The Brazilian Worker's ABC. Class Conflict and Alliances in Modern Sao Paulo* (Chapel Hill, NC [etc.], 1992); Alexandre Fortes, Antonio Luigi Negro, Fernando Teixeira da Silva, Hélio da Costa, and Paulo Fontes (eds): *Na luta por direitos. Estudos recentes em história social do trabalho* (Campinas, 1999).

72. "Um conflito de interesses entre patrões e operários", *A Noite*, Rio de Janeiro, 31 January 1931, p. 5; "Uma excursão do Ministro do Trabalho a Magé", 23 February 1931, p. 3; "Um comunicado do gabinete do Ministro do Trabalho", 27 August 1931, p. 2; "Solucionado o conflito entre operários e patrões da C. Fiação e Tecidos Mageense", *Diário da Noite*, Rio de Janeiro, 31 January 1931, p. 5; "As manifestações operárias ao Governo Provisório", *Diário Carioca*, Rio de Janeiro, 3 May 1931, p. 3; "O caso da fábrica de São Geraldo", *Diário de Notícias*, Rio de Janeiro, 13 August 1931, p. 13.

the government apparatus. At the same time, they were disposed to using the new institutional channels that were opening up to guarantee certain rights and legal regulations that the workers had been struggling for during decades, seeing these changes not as a deflection of these struggles, but as a form of their achievement. Furthermore, the shift towards the emerging corporatist unions created such momentum that even fierce critics of this development (such as the communists and several currents of dissident communist, including Trotskyists) proceeded to participate in these unions after 1933 in order to politicize them and dispute the hegemony of the Labour Ministry. However – as a long stream of literature on so-called populism, not only in Brazil, but also other countries in Latin America, has made clear – the regime and its corporatist arrangements gained the support of broad swathes of the working class. Far from being only a repressive manipulator of workers, Vargas obtained their consent in all parts of the country by offering opportunities and platforms for advancing workers' concerns and interests.[73] The figures studied here played a fundamental role in this process, both in mediating these opportunities (as well as their limitations) and in the process of legal codifications of these policies.

MULTIPLE WAYS OF BEING A SOCIALIST

In this article, we have sought to analyse the similarities and differences between the careers of socialist militants who saw a new and promising future coming in 1930, as well as the strategies that had guided their activities on behalf of workers in the previous decades. The comparison of the trajectories of the six socialists analysed in this article allowed us, on the one hand, to highlight common patterns among them, and, on the other, to identify differences that deconstruct supposedly coherent units such as "socialist during the First Republic" or "socialists in support of Vargas".

As for the similarities, all of them found an important space in the press for political activism and dissemination of ideas. In articles written both for the mainstream and workers press, they tried to raise workers' "consciousness" as well as establish a sort of exchange, even if sometimes controversial, with the representatives of other social classes as well as governmental institutions. In addition, the six individuals played important roles in workers associations, initially by trying to steer them towards socialist ideas, and, after 1930 (or even before, as in the case of Xavier da Costa) by prompting them to support incumbent governments when these had issued their proposals on the "social question". Furthermore, the six socialists also participated in strikes and insurrections before 1930 (some of them in a very militant fashion), while later, they intervened as mediators on

73. Angela Maria Carneiro Araújo, *A Construção do Consentimento. Corporativismo e tra-balhadores no Brasil dos anos 30* (São Paulo, 1998).

behalf of government in conflicts between bosses and workers. This role as intermediator was not entirely new, however: In Rio Grande do Sul, for example, due to various regional characteristics, especially the positivist influence in the ruling party, Xavier da Costa acted in such a function already during a strike in 1906. When Vargas came to power in 1930, all of them supported the new government's proposals in relation to labour issues. Some of them, however, were more organically involved in this process, by overtly intervening in the formulation and implementation of a labour legislation and by organizing and formalizing trade unions in accordance with the new labour law (such as Nazareth, Pimenta, and Moraes), while others had more indirect participation (Cavaco and Xavier da Costa).

As for the differences, these were most notable in the means of political intervention. Nazareth and Lacerda were prone to using conspiracy methods and insurrection strategies, involved, in one way or another, in the uprising of army officers in 1915–1916, 1922, 1924, and 1930. And in 1918, Nazareth was readily prepared to build alliances with anarchists such as José Oiticica (1882–1957), Astrojildo Pereira (1890–1965), and Everardo Dias (1883–1966) to promote a soldiers' and workers' uprising in Rio de Janeiro, clearly inspired by the Russian Revolution. Even the victorious general strike he led in 1919 in Salvador had an insurrectional profile according to some observers at that time. Cavaco, in turn, repeatedly used an inflammatory rhetoric, but did not take part in any insurrection. Moraes and Pimenta, meanwhile, being a criminalist and a law professor, respectively, nurtured an image of adhering to law and order. Xavier da Costa, despite some occasional aggressive speeches, most of the time also tried to present himself as "respectable" for bosses and rulers.

The trajectories of the six individuals after 1932 were quite varied: Nazareth continued his career at the MTIC, the Labour Court, and the Labour Public Prosecutor Office, retiring in 1959. He died in 1961. Pimenta remained in the Labour Court until 1937, when he changed to an academic teaching career, eventually dying in 1963. Moraes left the Labour Ministry in 1932, but never explicitly opposed the Vargas government. The most distinctive was Lacerda's course: He supported the Aliança Liberal rally in 1929 and took part in the Revolution of 1930, but never worked for the Labour Ministry or for the Labour Court, despite his legal career and the books he had written about labour law. In May 1930, he resumed his post as a Member of the Federal House of Representatives and worked as a Brazilian ambassador in Uruguay for a short period after Vargas came to power, but quit due to differences with the new government. He was again Mayor in Vassouras between 1932 and 1935 and took part in the Aliança Nacional Libertadora (National Alliance for Freedom), an organization that gathered anti-fascists and communists. After the end of the Estado Novo in 1945, however, Maurício de Lacerda became part of the União

Democrática Nacional (National Democratic Union), a party that gathered the same right-wing liberals that were later involved in the coup d'état that started the military dictatorship in 1964.

When attempting to understand why men who were socialist militants during the First Republic joined the campaign of the Aliança Liberal and later the Vargas administration, several recent studies have introduced interpretations that steer wide of the ideas of "selling out" and "betrayal". Focusing on Francisco Xavier da Costa and Carlos Cavaco, one of the authors of this article has underscored the need to replace moral judgements with historical analysis, concluding that these individuals did not see their support for the regime after the 1930 "revolution" as contradicting their own pasts. On the contrary, they believed that both stages of their trajectories were consistent with each other, and they drew a continuous line between their socialist activism prior to 1930 and their involvement in the government under Vargas, as the latter, in their view, was about to fulfil long-held, historic demands of the working class.[74]

Joseli Mendonça reached similar conclusions in her study of the lay lawyer (later solicitor) Evaristo de Moraes. She stressed that the former socialist activist saw the new situation as an opportunity to redefine relations between capital and labour through an actively intervening State. According to Mendonça, the creation of the MTIC and its considerable powers fulfilled a long-held, persistent demand of Moraes and many other socialist militants from the old regime, who since the early years of the First Republic had called for state intervention in relations between workers and employers, especially concerning labour contracts. Evaristo de Moraes was convinced that those relations were structurally biased in favour of the employers to the detriment of the employees. To establish a kind of balance between those two forces for the good of the country, it would be necessary for the state to intervene, protecting and safeguarding the more fragile and disadvantaged party through means that included labour laws. Moraes, Mendonça writes, has especially devoted himself to the elaboration of such legal frameworks during his short tenure as Collor's legal advisor (from December 1930 to March 1932): The famous Trade Union Act of 19 March 1931, which he co-authored with Joaquim Pimenta, were part of that effort.[75]

There were many ways of being a socialist in Brazil as this article has shown by highlighting different moments in the trajectory of six socialists during last decades of the nineteenth century through to the 1920s, and by analysing in more detail their activities in the early years after the "revolution" of 1930. All six socialists shared certain common activities and

74. Schmidt, *Em busca da terra da promissão*, pp. 429–434.
75. Mendonça, *Evaristo de Moraes, tribuno da República*, pp. 381–436.

concerns, particularly the work within unions, the attempt to form political parties, the journalistic work in both the movement-related and mainstream press, as well as the participation in strikes and uprisings. In that, the variation in experiences of radical militancy and confrontational intervention – variations among the six, yet also in the course of their single biographies – is remarkable. At the same time, this refutes any overly clear image of the "accommodating reformist". Also, these socialists operated in an environment in which the labour movement was partly dominated by syndicalist and anarchist traditions, constantly forming alliances with these groups and integrating some of syndicalism's tenets into their programmatic platforms. Even their relations with the communists, from the late 1920s on, clearly marked by hostility, were more ambiguous at the beginning, the recognition of the Soviet Union being part of their international demands.

The trajectories of the six socialists – both shared and varied – made them actively participate in the regime that arose after the "revolution" of 1930 and the new labour policies it launched. While their support for this new regime was neither unreserved, nor without conflict, they offered both their expertise, not least in legal matters, and their political capital to develop the specific kind of labour corporatism for which the Vargas era is known until today. In doing so, they greatly contributed to the drafting and enactment of Brazilian labour laws – a body of legal regulations which, even in global comparison, stands out as exceptionally fine-grained and comprehensive.

Translation: H. Sabrina Gledhill

IRSH 62 (2017), Special Issue, pp. 165–190 doi:10.1017/S0020859017000608
© 2018 Internationaal Instituut voor Sociale Geschiedenis

World War II and Brazilian Workers: Populism at the Intersections between National and Global Histories

ALEXANDRE FORTES

Universidade Federal Rural do Rio de Janeiro
Department of History
Av Governador Roberto da Silveira S/N
Nova Iguaçu, RJ, Brazil

E-mail: fortes.ufrrj@gmail.com

ABSTRACT: This article argues that World War II played a very important, and generally underestimated role in the rise of Brazilian populism. It starts with an overview of recent trends in the debates on the use of the concept of populism in Brazil, with particular attention to works that stress the years from 1941 to 1945 as a critical juncture. Secondly, it explores the connections between war effort, changes in labor regulations, and workers' political participation in different contexts. Finally, it summarizes how the economic and social effects produced by the involvement of Brazil in the War led to profound and accelerated changes in the nature of the regime of Getúlio Vargas and in the role of workers in Brazilian politics.

Populism is one of the most controversial terms in our political vocabulary. Used to describe a broad range of phenomena and bearing strong pejorative undertones, numerous scholars have questioned the concept. Attempts to discard it, however, have been in vain. The term re-emerges with each inflection of the global political scene, whether on the left, with the election of progressive governments in South America in the first decade of the twenty-first century,[1] or on the right, in our current moment, epitomized by the election of Donald Trump as president of the United States.[2]

Although the transnational character of these "populist waves" is self-evident, analyses of them generally echo the nationalist logic inherent in the

---

1. See, for example, the polemic between Laclau and Žižek: Ernesto Laclau, *On Populist Reason* (London [etc.], 2005); Slavoj Žižek, "Against the Populist Temptation", *Critical Inquiry*, 32:3 (2006), pp. 551–574.
2. For recent examples of two significantly different points of view, see: Christian Salmon, "Trump, Fascism, and the Construction of 'The People': An Interview with Judith Butler", available at: http://www.versobooks.com/blogs/3025-trump-fascism-and-the-construction-of-the-people-an-interview-with-judith-butler; last accessed 24 October 2017; Guillaume Erner, "Europe: The Return of the People, or of Populism. Interview with Jacques Rancière", available at: http://www.versobooks.com/blogs/2896-europe-the-return-of-the-people-or-of-populism; last accessed 24 October 2017.

object of study. Global processes, such as the impact of the Great Depression in the 1930s or the reaction to the social impact of globalization in the post-1989 era, are usually mentioned, and studies of populism often identify general, shared characteristics of the phenomenon. The study of each case, however, tends to prioritize domestic factors.

This article will probe this subject from a different perspective, analyzing Brazil's major historical experience of populism, *varguismo*, through the lens of country's involvement in World War II. The reign of Getúlio Vargas (1882–1954), the wealthy Brazilian rancher who was twice elected president and also ruled as a dictator from 1937 to 1945 under the so-called *Estado Novo*, I hypothesize, established a form of mass politics that can only be fully understood when taking the geopolitical, economic, and social impact of the most extensive armed conflict in the twentieth century into account. Thus, it will be possible to bring the subject of populism together with the debate concerning the relationship between total war and the period's transformations in social rights and labor relations. This article aims to illustrate how an attentive eye toward the relationship between national space and global processes can substantially alter the contours of a traditional object of study.

This article has three parts. First, I consider the relationship between workers, *varguismo*, and the historiographic debate about the validity of the use of the concept of populism in the Brazilian context. Next, the article will engage with scholarship that discusses the relationship between total war, citizenship, and social policies in other regions. In the third part, I pause to consider the significance of World War II in creating the conditions for the reconfiguration of the working class and in its formative role in Brazilian workers' political experience.

VARGAS, WORKERS AND POPULISM

In studies of twentieth-century Brazil, populism has been approached from many angles, yet one of the major concerns has always been to understand the ways in which workers were incorporated into political participation from the 1930s on. That is to say: why did so many workers support a political regime that, at least in the eyes of many academic observers, did not genuinely represent their interests? Although the adjective "populist" can be applied to a diverse spectrum of types of leadership, parties, and local governments, at the center of the debate over the validity of the concept is the final assessment of the political legacy of Getúlio Vargas's rule and that of his political heir, president João Goulart (1961–1964).[3]

---

3. Originally from the state of Rio Grande do Sul on the border with Argentina and Uruguay, Vargas ran in the presidential election of 1930 with the Liberal Alliance (Aliança Liberal), a coalition of regional oligarchies from the peripheries of Brazil that had the broad support of the

In the 1960s and 1970s, authors like Gino Germani, Otávio Ianni, and Francisco Weffort used the concept of populism to construct a general model used to explain the transformations unfolding in Latin America from the 1930s on, particularly in the three most iconic cases: the reigns of Lázaro Cárdenas in Mexico (1934–1940), Juan D. Perón in Argentina (1943/45–1955), and Getúlio Vargas in Brazil (1930–1945; 1951–1954).[4] These approaches took as their point of departure the impact of the Great Depression on agro-export systems, the crisis of hegemony within Latin American societies, and working- and middle-class dissatisfaction with the region's oligarchical republics. These factors combined, the classical analyses said, brought about the ascendancy of illiberal ideas, the establishment of a new economic model (import substitution industrialization), the acceleration in internal migration, and the emergence of charismatic leaders whose ascent was based on the manipulation of the working classes, particularly what was seen, following Germani, as the new and "immature" sectors of the working class. In these approaches, populism always appeared as manipulative and demagogic, and workers as tempted to follow a deceptive leader.

Although it remains influential in public opinion, this model did not survive either the conceptual revisions or the increase of empirical research

middle classes in the country's main urban centers, of the low-ranking officer class in the Army that had led various rebellions in the 1920s (the so-called lieutenants or *tenentes*) and of the reformists within the labor movement. The *aliancistas* (supporters of the Liberal Alliance) contested the monopoly of power held by politicians in the states of São Paulo and Minas Gerais since the beginning of the nineteenth century and defended the strengthening of centralized power, the adoption of policies that promoted industrialization, and the expansion of social legislation to avoid worsening labor conflicts. The candidate from the incumbent party, Júlio Prestes, was declared winner of the election, but before he could be sworn in as president, his government was overturned by a political-military movement that denounced the electoral results as fraudulent. Coming to power through this "Revolution of 1930", Vargas was proclaimed the head of the Provisional Government, and later elected the president of the Republic by indirect means through the National Constituent Assembly of 1934. In 1937, the presidential elections that had been planned for the following year were suspended, using as a pretext the supposed discovery of a communist conspiracy to take power. Instead, a dictatorial government known as the *Estado Novo* (New State) was installed, ushering in a corporatist regime that was one of the most authoritarian and ideologically most right-leaning of Latin America's "classical" populisms. It would last until 1945, when Vargas was deposed, beginning a period of electoral democracy. In 1950, Vargas became president of the Republic again, this time democratically elected, yet proving unable to withstand the pressure put on him by his opposition. In 1954, in the context of a crisis after a failed assassination attempt against his major political adversary, he committed suicide while still in office. The years after his death saw a continuation of many of the arrangements of *varguismo*. Taking office in 1961, President João Goulart, a left-wing nationalist, was about to renew the populist tradition in a more progressive and reform-oriented way. This was disrupted by a coup in 1964, which ushered in a military dictatorship that lasted until 1985.

4. Gino Germani, *Política y sociedad en una época de transición. De la sociedad tradicional a la sociedad de masas* (Buenos Aires, 1962); Otávio Ianni, *O colapso do populismo no Brasil* (Rio de Janeiro, 1968); *idem*, *A formação do estado populista na América Latina* (Rio de Janeiro, 1975); Francisco Weffort, *O populismo na política brasileira* (Rio de Janeiro, 1978).

on the worlds of labor and populism in Latin America, especially from the 1980s on. Inspired by British Marxist historiography, the studies that made up the "Latin American labor studies boom"[5] made it impossible to sustain that workers had been simply manipulated by the state or by leaders who represented the interests of other social classes. This revisionist historiography experienced an additional uplift in the 1990s when the destructive influence of neoliberalism was also felt in Brazil. Latin America's populist regimes were re-evaluated in a newly positive light, because of their role in the construction of more sovereign national states, regulatory systems of labor relations, and of social welfare. Influential authors came to see in the concept of populism an abusive and derogatory generalization. Allan Knight, a distinguished historian of the Mexican Revolution, defended abandoning the term, which, in his view, was incapable of contributing to the analysis of *cardenismo*, the presidency of Lázaro Cárdenas in post-revolutionary Mexico, or of what he called "many *cardenismos*".[6] In Brazil, the classic reference epitomizing the shifts in the debate was Ângela de Castro Gomes's *The Invention of Laborism* (*A invenção do trabalhismo*).[7] Gomes, it should be stressed, did not concentrate on the early Vargas years after the so-called Revolution of 1930 and the first years of the *Estado Novo*, but rather on the period after 1941, when the Vargas regime started to open up to a more "mobilization"-oriented form of politics and stronger labor participation. She argued that the late Vargas era allowed, to a limited but momentous degree, for the inclusion of important parts of the working classes in the realm of politics and society, and enabled the labor movement to articulate a new notion of "social citizenship".

---

5. John French, "The Latin American Labor Studies Boom", *International Review of Social History*, 45:2 (2000), pp. 279–308.

6. Alan Knight, "Cardenismo. Coloso o catramina?", in María Moira Mackinnon and Mario Alberto Petrone (eds), *Populismo y neopopulismo en América Latina. El problema de la Cenicienta* (Buenos Aires, 2011 [1998]), pp. 197–230.

7. Angela Maria de Castro Gomes, *A invenção do trabalhismo* (Rio de Janeiro [etc.], 1988). Just as with the word "labor" in English, the Portuguese adjective *trabalhista* and the noun *trabalhismo*, have a variety of connotations, referring, at times, to the world of labor broadly conceived (as in, *legislação trabalhista*, "labor legislation"), to the labor movement (as in *manifestações trabalhistas*, or "workers' demonstrations"), and also to the Brazilian Workers' Party, or the Partido Trabalhista Brasileiro (PTB), which was created by supporters of Vargas during the process of transition to democracy in 1945. In her analysis of the period between 1941 and 1945, Gomes integrates these three dimensions of the concept of *trabalhismo*, inasmuch as the period begins with various initiatives of the *Estado Novo* seeking to lend more vitality to the state-run labor union structure, moves on to the passing of Consolidation of Labor Laws (Consolidação das Leis do Trabalho) in 1943, and draws to a close with the creation of the PTB. Despite the relevance and originality of Gomes's book, her approach carries numerous risks, particularly when she fails to recognize the role of other political forces acting on labor during that period, such as the communists, thus potentially obscuring workers' agency.

It was only in the mid-1990s, however, that Gomes openly argued for the abandonment of the concept of populism, whose diffusion in Brazil, she claims, resulted from the work of a group of intellectuals in the mid-1950s, which set out to systematize what were essentially the prejudices of a liberal-conservative elite against the incorporation of the "inorganic popular sectors" into politics.[8] In a similar vein, Marxist-inspired interpretations during the 1960s and 1970s associated populism with the supposed structural weaknesses of the Brazilian working class, which made it vulnerable to a political force alien to it, or with the mistakes made by their organizations and leadership. In contrast to this, for Gomes (and many other revisionists), it would be more appropriate to interpret Brazilian populism, particularly the period from 1945 to 1964, i.e. after the first, mostly dictatorial reign of Getúlio Vargas, as a kind of "labor pact", a notion that describes a relationship between "unequal actors" based on the state's concession of material and symbolic benefits and their reception and interpretation by workers, "following the terms of their possibilities and experiences".[9]

Among those who contributed to this revisionist reading, criticism of the concept of populism quickly evolved into a vindication of the laborism of Vargas supporters. For Daniel Aarão Reis Filho, the "laborist tradition" (by which he means the whole period between 1930 and 1964) was the Brazilian variant of the Latin American "national-statist traditions", which the labor movement had embraced from Juan Perón to Fidel Castro. As part of this "tradition", workers' strikes and demonstrations were "sometimes protected and encouraged, sometimes contained, and even repressed, depending on the conjunctures and the governments" then ruling the country.[10] Jorge Ferreira, for his part, understands what is traditionally called "populism" as a "laborist project", in which "the state and the working class identified common interests".[11]

Removing the concept of populism from this scene, as pejorative, imprecise, and ideologically contaminated as it is, we would be left with the extraordinarily broad and comprehensive notion of *trabalhismo*, i.e. a certain kind of labor activism that emerged in the mid-twentieth century and overlapped with populism. As explained above, for authors such as Ferreira and Aarão, the phenomenon refers simultaneously to a pact

---

8. These intellectuals formed in 1952 as the "Itatiaia Group" and were sponsored the Ministry of Agriculture. Angela Maria de Castro Gomes, "O populismo e as ciências sociais no Brasil. Notas sobre a trajetória de um conceito", *Tempo*, 1:2 (1996), pp. 31–58.
9. *Ibid.*, pp. 51–54.
10. Daniel Aarão Reis Filho, "O colapso do colapso do populismo ou a propósito de uma herança maldita", in Jorge Ferreira (ed.), *O populismo e sua história. Debate e crítica* (Rio de Janeiro, 2001), pp. 319–377, 346.
11. Jorge Ferreira, "O nome e a coisa. O populismo na política brasileira", in Ferreira, *O populismo e sua história*, pp. 59–124, 103.

between workers and the state that expresses a particular form of class consciousness, yet also to a "tradition" that connects legal, welfare, union, and party structures to social mobilization (simultaneously combining contention from below and repression from above). Above all, however, *trabalhismo* involves charismatic leaders who are able to "express" the interests, beliefs, and values of their base.

The research of Gomes and others who have questioned the very notion of populism has been incorporated into recent international scholarship on Brazil. Oliver Dinius, for instance, taking the specificities of the reality of the steel-producing city of Volta Redonda, classifies *trabalhismo* during the Vargas era as a mere variation of "Catholic paternalism".[12] While suggestively pointing to the intricate relationship between the state and the Church during the Vargas years, such an analysis also illustrates the risk of separating *trabalhismo* from the wider dynamics of populism in Brazil: It should not be forgotten that Getúlio Vargas was an avowed agnostic, who named his first son with the decidedly un-Catholic name Lutero and, moreover, for whom one of the main achievements of his *trabalhista* politics was to avoid the formation of a confessional form of unionism in a country deeply shaped by Catholicism. That does not mean that religion was absent from politics during *varguismo*: As an older but very nuanced analysis of the role of religiosity during *varguismo* has demonstrated, the process of the construction of a popular base of Vargas supporters involved the channeling of popular religious feelings toward the state, by way of the development of a form of civic ritualism and a cult of the figure of the dictator.[13]

The trend to completely shun the concept of populism soon revealed further limitations. For instance, one of the characteristics of revisionist approaches is that it is fully based on "methodological nationalism".[14] The earlier sociological scholarship of the 1960s and 1970s had many blind spots, yet it was able to conceive the phenomenon as a continental one, thinking of Latin America as a collection of units generated by common historical processes and exposed to the same general conditions, within which similar processes were taking place. While this earlier research also proceeded to move on to the national level in the next step of its analyses (once formed, populisms evolved according to their respective national contexts and the peculiarities of their leaderships), the posterior revisionist approaches were much more limited in that regard. They tend to highlight each nation's specificities in such a way as to discard in advance the very

---

12. Oliver Dinius, *Brazil's Steel City: Developmentalism, Strategic Power, and Industrial Relations in Volta Redonda, 1941–1964* (Stanford, CA, 2010), pp. 72–76.

13. Alcir Lenharo, *Sacralização da política* (Campinas, 1986).

14. For a critique of "methodological nationalism" in labor history, see Marcel van der Linden, *Workers of the World: Essays toward a Global Labor History* (Leiden [etc.], 2008), pp 15–16.

possibility of comparative analysis or the production of conclusions that might extrapolate the limits of the nation state.

Furthermore, the substitution of populism for *trabalhismo* impedes the very understanding of the diversity of processes through which workers have been incorporated into Brazilian politics during that period. In São Paulo, for instance, this process of inclusion originated in the mass support of two local politicians rather than Vargas himself, Ademar de Barros and Jânio Quadros,[15] leaders of movements that, as John French explains, were essentially anti-*trabalhista* and anti-Vargas. Such phenomena indicate, that *trabalhismo* and populism had many overlaps, yet were by no means identical. French proposes taking a different path, one based on an interactive model of social class. Analyzed in such a way as to integrate the changes in the internal composition of the working class with the transformation that other social segments of Brazil's population (like the middle class) experienced, the author emphasizes the importance of interclass alliances, which, he insists, imply neither passivity, nor subordination of workers to charismatic leaders. These alliances would form the basis for a "populist political system". Similarly, in the analysis of Fernando da Silva and Hélio da Costa, rather than a "blind and active adherence" to populist politics, workers exercised "a pragmatic realism with an elevated sense of the calculus needed to weigh the possible gains and benefits", imposing "on the state and on their bosses concessions and duties by way of a language drawn from their own populist rhetorical resources".[16]

"Populism" cannot serve us as a self-sufficient conceptual instrument. Equally, the term should not be discarded in the name of the irreducible singularity of every individual political phenomenon. The explanatory capacity of this concept must be tested by analyzing the phenomena it describes as historical processes. Thus, the analysis of specific and contextually embedded mutations can be more productive than the search for essential characteristics. In the Brazilian case, a fundamental point of departure for this type of approach is, for instance, a differentiation between the lasting impact of the Vargas era, especially on labor, on the one hand, and the trajectory of *varguismo* as a political movement, on the other. It is a matter of general agreement among specialized scholars that the fifteen years of the first Getúlio Vargas government (1930–1945) set the basic

---

15. "Pensar a América Latina. Entrevista de Daniel James e John French", in Alexandre Fortes *et al.* (eds), *Na luta por direitos. Estudos recentes em história social do trabalho* (Campinas, 1999), pp. 189–196, 191; John D. French, *The Brazilian Worker's ABC. Class Conflict and Alliances in Modern São Paulo* (Chapel Hill, NC, 1992), pp. 199–224. For São Paulo, see also Paulo Fontes and Adriano Duarte, "O populismo visto da periferia. Adhemarismo e janismo nos bairros da Mooca e São Miguel Paulista (1947–1953)", *Cadernos AEL*, 11:20/21 (2004), pp. 83–121.
16. Fernando Teixeira da Silva and Hélio da Costa, "Trabalhadores Urbanos e Populismo. Um Balanço dos Estudos Recentes", in Ferreira, *O populismo e sua história*, pp. 205–271, 225.

framework for modern Brazil: a largely urban, semi-industrialized country with a strong nationalist culture and a comparatively independent foreign policy, in which the national state played an important role in both economic and social policy. The long-term survival of the country's system of labor relations that Vargas established still intrigues most analysts. It remained untouched after the dictator's fall in 1945, was reinforced when he returned as a democratically elected president five years later, remained in place after a military coup removed João Goulart from power in 1964, and suffered only minor changes when a new democratic constitution was promulgated in 1988. With the same basic features, it remains in place even after enduring fierce attacks by the neoliberal governments during the 1990s that promised to overcome the "Vargas legacy". As an organized political force, however, the Vargas phenomenon did not have the same level of endurance or consistency (in sharp contrast, for instance, with Peronism in Argentina where the movements is a major political actor up until today): Vargas governed for fifteen years without creating a political party or a general workers' confederation. When the transition to democracy became imminent in 1945, the dictator initially attempted to organize a workers' wing of the recently created Social Democrat Party (Partido Social Democrático, or PSD), which was led by rural oligarchs. The government supporters inside the labor movement and central figures of the social policies of the *Estado Novo* dictatorship (a group that included staff of the Ministry of Labor and members of the political police) revolted against this solution, eventually resulting in the formation of the Brazilian Labour Party (PTB).[17] Once deposed, Vargas entered into post-war electoral politics in the ambiguous position of honorary president of both of these two parties.

The intensification of political conflicts that brought on the political crisis of Vargas's second administration (ultimately leading the president to commit suicide in 1954) further accelerated profound changes in the PTB's orientation and identity. The party assumed a more radical and anti-imperialist position, in an intricate process of approximation with the communists.[18] The attempt to maintain some measure of programmatic

17. For an analysis of how this process played out in Rio Grande do Sul (one of the regional strongholds of *varguismo*), see Jorge Ferreira, "Sindicalismo, política e trabalhismo no Rio Grande do Sul. A trajetória de José Vecchio", in Daniel Aarão Reis Filho (ed.), *Intelectuais, história e política. Séculos XIX e XX* (Rio de Janeiro, 2000), pp. 182–218.
18. For a general overview of the PTB's development in those years, see Lucilia Delgado de Almeida Neves, *PTB, do getulismo ao reformismo, 1945–1964* (São Paulo, 1989). The regional dynamics again in Rio Grande do Sol are analysed in Miguel Bodea, *Trabalhismo e populismo no Rio Grande do Sul* (Porto Alegre, 1992). The Communist Party of Brasil (Partido Comunista do Brasil, PCB) had experienced only a brief (but politically very successful) period of legal existence from 1945 until 1947 when it was driven underground again. However, it continued to exert a major influence both on the union movement and intellectual life during the 1950 and early 1960s.

and organizational cohesion among Vargas's political heirs, however, did not survive the effects of the long dictatorship installed in Brazil in 1964. When political amnesty declared in 1979 set in motion the process of redemocratization, the PTB remained under the control of Vargas's conservative niece, Ivete Vargas. Another contender for Vargas's legacy, the former governor Leonel Brizola, saw himself as obliged to form a new political organization, the Workers' Democratic Party (Partido Democrático Trabalhista, or PDT). None of these parties, however, became a relevant channel for the political expression of Brazil's workers' movements. It was the new Workers' Party (Partido dos Trabalhadores, PT), that filled this role after 1980, a party whose leaders had, since the 1970s, stood up against the corporatist union structure that had been created during the Vargas era, creating the more participatory New Unionism, and who strove for their own representation in the electoral system without the mediation of professional politicians.[19]

Vargas's legacy, then, has traveled along several trajectories and reveals a particularly sharp contrast between the impact of its specific way of regulating the relations between labor, capital, and the state, on the one hand, and of its political movement, on the other. These two trajectories are also telling because they imply a marked dissonance between the innovative agenda of the "revolutionaries of 1930" (industrialization, labor legislation, strengthening of centralized power, and so on)[20] and the conservatism of their political methods: In the first decade of Vargas's rule, the regime made no effort to mobilize the masses of workers.[21] On the contrary, it was more Vargas's adversaries who had to resort to popular mobilization, particularly in the three most important attempts to overturn him: the so-called Constitutionalist Revolution of 1932 in São Paulo;[22] the insurrectionary movement of the National Liberation Alliance (Aliança Nacional Libertadora), led by the communist Luís Carlos Prestes, in 1935;[23] and the attempted coup carried out by Brazilian fascists who were part of the group Brazilian Integralist Action (Ação Integralista Brasileira) in 1938.[24]

19. Margareth Keck, "The New Unionism in the Brazilian Transition", in Alfred Stepan (ed.), *Democratizing Brazil: Problems of Transition and Consolidation* (New York, 1989), pp. 252–296.
20. On the "Revolution of 1930" and the role of socialists in the early Vargas years also the contribution by A.S. Castellucci and Benito Bisso Schmidt in this Special Issue.
21. Except if we consider the civic commemorations that the regime promoted as mass mobilizations. Maria Helena Capelato, *Multidões em cena. Propaganda política no varguismo e no peronismo* (São Paulo, 1998), pp. 51–72.
22. Barbara Weinstein, *The Color of Modernity: São Paulo and the Making of Race and Nation in Brazil* (Durham, NC, 2015), ch. 3,"The Middle Class in Arms? Fighting for São Paulo".
23. Anita Prestes, *Luiz Carlos Prestes e a Aliança Nacional Libertadora. Os caminhos da luta antifascista no Brasil, 1934/35* (Petrópolis, 1997).
24. Hélgio Trindade, *Integralismo. O fascismo brasileiro na década de 30* (São Paulo, 1979).

If we consider the incorporation of the masses as one of the main political resources characteristic for populist regimes, then it is the historical conjuncture of World War II that functioned as an initial moment of a metamorphosis in the political movement around Vargas. While several authors have remarked on the qualitative changes of the interrelation between the Brazilian workers' and the *Estado Novo* in the period from 1940 to 1943, these shifts have generally been understood as the result of a natural evolution arising from the progressive application of corporatist doctrines or as a reaction to changes in the domestic political scene.[25] Contrary to such an "internal" view, this article argues that it was Brazil's growing involvement in the global conflict that played the most decisive role in these changes. This manifested itself in two processes in particular: On the one hand, the war effort and the alliance with the United States created the conditions that set in motion a cycle of industrialization and diversification of economic activity in Brazil, which, in turn, generated important changes in the composition of the working class. On the other, episodes of aggression by the Axis forces mobilized nationalist sentiment, which gave rise to a new political dynamic that led both supporters and adversaries of the regime, including communists, to take to the streets, presaging the post-war democratic era to come.[26] The way in which Vargas and his supporters dealt with the economic, social, and political impact of Brazil's insertion in this critical global context helps us to understand the aforementioned paradox between the strength and longevity of the institutional legacy of the Vargas era and its comparatively lesser success in terms of political movement. The exceptional situation that the war created helped consolidate a form of national politics centered around the industrialization of the country and the corporatist system of labor relations. Yet, the reactive, belated character of Vargas's initiatives to promote mass politics created a political legacy that was both precarious and contradictory. Before developing these arguments examining the particularities of Brazil's insertion in the context of World War II, I will

---

25. See, for example, Luiz Werneck Vianna, *Liberalismo e sindicato no Brasil* (Rio de Janeiro, 1976); Armando Boito Junior (ed.), *O sindicalismo de estado no Brasil. Uma analise crítica da estrutura sindical* (Campinas, 1991).
26. I have analyzed elsewhere in a more detailed way the complex dynamic behind the wave of insurrections that swept the country from the North to the South in reaction to the sinking of Brazilian ships by German submarines (with Vargas supporters at the forefront and the communists involved clandestinely), especially on the night of 18 August 1942, resulting in the destruction of German, Japanese, and Italian companies, residences, and clubs and those of the descendants of these immigrant groups. Alexandre Fortes, "A espionagem Aliada no Brasil durante a segunda guerra mundial. Cotidiano e política em Belém na visão da inteligência militar norte-americana", *Esboços. Revista do Programa de Pós-Graduação em História da UFSC*, 22: 34 (2016), pp. 81–115, 103–109.

briefly sketch the international historiographical debate on the relationship between total war, labor relations, and social rights.

TOTAL WAR, CITIZENSHIP, AND SOCIAL POLICIES

Historical scholarship dedicated to a wide variety of periods and countries has examined the role of the exceptional circumstances that war in general and the totalizing wars of the twentieth century create, both in strengthening the modern state's ability to regulate the economy and incorporating different sectors of the population, yet especially the lower classes as citizens. Hobsbawm attributes the very survival of the French Republic of 1792 to 1794 to the Jacobins' invention of what he calls "total war" (a notion that many other scholars would only use for the industrialized wars of the twentieth century): Surrounded by the most powerful armies in Europe, the French achieved victory by resorting to the "total mobilization of the nation's resources", obtained "through conscription, rationing and a rigidly controlled war economy, and virtual abolition, at home or abroad, of the distinction between soldiers and civilians". The state of war triggered the period's proactive popular action in support of the revolutionary government, whose methods "brought social justice nearer", even though it soon became clear the militarization of the police and of society were incompatible with "decentralized voluntarist direct democracy" that the *sansculotterie* cherished.[27] Similar paradoxes repeatedly appeared in other historical contexts.

The US Civil War resulted in a further "radicalization" of war and represents one of the nineteenth-century armed conflicts that anticipated the total wars of the twentieth century, including a close connection between war, social policy, and citizenship. Theda Skocpol dedicated one of her most classic works to the analysis of a pioneering program that introduced generous social programs for elderly, disabled, and dependent citizens, which the federal government implemented during Reconstruction (1865–1877). The competitive party politics of the late nineteenth century, which was the result of the expansion of suffrage, led to the expansion of benefits for veterans and their families. Expectations that this social policy would be implemented and universally applied, however, lost ground in the country's political agenda as the generation that had lived through the war disappeared by the turn of the twentieth century.[28]

In the twentieth century, especially in World War II, modern, industrialized war further morphed into total war, affecting and mobilizing societies comprehensively. This created space for interventionist policies,

---

27. Eric Hobsbawm, *The Age of Revolution, 1789–1848* (New York 1996 [1962]), p. 67.
28. Theda Skocpol, *Protecting Soldiers and Mothers: The Political Origins of Social Policy in the United States* (Cambridge, MA [etc.], 1992).

even in political environments predominantly hostile to it, such as in the United States. John Kenneth Galbraith underscores that the resistance that Keynesian ideas met and the timidity of anti-cyclical measure taken during Franklin D. Roosevelt's first administration contributed to the fact that, as late as 1939, 9.5 million Americans (seventeen per cent) were still unemployed. US involvement in the war led to the multiplication of government spending and, in 1942, various sectors experienced labor shortages. Galbraith comments, speaking ironically, that Hitler "was the true protagonist of the Keynesian ideas".[29] Yet, it was more than the state's full mobilization of the economy. Analyzing the context of labor union action of this period, Nelson Lichtenstein emphasizes that although "war-era corporatist structures failed to win lasting institutional expressions", in contrast with Western Europe, during the war, labor conflicts pointed toward other possibilities for the future:

> [...] elite power at the top of the mobilization apparatus was repeatedly challenged by insurgencies from below that sought to take advantage of the unprecedented demand for labor while at the same time actualizing the pluralist, social-patriotic ethos that was the quasi-official ideology of the World War Two home front.[30]

Already during World War I, it became evident that the overwhelming demands created by the mobilization of millions of soldiers over numerous years and the volume of armaments and supplies used in combat stretched thin the labor force, thus giving industrial workers an exceptional lever, strengthening the unions, and generating waves of labor activism. The war also transformed the composition of the labor force, for example in incorporating women into industry.

Conceptions of political economy also changed when the great wars of the twentieth century ended what Karl Polanyi had called "a hundred years of peace". He pointed to the connection between the geopolitical "balance of power" mechanism, a self-regulating market, the liberal state, and the gold standard.[31] The rupture of the first of these pillars of the nineteenth-century's global order shattered the others. Great Britain, bastion of fiscal equilibrium, was never the same again after having waged two wars that were well beyond the country's means. Centralized economic planning almost became a conditio sine qua non, as Lenin understood in extracting lessons from the German war economy that were then applied to the centralized economy policies in the Soviet Union during the period of Wartime Communism (1918–1921). While in 1939 only Germany and the USSR

---

29. John Kenneth Galbraith, *The Age of Uncertainty* (Boston, MA, 1977), p. 221.
30. Nelson Lichtenstein, "Class Politics and the State During World War Two", *International Labor and Working-Class History*, 58 (2000), pp. 261–274, 261.
31. Karl Polanyi, *The Great Transformation: The Political and Economic Origins of Our Time* (Boston, MA, 1944), ch. 1.

possessed mechanisms for comprehensively controlling the economy, in the course of World War II, Western democracies had installed them as well (often even more effectively than the former). As a result, British children enjoyed better health at the war's end than at its beginning, workers' salaries were higher, and the sense of social justice was strengthened.[32] In various countries, furthermore, World War II forged a culture of solidarity based on an ethos of shared sacrifices, helping to create the conditions that would make possible a broad, consistent political alliance that favored redistributive reforms.[33] After the war, as Geoff Eley points out, "the major increments of general European democracy [...] depended on the prior conditions of societal breakdown or transformation produced by war".[34] Rights expanded considerably in several waves as the state intensified its "demands upon society, its resources and territorial population". While the militarization of society had undoubtedly a top-down and authoritarian dynamic, at the same time, war produced "new democratic capacities, which became organized into an impressive postwar legal, institutional, and political settlement", and the war effort "legitimized the voice of all those groups willing to situate themselves inside the consensus", such as an organized working class, women, youths, and soldiers. These contradictions are succinctly communicated in the expression, "cashing in of the patriotic check"; in other words, "the popular expectation of substantial social and political reform in return for the sacrifices required by the wartime mobilization".[35]

It is thus no coincidence that the impact of World War II on the working class in various parts of the world has become a recurring topic of debate, including a growing number of case studies for non-Western countries.[36] For instance, Peter Alexander has compared the impact of the war economy on the interrelation between race and class both in the United States and in South Africa. In both countries, "as a consequence of war-related industrialization and resistance, black workers joined labour movements en masse. [...] [It] was a period of extensive industrial conflict and rising union membership" and "the working class was transformed, becoming larger, younger, blacker and more female".[37] Both countries also similarly

32. Eric Hobsbawm, *The Age of Extremes: The Short Twentieth Century, 1914–1991* (London, 1994), p. 47.
33. Geoff Eley, *Forging Democracy: The History of the Left in Europe, 1850–2000* (Oxford [etc.], 2002), pp. 278–298.
34. *Idem*, "War and the Twentieth-Century State", *Daedalus*, 124:2 (1995), pp. 155–174, 162.
35. *Ibid.*, pp. 164, 165, 166.
36. See, for instance, the following two issues of *International Labor and Working-Class History* dedicated to these topics: "The Working Class in World War II", *International Labor and Working-Class History*, 38 (1990) and "Wartime Economies and the Mobilization of Labor", *International Labor and Working-Class History*, 38 (2000).
37. Peter Alexander, "South African and US Labour in the Era of World War II: Similar Trends and Underlying Differences", in Rick Halpern and Jonathan Morris (eds), *American*

experienced increased participation in the labor market that strengthened activists' self-confidence, as well as accelerated inflation, which intensified the pressure for higher salaries and thus resulted in strikes, which were generally successful. Agreements between organized labor, the government, and employers, although intended to decrease the number of work stoppages, further stimulated unionization, which in turn fomented the spontaneous growth of movements focused on claiming rights. In both countries, although many workers were still full of racial prejudice, multiracial strikes took place, which generated a higher level of organization among black workers and a more egalitarian tendency among white workers. The differences between the two cases, however, are equally striking: In the United States, the Executive Order 8802 banned racial segregation in hiring practices, while measure 145 in South Africa reinforced racial divisions. In this process, organized labor in South African was severely weakened, and the possibility of attaining working-class, interracial unity in the post-war period was substantially reduced.

Latin America's involvement in World War II was of a nature and intensity absolutely distinct from that of the main belligerent nations. While military conflicts have, in general, played a less important role in the formation of nation states in the region than in other parts of the world,[38] the subcontinent at first sight seems to have been peculiarly detached from the twentieth century's great wars: Latin America has not experienced the "gigantic catalyst" of the two world wars, which, in Europe, "radicalized unpolitical workers, multiplied trade union members, lifted working-class parties into office, unleashed social revolutions".[39] This manifested itself also in the way these have been rendered in public space: Despite Brazil's participation in World War II, "even in 1945, there appears to have been little effort to glorify" the Allied victory.[40]

The South African example mentioned above, however, suggests that the war effort can be important even for workers from countries with little or no involvement in combat. In her book on Chilean coal miners, Jody Pavilack demonstrates how World War II marked the high point of both the process through which workers conquered their rights and of their assertion as political protagonists, a process that had already been developing

Exceptionalism? US Working-Class Formation in an International Context (New York, 1997), pp. 244–270, 261.

38. This refers to wars between nation states. The picture changes dramatically if armed internal conflict, civil wars, anti-colonial mobilizations, and the internal colonization campaigns against indigenous populations are included.

39. Perry Anderson, "The Common and the Particular", *International Labor and Working-Class History*, 36 (1989), p. 31–36, 35.

40. Miguel Centeno, *Blood and Debt: War and the Nation-State in Latin America* (University Park, PA, 2002), pp. 86–87.

under the Popular Front governments since the beginning of the 1930s. This more leveled interaction between workers and representatives both of capital and the state manifested itself in a unique political conjuncture, in which ideological polarization between capitalism and communism temporarily became less important in the face of the conflict between the Allied and the Axis forces.[41] Pavilack exemplifies this spirit of Peoples Front anti-fascism in recounting the US Vice President Henry Wallace's speech in Lota, a mining city known as a communist stronghold, hailing the local workers and their leaders as "soldiers of democracy".[42] In Brazil, this profound change in the correlation of forces played out as well, although under the specific conditions of an authoritarian, corporatist regime.

INTERNATIONAL RELATIONS, INDUSTRIALIZATION AND SOCIAL RIGHTS: BRAZILIAN WORKERS AND WORLD WAR II

Brazil entered World War II at a relatively late stage, joining the Allies in August 1942 (before that, it had itself declared neutral). It contributed to the war effort with 25,000 soldiers sent into combat in Italy, of which 471 died.[43] In addition, 1,074 died when German submarines torpedoed ships off the Brazilian coast. The importance of Brazil's war involvement, however, goes beyond these numbers (which, compared to the death toll of the conflict as a whole, are miniscule): it produced transformations that would co-shape the course of the country's history in the second half of the twentieth century.

In an analysis of the international situation prepared by the Brazilian Minister of Foreign Relations, Oswaldo Aranha, for a secret meeting between the Brazilian president Getúlio Vargas and Franklin Roosevelt in the Brazilian city of Natal in 1943, one can find "a summary of Brazil's foreign and domestic policies in the following decades": The "secure and intimate cooperation with the United States" would be a condition for the development of sea and air power aimed at consolidating Brazil's military predominance in South America. This demanded the development of heavy and war industry, the stimulation of key industries for global post-war reconstruction, the expansion of railway and road systems, and an exploration of the country's reserves of combustible fuels.[44]

---

41. Hobsbawm, *The Age of Extremes*, p. 143.
42. Jody Pavilack, *Mining for the Nation: The Politics of Chile's Coal Communities from the Popular Front to the Cold War* (University Park, PA, 2011).
43. Approximately 12,000 were injured during the war, and accidents or illnesses later caused two thousand more deaths.
44. Frank McCann, "Brazil and World War II: The Forgotten Ally. 'What Did You Do in the War, Zé Carioca?'", *Estudios interdisciplinarios de America Latina y el Caribe*, 6:2 (1995), pp. 35–70, 46.

This was a radically new scenario. In previous decades, those responsible for steering the Brazilian economy had sought in vain Washington's assistance in signing commercial agreements that would have enabled them to secure the foreign currency necessary for the country's imports as well as for investments needed to boost its industrial development. The sudden willingness to bestow the status of strategic ally on Brazil came only in 1940, when British intelligence convinced the North American authorities that the Germans, making use of the open sympathies of the *Estado Novo* for European fascism, could cross the Atlantic along Dakar-Natal line, establish bases in north-eastern Brazil, and foment a wave of pro-Axis coups d'état in South America. The Americans, however, not only intensified the Good Neighbor Policy (which had already been announced for the whole of Latin America in 1933 by Franklin D. Roosevelt in his inaugural address and had become ever more important with the prospect of a new major war, aiming at cultural, economic, and other forms of international cooperation in the Americas); they also planned "Operation Pot of Gold" a "preventive" invasion of 100,000 soldiers, which would be set in motion should negotiations with Vargas fail.[45]

German economic influence in Brazil had grown in the previous period. In the early thirties, the collapse of coffee exports, a basic source of foreign currency, had initially forced Vargas to order a sharp devaluation of the Brazilian currency. Between 1933 and 1936, planned and controlled deficits as well as a series of other measures (a policy later summed up under the label "import substitution industrialization") led to average growth of eight per cent (13.4 per cent in the industrial sector). But both the United States and Britain condemned the new currency exchange rate, which differentiated between imports and the transfer of profits, and they made their renewal of credit conditional upon the "liberalization" of the Brazilian economy. By contrast, Nazi Germany offered Brazil a deal that attended to the interests of the agro-export and industrial sectors in a more balanced way. The "compensation marks" that the German economic Minister Hjalmar Schacht proposed in 1934 were deposited in accounts on behalf of the Banco do Brasil in the Reichsbank (the so-called Ausländer-Sonderkonten Für Inlandszahlungen – ASKI), without the losses that would have resulted from the currency's conversion into US dollars. These compensation marks were then used to acquire machinery and supplies, as well as new armaments for the outdatedly equipped Brazilian Armed Forces, which, at the time, the United States refused to supply. Between 1934 and 1939, German participation in Brazilian exports grew from twelve to twenty per cent, and the participation of the United States only from 21.2

45. *Ibid.*, p. 41.

to 25.5 per cent, while British fell from 19.4 to 10.9 per cent.[46] This had a lasting impact: Still in 1941, the US consul in Recife attributed the continuing sympathies in north-eastern Brazil for the Nazis to the memory of the "prosperity" and the "good times" the compensation marks had brought, which guaranteed favorable prices for local producers of commodities, in addition to access to the much sought after German industrial products.[47] Local affiliates of German and German-Brazilian companies created "Germanophilic" networks throughout the country, fostered the development of local Nazi groups, and supported German commercial, political, and military espionage.[48] German clubs rivaled the British ones as spaces of elite sociability in numerous Brazilian cities. In 1936, the flags of Brazil and of the Third Reich waved on the cover of the magazine of the Deutscher Klub of Pernambuco.[49]

Meanwhile, relations with the United States took a turn for the worse in the context of the US recession of 1937. The situation began to change precisely with the beginning of World War II in 1939 and the subsequent attempts by the US to gain Brazil as an ally. The Brazilian government continued their prior policy currency exchange controls, but this time without US opposition. On the contrary, a new agreement was made for the payment of Brazil's foreign debt and in 1940, the "Inter-American Coffee Agreement" was established which set quotas for Brazilian coffee. In 1942, the Washington Accords extended the policies of such quotas to a range of other Brazilian products including rubber, cocoa, cotton, Brazil nuts, iron ore, industrial diamonds, mica, quartz, jute, castor beans, etc., many of which had never been exported before. The economic rapprochement also meant a renewed increase in the importation of manufactured goods from the United States, while simultaneously new opportunities for Brazilian industrial growth arose in the context of the commercial blockade with Europe. Vargas exploited the global conflict to initiate the construction of the Volta Redonda Steel Plant (Usina Siderúrgica de Volta Redonda), allowing Brazilians to imagine turning their country, home of the largest iron ore reserves in the world, into a great steel producer. During its period

---

46. Marcelo de Paiva Abreu, "The Brazilian Economy, 1930–1980", Leslie Bethell (ed.) *The Cambridge History of Latin America, vol. 9: Brazil since 1930* (Cambridge, 2008), pp. 283–393, 302.

47. Walter J. Linthicum (American Consul) to Jefferson Caffery (American Ambassador), 11 February 1941, National Archives and Records Administration (Washington, DC) [hereafter, NARA], Record Group 84 – Records of the Foreign Service Posts of the Department of State [hereafter, Record Group 84], Entry 2154, Political Reports, compiled 1938–1949 (Recife), Box 1.

48. Stanley Hilton, *Suástica sobre o Brasil. A história da espionagem alemã no Brasil, 1939–1944* (Rio de Janeiro, 1977).

49. Walter J. Linthicum (American Vice Consul) to the Secretary of State, "Political activities in North-eastern Brazil", Recife, 13 February 1942, NARA, Record Group 84, Entry 2154, Political Reports, compiled 1938–1949 (Recife), Box 1.

of neutrality in the war, Brazil had discussed this project with the Germans, but the Allied blockade of the Atlantic since 1939 made such a partnership unviable. The United States refused to invest directly in the enterprise and to assume its management, as Vargas had wanted, but they offered decisive US financial and technical support for the creation of the plant as a state company.[50]

After the accords of 1942, supplying wartime demands generated an average growth rate of 6.4 per cent until 1945, with industry growing at a rate of 9.9 per cent per year. The state's room for maneuver was strengthened with the increase in tax revenues from both consumer goods and income, in addition to the emission of the War Bonus. The accumulation of foreign reserves made possible a definitive negotiation of Brazil's foreign debt in 1943, with a reduction of fifty per cent of its nominal value. The state assumed control of waters, minerals, and strategic industries, banks, and the insurance sector. Companies and properties belonging to the Axis governments were expropriated, including the powerful German and Italian banks. The Itabira Iron Company, founded by British investors in 1911 and the cause for long-drawn conflict with Brazilian authorities, became the state-owned and run Companhia Vale do Rio Doce. Meanwhile, the United States financed the construction of the railway connecting the gigantic iron mines of Itabira to the port of Vitória, capital of the southeastern state of Espírito Santo. Other state industries created during that period include the Companhia Nacional de Álcalis[51] and the Fábrica Nacional de Motores.[52] The management of the economy grew stronger with the creation of the Department of Public Administration (Departamento de Administração Pública), which modernized the budgetary system, of the Technical Economic and Finance Council (Conselho Técnico Econômico e Financeiro), and the Economic Mobilization Planning Commission (Coordenação de Mobilização Econômica). In the social policy realm, this was also a period that saw the creation of a body of labor regulations, most importantly the Consolidação das Leis do Trabalho in 1943 (Consolidation of Labor Laws) forging a coherent body of labor legislation out of the accumulated stock of previous regulations, the consolidation of a labor court system (Justiça do Trabalho), and the foundation of the Institutos de Previdência Social responsible for social security programs.

Relations with the United States, however, were rapidly changing. In 1943, once an Allied victory was assured, the United States proved to be less generous. While the local costs of coffee production were rising, the US resisted further

---

50. De Paiva Abreu, "The Brazilian Economy", p. 313; Dinius, *Brazil's Steel City*, ch. 1.
51. See one of the classics of the 1970s developmentalist literature: Octavio Ianni, *Estado e planejamento econômico no Brasil* (Rio de Janeiro, 2009 [1971]), pp. 24–32.
52. For the Fábrica Nacional de Motores with an emphasis on workers' struggles: José Ricardo Ramalho, *Estado-patrão e luta operária. O caso FNM* (São Paulo, 1989).

readjusting the price. Also, Brazil's protectionist rationing of imports in 1944 generated new waves of discontentment within the Alliance. On the political scene, Vargas's relationship with the US had been deteriorating at an accelerating pace, and the ambassador Adolf Berle would come to play a relevant role in the fall of the Brazilian dictator. The experience of a nationalist political project in alliance with the US, however, would have long-term consequences – Brazil, in that regard, was no exception on the subcontinent with many Hispano-American countries taking a similar path since the 1930s (although with different political regimes and varying degrees of assertiveness vis-à-vis the US). The nature of war would definitively strengthen the link between industrialization and national sovereignty. In Brazil, Vargas's "nationalist bargain" between the Axis and the Allies established a general orientation that sought to advance industrialization as the strategic objective and that would guide Brazilian foreign policy, then and for the next fifty years; this approach to foreign relations remained in force even through the great variety of different political regimes that characterized the second half of the twentieth century in Brazil.[53]

But just how did Brazilian workers experience this period of accelerated changes? To what extent were the connections between defense, foreign policy, economic policy, and conceptions of citizenship, which have been observed in other contexts, also present in Brazil? Comparing Brazil in 1940 – ten years after Vargas came to power – with what happened in this period in various parts of Latin America[54] makes evident the fact that neither the state, nor political parties or working-class movements in Brazil achieved the mass mobilization necessary to provide the regime with an organic political support. In the absence of an integrated nationwide organization, those Vargas supporters who were part of the labor movement did not play any significant role in the political system. Even the era's social and pro-labor legislation was fragmented and was often not complied with. The onset of the *Estado Novo* dictatorship under Vargas in 1937 further exacerbated this situation, since the labor unions, now rid of communists, suffered a severe loss of both members and effectiveness, given the

53. Ricardo Seitenfus, *O Brasil de Getúlio Vargas e a formação dos blocos, 1930–1942. O processo do envolvimento brasileiro na II Guerra Mundial* (São Paulo, 1985); Frank McCann, *The Brazilian-American Alliance, 1937–1945* (Princeton, NJ, 1974); Ricardo Seitenfus, *O Brasil vai a guerra. O processo do envolvimento brasileiro na segunda guerra mundial* (Barueri, 2003); Paulo Vizentini, *Relações internacionais do Brasil. De Vargas a Lula* (São Paulo, 2003).

54. The incorporation of the organized working class into the political system, combined with the active role of state regulation in working conditions, had seen its first beginnings in several Latin American countries during and after World War I, yet the most important advances were made since the 1930s (but not without some shifts and reversals). For suggestive studies on three major countries (Argentina, Mexico, and Chile), see: Juan Carlos Torre, *La vieja guardia sindical y Perón. Sobre los orígenes del peronismo* (Buenos Aires, 1990); Kevin Middlebrook, *The Paradox of Revolution: Labor, the State, and Authoritarianism in Mexico* (Baltimore, MA, 1995); Pavilack, *Mining for the Nation.*

government supporters' organizational weakness. In other words, in comparative perspective, the Vargas regime in Brazil until the beginning of the 1940s fell short of a major characteristic of Latin American populisms, namely the ability to mobilize or coopt a mass popular movement in support of the regime.[55]

The perception of the importance of total war, however, changed the *Estado Novo* leadership's understanding of the relationship between civilian and military activities, which, in turn, reverberated in the realm of labor politics. Even without hostilities on its own territory and without a military commitment beyond the 25,000 strong Brazilian Expeditionary Force (Força Expedicionária Brasileira), this new kind of war resulted in the identification of civilian manual labor with national defense (the "soldiers of production"),[56] generating contradictory dynamics that would bring both an assault on workers and important reforms in their favor. On the one hand, legislation geared toward economic mobilization, such as Law (*Decreto-Lei*) number 4639, passed on 31 August 1942, empowered the government to suspend labor and civil rights.[57] On the other hand, though, the image of the factory as the trenches enabled workers to appropriate nationalist discourse as an instrument in their quest for better working conditions and pay. If workers sacrificed for the nation, they deserved a dignified life.[58] At the same time, rationing, scarcity, speculation, the black market, and so on stimulated popular revolt against the "sharks" that exploited the sacrifice imposed on the nation during wartime to gain extraordinary profits, strengthening class consciousness.[59]

---

55. For a comparative analysis of historical populisms in Latin America see the contributions to: Mackinnon and Petrone, *Populismo y neopopulismo en America Latina*.

56. On the militarization in Brazil during World War II, see, for instance, Fernando Pureza, "Economia de guerra, batalha da produção e soldados-operários. O impacto da Segunda Guerra Mundial na vida dos trabalhadores de Porto Alegre (1942–1945)" (MA thesis, Universidade Federal do Rio Grande do Sul, Porto Alegre, 2009).

57. On the impact of wartime labor laws and workers reactions, see Sílvio Frank Alem, "Os trabalhadores e a 'redemocratização' (Estudo sobre o Estado, partidos e participação dos trabalhadores assalariados urbanos e do pós-guerra imediato) 1942–1948" (MA thesis, IFCH-Unicamp, 1981), chs I and II; Maria Celia Paoli, O trabalhador urbano na fala dos outros", in José Sérgio Leite Lopes (ed.), *Cultura e Identidade Operária. Aspectos da cultura da classe trabalhadora* (Rio de Janeiro, 1987), pp. 53–99; Joel Wolfe, *Working Women, Working Men: São Paulo and the Rise of Brazil's Industrial Working Class, 1900–1955* (Durham, NC, 1993), pp. 94–124, correctly argues that the militarization of labor limited even more the possibility that official labor unions might act as a mechanism for the representation of workers' demands in this period. He ignores, however, the possibilites that the aforementioned contradictory dynamics of anti-fascist nationalism opened up.

58. Hélio da Costa, *Em busca da memória* (Comissão de Fábrica, Partido e Sindicato no Pós-guerra) (São Paulo, 1995), pp. 15–20.

59. Paoli, "O trabalhador urbano", pp. 88–90.

In parallel with these wartime labor politics, Brazil's productive demands and accelerated growth (as well as the demands of its US ally) unleashed waves of large-scale internal migrations: The acceleration of industrial production attracted rural workers to the city and workers from less industrialized regions to more industrialized ones. Thousands of men and women from Brazil's north-eastern region were recruited and drawn to the Amazon region to become "soldiers of rubber".[60] Large masses of laborers migrated to uninhabited regions of the country, in which companies build large industrial plants like the aforementioned Usina Siderúrgica in Volta Redonda in the state of Rio de Janeiro, the Fábrica Nacional de Motores in Xerém, built in an area in the outskirts of the city of Rio de Janeiro called the Baixada Fluminense, as well as the Nitro Química in São Miguel Paulista, located on the periphery of the city of São Paulo,[61] or the manganese mines in the Serra do Navio in the northern state of Amapá.[62] Similarly, airports were built in Brazil's North and Northeast by the Airport Development Program, a project carried out by Pan American Airlines.[63]

An important reversal occurred, as well, with respect to conceptions of ethnic and racial hierarchies: German immigrants, who, until then, were seen as important contributors to the "whitening" of the country, became the greatest expression of the external ("the Axis") and internal ("a Fifth Column") enemy. As part of this process, the "imagined community" of the nation was redefined and centered around more "internal" sources, with policies that aimed toward the valorization of "popular culture", which, at the same time, were cleansed of its "disorderly" qualities.[64]

This "self-nationalization" of a society that, until recently, had celebrated the influx of a large numbers of European immigrants, among them a sizeable group of German-speakers, led to a series of conflicts and symbolical displacements: In Porto Alegre, for instance, which, at that time, was Brazil's third industrial pole, most industries were owned by Brazilians of German origin, generating a powerful association of ethnicity and class.

60. María Verónica Secreto, *Soldados da borracha. Trabalhadores entre o sertão e a Amazônia no governo Vargas* (São Paulo, 2007); on the debates inside the US government and Congress about the labor conditions and regulations in the wartime rubber production in the Amazon, see Seth Garfield, "A Amazônia no imaginário norte-americano em tempo de guerra", *Revista Brasileira de História*, 29 (2009), pp. 19–65.
61. Paulo Fontes, *Um Nordeste em São Paulo: Trabalhadores migrantes em São Miguel Paulista (1945–66)* (Rio de Janeiro, 2008), pp. 89–131.
62. Adalberto Paz, "Os mineiros da floresta. Sociedade e trabalho em uma fronteira de mineração industrial amazônica (1943–1964)" (PhD dissertation, UNICAMP, Campinas, 2011), pp. 21–60.
63. Rebecca Herman, "In Defense of Sovereignty: Labor, Crime, Sex and Nation at US Military Bases in Latin America, 1940–1947" (PhD, University of California, Berkeley, 2014), p. 305, ch. II, "Labor Rights", Part 2: "Brazil", pp. 105–134.
64. Adalberto Paranhos, *O roubo da fala. Origens da ideologia do trabalhismo no Brasil* (São Paulo, 1999), ch. II.

This was not simply a matter of prejudice against what among German communities was seen as "Brazilian" workers (who bore last names of Portuguese origin and were associated with interracial unions with Indigenous or Afro-descended people). The institutional structure of the "German colony" (clubs, schools, newspapers, churches, the German consulate, and so on) amplified the influence of the German-Brazilian business owner on a broad spectrum of aspects of local social life. The ability to speak the language and ties with families of German origin might open doors for jobs in large companies with relatively comprehensive welfare schemes, as well as for their upward social mobility in and outside the factories. Brazil's entrance into the war had a profound impact on this local social arrangement. One symbolic indication of this shift was the popular reaction against the torpedoing of Brazilian ships by German submarines in August 1942: In Porto Alegre's industrial district, the street signs in "Germany" and "Italy" Avenue were pulled down by the crowd and substituted by other signs with the names of the two ships that had been sunk by German torpedoes. The act was later officially endorsed by a formal renaming of the streets by the city's mayor's office. Department stores that were part of the Renner chain, associated with the largest industrial complex in the state and an example of "welfare capitalism", were stoned.[65]

If Brazilian descendants of Germans were concentrated in the south, their presence in the country's economic activity also reached other regions, strengthened by the tightening commercial relationship between the two countries between 1934 and 1939. In Bahia, Dannemann and Suerdieck, two of the most traditional cigar factories in the interior of the state region (known as the Recôncavo, otherwise dominated by cane cultivation) were owned by "subjects of the Axis" (in fact, Brazilians of German origin). They also became the target of mass popular attacks after the sinking of Brazilian ships by the German navy.[66] The largest industrial group in Pernambuco, Tecelagem Paulista, was owned by the Lundgren family, Swedish immigrants of German descent, who were under the powerful surveillance of domestic and international espionage because of their involvement with Nazism. As spokespeople for the north-eastern textile business world, in 1939 the Lundgrens, in a request to the authorities asking

---

65. Alexandre Fortes, *Nós do quarto distrito. A classe trabalhadora porto-alegrense e a Era Vargas* (Rio de Janeiro, 2004), ch. 5. That the sign of Avenida Italia was taken down simultaneously with the one of Avenida Alemanha allows for a second reading of the events: This popular action can also be seen as not targeting symbols of Germany per se but of the Axis powers and thus as driven in equal degree by a anti-fascist feelings.
66. See the eyewitness account of a worker of communist affiliation: João Falcão, *O Brasil e a Segunda Guerra Mundial. Testemunho e depoimento de um soldado convocado* (Brasília, 1998), pp. 25–42.

for protectionist measures in favor of their industry, invoked the supposed racial inferiority of their workers as a main argument. It is worth quoting this at length as it seems representative of a language that was ubiquitous among Brazilian elites until the mid-1940s (and which would vanish from official discourse thereafter):

> Among the populations of the North, primitive elements that entered into their amalgamation predominate – white, black, and indigenous, forming the so-called *mameluco* and *mestiço* [mixed] races, whereas in the South, because of the migratory movements, this has had a positive influence on the formation of Brazil's southern race.[67]

An ideology of racial supremacy was, of course, not limited to certain immigrant communities or those circles in Brazil that had sympathized with fascism or the Axis powers. As is well known, a racist prejudice against the ethno-racial composition of Brazil, especially the Afro-Brazilian population, was a cornerstone of positivism, the guiding ideology of the dominant elites since the abolition of slavery in 1888, which also had numerous followers in the early labor movements: "Whitening" the country through European immigration in order to ensure "progress" was the outspoken and tacit consensus among the propertied classes, state elites, and many immigrant communities.[68] In contrast, the war indeed redefined discourses concerning racial relations and their connections with class relations in Brazil. It marked the beginning of a new ideological framework replacing the old positivist ideas with the new image of Brazil as an essentially "mixed" nation that has constituted as a "racial democracy" and achieved harmony among the different groups. One of the major intellectual originators and advocates of this turn was the sociologist Gilberto Freyre (1900–1987), who, in his 1933 work *Casa-Grande e Senzala* (*The Masters and the Slaves*), boldly affirmed the Afro-Brazilian culture, at the same time painting an image of complementary symbiosis among the different groups of Brazilian society.[69] It is thus indicative of the shifts in the mid-1940s that Freyre, after publishing an article in this vein in 1942, was arrested by two police officials who were "openly sympathetic with the Axis". In his piece, Freyre denounced the "falsely religious" people who dedicated themselves to spreading "ferociously ethnocentric, anti-Christian, and anti-Brazilian doctrines",[70] and he concluded:

---

67. Cited in José Sérgio Leite Lopes, *A tecelagem dos conflitos de classe na "cidade das chaminés"* (São Paulo, 1988), p. 295.
68. Jerry Dávila, *Diploma of Whiteness: Race and Social Policy in Brazil, 1917–1945* (Durham, NC, 2003).
69. Gilberto Freyre, *The Masters and the Slaves (Casa-Grande & Senzala): A Study in the Development of Brazilian Civilization* (New York, 1946).
70. The "falsely religious" were former Franciscans from Germany who had been responsible for the Nazi propaganda coming out of precisely the Paulista Textile Company (Companhia de

In an era in which forms of political hatred and racial pride are superimposed on top of everything else, even forcing the religious to break with their fidelity to the Christian ideas of human fraternity, peoples, like the Brazilians, whose entire organization is built on racial mixing, concerning the rights of the black, indigenous, and mixed-race people to the same privileges as whites, one has to be vigilant.[71]

The emerging new consensus about racial relations enabled the Vargas regime to draw closer to a fundamental ideological component of a populist regime: the invocation of "the" people as a broad group of society that embodies the national idiosyncrasies and presupposes equality among each of the groups' members. To become effective, the regime thus had not only to include workers into the political project but also undo (or at least pretend to undo) the color line.

POPULISM BY FORCE OF CIRCUMSTANCES?

One major aspect of populism remains its mobilizational character – mobilizations that give a populist leader much of his legitimacy and power, and which this leader should, ideally, be able to control. As mentioned, the Vargas regime since the "Revolution of 1930", yet especially during the *Estado Novo* since 1937, had conspicuously lacked this mobilizational component. However, as mentioned above in relation to the renaming of streets in Porto Alegre, popular mass action driven by nationalist sentiments, with the support (or at least the complacent tolerance) of sectors of the state apparatus, started precisely with Brazil's involvement in World War II. Being then a novelty in the Brazilian political scene, at least on a national scale, these anti-Axis mass actions multiplied throughout the country, especially after 17 August 1942, when the U-507 German submarine sank various sea vessels off the Brazilian coast resulting in 551 deaths. In a limited way, this also resulted in a sensible ideological shift in the *Estado Novo* from exhibiting philo-fascist tendencies towards a kind of

Tecidos Paulista). See a Brazilian secret police report filed in the reports by the US consul in Pernambuco: "Secretaria de Segurança Pública. Denúncia sobre supostas atividades de religiosos estrangeiros em Pernambuco. Diligências da Delegacia de Ordem Política e Social para esclarecimentos", in NARA, Record Group 84, Entry 2154 (Recife: – Political Reports, 1938-49), Box 1. Curiously, in November 1942, twenty-three of the forty-seven German employees of the company were detained by the political police and sent to a prison camp built by that same company sixty kilometers away from Recife, where they were held until August of 1945 – a company whose owners had shown to be heavily involved with Nazism. See Priscila Perazzo, *Prisioneiros da guerra. Os "Súditos do eixo" nos campos de concentração brasileiros (1942–1945)* (São Paulo, 2009), pp. 112–132.

71. Gilberto Freyre, "O exemplo de Ibiapina", in *idem, Diário de Pernambuco*, 11 June 1942. Quoted from a clipping of a newspaper article filed among the reports of the US consul in Pernambuco, in NARA, Record Group 84, Entry 2154 (Recife: – Political Reports, 1938-49), Box 1.

anti-fascist nationalism. While much of this was tokenistic from the state's side it did open some opportunities for left-wing activists. Communist militants recount that the campaign in favor of Brazil's entrance in World War II helped break the left's isolation in the national political realm after the intense waves of repression in 1935 and 1937.[72]

As this article aimed to illustrate, Brazil's involvement in World War II helped to trigger a series of economic, political, social, and cultural changes. While historians studying post-1930 labor history have always converged on the years 1941–1945 – not least because of the consolidation of Vargas-era labor laws and the emergence of a new kind of working-class political participation – the impact of World War II on the Brazilian working class has only been studied in depth more recently. In these more recent studies, three concerns have attracted the attention: First, the changes that the war produced in the articulation of class and inter-ethnic relations. Second, the changes that the evolution of Brazil's involvement in the international conflict engendered among the political forces vying for the support of the growing numbers of urban workers in the country. Third, the connections between, on the one hand, the conflicts among the top hierarchy of Vargas's *Estado Novo* as Brazil moved toward declaring war against the Axis, and on the other hand the adoption of a more proactive policy of expanding workers' entitlements to the rights of citizenship.

This article has argued that, in order to fully understand the impact of World War II on the Vargas regime and its relation to labor, it is necessary to take the full range of processes into account. In this way, it becomes clear how total war was a powerful force of change, even in a country with no hostilities on its territory (and only some at its shores) and a relatively small military commitment: Economically, World War II enabled the regime to become part of the Allied war machinery, producing a series of highly valued raw materials and crops under relatively favorable conditions, at the same time initiating a program of further industrialization and seeing the local consumer industry expand. Socially, this led not only to the well-researched further inclusion of workers and the expansion of rights and legal regulations of labor, but also to momentous processes of internal migration, restructuring, and swelling the urban working classes. The corporatist arrangement already installed in the 1930s was thus strengthened and expanded. Culturally, it led to a certain re-shuffling of the ethno-racial hierarchies in Brazil, resulting in a symbolical move away from previously

---

72. The metal worker Eloy Martins, for instance, describes his shop-floor activism in the state workshops in Porto Alegre, recalling the collective reading of news from the war that took place after lunch: "Our work was so efficient that, as soon as the party became legal, we were able to build a cell with more than twenty sympathizers. The machine operator, who was an intransigent defender of Hitler, became a sympathizer of the socialist cause". Eloy Martins, *Um depoimento político* (Porto Alegre, 1989), pp. 72–73.

valued groups such as German immigrants, and the revaluation of Brazil as an essentially mixed nation of *mestiços*. Politically, meanwhile, Brazil's involvement in the war conditioned and enabled a mobilizational dynamics which was novel in Brazilian politics and which moved the Vargas regime – which had since 1930 been a "populism sui generis" without the systematic invocation or mobilization of the masses – closer to other populist regimes in Latin America, such as Peronism in Argentina or Cardenism in Mexico.

The notion of populism has justifiably been criticized as problematic because of its analytical vagueness and its negative connotations. However, the critical and revisionist response – to dispose of the notion altogether and to use *trabalhismo* in order to highlight processes of inclusion and entitlement, which took place in Brazil especially since the mid-1940s, has its own limitations: It tends to over-emphasize idiosyncratic specificities, it ignores transnational and global influences, and, above all, it mistakes a central component, *trabalhismo*, for the whole. This whole – for want of a better term, it remains useful to call it populism – only becomes fully comprehensible if other domains are included in the analysis, such as geopolitical constellations, inter-ethnic relations, ideological shifts, yet above all the incorporation of mass mobilization, under the aegis of nationalism, as an intrinsic part of politics. Of course, the role of workers and popular classes in this process should never be underestimated (and indeed has been pointed out in a series of excellent studies). At the same time, in Brazil an apparently "external" process, World War II, equally played a central role. It helped to push a regime that previously had tended to shy away from such a kind of politics towards actually adopting "populism". In this way, populism as a political system in Brazil was born during the conjuncture of the World War II.

Translation: Amy Chazkel

IRSH 62 (2017), Special Issue, pp. 191–216 doi:10.1017/S0020859017000591
© 2018 Internationaal Instituut voor Sociale Geschiedenis

The Local and the Global: Neighborhoods, Workers and Associations in São Paulo (1945–1964)

PAULO FONTES[1]

*School of Social Sciences of the Fundação Getulio Vargas
(CPDOC/FGV), Praia de Botafogo, 190 – sala 1422, 14° Andar
Botafogo, Rio de Janeiro
RJ, 22250-900, Brazil*

E-mail: paulo.fontes@fgv.br

ABSTRACT: This article aims to analyze residents' associations organized around specific working-class neighborhoods in São Paulo between the end of World War II and the Brazilian Military coup in 1964. It examines, in particular, the connections between neighborhood associations and labor union struggles. Based on the strong social networks and informal relationships created by workers, organizations like the Neighborhood Friends Societies (Sociedades Amigos de Bairro) were fundamental to the construction of political communities that had a powerful impact on electoral processes and on the formation of the state at the local level. Likewise, this article will show how, during that period, identities at the neighborhood level frequently developed in dialogue with processes of class formation, staking claim to a language of rights associated with the condition of being a worker and, simultaneously, a citizen. Finally, the piece suggests how analyses with such a localized scope, like those focused on specific working-class neighborhoods can intervene in debates concerning Global Labor History.

On 27 January 1954, Heitor Brugners, the director of the Friends of Vila Palmeira Society in a neighborhood to the north of the city of São Paulo, wrote a letter requesting that Jânio Quadros, São Paulo's mayor who would later be elected president of Brazil, intervene in an ongoing matter with São Paulo Light and Power, the Canadian company that held the concession for the city's public lighting. Brugners hoped that, with the mayor's help, the powerful concessionaire could be convinced to install streetlights in his neighborhood, in the far outskirts of the city.[2] In June of that year, residents of Vila Independência in the town of Ipiranga likewise directed a petition to

---

1. Paulo Fontes holds a research fellowship Pesquisador Bolsista Produtividade by the Conselho Nacional de Desenvolvimento Científico e Tecnológico (CNPq). I thank the participants in the two workshops carried out to develop this Special Issue. In particular, I would like to thank Adalberto Paz and David Mayer for their comments and suggestions.
2. Processo 071441/1954, Secretaria Municipal de Gestão (Prefeitura de São Paulo) – Divisão do Arquivo Municipal de Processos [hereafter, DGDP-2], Secretaria Municipal de Planejamento, Orçamento e Gestão [hereafter, SMPOG]).

their city's mayor by way of their local Neighborhood Friends Society (Sociedade Amigos de Bairro). This petition, like their counterparts in Vila Palmeira, asked the mayor to intervene with The São Paulo Light and Power Company, to request the installation of an external energy connection to power the existing streetlamps in their district[3] of "approximately 30.000 inhabitants", to achieve "JUSTICE" in "finding a solution to one of the most sensitive problems, since a large number of workers, young women and men, suffer all types of danger, from accidents to assaults".[4] And the president of the Vila Ipojuca Friends Society, in São Paulo's Lapa district, claiming to speak on behalf of residents, made a similar plea for public street lighting in his area, in a petition to the mayor dated 1 September 1954, which also included several other requests.[5]

These types of letters, requests, and petitions addressed to public authorities in São Paulo were common in the post-World War II period. In general, these communications were sent via so-called Neighborhood Friends Societies (Sociedades Amigos de Bairro, or SABs), a form of association for local residents that emerged and proliferated in the city from the late 1940s. From the end of the *Estado Novo* dictatorship, under Getúlio Vargas, in 1945, until a military coup in 1964 instated a dictatorship that would last for more than twenty years, Brazil lived through its first experience of mass democracy. In addition to regular elections, workers and popular sectors in general managed to significantly expand both their level of self-organization and their ability to make claims vis-à-vis the state, thus increasing their weight and say in public affairs.

In this context, the tendency to form popular associations based on neighborhoods (and the specific territorial space they defined) gained strength and came to characterize the history of social movements and political life in São Paulo and its surrounding industrial towns. Tenants' organizations, residents' associations, Neighborhood Friends Societies, *favelas* organizations (informal housing settlements), sporting and recreational clubs with strong local ties, etc. made up the exceedingly diversified and complex mosaic of the associative lives of urban workers, which had political and social repercussions that, at many points in the city's twentieth-century history, transcended the local level. This dynamic was fundamental to the city's class formation process, and it frequently developed in tandem with the more "classic" workers' movement defined by unions and political parties.

---

3. The basic administrative level in Brazil, both in the period analyzed in this article and today, is the municipality (*município*), each of which has its own government bodies. Municipalities may introduce subdivisions, such as districts, neighborhoods, or villages, yet these exist for purely administrative reasons, are often vaguely defined, and have no legal effect or political autonomy.
4. Processo 129598/1954, DGDP-2, SMPOG. Capitalization as in original.
5. See Processos 133526/1954 to 133524/1954, DGDP-2, SMPOG.

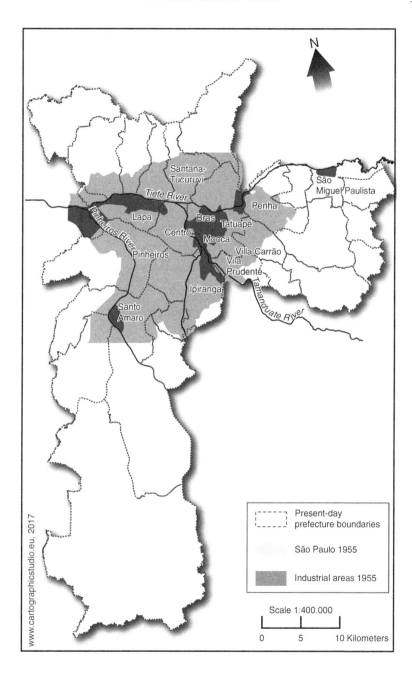

Figure 1. São Paulo's industrial areas in 1955.

Between 1940 and 1970, São Paulo and the cities that surrounded it
(in what would come to be known as the metropolitan region of "Greater"
São Paulo) experienced an industrial boom and an impressive urban and
population expansion (a process that would continue in the four decades to
follow), transforming São Paulo into one of the largest cities in the world.
Two characteristics of this vertiginous, dual process of industrialization
combined with urbanization stand out. First, São Paulo's twentieth-century
urbanization process is characterized by its tendency to segregate by class,
marked as it was by the intense and continuous expulsion of the poorer
classes from the central regions to the peripheries of the city. This
"peripheral pattern of urban growth", to use a term well-established in the
specialized literature, marked urban development in the post-war period:[6]
A large part of the working population came to live in peripheral areas that
were increasingly removed from the urban center and increasingly bereft of
urban resources, widening the geographical, social, and cultural distances
between the city's different social classes. The magnitude of the wave of
immigration during that period further accelerated the creation of neighborhoods in the peripheries, especially in the eastern and southern regions
of the city. A greater distance between one's home and work (although a
sizeable portion of the workers found jobs in these peripheral neighborhoods), a growing dependency on public transportation, in particular buses,
and individually owned houses constructed by their residents in peripheral
lots are some of the most distinctive characteristics of the daily experiences
of São Paulo's working class during this new era. A second feature of the
history of urbanization and industrialization in São Paulo concerns the
importance of these neighborhoods as spaces of conviviality and sociability,
especially for the popular classes.[7] They were fundamental spaces for the
formation of social networks and common experiences – in both the work
sphere and residential life. A place of residence, leisure, and labor, one's
neighborhood also contained the entire spectrum of personal relationships
with family members, friends, and neighbors, equipping workers with
knowledge and personal contacts that were essential to quotidian life.
Unsurprisingly, Jorge Wilheim, a famous Brazilian urbanist concerned with
urban planning between the 1960s and the 1980s, emphasized the strong
local identities that centered on neighborhoods: For him, the neighborhood

6. For studies using the notion of "peripheral patters of urban growth" in the case of São Paulo,
see, for instance, Lucio Kowarick (ed.), *Social Struggles and the City: The Case of São Paulo* (New
York, 1994); Teresa Caldeira, *City of Walls: Crime, Segregation, and Citizenship in São Paulo*
(Oakland, CA, 2000).
7. Such characteristics are in no way exclusive to São Paulo. In fact, it appears to be a common
feature of large Latin American metropolises that have gone through processes of rapid industrialization and urbanization, such as Buenos Aires, Mexico City, and Lima, among others,
making them appropriate for applying translocal, comparative analyses.

was "the urban unit, the most legitimate representation of the spatiality" of the population of the city of São Paulo.[8] Even today, the idea of a city historically forged by various local identities seems to have endured. The French anthropologist Oliver Mongin, for instance, recently stated that São Paulo is still "made up of multiple and varied neighborhoods, in which we feel a strong sense of autonomy".[9] In the decades following World War II, the experiences of residents of the neighborhoods in São Paulo's, especially, in the expanding peripheries, were powerfully marked by a general dearth of urban infrastructure. But disillusionment with the promises of urban progress and the growing perception that inequalities and exploitation also pervade the urban fabric provoked a burst of associative activity, for which the neighborhoods would provide a common thread and a central identity.

This article seeks to analyze these residents' associations organized around specific neighborhoods between the end of World War II and the coup in 1964. It examines, in particular, the veritable boom of associative activity that centered around SABs at the beginning of the 1950s and its relationship with local politics. In addition, this study explores connections between neighborhood associations and labor union struggles at the end of the 1950s and beginning of the 1960s, a period of major political polarization and the affirmation of a language of rights centered around the universe of labor. Based on strong social networks and informal relationships created by workers,[10] I argue that organizations like the Neighborhood Friends Societies were fundamental to the construction of political communities that had a powerful impact on electoral processes and on the formation of the state at the local level. Likewise, this article will show how, during that period, identities at the neighborhood level frequently developed in dialogue with processes of class formation, staking claim to a language of rights associated with the condition of being a worker and, simultaneously, a citizen. Finally, seeking to bring my own research agenda into dialogue with a transnational perspective, this article suggests how analyses with such a localized scope, like those focused on specific working-class neighborhoods, can intervene in debates concerning Global Labor History. Despite the broad recognition of the importance of neighborhoods and residential locales to processes of class formation, the body of research conducted from

---

8. Jorge Wilheim, *Projeto São Paulo. Propostas para a melhoria da vida urbana* (Rio de Janeiro, 1982), p. 63.

9. Oliver Mongin, "Metrópole para poucos", *Carta Capital*, 27 janeiro 2010, p. 21.

10. A more detailed analysis of the role of social networks and of informal relationships in neighborhood organization and in the labor union movement can be found in my book, Paulo Fontes, *Migration and the Making of Industrial São Paulo* (Durham, NC, 2016). See also, *idem* and Francisco Macedo, "Strikes and Pickets in Brazil: Worker Mobilization in the 'Old' and 'New' Unionism, the Strikes of 1957 and 1980", *International Labor and Working Class History*, 83 (2013), pp. 86–111.

a global studies perspective still appears to undervalue the comparative and transnational potential of "local" studies undertaken with a "micro-analytical" approach.

NEIGHBORHOOD FRIENDS SOCIETIES AND POLITICAL LIFE IN SÃO PAULO IN THE 1950s[11]

On 29 March 1954, Mayor Jânio Quadros's office received a letter with claims made by residents of a far-flung neighborhood in the north zone of the city. The missive was signed by Moacyr Lázaro Barbosa, Mario dos Santos Lourenço, and Magnólia Pires de Souza, respectively the president, council president, and the secretary-general of the Vila Gustavo Friends Society. The typewritten text, written on the Society's letterhead, which indicated that the entity had been founded on 20 June 1948, requested, "in the name of the approximately 1,500 members" of the organization, that the city provide "public illumination on Avenida Júlio Bueno, because this is a main, inter-neighborhood avenue [...] on which the Vila Gustavo buses travel". The authors of this brief letter closed by emphasizing their certainty that the mayor would attend to their "appeal that this Society is making to him", which aimed to "interpret and transmit to the appropriate authorities the anxieties of this forgotten, *proletarian* population, which, although humble, also contributed to São Paulo's development and its greatness".[12]

Requests such as this one, sent directly to the mayor, were common in those years. Indeed, every day the mayor's office was flooded with letters, messages, petitions, and claims authored by the newly formed and territorialized Neighborhood Friends Societies (Sociedades Amigos de Bairro, SABs).[13] It is difficult to trace the emergence of the first Neighborhood Friends Societies. Associations with this curious name, however, seem to have first appeared in the late 1930s and early 1940s, probably inspired by Friends of the City Society (Sociedade de Amigos da Cidade), an organization created in 1934 by engineers, urbanists, and other middle-class professionals (including Francisco Prestes Maia, the city's mayor from 1938 to 1945). These pioneers in shaping an association in São Paulo concerned with the city's development, in turn, seem to be have been inspired and

---

11. An earlier, preliminary version of this section was published as part of a larger research project, under the title "Trade Unions, Neighbourhood Associations and Working Class Politics in São Paulo, Brazil (1950s–1960s)", in Sabyasachi Bhattacharya and Rana Behal (eds), *The Vernaculization of Labour Politics* (New Delhi, 2016), pp. 63–82.
12. Processo 06447s/1954, DGDP-2, SMPOG. My emphasis. As we will see below, the use of such terms as "proletarians", "laborers", and "workers" was frequent in the petitions and similar documents, as a reference to the public that the Sociedades Amigos de Bairro claimed to represent.
13. Residents' organizations, such as the SABs, would be a fitting subject for analysis with a focus on the participation of women in civil society and political life. Future studies must develop in a more detailed way this fundamental aspect of neighborhood life.

influenced by the Friends of the City of Buenos Aires Society (Sociedad Amigos de la Ciudad de Buenos Aires) and by the local development associations (Sociedades de Fomento) that proliferated in the neighborhoods of the Argentine capital during that period.[14]

Yet, it was only during the years immediately following World War II that São Paulo would experience a visible surge in residents' organizations with an expressly local and territorial character. Particularly encouraged and influenced by the then-ascendant Communist Party (Partido Comunista do Brasil – PCB), the neighborhood-based groups quickly spread through working-class areas of the city, under the name of Democratic and Popular Committees (Comitês Democráticos e Populares – CDPs), expressing a wide-ranging set of demands for urban improvements, administrative decentralization, and democratization of urban governance.[15]

In the political vacuum brought about by the criminalization of the Brazilian Communist Party in 1947 and the consequent extinction of the CDPs,[16] some of those previously involved in them as well as other activists reoriented and organized themselves under the name of "Neighborhood Friends Societies". In this same vacuum, Jânio Quadros (1917–1992),[17] a previously obscure local assemblyman, managed to capitalize on and collaborate with this new civil society movement based in São Paulo's

14. On the Argentine influence on the constitution of the SABs in São Paulo, see an interview by Adriano Duarte with former community movement leader Eduardo Rosmaninho, 15 September 1999. The interview transcript has kindly been made available to me by the historian Adriano Duarte.

15. For the CDPs in São Paulo, see in particular Adriano Duarte, "Em busca de um lugar no mundo. Movimentos sociais na cidade de São Paulo nas décadas de 1940 e 1950", *Estudos Históricos*, 21:42 (2008), pp. 195–219. This phenomenon was also pronounced in Rio de Janeiro. Cf. Marcos César de Oliveira Pinheiro, *Os Comitês Populares Democráticos na cidade do Rio de Janeiro* (MA, Universidade Federal do Rio de Janeiro, 2007).

16. Having been legalized only in 1945, the PCB experienced a period of growth both in numbers and influence, and was banned again in 1947 in the context of the intensification of the Cold War. The communists nonetheless continued their activities in a more or less clandestine manner, depending upon the particular moment, and despite this illegality they would once again exert major influence on organized labor and intellectual and political life between the end of the 1950s and the military coup in 1964.

17. One of the most controversial politicians in Brazilian history, Jânio Quadros, a talented orator with a peculiar style of his own, zigzagged across the political spectrum: If his political career began on the left with the support of the Brazilian Socialist Party (including some Trotskyites) and the more progressive sectors of the Christian-Democrats, Quadros progressively moved to the right of the national political scene. Combining a rhetoric against administrative corruption with his frequent support for workers' demands for urban improvements in the city's poor suburbs, Jânio Quadros had a meteoric and impressive political career. In less than thirteen years, he was successively elected city council member, state congressional representative, mayor, governor, federal congressional representative, and president. His polemical renunciation of the presidency in August 1961, after only seven months in power, marked the beginning of a period of political instability that would be ended by the military coup in 1964.

working-class neighborhoods and cultivated an interrelation between these and the city's authorities as no other politician had before.

It was precisely in the context of his mayoral campaign in 1953 that the Neighborhood Friends Societies gained public prominence. The election of Jânio Quadros came as a surprise to the world of traditional politics. Quadros's victory would be called the "Revolution of March 22nd" by his allies, in a reference to both the date of the election and to the magnitude of the transformations that he sought. But the electoral triumph revealed, above all, the power of the vast support base he had built, in a relatively short time, through the SABs in São Paulo's working-class neighborhoods. During his exhilarating campaign, Quadros made the neighborhood residents' demands his own, and, receiving 65.8 per cent of the vote, he won an astounding victory, in particular in the city's peripheral districts. From then on, it would no longer be possible to pursue politics in São Paulo without taking seriously the SABs and their claims and demands.

Quadros's victory and the expectations it generated gave the existing SABs a huge boost: By way of mobilizations and claims sent directly to the new leader of the local government, the SABs tried to take advantage of the momentum created to demand improvements for their districts. Apparently, Quadros's victory also accelerated the formation of new residents' associations of this kind. Judging from the dates when these associations were created, found on the logos printed on the correspondence that they sent to the mayor, several of these "Sociedades de Amigos" were founded in the period immediately following the election of the new mayor.

Moreover, in the immediate wake of the election, a major wave of industrial strikes[18] reinforced the pressures on the new mayor, who had been elected as the "champion of the periphery". Aware of the political potential of these associations and clearly interested in keeping himself close to them, the mayor encouraged the neighborhood associations as they took on a more active role in public life in pursuit of their interests. The mayor's view of the SABs as welcome protagonists in São Paulo's urban politics, becomes clear, for instance, in a petition with more than 6,000 signatures,

---

18. One week after Jânio Quadros's election, an enormous strike paralyzed the city's main industries, as part of a broad protest movement that took over São Paulo for about a month. Known as the "Strike of the 300,000" the work stoppage was in large measure articulated and organized by the textile, metallurgy, and print industry workers, among others, and was made manifest both in factories and neighborhoods. The strike had a strong impact on the workers' movement in São Paulo and in Brazil generally, giving rise to a new phase in the organizational development and the public presence of unionism. For different interpretations of the Strike of the 300,000, see José Álvaro Moisés, *Greve de massa e crise política (estudo da Greve dos 300 mil em São Paulo, 1953–54)* (São Paulo, 1978); Hélio Costa, *Em busca da memória (Comissão de fábrica, partido e sindicato no pós-guerra)* (São Paulo, 1995); Joel Wolfe, *Working Women, Working Men: São Paulo and the Rise of Brazil's Industrial Working Class, 1900–1955* (Durham, NC, 1993); and Murilo Leal, *A reinvenção da classe trabalhadora (1953–1964)* (Campinas, 2011).

addressed to Quadros and sent by the Vila Izolina Mazei Friends Society. The residents of this neighborhood, defining themselves as "all poor workers", demanded that a series of improvements be made to the region and reminded the mayor of the speech "solemnly delivered at the Moinho Velho Friends Society, and published in the [newspaper] *A Gazeta*", in which Quadros had "called upon its residents to formulate their requests concerning public improvements whenever possible, by way of their NEIGHBORHOOD FRIENDS SOCIETIES".[19]

Many requests were sent asking the mayor to serve as an intermediary between neighborhood residents and companies holding concession contracts to provide telephone services (Companhia Brasileira de Telefones) or electrical energy (The São Paulo Light and Power Company, known simply as "Light São Paulo") in order to provide the neighborhoods with a telephone (to be installed, in general, in a local pharmacy or bakery) or with street lighting. These cases, which were dealt with in direct action-style on the part of the secretaries and departments of the mayor's office, were rather opportune occasions on which Quadros could don his hero's cape and apply pressure to utility companies like Light São Paulo, the target of his virulent attacks since his time as a city council member.

In this regard, speed seemed to maintain the mayor's image of a personal relationship with his constituents and his responsiveness to their needs. The directors of the Vila Olímpia Friends Society, for instance, in a letter dated 12 April 1954, requested that the mayor have a public telephone installed in a neighborhood bakery, reminding him that "as Your Excellency has already explained to us *verbally*, the lower part of the neighborhood has no telephone whatsoever, which makes urgent communications impossible".[20] Only two days later, Quadros responded to the Society, confirming that he had already placed a request to the company for the telephone line and the telephone itself.

The majority of these requests consisted of pleas to pave the streets, install telephones and public lighting, collect trash, create public markets to supply people with basic foodstuffs, and start or extend bus lines. The range of demands included the installation of a children's playground, a neighborhood daycare center, or the placement of curtains and blinds in a public school in the area. At times, this came with detailed information (including maps) about where these new establishments should, ideally, be located.[21]

Beyond their role in making claims on behalf of and mobilizing residents of the neighborhood, the Friends Societies were also sociable and leisure spaces.

---

19. Processo 175660/1954, DGDP-2, SMPOG. Capitalization as in original.
20. Processo 118840/1954, DGDP-2, SMPOG. Emphasis added by author.
21. Such as those requested by the SAB of the neighborhood Vila Guilherme in the first case and by the SAB of Vila Matilde in the second. Cf. Processos 162258/1954 and 122407/1954, DGDP-2, SMPOG.

Figure 2. Many SABs were created in connection with amateur football and recreational local clubs in the working class districts of the city.
Library of the São Paulo Chemical Industrial Workers Union. Used by permission.

As several studies show, many of these societies originated in or were asso-ciated with local sporting (particularly amateur soccer) and dance clubs and organizations devoted to entertainment in general.[22] Thus, it should come as no surprise to find amid these many demands for urban improvements a request for a license made by the Tremembé and Zona da Cantareira Friends Society, "to carry out four Carnival balls and two children's matinees, as part of the celebrations during the days of Carnival", in February of 1953.[23] Other local institutions and organizations also recognized the channels that opened up between the SABs and the municipal authorities and directed their own, particular appeals through neighborhood associations. This was the case, for example, in some local parishes of the Catholic Chuch. In Vila Palmeiras, Egisto Domenicali, the president of the local Friends Society, made a request on behalf of Father Antonio de Fillipo, asking the mayor "to pave the area in front of the parish church [of the neighborhood]".[24]

---

22. Cf. Adriano Duarte, "Neighborhood Association, Social Movements, and Populism in Brazil, 1945–1953", *Hispanic Historical American Review*, 89 (2009), pp. 111–139; Leal, *A reinvenção da classe trabalhadora*; and Paulo Fontes, *"Futebol de Várzea* and the Working Class: Amateur Football Clubs in São Paulo, 1940s–1960s", in Paulo Fontes and Bernardo Buarque de Holanda (eds), *The Country of Football: Politics, Popular Culture, and the Beautiful Game in Brazil* (London, 2014), pp. 87–102.
23. Processo 28232/1953, DGDP-2, SMPOG.
24. Processo 157177/1954, DGDP-2, SMPOG.

Public works were one of the most common demands, the pavement of roads in particular and construction projects in general. To have the street paved was generally a precondition for demanding further improvements, such as street lighting and public transportation. Again, this had been in part instigated by Jânio Quadros himself, who, as soon as he assumed the position of mayor, launched an "Emergency Plan" for carrying out these improvements, in particular paving the streets.

The language of most of these petitions and other communications directed to the mayor's office was far from begging for a "favor". The tone was, generally, respectful and formal. The gratitude and praise for the mayor – pointing to his "high public spirit" and "elevated sense of justice"[25] – was matched by references to promises made by the mayor during his candidacy or during a visit that he had made to a particular neighborhood. These pieces of correspondence, whenever possible, highlighted the personal contacts that had been previously made with politicians or visits that residents had paid to the offices of government authorities. When asking "*Doutor Professor* Alípio Correia Netto", Secretary of Hygiene in the Quadros mayoral administration, to install a public market in their neighborhood, for instance, the directors of the Vila Ipojuca Friends Society reminded him that the missive they were sending was simply intended to reinforce "what they had already had the opportunity to report to him in person".[26]

It was, however, through the use of the language of labor that the neighborhood residents represented in the SABs most insistently claimed their rights before the mayor. The authors of most of these petitions and letters mentioned repeatedly that theirs was a "working-class neighborhood", and phrasings such as "the large numbers of workers, men and women", living in Vila Independência in Ipiranga were not limited to this particular SAB. In a similar vein, the SAB of Vila Gumercindo emphasized that the neighborhood was made up of a "hard-working population of over ten thousand inhabitants", while the residents of Vila D. Pedro II called themselves "humble laborers", but ones who wanted "justice".[27] The examples are many and recur frequently in the documents. The world of labor had, admittedly, already been valorized by the state for some time – the reference to labor and its association with citizenship rights had been a central characteristic of Getúlio Vargas's government in the 1930s and 1940s (even if this was often only a rhetorical gesture). This continued and took on an even more complex and expansive dimension in the relatively democratic post-war period, when various political forces began

25. See, respectively, processos 160804/1954 and 118840/1954, DGDP-2, SMPOG.
26. Processo 104888/1954, DGDP-2, SMPOG.
27. See, respectively, processos 129598/1954, 118840/1954, and 139256/1954, DGDP-2, SMPOG.

to court workers. It is thus unsurprising that, under these circumstances, many workers (especially industrial workers), intensified their struggles for rights, tying these struggles to an identity and a language of class.[28] What is more remarkable, however, is how this identification was also embraced by a significant number of residents of poor neighborhoods, who underscored their condition as workers to express their demands for improved urban infrastructure and their part in the "progress" of the city. It was as workers, and not simply as individuals living in São Paulo, that an increasing number of residents demanded their rights to the city.

Jânio Quadros's connections with the SABs were decisive for structuring a reliable, well-oiled political machine that the future president could count on for many years. Several of the presidents and directors of the Friends' Societies remained ardent Quadros supporters, and some even built their own political careers. At the local level, the manifold claims and demands of neighborhood residents had established a stable channel of communication with the state, and, for neighborhood associations, this implied growing participation in urban politics. The capillary nature of the SABs' relations and connections thus increasingly became an object of desire for politicians across São Paulo's entire ideological spectrum. City Council members, in particular, whose electoral survival depended on securing a strong base in the neighborhoods, sought to establish their own privileged relationships with SABs and often tried to outdo each other in vocalizing and directing their demands to the executive authority.

Thus, from the mid-1950s on, it was not only Jânio Quadros and his followers that fought for representation in working-class neighborhoods by way of the SABs. The residents' associations were probably the most politically pluralistic social movement of that era. If, on the one hand, a class identity could be and was typically claimed by the "Friends Societies" (and could only be appealed to by those who shared it, or claimed to share it as well); on the other hand, a neighborhood identity, another central characteristic of the association, was more open and easily addressed and adopted by politicians of different stripes.

A considerable proportion of the existing studies of the political relationships between poor residents and political leaderships in cities going through accelerated urbanization processes have tended to characterize such relationships as clientelistic, based purely on the logic of the "exchange of material benefits for votes".[29] Thus, organizations like SABs functioned

28. There is an immense literature on this subject. Important examples include Wanderley Guilherme dos Santos, *Cidadania e justiça. A política social na ordem brasileira* (Rio de Janeiro, 1979); John D. French, *The Brazilian Workers' ABC: Class Conflict and Alliances in Modern São Paulo* (Chapel Hill, NC, 1992); and Alexandre Fortes *et al.*, *Na luta por Direitos. Estudos recentes em História Social do Trabalho* (Campinas, 1999).
29. Studies in this vein exist, of course, for the whole of Latin America (and indeed for other world regions). Typical representatives in the Brazilian context include José Álvaro Moisés,

only as institutional mediators for the political schemes of clientelistic networks. According to this reasoning, the SABs would be a prototypical example of the populist logic of manipulation and cooptation. An important conclusion of this type of approach is a presumed fragility of civic culture and the absence of a tradition of autonomous organization of civil society in Brazil (and, one can say, in Latin America in general), this being a central element in the country's lack of citizenship and democracy. In this type of analysis, however, the language and the actions of the Neighborhood Friends Societies and their constituents is typically neglected and subordinated to the logic of the state and its political leadership. Moreover, these studies seem to suggest a structural dichotomy between clientelistic networks and social mobilization. In contrast, the analytical efforts undertaken in this article aim to emphasize the perspective of the SABs and the agency of their participants. It is thus possible to understand how, in certain contexts, a language of rights associated with a discourse of class could be articulated and made binding even within a logic of domination and action that can be called clientelistic. Furthermore, following the trails blazed by such authors as Charles Tilly and Javier Ayero, neighborhood associations in São Paulo seem to confirm that "patronage and contentious politics can be mutually imbricated".[30] As we shall see in the following, the SABs' debates about decentralization and municipal autonomy and the approximation of neighborhood organizations with the labor unions and strike movements can offer interesting examples in this regard, as they point to attempts to develop other forms of action that were able to adapt to new constellations.

NEIGHBORHOODS, DECENTRALIZATION, AUTONOMY

Jânio Quadros only remained in the position of São Paulo's mayor for about two years, swiftly moving on to be the state's governor (1955–1959). While the principal constellation of considerable interaction between neighborhood associations and the city government continued under his successors, it is not surprising that the intense dynamic of the initial years soon wore off, not least because the city continued to expand and, with that, the number of new neighborhoods and urban challenges. In this situation,

Classes populares e protesto urbano (São Paulo, 1978); and Maria da Glória Gohn, *Movimentos sociais e lutas pela moradia* (São Paulo, 1991). A similar analytical scheme can be found in the more recent approaches of James Holston, *Insurgent Citizenship: Disjunctions of Democracy and Modernity in Brazil* (Princeton, NJ, 2008); and Leonardo Avritzer, *A participação política em São Paulo* (São Paulo, 2004).

30. Javier Auyero, "Poor People's Lives and Politics: The Things a Political Ethnographer Knows (and Doesn't Know) After Fifteen Years of Fieldwork", *New Perspectives on Turkey*, 46 (2012), pp. 95–107, 106. See also Charles Tilly, *Regimes and Repertoires* (Chicago, IL, 2006); and Javier Auyero, *Poor People's Politics* (Durham, NC, 2000).

a new orientation emerged among numerous neighborhood activists, one that no longer sought closer collaboration with the existing authorities but, on the contrary, a move away from them. In the course of the 1950s and the beginning of the 1960s, a series of movements calling for the administrative separation of working-class neighborhoods arose in various places in the São Paulo metropolitan region. These movements consisted of several actors; yet, in many cases, as we shall see, SABs played a central role in them. Basically, these movements demanded the separation of neighborhoods and entire regions from the administrative control of the city of São Paulo and their transformation into autonomous municipalities, each with its own budget.[31] These movements shared the idea that their areas had been the victims of abandonment and forgetting, and that only with administrative emancipation through a secession from São Paulo would it be possible to bring local power into line with the population's real necessities, especially in the poorest districts. The perception of a powerful injustice in the distribution of public resources on the part of the mayor's office, which benefitted the city's wealthiest, central neighborhoods to the detriment of the underprivileged periphery, was another common characteristic of the defenders of autonomy.[32]

For a district to call for political and administrative separation, it was necessary to fulfill several requirements stipulated in the federal Constitution of 1946 and to carry out a plebiscite, which needed to be authorized by the State Legislative Assembly. Even when autonomy was approved by a majority of local voters, however, strong political and juridical resistance from municipal mayor's offices confronted with such secessionist aspirations remained common, trying to prevent the territorial dismembering of their cities and the consequent loss of a population of constituents and of economic resources. Thus, the success of the processes of autonomy depended on a large and permanent popular mobilization, demanding both the build-up of political pressure as well as effective and proficient legal counseling.

This was the case with Osasco, probably the most famous and successful example of an autonomous district having seceded from the municipality of São Paulo. After its defeat in a first plebiscite carried out in 1953, the local

31. In the period being analyzed here, the Brazilian federalist system was composed of three government levels: federal, state, and municipal. Thus, administrative autonomy of a municipality implied the constitution of executive power (composed of an elected mayor and vice-mayor) and a local parliament (composed of elected city council members), in addition to its own budget. As mentioned before, "districts" or "neighborhoods" were (often quite informal) administrative subdivisions with no legal or budgetary consequence.

32. The social struggles for municipal autonomy in São Paulo are another topic of potential interest for comparative study. In many large cities in different countries, workers' districts in the areas surrounding the city and its suburbs have called for precisely the opposite, in other words for these areas' incorporation into the municipality.

autonomists reorganized themselves and managed to conquer the majority of votes when polling took place again in 1958. The São Paulo mayor's office appealed the voters' decision, followed by a long legal and political battle that inspired an impressive popular mobilization in the region. Osasco finally separated from the capital, becoming an autonomous city in 1962, when the newly formed municipality elected a mayor and city council members for the first time.[33]

Estimates indicate that, between 1945 and 1964, seventeen peripheral neighborhoods attempted to separate from São Paulo. Invariably, the attempts and campaigns for autonomy involved the local SAB. In reinforcing the elements of a local, communitarian identity, these campaigns also highlighted all of the dissatisfaction with the precarious conditions in working-class neighborhoods. At the same time, the campaigns clearly demonstrated a building pressure to extend democracy to the local level and a popular mobilization for citizenship. This went beyond the realm of labor and union organizing, with urban poverty serving as an important concern and reference point for the consolidation of the struggle for rights.

Legal and political difficulties, however, frustrated most of these attempts. But other arguments also influenced the results of some of the plebiscites in the few locales where they did take place: For instance, in an initial attempt at separation undertaken by the populous neighborhood of São Miguel, in the extreme east of the city, the worst damage to popular support for the campaign for autonomy were caused by rumors that a future city of São Miguel would be considered part of the state's hinterland, rather than an urban area and, as such, the salary index in force in this municipality would be held to a different standard from the capital city and other regions of the state and thus would be lowered. In contrast, the autonomists, trying to counter the arguments of the "No" campaign and, in particular, the salary question, demonstrated, for example, that in São Caetano do Sul (autonomous since the 1940s) the wages remained the same. What is remarkable about this dispute, however, is that both to defenders and opponents of separation the relevance of this labor-related issue seemed evident. Arguments directed at the residents as workers in this respect were broadly brought to bear on the campaigns, both pro and against autonomy.

At any rate, in the early 1960s, autonomist struggles in numerous neighborhoods resurfaced with great force, stimulated by the victory of the highly industrialized district of Osasco, which was officially made into an independent municipality in 1962. The vigorous mobilization and the victory of the autonomists in that locale served as an example of the possibility of secession and gave a strong stimulus to those that similarly argued

---

33. Concerning the autonomist movements in Greater São Paulo, see Moisés, *Classes populares e protesto urbano*, especially chs 7, 8, 9, and 10.

in favor of the emancipation of their neighborhoods in various parts of the São Paulo metropolitan area. In addition, the new mayor of Osasco, Hirant Sanazar, as well as several city council members from the recently created municipality, gave their explicit support to the various autonomist movements in the capital of the state of São Paulo. Present at an autonomist rally in São Miguel in June of 1963, for example, Sanazar attacked those who opposed secession and reminded the gathered crowd, "four years ago the São Paulo stepmother did nothing for Osasco, only taking care of the elegant neighborhoods", and, after enumerating a series of urban improvements in the newly autonomous municipality, like asphalted streets, health services, and urban cleaning services, he concluded, in a grandiloquent and messianic tone, that "autonomy means redemption".[34]

Beyond the uplifting example of Osasco, autonomy and the accompanying debate concerning administrative decentralization and the resolution of the urban problems that afflicted the residents of São Paulo's working-class neighborhoods appeared to be directly related to the general mood favoring change and mobilization, brought about by the proposals of the so-called Basic Reforms Plan (Reformas de Base). This wide-ranging set of demands, which not only included measures for land, tax, educational, and constitutional reform, but also proposals for a decentralization and democratization of urban areas, were advanced during the presidential administration of João Goulart (1961–1964), a left nationalist who enjoyed considerable support from the labor movement. It is no coincidence, then, that in the early 1960s many labor unions and leaders became actively involved in movements for autonomy in neighborhoods in São Paulo.

The military coup in 1964 put a stop to all of the mobilizations and initiatives for neighborhood autonomy in São Paulo. With the road to actual autonomy blocked, many turned their attention once more to the mayor's office, building up pressure (to the degree possible under dictatorship) for administrative decentralization as a way of attending, however partially, to the demands of peripheral neighborhoods. In fact, a decision, in 1965, by Faria Lima, the incumbent mayor, to create so-called Regional Administrations in many neighborhoods, sub-entities with the partial powers of a proper mayoralty, appears to have been a direct response to the

---

34. Cited from a report of the Department of Political and Social Order (Departamento Estadual de Ordem Política e Social – DEOPS), the organ of São Paulo's police in charge of the surveillance and investigation of all kinds of political and social movements and whose documentation offers unique (though, of course, very partial) glimpses of the activities of movements that have otherwise left few archival traces. DEOPS documentation gathers not only police papers and reports, but also an immense variety of original and unique sources from individuals, political parties, trade unions, and social movements apprehended by the police from the mid-1920s to the early 1980s. Dossiê 50-Z-591, fls. 64, Arquivo Público do Estado de São Paulo [hereafter, APESP], Departamento Estadual de Ordem Política e Social [hereafter, DEOPS].

mobilization of neighborhood entities and of the autonomist movement that had grown in São Paulo in the years just prior to the military coup. In the years to come, the SABs, which had not been proscribed by the military dictatorship, would come to play a fundamental role in urban politics. Although the political conditions were much more adverse than in the previous years, the socio-economic conditions of the neighborhoods compelled the SABs and other actors to continue their mobilizations and struggles. Consequently, the SABs increasingly went beyond the specific claims made by each neighborhood, and began to put the administration of the city as a whole and the role of the local government on their agenda.

SABs, LABOR UNIONS, AND STRIKES (1957–1964)

At the end of the 1950s and the beginning of the 1960s, in the context of growing social tensions and political struggles, workers were generally able to expand their space in the Brazilian public sphere. This was mainly true for (male) industrial workers in the cities and increasingly for rural workers in the countryside, but, as the example of the neighborhood associations illustrates, also included other groups of workers and the broader urban population. A nationalist, anti-imperialist rhetoric was powerfully articulated with a language of class that clamored for more inclusive economic development and deep social reforms in Brazil. Such political currents as the leftist nationalists and communists grew in the political scene. An overall picture that featured growing inflation, a wave of strikes, and protests characterized a period of intense political and social polarization that would come to a close with the military coup of 1964.

In that period, neighborhood organizations in São Paulo lived through a rapid process of radicalization and significant changes in the forms of action and political alliances in which they engaged. The year 1957 appears to have been a moment of particular importance for these changes. The SABs umbrella organization – the Federation of São Paulo Neighborhood Friends Societies (Federação das Sociedades Amigos de Bairros and Vilas de São Paulo, or FESAB), which had been created in 1954,[35] became stronger and began to act more consistently in conjunction with various other associations. For instance, in July of that year, a convention of SABs in São Paulo was organized, sponsored by the FESAB. Besides highlighting the accomplishments of the SABs so far, "in the sense of having achieved improvements in the general, immediate, or local order, such as: transportation, housing supply, water, illumination, sewage, pavement, mail delivery, telephone, public health, instruction, sports, etc.", the convention demanded the right of these entities to participate in the "master plan of the city [...] and in the administration of the CMTC [Companhia Municipal de Transportes – Municipal

---

35. "Fundada a Federação das Sociedades Amigos dos Bairros", *A Hora*, 24 August 1954.

Transportation Company]" and the formation of a "São Paulo metropolitan consumers' cooperative" to ameliorate the problems of furnishing the city with basic supplies.[36]

At the about the same time, the unions in São Paulo appear to have become increasingly attentive to the needs for workers beyond the shop floor and the need to organize workers in their neighborhoods. In a booming city like São Paulo, union leaders became ever more sensitive to the demands for urban improvements and increasingly sought strategies that accounted for urban geography. In the second half of the 1950s, various local unions, such as those of the chemical and metal workers, founded sub-headquarters in new neighborhoods with large concentrations of workers, as a way to bring unions closer to the laborers' residences and, thus, to facilitate activism and worker participation in the running of these organizations.

At that juncture, one could also perceive a tightening of the bonds between neighborhood associations and the labor union movement. This was illustrated, for instance, by the presence of the former in a meeting called by the Inter-Union Unity Pact (Pacto de Unidade Intersindical, or PUI)[37] to debate the growing cost of living in São Paulo.[38] Joint actions not only began to occur more frequently, but these two movements also started to articulate a common agenda of demands. The subjects of their claims for urban improvements slowly penetrated the union agenda and some union members began to participate more actively in neighborhood organizations. This was the case, for example, for Santos Bobadilha, a well-known leader of the Union of Dairy Workers of São Paulo, who, in those years, became an active militant in the Jardim São Vicente Friends Society.

The so-called Strike of the 400,000, carried out in October of 1957, represents an important moment for the strengthening of the ties of unity between these organizations. It also brought about the emergence of a shared language and agenda between unions and neighborhood

36. These quotations are from FESAB convention documents cited in a secret police report, Dossiê 50- J-138, fls. 145, APESP, DEOPS.

37. The Inter-Union Unity Pact (PUI) was created in 1953, bringing together the majority of the more militant trade unions in São Paulo. An alliance was consolidated between trade union leaders connected to the Communist Party (PCB), which was then illegal, but very active in the factories and neighborhoods, and trade unionists tied to the Brazilian Labor Party (PTB), which had Vargas-linked origins, but increasingly identified with the figure of Vice-President João Goulart. Equally significant was the political presence of labor leaders without ties to those parties or who were allied with other politicians, as in the case of the governor of São Paulo, Jânio Quadros (1955–1959). In addition to the defense of the workers' interests, it was a nationalist and anti-imperialist discourse that held this broad alliance together.

38. See the following report by US-American consul, an external but sensitively interested observer: Despatch 169 of February 1, 1957 from Amcongen, São Paulo, Brazil. Subject: Cost of Living meeting of São Paulo Labor, National Archives and Records Administration, Archives II (College Park, MD), General Records of the Department of State (GRDS), RG 59, Central Foreign Police Files (CFPF), LAB 3-3, Box 4308, Document 83201/2-2037.

Figure 3. The so-called Strike of the 400,000 in 1957 was an important moment for the strengthening of the ties of unity between the SABs and trade-unions. Many picket lines were organized in the neighborhoods.
Arquivo Público do Estado de São Paulo. Fundo Última Hora. Used by permission.

associations, which conceived workers also as residents of the city, and vice versa. Organized by a network of unions from various trades and industries, in particular the textile and metal industries, the strike, which took place at a moment when the economic plight of the poorer classes had caused widespread dissatisfaction, soon became a generalized labor action that paralyzed the whole city of São Paulo and other neighboring industrial cities. The movements took on the air of a popular rebellion: Picketing strikers took over the streets and several violent confrontations occurred in what is one of the most remarkable episodes in the labor history of São Paulo.[39] During this strike, the neighborhoods were one of the main locales that provided assistance for and sustained the work stoppage. Many picket lines, for instance, were organized in meetings convened in clubs and in residents' organizations in the industrial districts. In the months leading up to the strike, many SABs positioned themselves in defense of workers' rights and thus in favor of the unions' position against the high cost of living. In the middle of the October strike, the alliance forged among residents' associations and the union organizations of the city would be powerfully confirmed when FESAB released a manifesto expressing solidarity with workers, arguing that the "SABs are constituted in their absolute majority by workers from all industries and professions [...] and the struggle for a reduction in the cost of living is inherent in all of the people".[40]

39. For more details about this strike, see, among others, Paulo Fontes and Francisco Macedo, *Strikes and Pickets in Brazil;* and Leal, *A reinvenção da classe trabalhadora,* ch. 6.
40. Dossiê 50-J-138, fls. 126 and 193, APESP, DEOPS.

The approximation between neighborhood-based movements and labor unions continued in the following years. In June 1958, a new meeting of FESAB, which already included 196 popular associations that had joined together, debated such old demands as the paving of streets in the urban periphery, but they also discussed the "formation of a common front of action, between the [neighborhood] entities, the Interunion Unity Pact, and the State Union of Students [União Estadual dos Estudantes]".[41] Neighborhood problems and the demands of city dwellers were, in turn, increasingly discussed by union organizations, as in a meeting of the union of bank workers, in which union leaders and the SABs debated "the project of the city council member Norberto Mayer Filho concerning renewing the contract" of the Brazilian Telephone Company (Companhia Telefônica Brasileira).[42] Subjects like the problems of food supplies and cooperativism took an important place on the agendas of PUI meetings.[43]

The spike in the cost of living was one of the main topics that united the neighborhood associations and unions. At the end of the 1950s, these entities jointly organized various protests against inflation, the loss of purchasing power as a result of low wages, and the ensuing impoverishment. In June 1959, for example, the labor attaché of the British Consulate reported on the preparations for a "hunger march" that would bring a caravan of "unionists, students, and members of neighborhood associations" to Rio de Janeiro (then still the national capital).[44] This growth of FESAB and of the neighborhood movement in São Paulo as well as their alliance with the unions worried the authorities to such a degree that, when the entity actively participated in the organization of a strike movement in December, the Ministry of Justice authored a law closing down the FESAB and other SABs for ninety days, although it was never put into effect.[45]

In the effervescent period before the coup of 1964, the contacts and connections between neighborhood associations and unions appear to have deepened further. The importance of a kind of urban planning that was favorable to workers and poor urban residents in general began to take a more serious and important place on the union agenda. In July 1963, for example, some of the city's main unions, like the bank, metal, and textile workers, signed a manifesto calling for urban reform as an important part of the "Basic Reforms Plan" proposed by the João Goulart administration.

41. *Última Hora*, 16 June 1958.
42. Dossiê 50- J-138, pasta 1, APESP, DEOPS.
43. On the activities of the union movement concerning food supplies, cooperativism, and struggles against scarcity in the 1950s, see Leal, *A reinvenção da classe trabalhadora*, particularly ch. 4.
44. The National Archives [of the UK] (Kew), Foreign Office, São Paulo Consulate, Brazil, Correspondences, FO 371/139125.
45. Dossiê 50-J-138, fls. 323, APESP, DEOPS.

The overlapping interests between unionists, architects, and neighborhood organizations resulted in a seminar on the subject of housing and urban reform, which gathered a range of important actors from São Paulo's civil society. The questions of housing, the problems that neighborhoods suffered, and the very question of urban planning as a whole came to be seen by unions as a part of the world of labor.[46] The coup that took place in April 1964, evidently, dealt a death blow to these incipient initiatives. Subsequent attempts to match interests or coordinate activities now had to take place under the conditions of dictatorship.

The experiences of the SABs and of São Paulo's unions at the end of the 1950s and the beginning of the 1960s demonstrate a far greater political connection between the world of labor and urban questions than the older social science literature has generally recognized. For instance, in 1973, the sociologists Fernando Henrique Cardoso (later to become Brazil's president), Cândido Procópio Ferreira, and Lúcio Kowaric emphasized that, in the 1950s and 1960s,

> as a rule, the workers were absent from political life, at the level of urban demands. [...] The unions did not have the habit of [...] including in their programs questions connected to the urban problematic [...]. [At the same time], one cannot affirm that the Neighborhood Friends Societies represented workers. They represented much more the urban resident, a specific social category that the city created and whose action, during the process during which São Paulo became a major metropolis, attenuated if not completely dissolving class behavior.

Thus, the authors concluded, "the majority of the inhabitants of São Paulo remained politically marginal to municipal life". José Álvaro Moisés, for his part, also considered that, "for a long time", unions never demonstrated any interest "in the demands for urban living conditions for their members".[47] Yet, as this article has shown, workers' organizations and neighborhood organizations managed, at various moments, to unify their claims, transcending in practice the boundaries between the struggles in factories and in neighborhoods. In this process, a form of political action based on a much broader notion of class emerged, which included various dimensions of the lives of workers in São Paulo, in fact often overcoming the supposed division between worker and resident.

CONCLUSION

While the nexus between labor and urban issues has often not been fully acknowledged in a certain kind of sociological literature (in particular in the

---

46. On the seminar and the role of urban planning issues among São Paulo unionists at the time, see Leal, *A reinvenção da classe trabalhadora*, pp. 186–187.
47. Fernando Henrique Cardoso *et al.*, *Cultura e participação na cidade de São Paulo* (São Paulo, 1973), pp. 12 and 13; and Moisés, *Classes populares e protesto urbano*, p. 182.

case of big metropoles in the Global South), labor historians have been more observant in highlighting the important role of working-class neighborhoods in the process of class formation during different periods and in various national contexts (though, here too, the focus has been on experiences in the Global North). In particular, in the context of large cities propelled by industrialization from the nineteenth century on, many have underscored the dense sociability of working-class districts as fundamental to the mitigation of multiple social divides and the construction of a class identity, as well as its role in generating support for collective action. In a famous article, Eric Hobsbawm, for example, called attention to the labor movement's difficulties in large cities, "which are industrially very heterogeneous to have a unity based on labour" and "too broad to form true communities". The "communitarian potential" of working-class neighborhoods, however, transcended this "inhospitable environment", for it was here where "the true force of the working-class movement in megalopolises" resided.[48] Geoff Eley also reminds us that

> workers of whatever kind led lives beyond the workplace [...]. They lived in neighborhoods, residential concentrations, and forms of communities, cheek by jowl with other types of workers and alongside other social groups as well. [...] They came from diverse regions and birthplaces, spoke different languages or dialects, and bore profoundly different cultural identities from religious upbringing and national origins. They were young people and mature adults, and of course women and men.

Thus, "the rise of the urban working-class neighborhood", Eley argues, "was crucial" to the construction of a common working-class identity in Europe between the mid-nineteenth century and the beginning of the twentieth.[49]

To emphasize the roles of neighborhoods in processes of class formation implies a more serious consideration of both the spatial dimension and of constructions of different senses of community in historical analysis. In this respect, the British sociologist Mike Savage points out, in considering the centrality of what he calls "structural insecurity" in the working-class experience, "it is as important to look at the coping strategies used in urban neighborhoods and within households as at the labour process itself".[50]

While the mentioned authors have offered valuable clues for understanding the interconnection between neighborhood communities, the workplace, and class identity, there also numerous accounts, especially in

48. Eric Hobsbawm, "Labour in the Great City", *New Left Review*, I: 166 (1987), pp. 39–51.
49. Geoff Eley, *Forging Democracy: The History of the Left in Europe, 1850–2000* (Oxford, 2002), pp. 57–58.
50. Mike Savage, "Class and Labour History", in Lex Heerma van Voss and Marcel van der Linden (eds), *Class and Other Identities: Gender, Religion and Ethnicity in the Writing of European Labour History* (New York, 2002), pp. 55–72, 61.

older or "classical" studies of class formation, that lack attention to these spatial dimensions. This absence was polemically highlighted in Roger V. Gould's revisionist analysis of the famous Paris Commune of 1871. Gould asserts that the insurrection, contrary to the sacred mythology of the left, had little to do with class struggle and rather concerned the formation of communitarian urban identities in the context of the ongoing disputes over municipal freedoms, as opposed to the political centralization of France in the Second Empire.[51] David Harvey has refuted in minute detail both Gould's historical research methodology and the conclusions he draws, emphasizing how, in a variety of historical contexts (such as in the case of the Paris Commune) "there were class identifications related to local places, neighborhoods, and even communities [...]. The signs of class and class consciousness are as important in the space in which people lived as they are in people's work". Thus, Harvey continues, neighborhood institutions are spaces of social solidarity that are perfectly compatible and linked with social relations of class. In the context of the urban transformations of Haussmann's Paris, the city had "a community of class as well as a class of comunity" in Paris's working-class neighborhoods.[52]

Nonetheless, despite the intense debates and the evident weight of the mentioned discussions around working-class districts and their connections to class and communitarian identities, the international literature on these topics is very "parochial", exhibiting an evident lack of transnational or even comparative studies of neighborhoods. Conversely, the burgeoning field of Global Labor History – which precisely calls for an inclusion of such perspectives – conspicuously lacks sensitivity for the spatiality of the local. There seems to be little space for "place" in these more recent approaches, with few studies of local organizations or neighborhood workers' associations realized under their auspices.

One can outline some reasons for this absence. First, a significant part of Global Labor History appears to privilege a return to macro-narratives with an emphasis on economic processes on a global scale, with little interest in highly local studies, such as those at the neighborhood level. Second, a seeming lack of connections and transnationality between neighborhood associations confines their study to a level that, even within the municipal universe, can be considered "micro", making a more global analysis of the phenomenon difficult or, indeed, impossible. Third, although Global Labor History also has broadened our understanding in both time and space of what labor constitutes and who workers are – going decidedly beyond the forms of wage labor predominant in the Northern

---

51. Roger Gould, *Insurgents Identities: Class, Community and Protest in Paris from 1848 to the Commune* (Chicago, IL, 1995).
52. David Harvey, *Paris, Capital of Modernity* (London, 2003), particularly ch. 13.

Atlantic world from the nineteenth century on – one can still perceive the continuation of the old dichotomy and hierarchy between productive space and the spaces of social reproduction. The role that residential spaces and workers' neighborhoods have played in global development of labor is still underestimated.

Meanwhile, neighborhood associations have, since the 1970s, constituted one of the central concerns in studies about the so-called new social movements. Heavily influenced by such authors as Jürgen Habermas, Alain Touraine, and Manuel Castells, among others, a large part of the academic work on this topic has almost entirely fallen to geographers, sociologists, and political scientists emphasizing the "newness" of movements emerging in the 1970s. Beyond the supposedly shared values across these movements – autonomy vis-à-vis the state and the traditional political forces (including the labor movement), democratic, and participatory internal organization, etc. – this "newness" was said to manifest itself also in the emergence of social identities with little or no relation to class identities or with the world of labor. Such views have contributed to a segregation of research fields, with the study of neighborhoods and of territorialized popular organizations remaining largely outside the domain of labor history.

Yet, the study of neighborhood associations in Brazil and in Latin America in general holds many promises for labor historiography, including for studies inspired by the ideas of Global Labor History. Two interesting examples might illustrate the potential for comparative and transnational analysis in the study of neighborhoods and local workers' organizations.

The historiography of India, for instance, has been vigorously questioning the conventional notion that sees factories as spaces of change and modernity and neighborhoods as places of tradition and stasis, in particular those areas that are connected to their rural places of origin, to religion, and to caste. Numerous studies have been demonstrating how urban life at the neighborhood level, associated with the experience of places of work, continually redefined the rules of inclusion and exclusion established between the workers themselves. Neighborhoods also created feelings of belonging and emotional bonds, lending visibility to the workers and to a certain idea of common identity beyond traditional divisions. Workers' connections to their residential locales created the conditions for the emergence of leaderships and local organizations that demanded improvements for their districts and often forged links with union politics.[53] As one can see, despite great differences in culture and historical context, there are

53. See, for example, Nandini Gooptu, *The Politics of the Urban Poor in Early 20th-Century India* (Cambridge, 2000); Chitra Joshi, *Lost Worlds: Indian Labour and Its Forgotten Histories* (Delhi, 2003); and Aditya Sarkar, "The Tie That Snapped: Bubonic Plague and Mill Labour in Bombay, 1896–1898", *International Review of Social History*, 59:2 (2014), pp. 181–214.

interesting confluences in the construction of identities, the formation of organizations, and the making of collective action that unite the cases of neighborhoods in industrial cities in India and in Brazil. Research that takes into account the analysis of working-class neighborhoods beyond the local and the national has much to gain from understanding the processes and unexpected connections, even across long distances, particularly in countries that have gone through rapid and intense processes of urbanization, migration, and industrialization.

As previously stated, the great, industrialized urban centers of Latin America open up another and even more obvious possibility for comparative and transnational analyses, although labor historians have yet to tap adequately into this potential.[54] The example of Argentina is especially illustrative here. Just as in Brazil, a new generation of Argentine historians has recently been revisiting and adding new questions to the debate about urban popular associations in their county, particularly during the period during the rule of President Juan Perón (1946–1955).[55] A significant part of this literature contradicts the conventional vision, established in the 1980s, which saw the strong tendency to form associations at the neighborhood level in Buenos Aires in the 1930s (with the proliferation of neighborhood clubs, popular libraries, and *sociedades de fomento*[56]) as an expression of the supposed fact that the lower classes had outgrown primordial organizational forms based on class and ethnicity, which predominated in Buenos Aires until the 1920s. For this reason, these scholars avoided the use of the

---

54. Despite renewed interest among Latin American historians in the study of associative life and the political potential of working-class neighborhoods, there are still few initiatives that seek to analyze these phenomena from a regional and transnational perspective. For some interesting examples of recent studies of Latin American neighborhoods, see Alejandro Velasco, *Barrio Rising: Urban Popular Politics and the Making of Modern Venezuela* (Berkeley, CA, 2015); Paulo Drinot, "Moralidad, moda y sexualidad. El contexto moral de la creación del barrio rojo de Lima", in Scarlett O'Phelan and Margarita Zegarra (eds), *Mujeres, Familia y Sociedad en la Historia de América Latina, siglos XVIII–XXI* (Lima, 2006), pp. 333–354; Kenneth Maffitt, "From the Ashes of the Poet Kings: Exodus, Identity Formation, and the New Politics of Place in Mexico City's Industrial Suburbs, 1948–1975", *International Labor and Working Class History*, 64 (2003), pp. 74–90.

55. For some different perspectives, cf., among others, Omar Acha, "Sociedad civil y sociedad política durante el primer peronismo", *Desarrollo Económico*, 44:174 (2004), pp. 199–230; Rosa Aboy, *Viviendas para el pueblo. Espacio urbano y sociabilidad en el barrio Los Perales, 1946–1955* (Buenos Aires, 2005); Anahi Ballent, *Las huellas de la política. Vivienda, ciudad, peronismo en Buenos Aires, 1943–1955* (Buenos Aires, 2005); Hernán Camarero, "Consideraciones sobre la historia social de la Argentina urbana en las décadas de 1920 e 1930. Classe obrera y sectores populares", *Nuevo Topo. Revista de Historia y Pensamiento Crítico*, 4 (2007), pp. 35–60; and Omar Acha and Nicolás Quiroga, *Asociaciones y política en la Argentina del siglo veinte. Entre prácticas y expectativas* (Buenos Aires, 2015).

56. *Sociedades de Fomento* were residents' associations based on the territory of a neighborhood and began to proliferate in Buenos Aires and in other cities in Argentina from the 1920s on. They filled a role that was similar to Brazil's *Sociedades Amigos de Bairro*.

notion of "workers" and consecrated the term "popular sectors" for the subaltern residents of Argentina's capital. Implicit in these authors' analysis was the idea that the political culture of the Perón era, from the 1940s, with its emphasis on the use of the plebiscite, on state power, and with its tendency to articulate a certain language of class, has put an end to this prior civic culture and destroyed its popular associations as spaces where citizens would experience and experiment with democratic processes.[57] Contrary to such views, numerous historians have, especially in the last fifteen years, rejected the radical separation between civil society and the state that is implicit in the vision outlined above, and have shown how the Peronist state opened up space for the articulation and re-articulation of various popular demands.

The case of São Paulo in the 1950s and 1960s equally suggests that the phenomenon of urban associations has played an important role in the construction of a language of rights and in workers' political interaction with local authorities and with the municipality – and that this happened in a more complex manner than analyses emphasizing clientelistic logics have acknowledged. Examining this phenomenon allows us to observe a greater permeability and porosity of the state, which functioned as a site of conflicts and, under certain circumstances, was receptive to the demands from below, as was the case between the 1940s and the 1960s in Brazil. As this article has explained, a popular, neighborhood identity, on the one hand, and a laborer's, working-class identity, on the other, are not mutually exclusive. Despite their socio-occupational heterogeneity, many neighborhoods in São Paulo recognized themselves and were recognized by others as "working-class". "Popular", "working-class", and "resident" can be complementary identities and are not necessarily in conflict with each other.

---

57. The fundamental reference from this perspective is the book by Luis Alberto Romero and Leandro Gutiérrez, *Sectores populares, cultura y política. Buenos Aires en la entreguerra* (Buenos Aires, 1995). More recent reflection on this topic have been produced by Luis Alberto Romero and Luciano de Privitellio, "Organizaciones de la sociedad civil, tradiciones cívicas y cultura política democrática. El caso de Buenos Aires, 1912–1976", *Revista de Historia*, 1 (2005), pp. 1–34. Luciano de Privitellio, *Vecinos y Ciudadanos. Política y sociedade em la Buenos Aires de entreguerras* (Buenos Aires, 2003).

IRSH 62 (2017), Special Issue, pp. 217–243 doi:10.1017/S002085901700058X
© 2018 Internationaal Instituut voor Sociale Geschiedenis

Sugarcane Workers in Search of Justice: Rural Labour through the Lens of the State

CHRISTINE RUFINO DABAT

Universidade Federal de Pernambuco
Departamento de História, CFCH
Av. Prof. Moraes Rego, 1235
Cidade Universitária – CEP:50670–901
Recife, Brazil

E-mail: christine.dabat@ufpe.br

THOMAS D. ROGERS

Emory University
Department of History
361 S. Kilgo Circle
Atlanta, GA 30322, USA

E-mail: tomrogers@emory.edu

ABSTRACT: Drawing from case file records generated in rural labour courts in Brazil's north-eastern state of Pernambuco between 1965 and 1982, this paper demonstrates how these forums reified class-based exploitation, even as they purportedly protected workers' rights. The paper focuses on two districts in the state's sugarcane-growing region, both of which reveal a clear pattern of inferior treatment for rural as opposed to non-rural workers. Interpreting the evidence as a function of long-term patterns of social and economic relations in the region, the paper also sets this case in a larger context of rural labour history around the world.

Sugarcane agriculture has dominated the coastal area of the north-eastern Brazilian state of Pernambuco for almost half a millennium. The workers in those fields descend from many generations of cane workers, reaching back to those who toiled under a three-and-a-half-centuries'-long slave regime. Twentieth-century workers inherited not just the work, but also the culture created by and around the agro-industry, including patterns in the distribution and exercise of power based on land ownership. We have seen traces of this inheritance in the form of violent and highly racialized labour relations, persistent exploitation, and disdainful attitudes toward rural labour.

These features prevailed even after 1963, when the Rural Worker Statute (Estatuto do Trabalhador Rural – ETR) was passed under the left-nationalist President João Goulart in a context of heightened social mobilizations and progressive reforms. The bill extended to rural workers many rights already enjoyed by urban or industrial workers. The ETR rapidly extended labour courts (Juntas de Conciliação e Julgamento, JCJs) to rural areas to hear the complaints of rural workers and employers. Though it did not bring liberation, the law triggered the production of an invaluable cache of sources with which it is possible to explore the history of rural Pernambuco.

This paper answers a key question: To which degree did Pernambuco's rural labour courts reflect patterns of class-based exploitation, even though they were institutions created through an apparently progressive extension of labour rights? Cases heard in the courts between 1965 and 1982 comprise the empirical foundation of our analysis.[1] Non-rural workers had had access to the labour judiciary since the 1930s, when Getúlio Vargas came to power and initiated a long period of state interventionist politics that involved both a series of worker-friendly reforms and a high degree of state control over unions and the labour movement. The labour judiciary was institutionalized more reliably during the corporatist and dictatorial *Estado Novo* (1937–1945) with the Consolidation of Labour Laws (Consolidação das Leis do Trabalho – CLT) in 1943.[2] The mere fact of the twenty-year lag between the major legal interventions of the CLT and the ETR, a period when rural workers awaited their rights, indicates the consistency of state authorities' collective posture toward rural, as opposed to urban work: They not only recognized a difference between these arenas of labour, but also relegated rural labour to a position of inferiority relative to its urban-industrial counterpart.

We argue that these attitudes flowed from social structures with long histories, including slavery. And we suggest that this perspective had concrete effects. As this article will show, there clearly was a differential treatment accorded to rural and non-rural workers in the outcomes of the cases.[3] Even after gaining admission to labour courts, Pernambuco's cane workers suffered discrimination in their belatedly granted rights.[4]

---

1. We have both used Pernambuco's court archive in the past, publishing several works that appear in the footnotes below. The present article, however, draws on new research and a new cache of cases.

2. With the exception of domestic workers, who had to wait even longer than rural labourers.

3. We tend to use the adjective "non-rural" instead of "urban" because of the ambiguities of the latter. This is especially true of Catende, one of the two jurisdictions further analysed in this article, which was a typical company town. Just like the general judiciary, the JCJs were organized territorially, which means that they heard cases of both rural and non-rural workers, a fact that has allowed us to directly compare the treatment of each group by this institution.

4. An anthropology student's careful ethnography of one JCJ offers abundant evidence of the quotidian forms of discrimination: Moema Maria Marques de Miranda, "Espaço de Honra e de Guerra. Etnografia de uma junta trabalhista" (MA thesis, Universidade Federal de Rio de Janeiro, 1991).

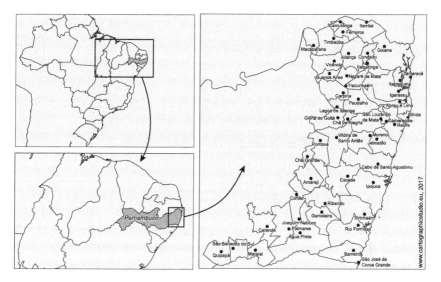

Figure 1. Pernambuco's sugar cane zone, 1960s-1980s.

We found considerable differences between rural and non-rural workers in the mode of calculating compensations and the amounts awarded for revoked contracts or complaints of unpaid benefits.[5] To explain these differences, we will further analyse the social and educational background of the judges rendering the court decisions. As will become clear, they were so closely linked to both the landed class and the state elites that it seems plausible to speak of a coherent class perspective, informed by the cultural imaginary of Brazil, which was especially pronounced during the military regime (1964–1985).

After addressing this material from Pernambuco's rural labour courts, we put three core themes from our interpretations into dialogue with rural labour scholarship from various places around the globe: First, we point to the blurred lines between free and unfree labour, a phenomenon registered prominently in more recent Brazilian historiography and which is, furthermore, at the heart of current debates in labour history worldwide.[6] Second, we see the labour courts as crucial sites for observing the actions of the state and the structural inequalities it reinforced. Third, we draw on

Marcelo Ferreira also adds context for the courts' culture: José Marcelo Marques Ferreira Filho, "Entre 'direitos' e 'justiça'. Os trabalhadores do açúcar frente à Junta de Conciliação e Julgamento de Escada/PE (1963–1969)", *Cadernos de História*, 6:6 (2009), pp. 211–247.

5. Revoked contracts were called rescissions by the courts and generally amounted to the employer firing the worker without just cause.

6. Alexandre Fortes *et al.*, *Novos olhares sobre a história do trabalho* (São Paulo, 2013); Ricardo Antunes, *Os sentidos do trabalho. Ensaio sobre a afirmação e a negação do trabalho* (São Paulo, 2009).

scholarship that engages cases like Brazil, where notions of modernity and archaism conflicted and overlapped. These themes are in conversation with work about India, Africa, the greater Caribbean Basin, and the United States.

RURAL WORKERS' STRUGGLE FOR JUSTICE: THE EMPIRICAL EVIDENCE

Background of the Labour Courts

It is possible to draw a detailed picture of rural workers' interactions with employers and judges by analysing a sampling of cases from two courts (JCJ's) situated in Pernambuco's cane zone: Catende and Nazaré da Mata, which lie, respectively, in the southern and northern sub-regions and which shared similarities and had significant differences (see Figure 1).[7] We examined four sample years, distributed in roughly six-year intervals across a generation after passage of the ETR: 1965, 1971, 1977, and 1982.[8] By gathering a large number of rural cases for each year and comparing them with around twenty non-rural cases, we were able to reveal the difference in treatment experienced by rural and non-rural workers, as well as changes over time (see Table 1).

The basic administrative level in Brazil is the district (*município*).[9] The jurisdiction of a single court may encompass several districts, as with Nazaré da Mata court, hearing cases from a large proportion of the northern sugarcane region. Catende's court, on the other hand, covered only a few districts.[10] Government records allow for a precise assessment of Catende and Nazaré's land ownership patterns in 1985.[11] The Catende Mill alone held 78.60 per cent of the land in that district. Counting its subsidiary properties, the mill owned ninety-six per cent of the land! Meanwhile, farmers with up to ten hectares represented forty-one percent of the total

---

7. Pernambuco's cane zone occupies the whole coastal area of the state, reaching approximately fifty kilometres inland. It comprises, in total, about forty municipalities and is traditionally divided in a smaller North (*Mata Norte*) and more sizeable South zone (*Mata Sul*).

8. During the whole period studied in this article, Brazil was governed by a military regime (1964–1985). The dictatorship claimed to abide by a constitutional structure, which helps to explain why the labour judiciary remained active throughout the period.

9. Although *município* literally means "municipality", it is the only official sub-state level administrative unit and roughly equivalent to a "district" in England or a "county" in the United States; we thus translate it as "district".

10. Catende had originally been overseen by a neighbouring court but with the passage of Law 5650 on 11 December 1970, gained its own.

11. The following numbers have been calculated based on data contained in the Land registries at the Federal Agency for Land Settlement and Agrarian Reform: Instituto Nacional de Colonização e Reforma Agrária (INCRA), Sistema Nacional de Cadastro Rural. Relação para Sindicato CONTAG, Exercício 1985. The data comes exclusively from owners' reports. We have had extreme difficulty obtaining these materials and are lucky to even have these numbers from 1985.

Table 1. *Comparing Rural and Urban Workers' Experiences in the Labour Courts (Catende and Nazaré da Mata). 1,221 cases total.*

	Rural award (Cr$)*	Non-rural award (Cr$)	Rural wages (Cr$)	Non-rural wages (Cr$)	Rural years employed	Non-rural years employed
1965 Catende (n=120)	40,778.03 (n=107)	291,391.05 (n=19)	1,812.5 (n=20)	2,012.33 (n=30)	6.9 (n=107)	5.48 (n=13)
Nazaré (n=493)	57,408.34 (n=453)	67,687.50 (n=16)	992.58 (n=111)	1,290.97 (n=24)	5.2 (n=288)	2.8 (n=28)
1971 Catende (n=110)	420.74 (n=25)	81.71 (n=2)	4.29 (n=75)	4.39 (n=5)	18.2 (n=93)	16.5 (n=10)
Nazaré (n=121)	625.77 (n=75)	1,080.74 (n=19)	3.93 (n=33)	6.87 (n=14)	7.8 (n=79)	5.1 (n=21)
1977 Catende (n=104)	11,949.14 (n=21)	9,209.58 (n=9)	33.10 (n=4+42†)	34.22 (n=7)	14 (n=47)	14.5 (n=27)
Nazaré (n=93)	4,386.15 (n=79)	8,413.29 (n=20)	**33.30** (n=2)	**21.22** (n=12)	9.5 (n=65)	6.4 (n=20)
1982 Catende (n=109)	210,013.03 (n=30)	294,666.58 (n=3)	479.55 (n=24)	598.99 (n=24)	11.6 (n=104)	13.2 (n=14)
Nazaré (n=61)	63,082.12 (n=34)	92,008.93 (n=16)	453.09 (n=9)	620.56 (n=13)	7.2 (n=34)	4.2 (n=19)

* Money amounts given in this table are to be taken with caution because of several currency changes during the period as well as the impact of inflation: In 1967 the *cruzeiro* (Cr$) was replaced with the *cruzeiro novo*, only to revert back the *cruzeiro* (Cr$) in 1970, starting, however, with a higher valuation against other world currencies. By 1977 and 1982 inflation had returned the currency to similar levels as in 1965. The money amounts thus serve mainly as a measure for the differences between rural and non-rural workers.

† Regional minimum salary (salário mínimo regional).

number of parcels, but held only 0.46 per cent of the total area. Middle-sized properties (ten to 100 hectares) held 3.67 per cent. The same pattern prevailed in many of the other districts of the southern cane zone; for instance, neighbouring Palmares had twenty-six small farmers, accounting for 0.3 per cent of land ownership, while medium farms held 3.97 per cent and the thirty-seven large estates enjoyed a near-monopoly of 95.73 per cent of the land. The ownership patterns of the northern cane zone are similar, but slightly less acute. In Nazaré da Mata, 4.23 per cent of the land was in the hands of small farmers, who owned 66.31 per cent of the properties. Forty-one large estates (14.38 per cent of all properties) owned 87.02 per cent of the land. Neighbouring Timbaúba and Vicência, two large districts in the northern area, have similar patterns, with slightly less property concentrated in large estates, although they still control around seventy-five per cent of the land.

Therefore, Catende and Nazaré da Mata differ slightly from one another, but match the prevailing norms for their respective sub-regions. Data for the whole cane zone reveals that in more than twenty of forty-six districts, properties larger than 100 hectares occupied eighty per cent or more of the land. As a result, for a majority of the population, there were very few local alternatives to wage labour on big estates.

We chose our two sample courts and four sample years with the intention of gauging relatively distinct conditions. In a southern cane area like Catende, the establishment and growth of the large productive mills (*usinas*) since the 1940s had been replacing the traditional plantations (*engenhos*). In the northern area, however, even in the 1960s a district like Nazaré da Mata had comparatively more small farms and a large proportion of workers still had access to personal garden plots. The domination and expansion of the mills was strengthened in the 1970s by several federal financing programmes, the most famous of which was the National Alcohol Programme adopted in 1975, which incentivized and subsidized the production of fuel ethanol. Finally, the redemocratization process from the beginning of the 1980s introduced another variable; the rural workers' unions of the cane zone organized major wage campaigns and region-wide strikes beginning in 1979 and these started to bear fruits.

In spite of all of these differences and the geographic and temporal variation, we found a stable pattern: lower wages and levels of compensation for rural workers than non-rural and less value accorded to rural workers' time of service. Furthermore, rural cases seem to have been treated with a cavalier attitude, with judges making less effort to carefully measure the plaintiffs' rights. Most plaintiffs were illiterate, of Afro-Brazilian descent, and they frequently went to court unassisted by their trade union.

The court case files comprise the only consistent and comparatively abundant source material that offers direct insight into these rural workers' lives during the period in question, especially the 1960s and 1970s. As we

Figure 2. Cane worker, Pernambuco, 1940s.
Acervo Fundação Joaquim Nabuco – Ministério da Educação. Used by permission.

have noted in previous publications, rural workers have left behind very few written sources that attest to their ideas, feelings, and experiences. They have existed in a predominantly oral culture, and the elite sources that we do have generally treat them as a bloc, or a mass; this includes such traditional historical sources as newspapers.[12] These labour court files, by contrast, track individual workers' paths as the court treated complaints, sometimes with transcribed individual testimony and personal details. For the particular sample years chosen for the two courts, we have considered all cases for which the files met certain requirements (such as adequate physical status of file, basic information on the workers and their reasons for being involved in a case, etc.).

The gross number of cases heard in a given court varied from year to year.[13] But from case to case, we also found significant inconsistencies in the

12. Thomas D. Rogers, *The Deepest Wounds: A Labour and Environmental History of Sugar in Northeast Brazil* (Chapel Hill, NC, 2010), p. 7. A valuable exception to this rule is the body of work produced by the school of anthropologists active at the Museu Nacional/Universidade Federal de Rio de Janeiro in the 1970s: Moacir Palmeira, José Sergio Leite Lopes, Lygia Sigaud, Beatriz Maria Alasia de Heredia, and others. See Sigaud citation below.
13. Based on an agreement with Pernambuco's Regional Labour Tribunal (Tribunal Regional de Trabalho), since 2004 about 130,000 cases of the state's labour courts covering a period from 1943

amount of information gathered. For instance, not every plaintiff or plaintiff's lawyer (the latter, when present, usually hired by the rural workers' union) stated the wages that the plaintiff earned. And plaintiffs often failed to mention how many years they had worked for an employer. Others, though, reported time of service with startling precision, as when a worker in Catende reported in 1965 that he had worked for three years, seven months, and fifteen days.[14] Finally, many of the paper files themselves have deteriorated over time, leaving us with incomplete or illegible records. Many of the cases did reach an end point, with a document outlining the terms of the conciliation. Many other cases were only archived (a phenomenon that we will further discuss below), and a smaller proportion were arbitrated directly by the judges. Despite its initial introduction through the efforts of a vigorous workers' movement, labour legislation made its most important advances in Brazil under the regime of Getúlio Vargas, particularly during the corporatist dictatorship of the *Estado Novo* (1937–1945) and thus retained a strong paternalistic streak at least until the adoption of a new federal Constitution in 1988.

A trained member of the judiciary acted as the presiding judge of each court. Called a president, he generally came from the educated, white upper middle class, often directly linked by patronage or family ties to the landed class, and he almost invariably had attended the Recife Law School many of whose graduates assumed high state functions (both in Pernambuco and the federal state) as well as positions in the labour courts.[15] Indeed, particular families maintained traditions of staffing the judiciary. Judges and the rural employers who were taken to the labour courts thus generally came from the same class background. Two additional lay judges assisting the president[16] were chosen by the respective professional organizations of workers and employers, thus reinforcing the central purpose of the courts: to conciliate between workers and employers as proclaimed since the CLT. The position of lay judge was often a sinecure for trustworthy union

---

until 1985 have been archived under the auspices of the Federal University of Pernambuco (Universidade Federal de Pernambuco, UFPE) under Prof. Antônio Montenegro's supervision. All archival material cited in this article stems from this Labour Court Archive at the UPPE, located in Recife. More details about the peculiarities of these files can be found in: Thomas D. Rogers and Christine Rufino Dabat, "'A peculiarity of labour in this region': Workers' Voices in the Labour Court Archive at the Federal University of Pernambuco", *Latin American Research Review*, 47 (2012), pp. 163–178.

14. Juntas de Conciliação e Julgamento Catende, UPPE Labour Court Archive (Recife) [hereafter, JCJ-Catende], 3208/65, Heleno Hizidorio de Lima.

15. Arianna Dawn Kinsella Coutinho, "Les étudiants de la Faculté de Droit de Recife et l'espace politique, 1944–1964" (Mémoire de Master 2, Paris, EHESS, 2011).

16. Lay judges were eliminated by Constitutional Amendment 24 of 12 September 1999, which transformed the JCJs into regular courts (which following the general notion for first instance jurisdiction are called *varas do trabalho*).

officials who had been fully integrated in the corporatist structures built under state auspices since the 1930s. Meanwhile, those chosen by employers shared the same class background with the academically trained presiding judges.

Judges and their class peers (even people who ostensibly supported workers) operated according to an epistemological framework that constructed the rural world as ontologically linked to backwardness and inferiority. In this stage-based historical imaginary, the predominant mode of production in rural areas – especially in the supposedly "feudal" cane plantation system – represented an era to be superseded. According to such views, the workers during the anachronistic slave-based labour regime until the end of the nineteenth century, as well as their descendants until the 1950s and again after the coup in 1964, lacked basic freedoms, especially the freedom of information, movement, and association, and even simply the freedom to assemble as a workforce on a plantation to develop and manifest a socially constructive class consciousness. These ideas informed and shaped the mentality of authorities in general and particularly the state apparatus, including the judges.

The roots of this framework run deep, into a centuries-old power structure that encompassed all dimensions of life. The consolidation of power by certain families had a social and class logic, and was deeply racialized. The more "progressive" elites of most of Brazil's federal states in the late nineteenth and early twentieth centuries turned to an adapted variant of positivism, which not only pledged allegiance to "progress", "science", and "law", but also supported a form of eugenic politics by "whitening" the country through European immigration, hoping that the past of a slave-based economy and, indeed, the whole Afro-Brazilian component of Brazilian society would vanish.[17] Offspring from the dominant class manned state posts throughout the post-independence eras of the Brazilian Empire (1822–1889) and the First Republic (1889–1930). But the main basis for the concentration of power in the cane region was, and remains, land ownership. As borne out in the statistics cited above, the overall pattern was of monopolistic domination. Military and police strength had enforced these concentrated landholdings since the period of colonization. Neither the land's original inhabitants hundreds of years ago, nor rural workers who hoped to become real farmers, had a chance of breaking the hold of the major landowners – not even in those historical moments since the 1930s when urban, industrial workers in other parts of Brazil were able to gain considerable concessions.

17. Carlos Alberto Cunha Miranda, "Saberes e Práticas do Movimento Eugênico no Brasil. Uma busca pela regeneração integral da natureza humana", in André Mota, Maria Gabriel S.M.C. Marinho (eds), *Eugenia e História. Ciência, educação e regionalidades* (São Paulo, 2013), pp. 156–179.

Findings from the Court Records

In August 1963, negotiations between employers and workers of Pernambuco's cane region produced a landmark document meant to standardize compensation, but effective wages could vary quite widely. The Ministry of Labour had jurisdiction over the document's enforcement but conducted little oversight. The parties renewed the agreement until 1965, when, in the wake of the right-wing military coup of 1964, it was effectively discarded until 1979; then, a strike by cane workers forced employers to participate in negotiating new guidelines for fieldwork. With or without such agreements, the overall picture revealed by the sample cases from Nazaré da Mata and Catende in 1965, 1971, 1977, and 1982 shows that rural workers generally earned lower wages, and worked longer periods for their employers than non-rural workers, as well as receiving lower settlements when going to court (see Table 1).[18] The near-invariability of the rural workers' inferior compensation and treatment supports our overarching argument that this group of workers faced pervasive discrimination.

The cases from Catende in 1965 document employers – and especially the district's dominant employer, the Catende Mill – reacting to the passage of the ETR.[19] The mill was involved in the vast majority of the cases from this year as it dismissed hundreds of workers in order to avoid compliance with the ETR's prescriptions. Without a formal employment relationship, the mill would not have to provide workers with the stipulated benefits such as distributing the end-of-year bonus, pay for holidays, etc. The mill also likely carried out a political cleansing following the coup, dispensing with workers who had joined Peasant Leagues or were seen as militant trade unionists. The uniformity of Catende Mill-related cases from this year differs from other years and other courts, in which the cases were of greater variety. In many of the 1965 Catende Mill firings, the workers received no compensation at all from the court.

We selected ninety-nine cases of the Catende JCJ from 1965, involving 107 individuals; all were dismissals and we have no data for wage levels. The rural workers received an average compensation of Cr$40,778.03. If we divide the awards rural workers received by the total years they worked, we find that they were given an average of Cr$5,880.30 per year of work, although amounts per year of service varied widely among rural workers. In fact, judges appear not to have weighted length of service, with awards bearing little relation to experience. A series of cases from November bears

18. As Table 1 shows (see the three instances highlighted in bold), there were a few exceptions to this general picture, when rural workers appeared to earn or receive more money. In each of these, the number of cases is very low, with one outlier likely throwing off the calculation.

19. Catende's cases were heard in the Palmares court for this year, but we separated the Catende cases from the rest.

Figure 3. Group of workers cultivating cane field, Pernambuco, 1940s.
Acervo Fundação Joaquim Nabuco – Ministério da Educação. Used by permission.

this out, as fourteen workers fired around the same time received the same award – Cr$40,000 – despite having experience ranging from three years to twenty years.[20] The apparent randomness of some of these compensation levels leads us to believe that many of the dynamics at play in the courtroom did not leave any traces in the case records (such as varying degrees of commitment by the lay judge for the workers' side, the intervention of a local priest, etc.). It is possible, too, that the lawyer of the mill, particularly in Catende, successfully argued that the certain cases' claims should be reduced or dismissed entirely.

We should note that the primary importance of comparing wage and compensation quantities lies in what they reveal relationally, between different groups of workers for instance. The currency suffered from high

20. JCJ-Catende 3208/65, Heleno Hizidorio de Lima vs. Usina Catende; JCJ-Catende 3219/65, Manuel Teixeira de Oliveira vs. Usina Catende; JCJ-Catende 3221/65, Antonio Maximiano vs. Usina Catende; JCJ-Catende 3236/65, Maria Luiza da Silva vs. Usina Catende; JCJ-Catende 3251/65, José João de Souza vs. Usina Catende; JCJ-Catende 3252/65, José Vicente da Silva vs. Usina Catende; JCJ-Catende 3286/65, Antonio Candido de Lima vs. Usina Catende; JCJ-Catende 3290/65, Josefina Vitor da Silva vs. Usina Catende; JCJ-Catende 3376/65, Manoel Sverino da Silva vs. Mendo Sampaio; JCJ-Catende 3398/65, José Alves dos Santos vs. Usina Catende; JCJ-Catende 3417/65, José Isídio vs. Usina Catende; JCJ-Catende 3422/65, José Carlos da Silva vs. Usina Catende; JCJ-Catende 3452/65, Juvenal Ferreira Campos vs. Usina 13 de Maio; JCJ-Catende 3457/65, Joel Luis Guimarães vs. Usina 13 de Maio; JCJ-Catende 3490/65, José Bezerra de Lima vs. Usina 13 de Maio.

inflation during the period and the government reacted with devaluations and by introducing new currencies. Brazil replaced the *cruzeiro* with the *cruzeiro novo* in 1967, but when the new currency fell prey to inflation, it shifted the name back to the *cruzeiro* in 1970. This *cruzeiro* began with a higher valuation against other world currencies, meaning that wage levels and prices were calculated in much smaller amounts. This explains why judgement and wage amounts appear markedly different between 1965 and 1971; one can also see that, by 1977 and 1982, inflation had returned the currency to similar levels as in 1965. To further contextualize the values from this paper, the average compensation cited above for rural workers in Catende 1965 came to $2,303.96 in US dollars from the time, or US$332.24 per year of work.[21] In terms of buying power, a kilogramme of dried meat (*charque*) cost between Cr$1,500 and 1,800 in March 1965. So the indemnification of a year's rural labour would buy a bit more than three kilos of meat.[22]

Non-rural workers going to the Catende JCJ were awarded an average compensation of Cr$291,391.05 (US$16,463.59). Because they tended to work fewer years for an employer than rural workers, their per-year award was much higher, averaging Cr$48,666.14 (US$2,749.64). Rural workers, then, earned about an eighth of the per-year rate of compensation of their non-rural peers. Even low-level non-rural workers, like unskilled casual workers (*serventes*) received larger settlements than rural workers. An unskilled worker with four and a half years of experience, for instance, received Cr$372,804, while a rural worker who had served the mill for ten years got only Cr$30,000.[23] Administrators, not surprisingly, received much larger compensations. Their higher prestige roles, placing them closer in the class strata to their employers, meant that the packages from the two cases we found in this year were much larger: Cr$180,000 and Cr$177,428 per year, respectively.[24]

For Nazaré da Mata in 1965 we gathered 453 rural cases with enough data to use and sixty non-rural cases. Among the rural cases, 265 ended in conciliations, eighty-five cases were archived because the plaintiff failed to appear, and for eighteen cases the plaintiff withdrew his or her complaint. On the non-rural side, we only have documented resolutions for twenty-nine of the cases. Of those, nineteen ended in conciliations, eight were

---

21. The exchange rate in August 1965 between the cruzeiro and the US dollar was 0.0565. Stock Quote 15 – [no title], *New York Times (1923–Current File)*, 7 August 1965, available at: https://login.proxy.library.emory.edu/login?url=https://search-proquest-com.proxy.library.emory. edu/docview/116955305?accountid=10747; last accessed 18 October 2017. Please note, an Emory Univ. login is required.

22. *Diário de Pernambuco*, 27 March 1965, p. 9.

23. JCJ-Catende 2860/65, José Rui Cordeiro da Silva vs. Usina Catende; 3139/65, Marina Maria da Conceição vs. Usina Catende.

24. JCJ-Catende 3442/65, Manoel Pereira de Lucena vs. Usina 13 de Maio; and 3445/65, Manoel Joaquim da Silva vs. Usina 13 de Maio.

archived, and the plaintiff withdrew from two cases. The average judgement on non-rural workers for 1965 was Cr$67,687 (US$3,824.32), while the average rural judgement was Cr$57,408 (US$3,243.55). The average non-rural wage for 1965 was Cr$1,290.97 per month (US$72.94), with an average of 2.8 years of service. The average rural wage was Cr$992.58 (US$56.08) and rural workers had worked an average of 5.2 years for their employers.

We have 110 cases from the Catende court for 1971, and for a plurality of these the Catende Mill was listed as the defendant (thirty-six of the ninety-nine rural cases and seven of the ten non-rural cases). The other defendants in the non-rural cases were the Roçadinho Mill, twice, and a tile factory. The non-rural workers were three unskilled casual workers, a carpenter, a mason, a brakeman (presumably for the mill's railroad), a locksmith's assistant, a forest guard, a tile maker, and a foreman. All ninety-nine rural plaintiffs were given the generic "rural worker" label. Among these, fifty-six were archived and thirty-three were conciliated. Twelve were either judged in favour or against the plaintiff. These numbers exceed ninety-nine because some of the cases included more than one plaintiff, while the different workers experienced different resolutions, a typical pattern in these courts. In all, seventeen of the rural cases were collective complaints. Only eleven of the rural plaintiffs could sign their names; the others marked the court documents with a thumbprint. For only two of the non-rural cases a determination of the signature mode could be made: one signed, the other did not. For the region as a whole, these were fairly typical ratios for literacy (or at least the capacity to write one's name).

For only twenty-five of the ninety-nine Catende 1971 rural cases do we have a clear monetary award recorded for the plaintiffs. For five of those, we also have the claim made by the plaintiff and in each of these cases the award was far lower than the claim. On average, rural plaintiffs were only awarded about eight per cent of their initial claims. In one example, the worker demanded Cr$3,641 (US$191.52) and ended up receiving only Cr$97 (US$5.10).[25] Interestingly, Catende in 1971 represents an exception to the general structural gap in wages between the different groups of workers, with both rural and non-rural workers earning around Cr$4.50 per day (US$0.24). In the same vein, the average time of service for the rural and non-rural workers was quite similar: eighteen years for the former group and 16.5 for the latter.

25. JCJ-Catende, 78/71, Izabel Maria Barbosa da Silva e outras (3) vs. Engenho Caroba. The August 1971 exchange rate from cruzeiros to US dollars was 0.0526. Stock Quote 12 – [no title], *New York Times (1923–Current File)*, 13 August 1971, available at: https://login.proxy.library. emory.edu/login?url=https://search-proquest-com.proxy.library.emory.edu/docview/119146205? accountid=10747; last accessed 18 October 2017. Dried meat cost Cr$5.50/kg at this time. *Diário de Pernambuco*, 7 April 1971, p. 6.

In Nazaré da Mata in 1971, however, differences between rural and non-rural workers were marked in all matters: We have twenty-one non-rural cases, of which nineteen ended in conciliations (and one withdrawal and a judgement). Among the 100 rural cases for 1971, seventy-five reached conciliations and sixteen were archived when the plaintiff failed to appear (and two withdrawals and five judgements). As for the average compensation awards, the rural workers, were granted only fifty-eight percent of the money their non-rural peers received. The average time of service for the rural awardees in 1971 was 7.8 years, while the average time of service for non-rural workers was five years. The average daily rural wage was Cr$3.93, while the average non-rural wage was Cr$6.87.

While rural employers fired workers en masse following the passage of the ETR, they later devised other ways to avoid legal obligations to their employees. Some of these 1971 cases offer insight into the range of strategies employers used to manipulate work conditions and push workers off their contracted rolls: For instance, workers often complained about field foremen demanding tasks too large to complete, which would cause the worker to lose Sunday's paid rest.[26] The inverse of this strategy consisted of refusing to assign workers any task at all, forcing them to seek work elsewhere.[27] Similarly, the mill might assign only five days of work instead of six, or demand six when the worker wished to work five.[28] More commonly, mills would deliberately pay less than the minimum wage, forcing workers to appeal to the courts for assistance. In one instance in 1971, thirty-one plaintiffs filed one case together in relation to this complaint.[29] Finally, some cases from 1977 also mention a list of casual off-the-books workers (a *"folha extra"*) deprived of the benefits won through collective bargaining results (and allegedly not entitled to make any claims before the labour courts).

Among employers' strategies in their repertoire for evading labour law, especially in the southern cane region, mills would find renters who had contracts to manage some mill land. These arrangements aimed to obfuscate the question of who bore responsibility for the long-term rights of the wage earners. The mill would argue that it had no responsibility since the renter

26. JCJ-Catende 59/71, João Firmino da Silva vs. Usina Catende.
27. JCJ-Catende 100/71, Antonio Francisco da Silva vs. Usina Catende. For similar cases from 1982 see JCJ-Catende 171/82, Maria José Ferreira and 287/82, Antônio Barbosa dos Santos both vs. Usina Catende.
28. JCJ-Catende 142/71, José Eloy Barbosa vs. Usina Frei Caneca.
29. JCJ-Catende 60/70, Antonio Avelino da Silva e outros (31) vs. Usina Água Branca, 20 de setembro 1971.The next two cases (61 and 62), filed on the same day on behalf of thirty and twenty plaintiffs, respectively, levelled the same complaint and also named Usina Água Branca as the defendant. This strategy was already highlighted in an anthropological study realized at the time: Lygia Sigaud, *Os Clandestinos e os Direitos. Estudo sobre Trabalhadores da Cana-de-Açucar de Pernambuco* (São Paulo, 1979), 90, 97.

Figure 4. Group of workers harvesting cane, Pernambuco, 1940s.
Acervo Fundação Joaquim Nabuco – Ministério da Educação. Used by permission.

was the actual employer. After only a few years, though, the renter would end the rental arrangement and abandon all obligations vis-à-vis the workers. In addition, mills often expected renters to eliminate traditional claims such as access to a plot for planting food crops and "clear" the land of workers. The period we are analysing is considered the height of this process of expulsion from gardens.[30] Technological changes, such as increasing mechanization and the use of agricultural chemicals, also arrived during this period, progressively diminishing the demand for rural workers. At the same time, the area under cultivation expanded since state subsidies for land planted with sugarcane were available and planters filled all available space with cane. Improved road conditions allowed workers to shift more rapidly from countryside to city according to seasonal labour demands, and both processes together meant an increasing casualization and urbanization of rural workers.[31]

Our files for Catende in 1977 include seventy-seven rural workers' cases and twenty-seven non-rural workers. Very few of the latter have complete data, unfortunately. Compensation judgments range widely, the lowest

30. See a study realized in the period pointing to the central role of these enclosures in the constant undernourishment of poor rural workers: Robert Linhart, *O açúcar e a fome* (Rio de Janeiro, 1979).
31. Espedito Rufino de Araujo, *O trator e o "burro sem rabo". Consequências de modernização agrícola sobre a mão-de-obra na região canavieira de Pernambuco* (Genève, 1991).

being merely eight per cent of the highest, as do wage levels, from Cr$250 (US$16.95) to Cr$500 (US$33.90) per week to only Cr$16 per day (US$1.08).[32] Variations among non-rural workers were even more marked.[33]

A large number of women among the rural workers in this year's cases (forty-one out of ninety-one) may have been the result of a Usina Catende policy of firing female employees. The mill would target women as a means of pressuring families to leave the property and give up their garden plots.[34] Some were dismissed for pregnancy and child birth. Severina Alexandre da Silva explains that she "gave birth and was fired", even though she had been working for the mill for five years.[35] Other workers claimed that they were threatened, probably by employers seeking to expel them from plantation property. José Alves da Silva, for instance, who had worked more than twenty years for his employer, stated that the Esporão-Canhotinho Plantation's owner had threatened and tried to push Silva to accompany him to the police station (his case was archived as he did not show up at court).[36]

Many cases deal with a specific request: workers sought categorization as industrial rather than rural workers. Lawyers brought the demand so often for workers that they phrased it in consistent language in the case files and brought mimeographed copies of the section of the CLT that pertains to the sugar industry. They also cited a decision by the Supreme Labour Court (Tribunal Superior de Trabalho, TST), holding that all those employed by a firm with an industrial activity should be considered as industrial workers, whether they worked in a mill or not.[37] A change of category could win a worker a higher minimum wage. The argument shows the ingenuity of workers and their union lawyers in defending their interests and countering employer abuse and intransigence.

---

32. See the compensations awarded in: JCJ-Catende 407/77, Edvaldo José Belchior vs. Usina Catende; 413/77, Luiz Roberto da Silva vs. Usina Catende; JCJ-Catende, 304/77, João Pedro da Silva vs. Usina Catende. The August 1977 exchange rate from cruzeiros to US dollars was 0.0678. Foreign Exchange, *New York Times (1923–Current File)*, 24 August 1977, available at: https://login.proxy.library.emory.edu/login?url=https://search-proquest-com.proxy.library.emory.edu/docview/123264095?accountid=10747; last accessed 18 October 2017. Please note, an Emory Univ. login is required. Dried meat cost Cr$28.29 at this time. *Diário de Pernambuco*, 23 March 1977, p. 6.

33. JCJ-Catende, 388/77, José Mendes Barbosa vs. José Ferreira de Amorim; and 304/77, João Pedro da Silva vs. Usina Catende. While Mendes got Cr$18,860.30 for nine years of service, da Silva was only awarded Cr$1,000 for six years of service.

34. Renata Cahú, "Defendendo espaços conquistados. Dificuldades e discriminações enfrentadas pelas trabalhadoras rurais na Zona da Mata Sul de Pernambuco", *Anais do Encontro estadual de História da ANPUH – PE* (Recife, 2016), pp. 2080-2090.

35. JCJ-Catende, 422/77, Severina Alexandre da Silva vs. Usina Catende. All translations are by the authors.

36. JCJ-Catende, 411/77, José Alves da Silva vs. José Ferreira de Amorim.

37. See the corresponding court rulings: Súmula 196, available at: http://www.tst.jus.br/sumulas; last accessed 18 October 2017. Súmulas do TST, Enunciado no. 57, available at: http://www.Soleis.adv.br/sumulastst.htm; last accessed 18 October 2017.

Such attempts to change legal status are hardly surprising, considering the court decisions on compensation: In Nazaré da Mata in 1977, the average compensation for rural plaintiffs was Cr$4,386.15 with the average time of service being 9.5 years. The non-rural workers, on the other hand, received awards averaging nearly twice as much while generally working fewer years for their employers (6.4 on average). However, non-rural cases reached conciliation much more regularly (eleven of the twenty), while eight were judged and one ended in the plaintiff's withdrawal.

In 1982, of Nazaré da Mata's twenty non-rural cases, fourteen ended in conciliations. Two others ended in judgements by the court judges, two were archived, one plaintiff withdrew, and we do not know the outcome of the final case. We have forty-one rural cases, twenty-five of which reached conciliations. Nine others reached judgements and we lack data for the other seven. There was a difference of thirty-two per cent in the average compensation levels between rural and non-rural workers (roughly Cr$63,000 against Cr$92,000, or US$346.50 and US$506).[38] On average, non-rural workers made Cr$620.56 per day, while rural workers earned Cr$453.09 per day (US$3.42 and US$2.49, respectively). This represents a similar gap between non-rural and rural workers to that seen with the compensations, with the latter earning only seventy-three per cent of their non-rural counterparts' wages. The rural plaintiffs had given an average of 7.24 years of service and the non-rural workers 4.16 years.

A Nazaré da Mata case from early 1982 offers some additional insights into the conditions and culture workers faced in the courts: Antonio José da Silva brought a complaint against the plantation Gameleirinha in January, claiming he was fired without prior warning and asking for support because he had been absent from work for a month through illness. In testimony before the court, Silva said that his pay records did not accurately reflect all of the work he had done, but he refrained from pursuing that complaint because he feared physical reprisal from the plantation renter, Marcelo Ibernon de Albuquerque Cavalcanti.[39] In fact, Silva testified, Cavalcanti had explicitly threatened to do so. In this case and others, we glimpse the pervasive climate of violence surrounding rural workers every day. That violence buttressed and policed very pronounced class divisions that separated workers from their social superiors. And the latter group did not

---

38. The August 1977 exchange rate from cruzeiros to US dollars was 0.0055. Stock Quote 4 – [no title], *New York Times (1923–Current File)*, 15 August 1982, available at: https://login.proxy.library.emory.edu/login?url=https://search-proquest-com.proxy.library.emory.edu/docview/121996280?accountid=10747; last accessed 18 October 2017. Please note, an Emory Univ. login is required. Dried meat cost Cr$419 at this time. *Diário de Pernambuco*, 6 March 1982, p. 10.

39. Juntas de Conciliação e Julgamento Nazaré da Mata, UPPE Labour Court Archive (Recife), 47/82, Antonio José da Silva vs. Engenho Gameleirinha.

just include the plantation and mill owners, but the judges and lawyers in the court as well.

The perpetually lurking violence workers faced, we contend, was one of the main reasons for the high rate of attrition observed for all years. A large proportion of cases were listed as archived, or cancelled, because of the plaintiffs' failure to appear for hearings after lodging an initial complaint. This could make up more than half of the cases, as in Catende in 1971, when fifty-six out of ninety-nine cases were archived. In addition to the climate of violence, the onerous distances workers had to travel to the court and attend hearings also impeded cases from reaching a conclusion. Workers would lose a day of work and their paid weekly rest.

Finally, numerous cases made clear that workers sensed that the courts were biased or constituted a space that actually made them more vulnerable. Sometimes, this becomes visible when workers asked to be heard by another court, as José Manuel de Lima did in 1977, requesting that his complaint be forwarded to the Regional Labour Representative, because "it is very hard to win a labour complaint" in the Catende court.[40] In more general terms, the mere numbers indicate the degree to which courts were a space of risky exposure for workers. We analysed 104 cases of rural workers in Catende in 1982, and half of the workers seeking compensation failed to receive it. We see familiar reasons for the failures, such as one worker testifying that he had received a death threat,[41] while Josefa Maria da Conceição testified that she had been fired after her husband filed a complaint against their employer.[42]

At the same time, Catende in 1982 stands out from other years as some of the usual patterns between the two major groups of workers are reversed: Rural workers spent an average of 11.6 years with their employers, while the non-rural average was 13.2. Also, the average annual compensation for rural workers was even slightly higher than for non-rural workers. Important changes had taken place which explain this turn: The amnesty of 1979 and the progressive return to a democratic system coincided with workers' organizations (both rural and non-rural) pursuing more explicit avenues for claiming their rights. Pernambuco's sugarcane area was a pioneer in this respect, as cane workers mobilized extensively and mounted a large strike in 1979. The 1980s brought a successful effort to democratize unions.[43]

40. JCJ-Catende 300/77, José Manuel de Luna vs. Usina Catende.
41. JCJ-Catende 401/82, Cicero Mendonça da Silva vs. Engenho Novo Horizonte.
42. JCJ-Catende 355/82, Josefa Maria da Conceição vs. Engenho Cangalia.
43. On the shifts at the beginning of the 1980s see, for instance: Marcela Heráclio Bezerra, "Mulheres (des) cobertas, histórias reveladas. Relações de trabalho, práticas cotidianas e lutas políticas das trabalhadoras canavieiras na Zona da Mata Sul de Pernambuco (1980–1988)" (UFPE, PPGH, dissertação de mestrado. 2012), available at: http://repositorio.ufpe.br/handle/123456789/11042; last accessed 18 October 2017.

INTERPRETATIVE AND COMPARATIVE PERSPECTIVES: HISTORIOGRAPHY OF THE PAST FIFTEEN YEARS

This section places our empirical findings in dialogue with historiography from Brazil and other parts of the world, primarily Africa, India, the Caribbean Basin, and the US. Three central themes emerge from our work: free and unfree labour, the role of the state in labour relations, and the tension between backwardness and modernity in the treatment of rural workers.

Rural labour occupies a curious place in Brazilian historiography. One of its peculiarities is that the volume of work on rural slaves in colonial and post-independence times far outstrips the more modest literature on free rural workers after abolition. This, however, not only constitutes an imbalance, but also speaks to an analytical opportunity, since continuities between slavery and free labour mark Brazilian history. As scholars have long observed, bonded and free labourers can be placed within the same analytical frame. The first main interpretation of our evidence drawn from the labour court documents is that the line between free and unfree labour is, across time, both fundamental and often blurred, and rural workers' experiences after the ETR bear out that fact. João José Reis's careful research about a major strike by mostly black workers in Bahia in 1857 offers a nineteenth-century example, as he describes a labour market where slaves and freedmen routinely worked side by side and found themselves confronting shared challenges. While this strike shows us the porosity of the slave/free boundary, it also points to how the status of labourer was inextricably mingled with other identifications: Ethnicity, and specifically anti-African prejudice, proved a more salient variable for these workers than the question of freedom. They were not blind to the difference, obviously, and slaves had to abandon the strike soon in response to their masters' orders. But slave or free status was one among many axes of difference, with ethnicity and occupation playing roles too.[44]

Just as blurry as the line between slave and free for people of African descent until abolition in 1888 is the divide between the era of slavery and the age of freedom. When did slavery end, and for whom? Beatriz Mamigonian and others have shown that the path to freedom in the years preceding the definite end of slavery could be circuitous, even for groups legally entitled to their emancipation.[45] Even after official abolition, in 1888, patterns of unfreedom – marked by coercion and exploitation – persisted in

---

44. João José Reis, "A greve negra de 1857 na Bahia", *Revista USP*, 18 (1993), pp. 8–29; *idem*, "'The Revolution of the Ganhadores': Urban Labour, Ethnicity and the African Strike of 1857 in Bahia, Brazil", *Journal of Latin American Studies*, 29 (1997), pp. 355–393, 383, 392.
45. Beatriz Gallott Mamigonian, "Do que 'o preto mina' é capaz. Etnia e resistência entre africanos livres", *Afro-Ásia*, 24 (2000), pp. 71–95, 72.

Brazil and beyond.[46] Yet, it is not only the real continuities of unfreedom in different forms and degrees that compel the use of the labour history of slavery to address the field of rural labour history – indeed to merge these fields. In addition, the fluid categories used to describe these realities under slavery remained fluid after its end, as Sidney Mintz has shown.[47] In the case of the rural workers analysed in this article, the category "wage-earner" has a dubious specificity as a label. Instead of (or in addition to) an identity defined by race, this one was (and is) defined by what these people were doing to earn money, namely agricultural labour.

In his study of rural labour in a Puerto Rican sugarcane district during the period of emancipation (slavery there was only abolished in 1873), Luis Figueroa describes how *libertos'* actions and their interpretation by others depended on the larger system in which they made their decisions. "Slavery, of course, constituted not simply a labour system", Figueroa points out, "but also a system of power relations, of behavioural codes that provided a powerful justification for domination, for sorting people out in particular ways, even if those codes were not always followed". The apparent exercise of freedom by *libertos* concerned Puerto Rican elites, who reacted by labelling their mobility as vagrancy or worse. They moved swiftly to erect new barriers to restrict the freedpeople's options.[48]

Sidney Chalhoub, another of the eminent scholars on this question, analyses an oppressive reality beyond the freedom–slavery dichotomy. Although freed Afro-Brazilians constituted a sizeable group in Brazilian society in the last decades before abolition, "[b]lack people saw their life marked by the threat of enslavement", Chalhoub writes, and his work shows that free persons of African descent or freed ex-slaves consistently faced this danger.[49] Many of the post-independence authorities' administrative measures, such as the census, were interpreted (even if mistakenly) as hidden manoeuvres to achieve such ends. This was reinforced by the persistence and naturalization of racialized thought, which filtered into public policy and found a forceful expression in the preference for "white" immigrant workers.

We see the treatment of rural workers by the state – from the beginning of the First Republic in 1889 through the state-interventionist period since

---

46. John D. French and Thomas D. Rogers, "Slavery as a 'Sinister Principle' of Authority: Continuities between Slavery and Freedom in the Making of Modern Brazil", unpublished manuscript.

47. Sidney W. Mintz, "Was the Plantation Slave a Proletarian?", *Review (Fernand Braudel Center)*, 2:1 (1978), pp. 81–98, 97, fn. 31. In response to the question he poses in his title, Mintz responds "It is the titles which are abstract"; we must look to lived reality.

48. Luis A. Figueroa, *Sugar, Slavery, and Freedom in Nineteenth-Century Puerto Rico* (Chapel Hill, NC, 2005), pp. 144–145.

49. Sidney Chalhoub, *A força da escravidão. Ilegalidade e costume no Brasil oitocentista* (São Paulo, 2012), p. 18.

1930 to the years of military dictatorship from 1964 on – as an extension of this principle, following Igor Kopytoff's proposal that "slavery should not be defined as a status, but as a process of transformation of a status that can last a whole life or even spread down to further generations".[50] Proof of it lies in rural workers' exclusion from legal protections until 1963 with passage of the ETR, as well as the differentiation in minimum wage and pensions, which for rural workers was just half of the non-rural level.

Scholarship on the Caribbean offers additional insight into government-enforced systems of exclusion that persist even when they clash with the state's declared principles. Miranda Spieler has shown this for the French in Guiana, with a broader range of categories of people subjected to exploitation and discrimination, including in and by court systems.[51] She documents the travails of Amerindians, African slaves, African immigrants, their descendants, political and common law European prisoners, and former prisoners. Among the common dimensions of this downtrodden population, the lack of access to the ownership of land is the most salient.[52]

The range of victims of this French system, coming from so many origins, suffering in spite of the nation's long tradition of revolutions and reiterated declarations of human rights, reveals one of the essential features of the phenomenon we study in Brazil: The French Third Republic's ideology enshrined the idea of a nation in which small farmers and soldiers occupied a central place. In Guyana, however, it was particularly these groups who were subject to open discrimination and could only serve as field hands, not independent farmers. Authorities of a theoretically progressive state, then, created a "new sort of historical subject", nominally free but without citizenship "who lived with considerable legal incapacities and was struck by policing mechanisms that narrowed the difference between slavery and freedom".[53]

One can make compelling comparisons along these lines with the United States.[54] Historian Greta de Jong's descriptions of African-American experiences in twentieth-century Louisiana could have come from Pernambuco. "The plantation elite's control over people and resources in

50. Igor Kopytoff, "Slavery", *Annual Review of Anthropology*, 11 (1982), pp. 207–230, 221–222.

51. Miranda Spieler, *Empire and Underworld. Captivity in French Guyana* (Cambridge, MA, 2012).

52. *Ibid.*, pp. 176–177. Even under the Third Republic, administrative employees acted on their opinion of the "African race" of "primitive ignorance". This attitude cleaves closely to that of the Brazilian elite, referenced above in relation to eugenics.

53. Miranda Spieler, *Empire and Underworld*, p. 221.

54. Much rural labour history in the US focuses on California, with special attention given to the 1960s–70s farmworkers movement. However, there were other moments of rural militancy, such as the 1930s, when the country saw more than 275 agricultural strikes (half of them in California). Dionicio Nodín Valdés, *Organized Agriculture and the Labour Movement Before the UFW: Puerto Rico, Hawai'i, California* (Austin, TX, 2011), p. 6.

rural Louisiana was never absolute", she writes, "but it often seemed close to being so. Some parishes resembled personal fiefdoms, governed by a few individuals or families whose influence extended over everyone in the community, white or black."[55] De Jong writes, "[p]overty, inadequate education, disfranchisement, and the threat of violence discouraged organizing efforts, while plantation owners' control over economic resources, political offices, and the law enabled them to stifle most challenges to the system".[56] Pernambuco's rural workers suffered a similar lack of access to education and almost complete exclusion from political processes, since literacy was required to vote until 1988. And of course De Jong's reference to control of the courts resonates with our study. Furthermore, there are parallels in the historical shifts of labour relations in sugar cane: By the 1930s, eighty per cent of Louisiana sugar plantations workers earned wages, as opposed to working through traditional arrangements. Earlier norms had kept workers tied to their employers through access to land for gardens, firewood, and houses, just like similar tenancy agreements in Pernambuco. There, the transition began around the same time, but arguably culminated only during the period we study in this paper.[57]

Our second interpretative theme revolves around essentially the same question from a different perspective. In this case, we focus on how patterns of rural labour exploitation persist through and because of state action and complicity. We see helpful guidance in Ranajit Guha's approach from his famous work on peasant insurgencies in India. He interprets colonial bureaucratic documents as constituting a particular genre. District officials writing about episodes of peasant revolt and insurgency actually composed narratives, or history, Guha writes. These descriptions and explanations obeyed a coherent logic that negated the possibility that the peasants had a larger project than violence and reaction and thereby negated their actions' political content. Famously, to tease out these contents, Guha employs a method to read the documents "against the grain", as evidence of the ideas and motivations of the peasants.[58]

Like these colonial documents and their discursive logic, our court cases employ the language of power and the state. The cases' results and the figures involved in the compensation sometimes offered to workers at their conclusion can be understood as effects of the visions of power and culture held by their authors – the judges. Rural workers' visits to courts had

---

55. Greta de Jong, *A Different Day: African American Struggles for Justice in Rural Louisiana, 1900–1970* (Chapel Hill, NC, 2002), p. 36.

56. *Ibid.*, p. 5.

57. *Ibid.*, p. 27. Three quarters of those wage labourers in 1930 Louisiana were African Americans.

58. Ranajit Guha, "The Prose of Counter-Insurgency", in Ranajit Guha (ed.), *Subaltern Studies II. Writings on South Asian History and Society* (Dehli [etc.], 1983), pp. 1–42. See also, Ranajit Guha, *Elementary Aspects of Peasant Insurgency in Colonial India* (Durham, NC, 1999), pp. 1–17.

predictable outcomes, in part because of the class perspective of the judges. Following Guha, we argue that there *were* patterns, that the "prose" of those in power was coherent and followed a logic. Our documents mirror Guha's "primary discourse", which he says came almost entirely from the realm of officials, revealing the structures of power that their authors served. However, different from the specific instances of Guha's study (which focuses on moments of rebellion and counterinsurgency in a context of colonial domination) the rural workers in Pernambuco dealt with an institution that was imbued with a language of rights leaving, despite all limitations, a larger margin to the workers to bring in their own logic and employ the official discourse to their benefit.

The crucial role of the state is borne out in the sugar cane plantations of Louisiana mentioned earlier. Whereas workers in Pernambuco had to wait for the ETR (1963) to unionize and collectively negotiate with planters, the Louisiana Farmers' Union (LFU) was formed in 1937. Its influence over the conditions workers faced was limited, but it began the process of challenging planters' power. The LFU's complaints were very similar to those rural workers' unions lodged in Pernambuco in the 1960s and 1970s: inadequate wages, receiving pay in coupons for the plantation store, excessive prices at those stores, and a lack of access to land to grow their own food.[59] Mechanization began to spread in Louisiana in the 1940s, whereas it would only come to Brazil in the 1980s and later.

Douglas A. Blackmon's work on Alabama echoes De Jong's on Louisiana and provides another powerful comparison to Pernambuco. He describes how post-abolition Lowndes County, Alabama, became a region where "the war seemed to have had little effect on the question of whether slavery would continue there [...] [T]he landholders who remained reforged an almost impenetrable jurisdiction into which no outside authority could extend its reach."[60] This characterization also captures Pernambuco's sugar cane during the military dictatorship until the late 1970s when the rural workers managed to organize and launch successful mobilizations. As Blackmon puts it, the county's African American residents were "no longer called slaves but liv[ed] under an absolute power of the whites nearly indistinguishable from the forced labour of a half century earlier". As in Brazil and Guiana, land concentration helped perpetuate the problem. "Black land ownership in the county was inconsequential", Blackmon writes. "Where it existed on paper, the appearance of independence was a chimera behind which local whites continued to violently control when and where blacks lived and worked, and how their harvests were sold."[61]

---

59. De Jong, *Different Day*, pp. 100–104.
60. Douglas A. Blackmon, *Slavery by Another Name: The Re-Enslavement of Black Americans from the Civil War to World War II* (New York, 2009), p. 271.
61. *Ibid.*

He also touches on the difficult subject of sexual exploitation of women, and emphasizes the "environment of overt physical danger that existed in Lowndes County".[62] As we have mentioned, violence rarely breaches the surface of our court files, yet its pervasiveness was well known. The same can be said for the obstacles that landlords both in Alabama and Pernambuco erected against any educational effort.[63] Although a national law had, since 1973, obliged employers of fifty or more wage-earning workers to open a school,[64] few employers complied, even after redemocratization in the mid-1980s.

Despite the sweeping and largely progressive nature of the Brazilian labour law introduced during the corporatist Vargas years and after (CLT 1943; ETR 1963), workers' and unions' attempts to secure its fruits have met with only limited success, especially in those regions of the country that were based on a near-monopoly of land and cheap agrarian labour. To explain this gap, John D. French argues that Brazilian legal culture generally is marked by fluidity and regional differences. Other aspects of social organization – the ongoing power of patronage networks, the social weight of prestige, etc. – militate against full compliance with labour law.[65] Along these lines, Antônio Montenegro pointed out in a study about a Pernambucan plantation that the class origin and educational background at the Recife Law School of the rural judges formed a convergence of values and criteria.[66]

James Scott's work offers a useful reminder of the relationship of bureaucrats to the populations they supposedly serve. Speaking of "the growing armory of the utilitarian state",[67] he stresses that "officials of the modern state are, of necessity, at least one step – and often several steps – removed from the society they are charged with governing. They assess the life of their society by a series of typifications that are always some distance from the full reality these abstractions are meant to capture".[68] We can understand the rural judges taking a detached, bureaucratic perspective along these lines as they discriminated between rural and non-rural cases.[69]

---

62. *Ibid.*, p. 173.
63. Christine R. Dabat, "Os Primórdios da Cooperativa Agrícola de Tiriri", *Clio. Revista de Pesquisa Histórica*, 16 (1996), 41–63.
64. Article 16 of law no. 5.889 of 8 June 1973 (Regulamentado pelo Decreto n° 73.626/74. Estatui normas reguladoras do trabalho rural). Published in *Diário Oficial da União*, 11 June 1973, available at: http://www.guiatrabalhista.com.br/legislacao/l5889.htm; last accessed 14 December 2017.
65. John D. French, *Drowning in Laws: Labor Law and Brazilian Political Culture* (Chapel Hill, NC, 2004), pp. 97–120, 151–154.
66. Antônio Torres Montenegro, "Trabalhadores rurais e Justiça do Trabalho em tempos de regime civil-militar", in Ângela de Castro Gomes and Fernando Teixeira da Silva (eds), *A Justiça do Trabalho e sua história. Os direitos dos trabalhadores no Brasil* (Campinas 2013), pp. 303–348.
67. James C. Scott, *Seeing Like a State: How Certain Schemes to Improve the Human Condition Have Failed* (New Haven, CT, [etc.] 1998), p. 51.
68. *Ibid.*, p. 76.
69. Some could be individually persecuted for political reasons, however, as Marcília Gama showed: "História, Política, DOPS-PE e os Processos Trabalhistas. Uma Contribuição à Memória

Alejandro Gomez and Michel-Rolph Trouillot's studies of the impact of the Haitian Revolution and other rebellions on nineteenth-century slave societies also demonstrate the degree to which fear informs the state in such unequal societies. In their case, a dominant class – planters – played a significant role within the ideology of the state apparatus regarding rural workers, contributing to "structure an imaginary based on [a] lesson from the past", about the looming danger of popular revolution.[70]

Gomez's observation points us toward our final interpretative theme. In describing how planters collude with the state in drawing forward this "lesson from the past", he gestures toward the ways that modernity and archaism can blur into one another. This phenomenon, in turn, helps reinforce our previous exploration of the indistinct boundary between free and unfree labour and the importance of the state. Pernambuco's labour courts exercised their function according to a specific kind of what Scott calls "high modernist ideology".[71] At the same time, they were vulnerable to the influences of personal class origins and a predominant cultural heritage that systematically took the extremely unequal distribution of assets, income, and power for granted while underrating whatever is rural, even in a region that derives its wealth from this sector, as in India, the southern US and colonial France, evoked above. Although governed by modern states by any measure, these places subjected rural workers of various origins to subaltern legal status, preventing them from enjoying the exact same treatment as urban-industrial proletarians. Rural court cases reveal a trend also visible with surprising consistency across various chronologies in other capitalist countries with comparable state ideologies and the realities they produce. Sidney W. Mintz discusses the condition of Chinese, Javanese, and Indian contract workers transported to the Caribbean. Their situations and conditions are similar to those Miranda Spieler describes, as well as what Paulo Terra has shown about distinctions between workers as blind spots for questions of ethnicity or juridical status.[72] It could be understood in parallel with Ravi Raman's study of tea plantations in India (another Eurocentric production process, like cane in Brazil), where a system, sometimes called "patriarchal", disciplined *dalits* in a social hierarchy rooted in a racialized division of labour.[73]

e a Historiografia", paper presented at *VI Simpósio Trabalho Historiografia e Fontes Documentais*, Universidade Federal de Pernambuco, 1–2 September 2016, Pernambuco.

70. Alejandro E. Gómez, *Le spectre de la Révolution Noire. L'impact de la Révolution Haïtienne dans le monde atlantique, 1790–1886* (Rennes, 2013), p. 265. For a similar observation in Trouillot's book see: Trouillot *Silencing the Past: Power and the Production of History* (Boston, MA, 1997), p. 69.

71. Scott, *Seeing Like a State*, pp. 4–5.

72. Paulo Cruz Terra, "Hierarquização e segmentação: carregadores, cocheiros e carroceiros no Rio de Janeiro nos fins do século XIX", in Marcela Goldmacher, Marcelo Badaró Mattos, and Paulo Cruz Terra (eds), *Faces do Trabalho. Escravizados e livres* (Niterói, 2010), pp. 59–83.

73. K. Ravi Raman, *Global Capital and Peripheral Labour: The History and Political Economy of Plantation Workers in India* (London, 2010), pp. 66–67.

Mintz affirms that such situations present a challenge to moral logic. He argues that the extreme exploitation and mixture of peoples represent, as in Pernambuco's cane fields, "precocious modernity", even if it went unnoticed at the time and later. Observers could ignore it, because it was

> happening to people most of whom were forcibly stolen from the worlds outside the West. No one imagined that such people would become 'modern' – since there was no such thing; no one recognized that the raw, outpost societies into which such people were thrust might become the first of their kind.[74]

In a sense, following Mintz, Achille Mbembe provocatively suggests the *"Becoming Black of the world [le devenir-nègre du monde]"*.[75] African slaves and others who endured similar conditions were just the first ranks of a world proletariat. From such a perspective, legal protections and workers' rights, though long seen as signs of social evolutionary progress, ineluctable and universal in range, as societies reach development and democracy are, arguably, little short of a parenthesis. Mbembe suggests that "the system[ic] risks experienced specifically by Black slaves during early capitalism have now become the norm for, or at least the lot of, all of subaltern humanity".[76] As Mintz suggested, modernity first appeared on the sugar plantations of the Americas and is now global. Mbembe bears out the argument that the globalization of capitalist modernity has placed "subaltern humanity" at the mercy of the same risks African slaves faced.

Our files show a continuity of this logic of radical exploitation and the attempt by the modern Brazilian state, on its way to "development" and "democracy", to create a legal façade for such a logic. But, for rural workers, this veneer always remained quite thin. Employers often responded with immediate non-compliance vis-à-vis requirements, such as the registration of wage earners and resorted to even further marginalizing the rural workers through casualization and eviction from garden plots, reducing them to the status evoked by Mbembe.

Thus, while the Brazilian state displayed a strong thrust towards modernizing society – which, among other things, allowed for the installation of an "inclusive" institution such as the rural labour courts – the mindset of local public officials, conforming to a specific class perspective and complicated by various prejudices, remained faithful to the social realities of their regions. In that, they reproduced deeply rooted ideas about the distinction between rural and urban, agricultural and industrial, archaic

---

74. Sidney W. Mintz, "Enduring Substances, Trying Theories: The Caribbean Region as Oikoumenê", *The Journal of the Royal Anthropological Institute*, 2:2 (1996), pp. 289–311, 298.

75. Achille Mbembe, *Critique of Black Reason* (Durham, NC, 2017), p. 6; *Critique de la raison nègre* (Paris, 2017), p. 9. Emphasis and capitalization in original. We have inserted the French for better intelligibility for those who can read it.

76. *Ibid.*, p. 4. We have rendered "systematic" as "systemic" because it is "systémique" in the French. Mbembe, *Critique of Black Reason*, p. 14.

and modern. This resulted in a state ideology in which the city and industry seem privileged sites of civilization, and in which urban activities are presented as inherently superior to rural. The JCJs of Pernambuco demonstrate the ambivalent simultaneity of the "archaic" and the "modern" and in their findings their judges served more to conceal than to attest to the fundamental facts of the lives of rural cane workers in Pernambuco and so many other workers in most world regions: a permanent exposure to, as Mbembe calls it, "systemic risks" and the pervasive experience of physical violence.

IRSH 62 (2017), Special Issue, pp. 245–269 doi:10.1017/S0020859017000578
© 2018 Internationaal Instituut voor Sociale Geschiedenis

Looking at the Southern Cone: American Trade Unionism in the Cold War Military Dictatorships of Brazil and Argentina

LARISSA ROSA CORRÊA

Departamento de História
Pontifícia Universidade Católica of Rio de Janeiro
R. Marquês de São Vicente, 225 – Gávea
Rio de Janeiro – RJ, 22430-060, Brazil

E-mail: larissa_correa@puc-rio.br

ABSTRACT: This article analyzes the AFL-CIO's anticommunist international policy in the period just before and after the overthrow of democratic regimes in Brazil (1964) and Argentina (1966–1976). It focuses on the activities of the American Institute for Free Labor Development (AIFLD), a labor organization closely associated with US foreign policy interests. By highlighting similarities, differences, and direct connections between US labor activities in these two South American countries, I argue that Brazil's 1964 coup and subsequent dictatorship were key experiences for US trade unionists as they formulated an AFL-CIO labor policy for Argentina and the rest of the Southern Cone.

In May 2016, Brazil was approaching the climax of its worst political crisis in half a century. The month before, the lower house of Congress had voted to impeach center-left President Dilma Rousseff on trumped-up charges, and by May a judicial-parliamentary coup was in full swing.[1] Like many other foreign leftist organizations, the AFL-CIO came out strongly against the impeachment. In an online statement, the union drew comparisons to Brazil's 1964 coup, identifying it as a civilian-military movement headed by conservative elites to overthrow President João Goulart. The result of this intervention, they stated, was the death, disappearance, or torture of hundreds of the regime's opponents. Now, more than fifty years later, these same elites had engineered a movement to remove another

---

1. Those who consider Rousseff's impeachment a coup still do not agree on the proper terminology. Some have called it a judicial-media coup, because it enjoyed the support of the country's major media outlets. For Rousseff's opponents, her impeachment was both legal and democratic.

president, Brazil's first female head of state.[2] Yet, amidst all the parallels the AFL-CIO drew with 1964, they remained conspicuously silent about their own reaction to the coup that had overthrown Goulart. For in 1964, the union had sided with the very elites whom they now condemned, which marked the beginning of over a decade of support for military coups and right-wing dictatorships across Latin America.

Throughout the 1960s and 1970s, the AFL-CIO invested in union education programs and social development with the aim of promoting "free unionism" in Latin America. In the Southern Cone, the main targets for American trade unionism were Argentina, Brazil, and Chile, seen as strategic countries to contain the advance of communism.[3] In each country, they intensified their activities immediately preceding and following the military coups: Brazil in 1964, Argentina in 1966 and 1976, and Chile in 1973. This article compares the approaches of American unionism in Brazil and Argentina. It is part of a larger, ongoing project that compares the activities of American trade unionism in all three countries.[4] More broadly still, it also has implications for the way scholars understand the role of the United States in other Latin American countries. The first part of the article offers a general overview of the principles, goals, and characteristics of the American Institute for Free Labor Development (AIFLD), the AFL-CIO's main representative in Latin America. It will then analyze in more detail the AIFLD's role in Brazil in order to offer some comparisons with the Argentine case.

My previous research on the AFL-CIO in Brazil in the 1960s and 1970s uncovered a series of diplomatic agreements and disagreements concerning the conflicts and alliances forged and thwarted between unionists and Brazilian and American political authorities.[5] Using reports produced by the AFL-CIO, Brazilian and international union publications, analyses written by diplomats at the American embassy, interviews, police records, and newspapers, I traced Brazilian–American labor relations until 1979, when Brazil's military dictatorship entered a phase of gradual democratic opening called *abertura*. This previous research serves as a point of departure from which to draw comparisons with Argentina, thereby offering a deeper

---

2. Brian Finnegan, "AFL-CIO Stands with Brazilian Workers and Democracy", 24 May 2016, http://www.aflcio.org/Blog/Global-Action/AFL-CIO-Stands-with-Brazilian-Workers-and-Democracy; last accessed 15 October 2017.

3. For reasons of convenience, "American" is used here as a short-hand for "US-American", although it is clear that "America" is a large continent made up of thirty-five nation states (and a number of dependent territories). Similarly, "Southern Cone" is used in this article including the whole of Brazil although most definitions only see some of the southern Brazilian states as part of this macro-region.

4. The project, financed by Pontifícia Universidade Católica of Rio de Janeiro, is titled "Relações sindicais Estados Unidos e América Latina. A atuação do sindicalismo norte-americano nas ditaduras militares do Brasil, Argentina e Chile".

5. See Larissa Rosa Corrêa, *Disseram que voltei americanizado. Relações sindicais Brasil e Estados Unidos na ditadura militar* (Campinas, 2017).

understanding of both the similarities and differences between these national contexts, and the general orientations of AFL-CIO policy in the region.

In order to create a concrete basis for comparison, I focus here on three questions: First, which Brazilian and Argentinian unions were involved in the AFL-CIO's international education program and what was the character of these unions? Second, what sorts of social projects did the American union finance and how many students were involved in the union's educational programs, and what were the contents of their training courses like? Third, what sorts of other activities did the AIFLD spearhead? Answering these three questions enables us to understand the reach and possible impacts of programs intended to establish "free" trade unionism in Argentina and Brazil.

As this article will show, the Americans' experiences after Brazil's 1964 coup to a great extent influenced the AFL-CIO's "free and democratic" activities in Argentina in 1966 and 1976, as well as in Chile in 1973. By the time the AIFLD expanded its operations in Argentina with an office in Córdoba in 1968, American union leadership not only knew about the Brazilian generals' political and economic project and the repression they had unleashed against activists and workers; they also had developed a specific stance towards regimes of this kind: tacitly accepting them in their anti-communist thrust, the American representatives hoped to influence the officers and civilians that ran the regimes in terms of what they saw as an appropriate labor policy.[6]

It is not possible to understand the policies of American unions toward Latin America without considering the specific national political contexts, permeated, on the one hand, by the ideological struggle between the countries of the, as it was called then, First and Second Worlds during the Cold War, and, on the other, by the different types of political-economic projects carried out by the dictatorial regimes. As Victoria Basualdo observes, "interpretations of the Cold War that focus solely on the two sides of the ideological dispute are neither sufficient nor useful for understanding the Latin American dynamic." To conduct a transnational and comparative analysis about the impact of the Cold War on Latin America, it is essential to be aware of the interests and internal logics of the countries that were targeted by international bilateral politics, not simply the positions they took in the central conflict.[7]

Moreover, as Barbara Weinstein points out, "much of the literature about the relations between the US and Latin America has been written from the

---

6. The Brazilian military started immediately after the coup to imprison and torture those it considered "enemies of the country". These violations were denounced early on by the journalist and future federal deputy Márcio Moreira Alves in *Tortura e torturados* (Rio de Janeiro, 1966). Meanwhile, the Brazilian press, still free of military censorship, condemned the abuses committed by the regime's political police already shortly after the coup. The first references to torture appeared in *Correio da Manhã*, 7 April 1964.

7. Victoria Basualdo, "El movimiento sindical argentino y sus relaciones internacionales. Una contribución sobre la presencia de la CIOSL y la ORIT en la Argentina desde fines de los '40 hasta comienzos de los' 80", *Revista Mundos do Trabalho*, 5:10 (2013), pp. 199–219, 200.

top down, that is, from the perspective of the US, with Latin Americans generally portrayed as passive or unlucky victims of US policy."[8] Similarly, Hal Brands argues, "[m]ost scholarship by US diplomatic historians focuses on the view from Washington, as is the case with even the best accounts of US–Latin American affairs." In contrast, Brands has pointed to the diversity of meanings that the ideological discourses produced by the global powers during the Cold War had in Latin American countries.[9] Recent scholarship has gone beyond the conventional field of diplomatic studies of the Cold War, as researchers have begun to offer a broader and less Manichean perspective on US-Latin American relations. Their multidimensional, transnational perspectives have decentered the US and incorporated a variety of national and regional actors, including governments, political parties, and an assortment of left- and right-wing movements. In so doing, they have uncovered a series of overlapping conflicts in a tangled web of interests both political and economic, regional and national, all competing with the interests of the global superpowers.[10]

To analyze relations between the US, Brazil, and Argentina during the Cold War, it is also necessary to take into account the national-developmentalist projects of industrial modernization orchestrated by Brazil and Argentina's mid-century populist leaders, Getúlio Vargas (1930–1945) and Juan Perón (1946–1955). The search for a "third way" that could escape the stark options offered by the capitalist–communist binary through emphasizing national interests might be key for a better understanding of the dynamics of Cold War conflicts between the US and Latin America. Whenever political, economic, and social tensions ran high, nationalism and anti-Americanism served as a point of convergence for union leaders, workers, political authorities, and even domestic business leaders.

To a great extent, this "third way" was, amongst other references, the result of the dissemination of the ideals of Catholic social doctrine, by this time well established in the Latin American labor movement, which caused many union leaders and rank and file workers to reject or at least mistrust the "free" unionism so touted by the Americans. In that regard, both catholic labor organizations and those of the non-religious left shared common ground. American authorities and union leaders certainly knew

8. Barbara Weinstein, "Foreword", in Carla Simone Rodeghero, *Capítulos da Guerra Fria. O anticomunismo brasileiro sob o olhar norte- americano* (Porto Alegre, 2007), [unpaginated]. A recent example for such US-centered perspectives is Kim Scipes, *AFL-CIO's Secret War against Developing Country Workers: Solidarity or Sabotage?* (Lanham, MD, 2010).

9. Hal Brands, *Latin America's Cold War* (Cambridge, MA, 2010), p. 2.

10. The body of literature using such extended perspectives on the Cold War in Latin America is growing rapidly. See, for example, Tom Long, *Latin America Confronts the United States: Asymmetry and Influence* (Cambridge, 2015); Tanya Harmer, *Allende's Chile and the Inter-American Cold War* (Chapel Hill, NC, 2011); Jeffrey Taffet, *Foreign Aid as Foreign Policy: The Alliance of Progress in Latin America* (New York, 2007).

that nationalism and anti-Americanism created serious obstacles for them in the Southern Cone. It was not by happenstance that American authorities went out of their way to clarify for Latin Americans that John F. Kennedy's Alliance for Progress did not constitute US intervention, but rather inter-American cooperation. Typically for its time, a Brazilian worker stated categorically in an interview for a major national newspaper, "Neither Prague, nor Geneva", pointing to the seat of the "Eastern" World Federation of Trade Unions (WFTU) in Prague, yet mistakenly associating "free unionism" with "Geneva" (the seat of the UN-affiliated International Labour Organization), while the "Western" International Confederation of Free Trade Unions (1919–2006) had its headquarters in Brussels. In any case, the worker added wittily, "Couldn't it be Prague, Geneva, or Brasília?"[11]

FOUNDING AND EARLY YEARS OF THE AIFLD

In 1961, after the fiasco of the Bay of Pigs invasion, President John F. Kennedy became convinced of the importance of trade unions as a key factor in economic and social development, as well as a constraint on the influence of communism and nationalism in Latin America. Thus, the Kennedy administration decided to invest in a regional labor education program under the supervision of the AFL-CIO. The same year, still in the shadow of the 1959 Cuban Revolution, Kennedy launched the Alliance for Progress in Latin America. It aimed to improve economic, social, and political conditions in the region over a ten-year period with a heavy infusion of US aid.[12]

For the US government, the situation in Brazil in the early 1960s was dangerous and worrying. A political atmosphere of dissatisfaction, they argued, made Latin America in general an "easy target" for communism. Due in no small measure to their mistreatment at the hands of the region's elites, Latin America's working class was a potential revolutionary force. To stave off this frightening possibility, the American government felt an urgent need to export the US model of capitalist democracy, seen as the antidote to both the oligarchic and often state-directed capitalism of Latin

---

11. After participating in an event organized by the National Confederation of Communication and Advertising Workers (Confederação Nacional dos Trabalhadores de Comunicação e Publicidade) the interviewed union activists José Mauro Ribeiro Lobo asserted that the relation between his union and the International Federation of Petroleum and Chemical Workers caused distrust to him, adding that a genuinely Brazilian labour movement needed to be built, in which "the workers are freed from the illussion of either the right or the left". Interview extracts are cited from a parliamentary commission report about "foreign entities" in Brazil: Câmara dos Deputados, "Relatório Final da Comissão Parlamentar de Inquérito sobre as entidades estrangeiras no Brasil", *Diário do Congresso Nacional*, seção I, 28 de agosto de 1970, 102.
12. The Alliance for Progress provided technical and financial aid targeted at primary education, agrarian reform, healthcare, housing, currency stabilization, and various cooperative programs. For a general assessment see the contributions to: John E. Dreier (ed.), *The Alliance for Progress: Problems and Perspectives* (New York, 1987).

America's elites and the totalitarian socialism of global communism. They thus sought to shape a new Latin American working class that would buy into the US model of labor relations and workplace regulation. This so-called free and democratic trade unionism was also expected to lead to a better relationship between native workers and foreign employers, since Latin America was being targeted by US corporations eager to expand their business.[13]

In this political context, the Alliance for Progress boosted the AFL-CIO's labor education program for Latin America.[14] US policymakers also saw Brazil as a key regional power that should play a vital role in achieving the Alliance's goals.[15] Until the early 1960s, the AFL (with the support of the CIO) already had promoted sporadic visits of Brazilian trade unionists to the United States and vice versa. Furthermore, some exchange activities were undertaken in cooperation with the International Confederation of Free Trade Unions (ICFTU) and the Interamerican Regional Organization of Workers (ORIT).[16] The new policy, however, led to a dramatic expansion of the reach of American trade unionism in the region. In 1962, the AFL-CIO founded the American Institute for Free Labor Development (AIFLD) pooling substantial financial means from different sources.[17] Seeking to establish ties with Latin American trade unionists, the AIFLD soon started to finance exchange programs and regular visits to the United States, amongst other activities.[18] In the words of the AFL-CIO president George Meany, "[t]he AFL-CIO maintains the AIFLD to bring the example of the US trade union movement to workers in Latin America and the Caribbean."[19] In practice, these actions counted on

13. This position, including the noteworthy critique of the Latin American elites, was staked out for instance, in Robert H. Dockery, *Survey of the Alliance for Progress: Labor Policies and Programs [A Study Prepared at the Request of the Subcommittee on American Republics Affairs and Committee on Foreign Relations of the United States Senate]*, (Washington, DC, 1968), p. 6, available at http://http://pdf.usaid.gov/pdf_docs/pcaaa242.pdf; last accessed 30 November 2017.

14. Hobart A. Spalding Jr., "US and Latin American Labor: The Dynamics of Imperialist Control", *Latin American Perspectives*, 3:1 (1976), pp. 45–69, 52.

15. There is an extensive literature published during the 1960s and 1970s on social issues in Latin America. For a typical example see: John Gerassi, *The Great Fear in Latin America* (New York, 1963).

16. For an overview of the ORIT and the first contacts between the US labor confederations and Latin American trade unionists, see Robert J. Alexander, "Labor and Inter-American Relations", *Annals of the American Academy of Political and Social Science*, 334 (1961), pp. 41–53.

17. Similar institutions were also founded for other world regions: The African-American Labor Center was created in 1964, followed by the Asian-American Free Labor Institute four years later. The latter focused on the Vietnamese labor movement. Beth Sims, *Workers of the World Undermined: American Labor's Role in US Foreign Policy* (Boston, MA, 1992), p. 3.

18. Substantial documentation originating from AIFLD is available to researchers as part of the George Meany Memorial AFL-CIO Archive at the University of Maryland. For more details about the accessible source see: https://drive.google.com/file/d/oB27oiiodc9t9UE9zSXJXO W5EY1k/view; last accessed 15 October 2017.

19. American Institute for Free Labor Development [hereafter, AIFLD], *1962–1972: A Decade of Worker to Worker Cooperation* (Washington, DC, 1972), p. 21.

the support of the most anti-communist and conservative sectors in the Latin-American trade union movement. The AIFLD over the years also established offices in Argentina, Chile, Uruguay, and Bolivia, along with other Latin American and Caribbean countries.

The AIFLD was sustained with means from different funders (which also changed according to its activities), including, American corporations, the AFL-CIO, and different US government agencies and initiatives, such as USAID, the Alliance for Progress, etc.[20] The institute was a private, non-profit organization, led by Serafino Romualdi, an ardent anti-communist with a long relationship with conservative Brazilian trade unionists.[21] During the 1940s and 1950s, Romualdi had served as an official Latin American representative, first of the AFL, then of the AFL-CIO, tasked with forming alliances with local unionists and the authorities. He had been particularly active in Brazil and Argentina, where he had opposed the governments of Vargas, Perón, and later, João Goulart. His track record in both countries was highly controversial. Banned from entering Argentina by order of Perón, Romualdi had been constantly accused of attempting to interfere in the Argentine labor movement.[22]

Latin American trade unionists were invited to take part in an intensive three-month labor course at the Front Royal Institute in Virginia. The site could accommodate up to forty guests at a time. The Institute functioned like a boarding school, with the students spending all their time there, all expenses paid by the AIFLD. They were trained in leadership techniques, labor education, finance, history of the international labor movement, economics, statistics, English, and, most importantly, collective bargaining techniques. Later, these courses were moved to Loyola University in New Orleans and Georgetown University in Washington.[23] All told, the Alliance for Progress oversaw the allocation of $24 million to AIFLD and another institution, International Technical Assistance Corps of the Department of Labor (DOLITAC),[24] to invest in the Latin American labor movement.[25]

20. Hundreds of US companies sponsored AIFLD activities in Latin America. This also manifested itself in AIFLD's governing bodies: In 1965, for instance, Charles M. Brinckerhoff (Anaconda Corporation), William Hinckley (United Corporation), Robert Hill (Merck and Company), Juan T. Trippe (Pan American World Airways), Henry Woodbridge (Tru-Temper Copper Corporation), and J. Peter Grace (W.R. Grace Corporation) were all members of the AIFLD Executive Board.

21. See his autobiographical account: Serafino Romualdi, *Presidents and Peons: Recollections of a Labor Ambassador in Latin America* (New York, 1967).

22. *Ibid.*, p. 58.

23. AIFLD, *1962–1972: A Decade of Worker to Worker Cooperation*, p. 23.

24. In 1964, the Department of Labor initiated the International Technical Assistance Corps (DOLITAC), which was made up of US experts who served abroad helping foreign countries solve labor problems in a more technocratic vein, i.e. in terms of traning, intermediation, addressing labor market deficiencies, etc.

25. Dockery, *Survey of the Alliance for Progress*, p. 10.

Soon after its foundation, the AIFLD began to work more closely with the Inter-American Regional Organization of Workers (ORIT). Founded in Mexico in 1951 as the regional federation of Latin American ICFTU members, the ORIT also collaborated with the Alliance for Progress. In the 1960s, ORIT, headed by Arturo Jáuregui, a trade unionist with ties to the CIA and member of the AIFLD executive board, was tasked with enacting the AIFLD's agenda in each of the targeted Latin American countries.[26] In Argentina, organizations belonging to the ORIT included the Confederation of Municipal Workers of the Argentine Republic, the General Confederation of Commercial Employees, and the National Bank Workers' Association, while in Brazil, ORIT affiliates included the National Industrial Workers' Confederation, the National Commercial Workers' Confederation, and the National Ground Transports Workers' Confederation.[27] In this collaboration, ORIT and AIFLD specialized in organizing regional seminars intended to strengthen local unions. The courses generally addressed issues related to the world of trade unionism, such as trade union organizational structures, labor legislation, collective bargaining, trade union administration and finance, the union press, as well as many others. In addition to the AIFLD, other international union organizations such as the industry branch federations of the International Trade Secretariats (ITS), also dedicated themselves to sowing the seeds of "free and democratic unionism" across Latin America.[28]

By the late 1970s, the AIFLD was offering labor education classes to approximately 23,000 workers across Latin America and the Caribbean annually and maintained offices in 18 countries. By June 1978, a total of 338,000 Latin American unionists had participated in the organization's _in situ_ courses, where they learned about fundamental principles of trade unionism and organizational techniques, along with more complex issues

26. On the links between the CIA and ORIT, see Peter Gribbins, "Brazil and CIA", _CounterSpy_ (April–May, 1979), pp. 4–23.
27. ORIT/ICFTU, "Report to the Sixth Continental Congress of ORIT", Mexico City, 2–6 February 1965, 17. The original names of these organizations are, for Argentina: Confederación de Trabajadores Municipales de la República Argentina, Confederación General de Empleados de Comercio e Asociación Bancaria; and for Brazil: Confederação Nacional dos Trabalhadores da Indústria, Confederação Nacional dos Trabalhadores do Comércio, and Confederação Nacional dos Trabalhadores em Transportes Terrestres.
28. Among the ITS members who were particularly active in Latin America were the International Transport Workers' Federation; International Miners' Federation; International Agricultural Workers' Federation; International Hotel and Restaurant Workers' Union; International Postal, Telephone, and Telegraph Workers' Organization; International Technical and Bureaucratic Workers' Federation; International Federation of Petroleum Workers' Unions; and International Federation of General Factory Workers' Unions. See: Robert J. Alexander and Eldon M. Parker, _International Labor Organizations and Organized Labor in Latin America and Caribbean: A History_ (Santa Barbara, CA, 2009), p. 254.

like trade union participation in economic development decision-making and interregional integration. The AIFLD also selected union leaders for intensive six-week programs at the George Meany Center in Silver Spring, Maryland.

Significantly, the AFL-CIO's education policy in the 1960s and 1970s ignored one important group of workers: women. Only in the mid-1970s did they begin to be chosen for scholarships and specialized courses. In the wake of International Women's Year and the UN's World Conference on Women in 1975,[29] the February 1976 edition of AIFLD's own journal, *The AIFLD Report*, highlighted a meeting for female union leaders, held in Asunción, Paraguay, part of the First International Women's Labor Leaders Congress.[30] By 1977, sixty-nine women's groups from Latin America and the Caribbean enjoyed the full support of the AIFLD.[31]

The major part of the financial resources channeled through AIFLD, however, were not spent on education but social projects. For instance, nearly ninety per cent were dedicated to the construction of low-cost housing for workers. USAID, the second major funder of AIFLD, also allocated substantial means to this end. The Department of Social Projects, which was responsible for construction, had a partnership with Louis Berger and Associates, of Orange, New Jersey. In the late 1960s, accusations of corruption in Mexico led Berger to be investigated by Brazilian police.[32] Still, construction continued, and by the end of 1978, the AIFLD estimated that it had completed 18,048 homes in thirteen countries, at a total cost of $77,313,060. Funds coming from USAID were, in some cases, funneled through the Regional Revolving Loan Fund (RRLF), which had been created in 1968 to manage funding for international social projects. According to the AIFLD, since the RRLF's creation in 1962, the organization had obtained $1,425,544 from it to invest in

29. On International Women's Year, see Jocelyn Olcott, *International Women's Year: The Greatest Consciousness-Raising Event in History* (New York, 2017).
30. "Important International Women's Meeting", *The AIFLD Report*, 14:2 (April–May 1976), p. 2. *The AIFLD Report* was launched in 1963 and constitutes one of the major sources available documenting the organizations' the full scope of activities.
31. See the following self-representation booklet published in 1980: AIFLD, *American Institute for Free Labor Development: A Union to Union Program for the Americas* (Washington, DC, 1980), pp. 21–25.
32. According to a report by Brazil's notorious Department of Political and Social Order (Departamento Estadual de Ordem Política e Social), the police department in charge of the surveillance of all kinds of political and social movements, Berger was responsible for promoting projects of AIFLD interest in Latin America. His business had been expelled from Mexico, the report claimed, accused of corrupt dealings surrounding the construction of 3,100 residences in Mexico City. "Relatório sobre o Iadesil", 4 August 1972, Arquivo Público do Estado de São Paulo (APESP), Departamento Estadual de Ordem Política e Social (DEOPS), Dossiê, 52-z-0, doc. 5861.

social projects in Latin America and the Caribbean.[33] The AIFLD oversaw the construction of the following number of houses, divided by country:

Table 1. *Number of houses built in low-cost housing projects financed through AIFLD, per country, 1962–1978.*

Country	Houses
Argentina	6,227
Barbados	3
Brazil	488
Colombia	2,106
Costa Rica	128
Dominican Republic	110
Ecuador	14
Guyana	362
Honduras	1,185
Mexico	3,104
Peru	2,979
Uruguay	425
Venezuela	920

It is noteworthy that AIFLD investments in housing in Brazil were comparatively insignificant, only providing financing for 488 houses between 1962 and 1978. If funding for housing alone is considered, Argentina was the largest recipient. Nevertheless, upon considering other investments like community centers, union headquarters, hospitals, and co-ops, Brazil received more AIFLD funding than any other country. In this total account of all funding, Argentina still came in second place, with means awarded for social assistance for workers, credit cooperatives, printing equipment, technical schools, and mutual aid funds. Other countries that "benefited" included Mexico, Peru, Colombia, Honduras, and Venezuela.[34]

US LABOR EDUCATION IN BRAZIL: AIFLD'S ACTIVITIES IN DETAIL

The AFL's foreign outreach to Brazil began after World War II. Between 1945 and 1952, AFL trade unionists and government officials established contacts with local trade unionists, a challenging task as the aim was to look for a sector that was both non-communist and not too deeply affiliated with the corporatist tradition established during the Vargas era (1930–1945),

33. AIFLD, *A Union to Union Program for the Americas*, p. 25.
34. *Ibid.*, p. 34.

or at least not too committed to its ideological tenets of populism and nationalism. In the 1950s and early 1960s, the AFL strengthened their collaborations with local trade unionists, hoping to train new leaders willing to implement so-called free and democratic trade unionism.[35] To that end, the AIFLD financed exchange programs and regular visits to the United States. Their efforts enjoyed the support of the most anti-communist and conservative sectors of the Brazilian trade union movement, including the so-called *pelegos*, union leaders infamous for their willingness to ally themselves with whoever had power and money.[36] Starting in 1962, the US government and AFL-CIO leaders openly supported the opponents of the pro-labor and nationalist President João Goulart (1961–1964). From 1962 to 1964, the US formed alliances with conservative civilian and military forces, which were in the process of orchestrating a plan to overthrow Goulart.[37]

There is even some evidence indicating that the AIFLD trained a select group of right-wing Brazilian union leaders who participated in an ancillary role in the conspiracy that led to the civilian-military coup that overthrew Goulart on 1 April 1964: In the months before, the AIFLD was training thirty-three trade unionists in the US who returned to Brazil in early 1964 tasked with teaching "democratic" trade unionism in rural areas. Other groups of unionists, as Peter Gribbin has discovered, went to urban centers like Rio de Janeiro, São Paulo, and the port city of Santos.[38] And several months after the coup, an interview given by William Doherty, representative of AFL-CIO International Affairs, publicized the involvement of US labor organizations in the coup.[39] Doherty, however, may have overestimated the role of the US trade unionists in Goulart's ousting. Aside from the case of Rômulo Marinho, member of the Telegraph and Telephone Workers' Union of Guanabara, the activities of US-trained union leaders during those months so far remain shrouded in mystery. After taking classes in the United States, Marinho organized several anti-communist labor

---

35. Clifford Welch, "Labor Internationalism: US Involvement in Brazilian Unions, 1945–1965", *Latin American Research Review*, 30:2 (1995), pp. 62–89.

36. The term *pelego* is closely associated with the corporatist labor system established under Vargas. It refers to those conservative labor leaders who were central to the corporatist arrangement yet who did not buy too much into its ideological claims while acting compliantly under the direction of the federal Ministry of Labor, or who otherwise acted at the behest of politicians or entrepreneurs.

37. For the involvement of the US in the 1964 coup in Brazil see Phyllis Parker, *Brazil and the Quiet Intervention, 1964* (Austin, TX, 1979); Jan K. Black, "Lincoln Gordon and Brazil's Military Counterrevolution", in C.N. Ronning and A.P. Vannucci (eds), *Ambassadors in Foreign Policy: The Influences of Individuals on US-Latin American Policy* (New York, 1987), pp. 95–113.

38. Petter Gribbin, "Brazil and CIA".

39. Michael J. Sussman, *AIFLD, US Trojan Horse in Latin America and the Caribbean* (Washington, DC, 1983), p. 4.

seminars aiming to prepare workers for an impending political crisis.[40] Still, we know very little about the details of this operation. At any rate, "democratic" union leaders joined forces with other conservative sectors, such as military officers, right-wing political parties, students, and associations claiming to represent Catholic housewives, all of them eager to the celebrate the military intervention.

After 1964, the workers' movement was strongly repressed. Immediately after the coup, the new regime launched "Operation Clean-up", which resulted in an "intervention", i.e. a series of state measures against and purges in hundreds of rural and urban unions.[41] Between March and April 1964, in the first weeks after the coup, the Ministry of Labor nominated 235 new union officials (called *interventores*) considered reliable by the regime. The Ministry was also granted the power to annul union elections and to veto the candidacy of any union leader, if it was deemed necessary.[42] About seventy per cent of the unions with 5,000 members or more suffered this kind of state assault, and altogether, 536 organizations faced some form of "intervention" or repression between 1964 and 1970. According to the investigation conducted by the National Truth Commission (Comissão Nacional da Verdade – CNV), which, between 2012 and 2014, investigated human rights violations committed during the military dictatorship, about 10,000 union leaders were purged, although there is still some disagreement regarding this data.[43] The coup of 1964 seemed an important opportunity for US international union organizations to launch educational and welfare initiatives in unions across Brazil. The AIFLD hoped to contribute to the dismantling of the leftwing labor movement by forming a new generation of young unionists trained in the United States to replace the nationalist and Communist leaders. With the military in power, the number of training and union activities financed by AIFLD increased, developing the panoply of activities described above.

Meanwhile, the Brazilian military dictatorship, one of the longest in Latin America during the twentieth century, ending only in 1985, was not a homogenous phenomenon throughout its existence. It changed several times some of its political and economic orientations and always pretended to observe a certain constitutional framework. These changes had important repercussions on the opportunities for unions in general and the conditions under which the American labor bodies acted. In 1968, after months of

---

40. These activities were reported in a *Reader's Digest* article: Eugene Methvin, "Labor's New Weapon for Democracy", *Reader's Digest* (October, 1966), p. 28.

41. It should be added that the state prerogative to "intervene" into unions in all relevant matters was a legacy of the Vargas era.

42. Maria Helena Moreira Alves, *State and Opposition in Military Brazil* (Austin, TX, 1985), p. 70.

43. See CNV's final report: Relatório Final do Grupo de Trabalho Ditadura e Repressão aos Trabalhadores e ao Movimento Sindical da Comissão Nacional da Verdade, 2014, p. 59.

anti-dictatorship mobilization that included large student demonstrations and labor strikes in important industrial cities, the regime's hardliners pushed for the enactment of Institutional Act number no. 5 (Ato Institucional Número Cinco – AI-5), issued on 13 December.[44] During this period, the regime intensified state repression and retreated somewhat from its strategic partnership with the United States (without ever ending it entirely). After General Artur da Costa e Silva became president in 1967, the relationship between Brazil and the United States became increasingly tense: Costa e Silva was seen as being linked to the least democratic sectors of the military high command, the so-called hardliners. While the hardliners were ardently anti-communist, they also had a strong nationalist streak and resented the high degree of economic dependence on the US fostered by the outgoing administration of General Humberto de Alencar Castelo Branco. The new Costa e Silva administration was more interested in obtaining loans to stimulate economic growth. His government, supported intellectually by developmentalist thought, which had considerable influence in Brazil at the time, sought a greater degree of independence from the US. Costa e Silva was not content with the funds offered by the US government through the Alliance for Progress. He and his supporters criticized the fact that most of the US funds were aimed at social assistance, especially to purchase basic necessities for the poor, such as food, medicine, and housing. The clash of interests provoked a gradual political distancing between the two governments, although US economic interests were maintained throughout the period.

The new political and economic project led by General Costa e Silva had a considerable impact on relations between Brazilian and US trade unions: After 1967, many conservative trade unionists, supporters of the military regime, began to question the interference of foreign trade unionists in local matters. They also questioned the effectiveness of the exchange program offered by the AIFLD, as well as the courses offered in the United States. The idea that the Americans were interfering too much in internal union affairs led in October 1967 to the opening of an inquiry in the Chamber of Deputies into the actions of foreign labor organizations in Brazil.[45] In the wake of this investigation, the military government decided to monitor more carefully the AIFLD in Brazil. They expelled several American union leaders and urged the main Brazilian trade confederations to adopt a more anti-American posture. Unease with the strong influence of the US and, more specifically, with its interference in domestic politics, especially its criticisms of the regime, became

---

44. AI-5 suspended constitutional guarantees and increased the dictatorial powers of the president. It also empowered the president to close Congress.

45. For more detailed information on this inquiry, see Larissa Rosa Corrêa, "'Democracy and Freedom' in Brazilian Trade Unionism", in Geert van Goethem and Robert Waters (eds), *American Labor's Global Ambassadors: The International History of the AFL-CIO during the Cold War* (New York, 2013), pp. 177–199.

more widespread. Anti-Americanism became a trait that was no longer limited to leftist groups or the remnants of the corporatist nationalism of the Vargas era but also began to be identified with the authoritarian nationalism of the conservative civilian and military groups.

The Latin America visit of New York governor Nelson Rockefeller in 1969 is representative of the region's anti-American movement: Rockefeller, who maintained good relations with US-trained trade unionists, especially Serafino Romualdi, had been asked to lead a mission to Latin America and, based on what he observed there, make new policy suggestions to its governments. Months before his arrival in Brazil, Rockefeller had granted a \$75 million loan for Alliance for Progress initiatives through USAID. Nevertheless, he was met with a chilly reception and even protests in most countries, and the welcome in Brazil was not the warmest either. The Brazilian government still censored any negative reporting about his visit.[46]

In the early 1970s, as the AIFLD encountered strong resistance in Brazil, it turned its efforts to the development of educational programs designed to promote "free and democratic unionism" in Argentina and Chile.[47] However, the AIFLD maintained dialogue with the Brazilian government and continued channeling resources to the country, despite their awareness of the regime's acts of repression and of the impossibility of implementing the American model in a country whose labor relations were governed by corporatist legislation. Repression by the dictatorship was not only increasingly denounced; such accusations also gained a new weight with the rise of the "human rights" discourse and the corresponding notion of "human rights violations" in the 1970s. In the face of these shifts, AFL-CIO representatives worried that their apathy might earn them criticism in Brazil and abroad. Notwithstanding accusations of torture, the government of Emílio Garrastazu Médici (1969–1974) presided over a period of "economic miracle", when growth exceeded, on average, ten per cent per year.

Brazil's growing economic clout rekindled the old friendship between Brazil and the US, American foreign policymakers believed that Brazil was on the cusp of becoming a regional leader and, in so doing, could project American influence in the region. This created a quandary for

---

46. On the visit itself, see for instance: "Dúvidas sobre a vinda de Rockefeller", *Correio da Manhã*, 3 June 1969, p. 3. On Rockefeller's relations with Brazil more generally, see Elizabeth A. Cobbs, *The Rich Neighbor Policy: Rockefeller and Kaiser in Brazil* (New Haven, CT, 1992).

47. On the activities of American organized labor in Chile and Argentina, see Angela Vergara, "Chilean Workers and the US Labor Movement: From Intervention to Solidarity, 1950s–1970s", in Van Goethem and Waters, *American Labor's Global Ambassadors*, pp. 201–214; Pablo Pozzi, "El sindicalismo norteamericano en América Latina y en la Argentina. El AIFLD entre 1961–1976", *Herramienta*, 10 (July, 1999), available as a non-paginated html-version at: http://www.herramienta.com.ar/revista-herramienta-n-10/el-sindicalismo-norteamericano-en-america-latina-y-en-la-argentina-el-aifld; last accessed 15 October 2017.

American trade union leaders, divided between the growing pressures of public opinion, which was goading them to take a position opposing the military's regimes human rights violations, and US political and economic interests.[48] Thus, while AFL-CIO leaders publicly stated their wish to maintain a balanced view of the torture of political prisoners, they privately recognized, "[w]e cannot ignore the facts contained in these reports [from Brazil], which we have the privilege of reading."[49]

Why did the Alliance for Progress and AIFLD continue to invest so many resources in Brazil, even as its position had become complicated, first because of tensions mounting between the two countries' governments and then because of the increasing public criticism of the regime's repressive politics? To be sure, the country was still attractive to American business interests. But perhaps equally importantly, Brazil was also seen as a strategic site from which to monitor armed leftist groups in Argentina and Chile, above all during the government of Salvador Allende. We do know that the Brazilian dictatorship, despite the previous alienation vis-à-vis the US, allied with the Nixon administration (1969–1974) and provided technical and military support to coups in Bolivia, Uruguay, Chile, and, later, Argentina, even as it helped create a network of transnational repression in the Southern Cone, Operation Condor, which was tasked with exterminating leftist guerrillas.[50] Brazil was a key ally for the US in the region's stabilization, and, despite all odds, American unionism continued to collaborate closely with US foreign policy in the fight against what was considered to be a uniform threat of "communism".

AMERICAN "FREE UNIONISM" IN ARGENTINA

Like in Brazil, the relationship between American trade unionism and the Argentine labor movement began in the immediate post-war years, through contacts made by Serafino Romualdi. In Argentina, however, as Pablo A. Pozzi has pointed out, between 1946 and 1960, the AFL-CIO labeled Peronist union leaders as "fascists".[51] Basualdo's study of the relationship between the ICFTU, ORIT, and Argentine unions similarly paints a picture of frequent conflict, particularly during the rule of Perón, between 1946 and

---

48. On opposition to the Brazilian military dictatorship in the US, see James Green, *We Cannot Remain in Silent: Opposition to the Brazilian Military Dictatorship in the United States* (Durham, NC, 2010).

49. Andrew McLellan, AFL-CIO inter-American representative, to Alan Silberman, labor officer at the US embassy, 20 January 1970, George Meany Memorial AFL-CIO Archive (University of Maryland, College Park, MD), RG 18, series 4, box 16.

50. J. Patrice McSherry, *Predatory States: Operation Condor and Covert War in Latin America* (Lanham, MD, 2005).

51. Pozzi, "El sindicalismo norteamericano en América Latina".

1955.[52] However, Perón's fall in 1955 and the Cuban Revolution 1959 were game changers, and American authorities, instead of treating the Peronist labor movement as a homogenous group, began differentiating between what they considered as "communists" and "anti-imperialist nationalists", i.e. a more militant and left-leaning current within Peronism and a less left-wing one, which the Americans hoped to win for their cause.[53]

After 1961, Romualdi broadened his contacts among Argentine union leaders, establishing a fruitful alliance with specific Peronist sectors, especially Augusto Vandor (1923–1969), who became one of his primary interlocutors until mid-1960s. These relationships were also fundamental for the AIFLD in its efforts to gain a foothold in Argentina after its foundation in 1962. The increasingly cozy relations between the AIFLD and the largest Argentine labor confederation, the General Labor Confederation (Confederación General del Trabajo – CGT) enabled the implementation of a labor education project, which the AIFLD had wanted to launch in Argentina already for some time. As Gabriela Scodeller has shown, labor education was a field of dense competition and site for major conflicts among the various factions of the Argentine labor movement.[54] Union education was seen as a privileged medium for efforts to promote the political-ideological agenda of each current and it was an important step forward for AIFLD to gain access to this field via the CGT.

Throughout the 1960s, the AIFLD developed a complex and controversial relationship with the Argentine anti-communist trade unions through both social programs and a series of courses intended to train "authentic" leaders. The goal was to halt the radicalization unleashed by the local influence of different left-wing currents (erroneously) subsumed under the label of "communism" and Peronism on the workers' movement.[55] In Brazil, things were no different; in both countries, the AIFLD saw shifting alliances and fallings out with local union leaders, but the constant was that the local leaders

---

52. Victoria Basualdo, "El sindicalismo 'libre' y el movimento sindical argentino desde mediados de los años '40 a mediados de los años' 50", *Anuario IEHS*, 28 (2013), pp. 279–294.

53. Pozzi, "El sindicalismo norteamericano en América Latina". It should be added that – despite the Americans major concern with "communism" and "communist infiltration" – by the 1950s, the Argentine Communist Party (PCA) had lost most of its previous allegiance within the local labor movement. "Communism" should thus be taken as an imprecise signifier for a broad spectrum of different left-wing currents.

54. Gabriela Scodeller, "El Instituto de Capacitación y Formación Social Sindical. Una experiencia de formación politico-sindical en un contexto de intensa conflictividad social (Argentina, 1963–1965)", *Revista Mundos do Trabalho*, 5:9 (2013), pp. 239–258.

55. Juan Alberto Bozza, "Cooperación y cooptación. Agencias norteamericanas sobre el sindicalismo peronista en los sesenta", paper presented at the Segundo Congreso de Estudios sobre el Peronismo (1943–1976), 4–6 November 2010, at the Universidad Nacional de Tres de Febrero, Sede Caseros II (Provincia de Buenos Aires). See also Juan Alberto Bozza, "Trabajo silencioso. Agencias anticomunistas en el sindicalismo latinoamericano durante la Guerra Fría", *Conflicto Social*, 2:2 (2009), pp. 49–75.

with whom the American organization dealt were usually of a non-militant, non-bottom-up type whose vision of defending workers' interests was striking deals with employers and whoever had political power.

In the social arena, it is noteworthy how much the organization spent on "Operation AFL-CIO", which planned to build hundreds of homes for Argentine workers with a budget of $17 million. This amount shows just how important Argentina was to the AFL-CIO and, according to Pozzi, it consolidated the AIFLD's position in the country. By 1965, on the eve of the coup that overthrew president Arturo Illia (1963–1966), the AIFLD had two main goals in Argentina: 1) to deepen the divisions between Peronists and the left within the labor movement (which, as many Peronist labor activists increasingly leaned to the left, meant supporting the more right-wing currents within Peronism), through training and promoting "democratic" leadership, and 2) to introduce the American model of "business unionism" through labor education courses and social programs.[56]

Most AIFLD courses were conducted for small groups of workers, like the lumberjacks near the forest of Santiago del Estero, or farm workers in San Juan and villages in the Pampas interested in new agricultural techniques. Intensive "second-level" regional seminars lasted fifteeen days and were held in the late 1960s in cities like Comodoro, Rivadavia, Jujuy, Ingenio, Ledesma, Córdoba, and Mendoza. They were targeted at a vast array of professions: textiles and clothing, hospitals, entertainment, the maritime service, wine making, food service, petroleum, electricity, glass, leather, banking, insurance, government employment, postal and telephone services, transportation, commerce, printing, metal working, and auto making.[57]

In 1968, the AIFLD further expanded its operations in Argentina with an office in Córdoba, one of the country's industrial centers and site of intense mobilization for both the labor and student movements, which would explode the following year into the *Cordobazo*.[58] *The AIFLD Report*, the organization's periodical, in 1969 celebrated the great impact its social and educational programs had had on Argentina. Like in Brazil, these programs were carried out mainly in smaller cities or rural areas, places whose unions had little or no influence in the organized labor movement nationally. For example, the *Report* highlighted a seminar for journalists held in the northwestern city of Tucumán. It was co-sponsored by the local branch of

56. Pozzi, "El sindicalismo norteamericano en América Latina".

57. Charles Wheeler, "AIFLD's Programs in Argentina Underscore Friendship between Hemispheric Unionists", *The AIFLD Report*, 7: 9 (1969), pp. 5–6.

58. The goal of the new office in Córdoba was to support Alejo Simó of the Metal Workers' Union of Córdoda (Unión Obrera Metalúrgica – UOM) in his power struggle with Agustín Tosco, the legendary militant union leader of Córdoba's section of the Electric Energy Workers' Union (Federación Argentina de Trabajadores de Luz y Fuerza – FATLyF) and the CGT. Pozzi, "El sindicalismo norteamericano en América Latina".

the Press Association and Journalists' Federation of Argentina (Federación Argentina de Periodistas – FAP); the main participants were university professors and members of the local press.[59] But these locations, which in the Argentinian context were rather peripheral, and the social composition of these courses indicate how difficult it was for AIFLD to intervene in a country where the labor movement was disputed mainly among the left and left-leaning Peronists. Also in 1968, the AIFLD financed the fifth version of a national labor education course attended by fifty students from thirty local unions around La Plata, Pergamino, and Mercedes.

The AIFLD curriculum officially consisted of sociology, human relations, and public speaking. In practice, it emphasized economics, collective bargaining, job evaluation, productivity, and cooperativism. By the end of the 1960s, the organization had thirteen social projects underway in the regions of Buenos Aires, La Plata, Bahia Blanca, and Santa Fé. In 1969, the AIFLD provided loans of $13.5 and $4 million for private investors to develop a workers' housing initiative, backed by USAID and the National Mortgage Bank of Argentina.[60]

As the 1960s drew to a close, the AIFLD evaluated its track record in Argentina positively: With the country's labor movement largely held down by the right-wing dictator General Juan Carlos Onganía, the AIFLD was free to carry out its program as it saw fit. Charles Wheeler, director of social projects since 1965, had been fairly successful in his task of uniting all the "democratic" unions of the Argentine labor movement, which, in practice, meant leaders who were both anti-communist and anti-Peronist.[61] In spite of the resistance of both groups to "free" unionism, the extent to which AIFLD quickly came to influence labor in the country as a whole, particularly through its alliance with groups tied to Augusto Vandor, should not be underestimated. A significant proportion of union leaders who were able to develop a more stable activity during the last two Argentine military dictatorships (1966–1973 and 1976–1983) were trained in programs in the US. They came from unions like the Postal and Telecommunication Workers and Employees' Federation, the Confederation of Municipal Workers of the Argentine Republic, the Argentine Light and Power Workers' Federation, the Bank Workers' Association, the Argentine Confederation of Transport Workers, the Railroad Union, and The [train driver's] Fraternity.[62]

---

59. Anon. "Journalists hold Labor Seminar, Tucumán, Argentina", *The AIFLD Report,* 7:1 (1969), p. 3.
60. Charles Wheeler, "AIFLD's programs in Argentina Underscore Friendship...", pp. 5–6.
61. *Ibid.,* pp. 4–5.
62. The original names are as follows: Federación de Obreros y Empleados de Correos y Telecomunicaciones, Unión de Obreros y Empleados Municipales, Federación Argentina de Trabajadores de Luz y Fuerza, Asociación Bancaria, Confederación Argentina de Trabajadores del Transporte, Unión Ferroviaria, and La Fraternidad.

Members of the CGT, who denounced "imperialist" infiltration in their ranks in the late 1960s, estimated that close to 80,000 union members had taken the AIFLD's labor education courses. Many collaborated with the Onganía dictatorship despite its openly anti-labor policies and were on friendly terms with the local branches of American corporations that helped fund the AIFLD. As Juan Alberto Bozza has argued, "[i]n the 1960s, challenged at the grassroots level by combative associations and activists, the most vigorous internal currents within Peronism, the 'Vandorists' and 'participationists', revived their latent McCarthyism."[63] Among the allies of the American unions were Juan Racchini, of the Carbonated Water Workers' Union (Sindicato Unico de Trabajadores de la Industria de Aguas Gaseosas de la Argentina – SUTIAGA), and the Insurance Union, led by José Báez, a "technocrat" who had received training in AIFLD courses. And as the conflicts within the Argentine labor movement intensified, groups like the Argentine Light and Power Workers' Federation (Federación Argentina de Trabajadores de Luz y Fuerza – FATLyF), headed by Juan José Taccone, deepened their ties with the AIFLD.

AIFLD publications were full of optimism, often masking a much less glowing reality. The general mistrust by Argentine unionists and workers never abated, and the ill-fatedness of some of AIFLDs projects further undermined its credibility. For instance, the project aimed at building housing for workers was a failure and became the object of severe criticism, not only in Argentina, but also in Brazil. For example, as Pozzi has found, although the homes were budgeted at $3,200, their final cost varied between $6,000 and $11,500. Something that was supposed to be a grand gesture of support for Argentine workers ended in mistrust and conflict, not only due to the cost overruns, which suggested malfeasance and self-enrichment by union officials, but also due to the relatively limited benefits that a few thousand houses had for workers as a class.[64]

The AIFLD was surprised by the most important workers' uprising in South America in the 1960s, the *Cordobazo*,[65] and the subsequent labor conflicts that toppled Onganía in 1970. The heightening of political tension, along with fear of what it saw as "communist" infiltration in the Peronist

63. Bozza, "Trabajo silencioso", p. 68.
64. Pozzi, "El sindicalismo norteamericano en América Latina".
65. The *Cordobazo* was a general strike and uprising in Córdoba, Argentina's second biggest city, in May 1969. It saw the city's industrial workers (especially from the car industry) as well as radicalized students and major parts of the general population enter into strike and challenge the dictatorship's authorities. It was greatly shaped by the long tradition of militant, left-wing Peronist unionism, embodied by Augustín Tosco, and a small but significant array of radical leftist groups that had emerged in the wake of the Cuban Revolution. See James P. Brennan and Mónica Gordillo, "Working Class Protest, Popular Revolt, and Urban Insurrection in Argentina: The 1969 Cordobazo", *Journal of Social History*, 27: 3 (1994), pp. 477–498. Also see the more recent: James P. Brennan and Mónica B Gordillo, *Córdoba rebelde. El cordobazo, el clasismo y la movilización social* (La Plata, 2008).

labor movement and the strong reaction of the working class to Onganía's anti-labor policies, led the AIFLD to modify its internal structure and programs. The growth of guerrilla groups and the assassination of AIFLD ally August Vandor in 1969 (not accidentally by a competing left-wing Peronist faction) only worsened the situation. Wheeler was replaced as director of social projects by James Holway, a lawyer and former American consul-general in Brazil in 1960–1964, who maintained strong ties to the State Department. Holway closed the Córdoba office and cut the housing programs, opting instead to invest further in labor education and in worker credit cooperatives.[66]

The restoration of democracy in 1973 and the powerful opposition of Argentine labor to AIFLD caused the organization to practically close its doors by 1974. But the new coup of 1976 would create a more amenable climate, once again making clear the intimate relationship between the AIFLD and Latin American authoritarian regimes. After all, the temporary interruption of its activities hardly meant that the AIFLD had abandoned Argentina. The organization had spent eleven years building its influence and developing a network of contacts, and these were reactivated after the coup of 1976.

The dictatorship established under Jorge Videla in 1976, however, ushered in a period of state terrorism with massive repression targeting activists of all currents and using forced disappearances in a systematic way to physically exterminate any kind of social movement. Facing this situation, which also saw AIFLD contacts under attack, as well as under the influence of the international "human-rights-turn", AIFLD changed course. Now, its contacts would start to function as a base of support and financing for important union leaders from the leftist CGT, long-time opponents of the AIFLD. American labor assumed a new role in Argentina and, like the International Labor Organization (ILO), which had an important role in denouncing the regime's human rights violations against Argentine workers and union leaders and its termination of union autonomy, the AFL-CIO also sought to apply pressure.[67] Thus, even as the organization once again consolidated its position as one of the most important influences on the Argentine labor movement, it also began to oppose and even internationally criticize the regime's serious human rights violations. Soon after the military seized power, George Meany, president of the AFL-CIO, sent Videla a telegram asking for the release of imprisoned unionists, the return of union autonomy, and the re-establishment of civil and workers' rights.[68]

66. Pozzi, "El sindicalismo norteamericano en América Latina".
67. Victoria Basualdo, "The ILO and the Argentine Dictatorship (1976–1983)", in Jasmien van Daele *et al.* (eds), *ILO Histories: Essays on the International Labour Organization and Its Impact on the World During the Twentieth Century* (Bern, 2010), pp. 401–421.
68. Anon., "US Labor Concerned with Situation in Argentina", *The AIFLD Report*, 14:3 (1976), p. 9.

The ORIT equally expressed its disapproval of the junta's repression. Almost one month after the coup, members of the group visited Buenos Aires to take stock of the situation of Argentine workers and converse with union leaders who had not been imprisoned. The ORIT also sent various telegrams to the military government expressing its disapproval "of the strong hand tactics used against labor leaders and their organizations".[69] In mid-1977, the AFL-CIO Executive Council announced its enthusiastic endorsement of President Jimmy Carter's (1977–1981) decision to make human rights the cornerstone of American foreign policy. Consequently, the AFL-CIO expressed its concern with the political situation in South Africa, Chile, Uganda, and, of course, the Soviet Union. Argentina was not cited, whether intentionally or not. Thus, the American union stated a position that was meant to represent a turn of position, yet which also aptly captured its decades-long interventionist stance towards Latin America: "There are no longer any purely internal affairs."[70]

RETHINKING US-SOUTHERN CONE LABOR RELATIONS

The actions of AIFLD and other international bodies of American labor during the 1960s and 1970s have been the object of controversy early on. One of the most influential scholars on labor in Latin America at the time, Robert Alexander, both a nuanced observer of the subcontinent's realities and a staunch defender of "free unionism", exculpated AIFLD's role by arguing that it faced the opposition of a series of undemocratic governments hostile to "free" trade unionism. In these situations, he said, the organization had to decide whether to continue its activities or leave the country. In places where hostility was limited to certain sectors of the economy, it was possible for the AIFLD to simply shift its focus to other sectors. In dictatorial countries where it was not possible to promote "free" unionism in any area of the economy, it still might be possible to maintain educational projects and wait for political change. Finally, in countries where all union activity was repressed by authoritarian regimes, Alexander argued together with Eldon Parker that the AIFLD, through its ties to USAID and the American government, could still "provide some kind of protective covering for unionists who were trying to offer some resistance to the complete suppression of a free labor movement".[71] Although Alexander had little to say about the cozy relationship the AIFLD long maintained with dictatorial regimes, especially in Latin America, he did mention that the organization was forced to deal with critics who considered it an accomplice of authoritarians and tyrants.

69. *Ibid.*
70. Anon., "AFL-CIO Executive Council Endorses President Carter's Human Rights", *The AIFLD Report*, 15:2 (1977), p. 3.
71. Alexander and Parker, *International Labor Organizations and Organized Labor*, p. 277.

A number of other scholars recognized early on how closely the AFL-CIO tied itself to Latin American military dictatorships.[72] Yet, the finer grained strategies employed and difficulties endured by the United States' largest labor union and its Latin American counterparts have remained largely in the dark. Even the inspiring set of more recent works, which have examined the role of the AFL-CIO in the region in more detail, have not sufficiently analyzed its effects on local workers and union members, whose interests were shaped by the political, social, and economic transformations experienced by their own countries, and whose relationships with US organized labor could shift suddenly and unexpectedly.[73] Many issues and dimensions remain yet to be explored here: For instance, even if it is possible to give a quite detailed picture about AIFLD's educational activities we do not know yet how and to what extent union leaders incorporated the things they had learned in their courses on "free" unionism. Similarly, there remains much to be discovered about how workers and their unions in Brazil and Argentina reacted in the face of the ambiguous positions – characterized by their simultaneous collaboration with and opposition to the regimes – that the AIFLD took later on at the most repressive moments of dictatorial rule.

This article has aimed to start a scholarly conversation about these issues by suggesting that there is a lot to gain from returning to a systematic comparison of American union activities in different countries. Choosing two main cases from the region, Brazil and Argentina, which in the period studied were most of the time ruled by military dictatorships, it has pointed to a series of similarities and some significant differences. Following the ongoing debates in the study of international organizations, the Cold War, and the relations between the US and Latin America, I have contended that the interaction between international bodies of American unionism and local unionists in Brazil and Argentina was much more intermingled and contradictory than envisaged in such notions as "cooperation", "co-optation", "domination", or "autonomy".

I began this article with three questions. The first asked what kind of unions were involved in the AFL-CIO's labor education program: The evidence indicates that these tended to be the least influential unions, whose leaders carried little weight in the more militant national movement dominated by nationalists and leftists. In other words, in both countries it was

---

72. Fred Hirsch, *An Analysis of the AFL-CIO Role in Latin America, or, Under the Covers with the CIA* (San Jose, CA, 1974); Hobart A. Spalding, "US and Latin American Labor: The Dynamics of Imperialist Control", *Latin American Perspectives*, 3: 1 (1976), pp. 45–69; Michael J. Sussman, *AIFLD, US Trojan Horse in Latin America and the Caribbean*.

73. Bozza, "Trabajo silencioso"; Pozzi, "El sindicalismo norteamericano en América Latina"; Scodeller, "El Instituto de Capacitación y Formación Social Sindical"; Basualdo, "El movimiento sindical argentino y sus relaciones internacionales".

difficult for the American actors to find an actual interlocutor. Most of the trade unionists considered "democratic" due to their alignment with American unionism were at the margins of the Argentine and Brazilian labor movements. In Brazil, the AIFLD's social and educational projects ultimately did not succeed in altering the increasing support enjoyed by the communists and nationalists in the unions. The situation was similar in Argentina during democratic periods, or when the Peronists were on the rise. Both countries had been marked by a long tradition of corporatist arrangements between the state, the unions, and the employers (*trabalhismo* under Vargas in Brazil, Peronism in Argentina), by a heightened social conflictivity, and by the coming to power of military regimes. There is clear evidence that AIFLD transferred strategies it had tried and tested in Brazil during the first half of the 1960s to Argentina where its engagement intensified only from the mid-1960s on. In both countries, it was most successful in attracting unionists who were both part of the corporatist arrangement, yet had no (or less) allegiance to a corporatist ideology and nationalism. In transferring their strategies, however, AIFLD had to struggle with two significant differences between the two countries: First, the support for Peronism among unions and the currency of an outspokenly left-wing Peronism in Argentina went beyond the corporatist legacy in Brazil and made it more difficult to find appropriate interlocutors. Second, while the influence of "communism" had to be exaggerated already in the case of Brazil (where the communists had some notable currency among more militant unions), the Argentine realities saw a broad array of left-wing currents within and outside of the labor movement, numerous of them claiming a revolutionary orientation and sympathizing with Cuba, yet the communists proper by the 1960s had lost most of its support and were a comparatively marginal group.

It is undeniable, however, that the supposedly "democratic" trade unionists encountered increasing opportunities during the periods of political instability before and after the coups in Brazil (1964) and Argentina (1966 and 1976). As Bozza points out, American trade unionism, acting through the AIFLD, specialized in exploiting situations of "[military] intervention or destabilization of leftist and progressive governments".[74] Indeed, the evidence shows that the AIFLD ramped up its investments and activities during the periods that immediately preceded the military coups and during the dictatorships themselves. The investments in labor education courses proved useful for advancing American labor's anti-communist agenda when those who had participated in such courses took up leadership positions in their unions after their leftist or nationalist colleagues, now considered enemies of the state, had been removed.

---

74. Bozza, "Trabajo silencioso", p. 49.

The second interest of this article was to analyze and compare the kind of concrete activities developed in Brazil and Argentina. In both countries, the AIFLD invested millions of dollars in two types of projects: training of union leaders and social projects intended to improve the living conditions of workers committed to "free" unionism. However, in Argentina, the AIFLD spent liberally on housing for workers, while in Brazil, assistance took more the form of loans, construction of union headquarters, hospitals, and credit cooperatives. In fact, when compared with AIFLD expenditures in other countries, Argentina received the highest funding for housing of any country in Latin America. One possible explanation is that the Americans considered the Argentine labor movement to already be highly organized, and thus focused their efforts not on strengthening the unions themselves, but rather on conquering the "hearts and minds" through initiatives more directly targeted at workers. Beneficiaries of AIFLD housing were to be carefully tracked so that they could be called upon when needed to collaborate with "free" trade unionism.[75]

As to the educational programs and their impact, it seems clear that in both countries AIFLD offered abundant incentives to workers and trade unionists who were both anti-communist and against a left-wing interpretation of the corporatist legacy of either Peronism or Vargas: trips to US schools for specialized courses, events at the US embassy, opportunities for favors or loans for local unions, often enabling these individuals to gain a higher position. In exchange, AIFLD beneficiaries served as part of a wide network of contacts that not only included union officials at different levels, but also representatives of laborist institutions like the labor court system and Labor Ministry, officials at the American embassy, national and multinational business leaders, journalists, and academics. This network, in turn, enabled the US to gather and report information on the labor movement in both countries.

As it formulated its Cold War strategy for Latin America and the policy orientations for such international actors as AIFLD, the AFL-CIO was shaped by its experiences in Brazil immediately before and after the coup of 1964. Undeniably, by the mid-1960s the American unionists and authorities were aware of the consequences of military regimes that were installed against nationalist and leftist Latin American governments as well as of the implications of supporting such regimes. Through their complicity, or even outright collaboration, more than twenty years later with the 1976 Argentine coup, the people that had dominated the AFL-CIO for more than four decades showed once again that their overriding foreign labor policy concern was anti-communism.

Yet, the close relationships that the AFL-CIO built with authoritarian regimes created a quandary and resulted in countervailing dynamics which

75. Pozzi, "El sindicalismo norteamericano en América Latina".

complicate any assessment of its actions: At the same time that the organization depended on conservative governments to help them increase their reach and influence upon local labor movements, the AFL-CIO started to commit meaningful acts of solidarity with and assistance for Latin American workers at the very moment when the regimes were at their most repressive. Becoming part of the human rights-turn in international politics, the American unions shifted from supporting these military dictatorships to criticizing them. It was in this way, at least in Brazil and Argentina, that the American labor movement at first supported military coups, only to later condemn the dictatorships and denounce their attacks on union autonomy.

Translation: Bryan Pitts